THE
Old Farmer's Almanac

CALCULATED ON A NEW AND IMPROVED PLAN FOR THE YEAR OF OUR LORD

2001

BEING 1ST AFTER LEAP YEAR AND (UNTIL JULY 4) 225TH YEAR OF AMERICAN INDEPENDENCE

Fitted for Boston and the New England States, with special corrections and calculations to answer for all the United States.

Containing, besides the large number of Astronomical Calculations and the Farmer's Calendar for every month in the year, a variety of

New, Useful, and Entertaining Matter.

Established in 1792

by Robert B. Thomas

Earth endures;
Stars abide—
Shine down in the old sea.
–Ralph Waldo Emerson

ORIGINAL WOOD ENGRAVING BY RANDY MILLER

Cover T.M. registered in U.S. Patent Office

Copyright 2000 by Yankee Publishing Incorporated
ISSN 0078-4516

Library of Congress Card No. 56-29681

Address all editorial correspondence to
THE OLD FARMER'S ALMANAC, DUBLIN, NH 03444

Contents

Weather

Features

A Special Report

(continued on page 4)

12 Great Reasons to Own a Mantis Tiller

1. Weighs just 20 pounds. Mantis is a joy to use. It starts easily, turns on a dime, lifts nimbly over plants and fences.

2. Tills like nothing else. Mantis bites down a full 10" deep, churns tough soil into crumby loam, prepares seedbeds in no time.

3. Has patented "serpentine" tines. Our **patented** tine teeth spin at up to 240 RPM – twice as fast as others. Cuts through tough soil and vegetation like a chain saw through wood!

4. Weeds faster than hand tools. Reverse its tines and Mantis is a precision power weeder. Weeds an average garden in 20 minutes.

5. Digs planting furrows. With the optional Planter/Furrower, Mantis digs deep or shallow furrows for planting. Builds raised beds, too!

6. Cuts neat borders. Use the optional Border Edger to cut crisp edges for flower beds, walkways, around shrubs and trees.

7. Dethatches your lawn. Thatch on your lawn prevents water and nutrients from reaching the roots. The optional Dethatcher quickly removes thatch.

8. Aerates your lawn, too. For a lush, healthy carpet, the optional Aerator slices thousands of tine slits in your lawn's surface.

9. Trims bushes and hedges! Only Mantis has an optional 24" or 30" trimmer bar to prune and trim your shrubbery and small trees.

10. The Mantis Promise. Try any product that you buy directly from Mantis with **NO RISK!** If you're not completely satisfied, send it back to us within one year for a complete, no hassle refund.

11. Warranties. The entire tiller is warranted for two full years. The tines are guaranteed forever against breakage.

12. Fun to use. The Mantis Tiller/Cultivator is so much fun to use gardeners everywhere love their Mantis tillers.

For FREE details, call
TOLL FREE 1-800-366-6268

Contents

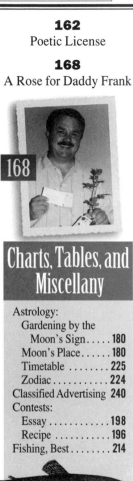

Forecasts, fads, fashions, and facts for 2001, researched and written by Jamie Kageleiry.

Fashion News

"Upcoming trends for fall-winter 2000 and into 2001: autumn colors such as red-brown, purple, olive, brass, and mid-tone brights like lilac, turquoise, coral. Some important fabrics: animal skins (real or fake), suede, lizard, leopard. You'll see flannel, felt, boiled wool, big chunky sweaters. The fuller the better in silhouettes, which means tunics, big shirts, full skirts for women."

—Aimee Marchand, designer at Liz Claiborne

WOMEN'S DEPT.

■ It's a fun time to be a girl. The multicultural trend is showing up all over fashion with the appearance of **bright, rich colors and embellishments** like embroidery, mirrors, and flounces.

The Wall Street Journal reports that **pajama sales are way up:** Women are buying men's pajama bottoms, wearing them with camisoles and a pair of mules, and going out of the house!

Not all of the next year's fashion will be loud: White will be popular, especially for jeans. **Navy will still be an important neutral.** And pant suits are back in.

Used vintage clothing—from the 1940s through the 1970s—will remain popular. Another trend: People who can afford anything they want are shopping at trendy but inexpensive stores such as Target.

TIME TO PUT AWAY: All-black outfits; knee-length khaki capris; thick black platform sandals; nylon shoulder bags.

FRESH FROM THE PATENT OFFICE

■ HBN Shoe of Manchester, New Hampshire, has patented the "Insolia Invisible Comfort

System," designed to prevent high heels from hurting by transferring a woman's weight from her toes to the back of her foot. We're not sure how that looks, but it sounds good.

And for the best of both possible worlds: DuPont has created "toeless hosiery"—stockings that cover your legs, but bare your toes. A little loop anchors them to your big toe.

MEN'S DEPT.

■ Watch that upper lip—**the mustache** is back (preferably trimmed, no wax).

As for clothing, **men will be wearing louder patterns, brighter colors.** Men who want the same costume for both work and play can choose the "dressy casual" suit: no upper chest pocket, flat-front slim trousers, smaller lapels, unlined jacket. **Clunky watches and not-so-clunky soled shoes** are in.

TIME TO PUT AWAY: Khakis, especially baggy ones with cargo pockets; polo shirts in white or beige; lug-soled black shoes.

The Home Front

"The 90s was such a black, gray, and white decade. Coming on the heels of the cool colors of the 90s is a demand for warm color—pinks, oranges, reds. The big story for the next year is lilacs and plums, often used with brown. We have gone from the minimalism and functionalism of high-tech to a look that embraces the sensual—we'll surround ourselves with color and texture. In this 'multi-culti' atmosphere, color is a universal that everyone can dip into. Even neutrals will be saturated, like vintage tea-stain."* –Ellen Sideri, CEO and founder of forecasting firm ESP, Inc.

■ **Bold colors and rich patterns** will be everywhere. Choose lots of ethnic looking, colorful accessories—pillows, throws, table settings. Tableware will feature unexpected juxtapositions: a quilted tablecloth, sisal mats, cut glasses, brushed metal underplates, and embroidered linen napkins.

Until recently, the number-one home plan sold by HomeStyles.com, a service that sells over 25,000 house plans a year, measured 3,000 square feet. But just recently, a design under 2,000 square feet jumped into first place, indicating the beginning of a trend. **Cozy is back,** complete with built-in nooks and alcoves.

(continued on page 10)

Here's Why Your Plants Will Grow Better In The EarthBox!

2½ feet long
15 inches wide
1 foot tall

Patented

Mulch Cover Stops weeds so there's no need for herbicides. Keeps the soil warm for earlier planting. Protects from rain and drought.

Fertilizer Band A lifetime supply of nutrients with just one application. There's no additional fertilizing schedule and never any guessing.

Potting Mix Eliminates fungus and soil borne disease. Transfers the ideal moisture to your plants - correctly from the bottom up. Forget about rocky or poor soil conditions.

Aeration Screen Supplies oxygen to the roots to prevent stagnation and root rot found in other containers. Keeps the soil above the water so it's impossible to over water.

Water Reservoir It's self watering, so go away for the weekend! The EarthBox automatically provides the ideal amount of water.

Tough, UV Resistant Container Resists even desert sun for years. Portable, reusable, recyclable. Good for our environment.

Large enough for 20 stalks of corn!

This doesn't mean that grandeur will go away completely—there's still plenty of call for **huge houses, and plenty of narcissism** (e.g., monogrammed furniture) fueling mansion construction. But there's a simmering desire for simplification, "unclutter" (thus the popularity of using Feng Shui methods of decorating), and comfort instead of grandeur.

Furniture will shrink some, too. Overstuffed **eight-foot sofas will be replaced with sleek seven-footers.** Even those giant hulks of kitchen ranges are losing favor to smaller, homier-looking retro-style (and red!) stoves.

HOT DESIGNS: Everyday items like **can openers and garlic presses** can be works of art. Toothbrushes, with their curves, arches, waves, squiggles, and ergonomic handles, are now winning design awards.

Brooklyn designer Oliver Beckert has come up with a **toilet tank that doubles as a fish aquarium.** Don't worry—your guppies won't end up in the sewer when you flush: The tank is sectioned so that the fish stay put.

CAR COLORS: White is still the most popular, but **second place now goes to silver, which replaces green.** DuPont, which manufactures automobile paints, predicts that shades of gold will be the next hot colors.

THE HOME SCENE: WHAT'S IN, WHAT'S OUT

IN	OUT
Comfort	Grandeur
Varied-height flat ceilings	Cathedral and vaulted ceilings
Porches	Roman and Greek columns
Window seats	Two-story foyers
Transom windows	Palladian windows
Alcoves	Curved staircases
Great rooms	Formal living rooms
Bold, warm colors	White, beige, or cool neutral walls
Laundries on the first or second floor	Basement laundries
Dust mops	Electrostatic dusters
Platinum or silver accents in place settings	Gold accents in place settings

Gardening Trends

"Sustainable gardens can take care of themelves—people can use more native plants that are already adapted to the climate, versus fussy tropical, non-native plants. If the plants are local, they'll grow well with the local precipitation, and you won't

(c o n t i n u e d)

need to amend the soil. It's less daunting, more approachable, more doable; it's working with what you have."

—Alysse Einbender, Philadelphia landscape designer

■ Ms. Einbender forecasts an increase in the number of edible components—**blueberry bushes, cherry tomatoes, herbs used as edging plants**—freely integrated with flowering plants in one garden.

Gardening is a hugely important part of our culture now. Thirty billion dollars was spent on gardens and lawns in 1998; there are about 160 different gardening magazines. **Gardening has gotten the ergonomic edge:** Tools have grips that are designed to prevent hand injuries.

So many people want a garden as a design element in their yard (and to look out upon) that the hobby aspect of it will diminish as more garden work is hired out, at least the harder work of preparing beds and installing plants.

BRINGING THE OUTSIDE IN: Lawn furniture and pots (from Tuscan terra-cotta to Vietnamese pottery) intended for the garden or patio will end up in the living room, including such nostalgic pieces as porch gliders and bent-metal lawn chairs.

Hot Collectibles

■ In general, **antiques and collectibles are being snapped up,** often with no dickering on price, by new, young, wealthy consumers. Dealers are broadening their definition of antiques and art just to stay in business, and collectors are expanding into new areas.

This explains, perhaps, the sudden interest in **graffiti art.** Watch that kid with the spray can—his or her art might be worth tons of money someday. No longer just a criminal activity, graffiti is beginning to be taken seriously. Some "pieces" in New York and Los Angeles have been sold for several

thousand dollars. Demand for any "difficult" (or controversial) art is up.

THE JOY (AND VALUE) OF COOKBOOKS
■ Hang on to that **red plaid Betty Crocker cookbook** your mom handed down to you. "Antique cookbooks are soaring in value," reported *The Wall Street Journal* recently, **"perhaps the hottest sector in the rare-book field."** Though some of this is due to baby boomers' desire to **own anything that reminds them of their youth,** much of the reason lies in the academic interest in social history— the details of everyday life, how

(c o n t i n u e d)

people lived, what they ate.

Old cookbooks are good sources for this. How far back do you need to look? A copy of Julia Child's *Mastering the Art of French Cooking,* volume 1, from 1963 may fetch $300. And that ratty old *Joy of Cooking*? If you have a first edition published by a small firm in 1931, you might get $3,000 for it.

What the Soothsayers Are Soothsaying About the Next Century and Beyond

■ Mars will become the hot new vacation spot, *ABC News* speculated.

■ Human reproduction, says chemist Carl Djerassi, will become automated, and sex will be reserved for purposes of lust.

■ We will be able to make ourselves more beautiful in the next few decades, reports *The Wall Street Journal:* Simple cosmetic procedures will modify skin color, muscle strength, bone hardness, and facial shape. Tiny robots will circulate through the body to repair aging tissue.

■ A new space age will emerge in the years

2500 to 3000, says Graham Molitor of the World Future Society. "Extraterrestrial enterprise will become an important feature of the world economy."

BEYOND ROSE-COLORED GLASSES

■ In the next centuries, you will be able to don glasses that filter out things you don't want to see, like sun or dirt or your old boyfriend. After that, this technology could get surgically embedded into your own eyelids, with programs that would recognize approaching humans and remind you who they are and where you met them. (New hope for the forgetful!)

Eating In and Eating Out

"*Latin ingredients will keep pace with the exploding Latin music scene as guava paste, cassava, and Scotch bonnet chilies become supermarket staples. Cooks are also turning to nut oils, especially almond and pistachio, for mixing into vegetable purees, drizzling on roasted fish, and even spooning over ice cream. In fact, fat in all its guises—especially butter from France, Italy, and Scandinavia—will make a comeback in the 21st century.*"

–Kate Krader, *Senior Editor,*
Food & Wine *magazine*

(continued)

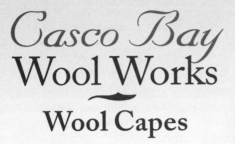

HOW SWEET IT IS

◾ Not only will fat be in style again, but so will sugar! **Look for some unusual sugars at the grocery store:** Pale golden turbinado is mild and works in gingerbread or coffee; Demerara is sticky and brown, great for glazing ham or adding to a cup of tea or coffee; piloncillo is dark brown and unrefined with a strong molasses taste.

But, you ask, isn't sugar evil? As with most vices, not in moderation.

As a matter of fact, the FDA has concluded that although it can cause cavities, **sugar is not to blame for diabetes, heart disease, or obesity.** And a study in the *Journal of the American Medical Association* found that sugar has no effect on kids' behavior (there goes that excuse). Not only that, another study proved that sugar helps people to think better! And in 19 of 20 cases, a spoonful of sugar did indeed cure hiccups.

Now, how do you like them apples? Candied, perhaps?

WHAT'S HOT AND WHAT'S COLD IN FOOD TRENDS

◾ **HOT**

Flowers (marigolds, nasturtiums, lavender, chive flowers) in salads and snacks
Soy—in everything from drinks to cereal
Beef and pork
Deep fryers
Slow cookers
Fish houses
Smoothies, tea, and hot chocolate

Breath mints, especially Altoids
Wine bars
Martinis (still!), rum drinks, Belgian beer, absinthe (be careful), and sake
Movie theaters serving dinner and drinks
Eastern European cuisine
Colorful restaurant decor, and restaurants accommodating children

◾ **COLD**

Carbohydrates
Low-fat food
Microwave ovens
Lattes
Cigar bars
Huge pasta entrées
The vertical layered look: components of entrées piled high on a plate
Beige interiors of restaurants

Cooking itself is HOT. Enrollment at culinary schools and in high-school cooking programs has soared—partially due to the cachet and celebrity that is accorded to chefs.

Home cooks will be trying their hand at **wood roasting or grilling whole fish** (it stays moister than other cuts), especially sturgeon and arctic char.

SOME NEW SEASONINGS:

Japanese sansho pepper and dried fennel pollen. A company called Wild Things offers cooking oils scented with marjoram, ginger, and pepper.

(c o n t i n u e d)

Demographica

"As boomers move into the empty-nest and peak-earning years, their discretionary income will rise, creating new marketing opportunities for retailers. By 2003, there will be 1.5 million more households with incomes over $100,000, a 16 percent increase from 1998. The millionaire ranks are growing fast, too. The number of households worth $1 million rose 36.6 percent from 1995 to 1998."

> –Diana Holman and Anne Marshall,
> *publishers of* WomanTrends

◼ As usual, baby boomers and their maturing teenagers will dominate our demographics and drive decisions by retailers and marketers.

Car companies are redesigning prototypes for future models so that one car can appeal to aging boomers and young drivers alike. Sleek-looking vehicles, such as the "TransG" (for transgenerational), will have power swivel seats that rotate for easy access; oversize door handles; seatbelt systems that don't require reaching over one's (arthritic) shoulder; rolling platforms in the back that ease strain on the back when unloading groceries.

Watch for increases in products for over-50's: Adult incontinence products have jumped 50 percent in the last five years; books and research on menopause are ubiquitous.

By 2025, life expectancy for newborn girls could reach 82; for boys, it could reach 79.8. **Centenarians are a booming section of the population:** There will be about 70,000 of them alive in the country this year, versus 37,000 in 1990. The number could reach a million by 2050. Studies have found that up to a third of them stay robust and mentally sharp through their tenth decade.

WomanTrends notes that "the trend of fleeing country life for city life has reversed. In the last decade, 71 percent of rural counties have gained population. The biggest growth is in those areas with retiree and recreation amenities."

WE'VE COME A LONG WAY

◼ In 1900, only 3 million Americans were 65 or older, compared with 34 million in 1997.

◼ **The average household had 4.8 people in 1900; in 1998, there were 2.6.**

◼ The revenue of the U.S. government in 1900 was $567 million versus $1.7 trillion in 1999.

◼ **There were 36 highway traffic fatalities in 1900 and almost 42,000 in 1997.**

(c o n t i n u e d)

■ Four times more adults receive their high school diplomas now than did in 1900.

■ **Accidental deaths have dropped by 61 percent since 1900, despite the millions of** people riding on planes and in cars.

■ The average work week has gone from 50 hours in 1909 to 35 hours now, and we spend twice as much time at leisure as did our great-grandparents.

It's Good for You

WINE (THE LATEST REASON): It has anti-aging properties. Grape seeds are used to firm skin, a spa treatment called "vinotherapy." Other foods used in skin-care products: olives, caviar, ginger, salt, sugar, and soy beans (which mimic estrogen's skin-softening properties).

ROOMMATES: Gerontologists have confirmed that elderly people who share their home with a roommate are happier, healthier, and feel their lives are better overall.

SONG: Music therapy is now reimbursable under Medicare and has been found to be as effective for anxiety as five milligrams of Valium.

LOWERING YOUR EXPECTATIONS: Ed Diener, of the University of Illinois, reported that happy people say they have mild to moderate pleasant emotions "most of the time" rather than intense positive moments some of the time. "One lesson from these findings," writes Diener, "is that if people seek ecstasy much of the time, whether it be in a career or in a love relationship, they are likely to be disappointed." Age, gender, and income, by the way, were found to have no correlation with a person's sense of happiness.

Happiness itself is good for you, no matter how you get there: In a study spanning three decades, Mayo Clinic researchers found that optimists live about 19 percent longer than pessimists.

Bad for You

STRESS: You already know this, right? But here is one more downside to stress: **It can give you dandruff, caused by stress-induced hormone surges.** Oh! We almost forgot! Stress also can make you forgetful. The hormone cortisol, released during periods of stress, **inhibits short-term memory.** This helps explain why we so quickly forget the things we learn while anxiously cramming for a test.

HEADACHE CURES: Unfortunately for many headache sufferers, overuse of pain relievers can cause "analgesic rebound headaches." How much is too much? New labels on medication will soon tell you not to take the drug for more than 48 hours— that's what starts the cycle.

BAD HAIR: According to a study at Yale, a bad hair day can lower your self-image and inspire feelings of incompetence and self-doubt. The hair conditions with the most profound impact: "sticks out," "needs cutting," "frizzy," "poofy," "bad haircut."

(continued on page 24)

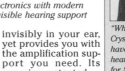

Pet News

■ A company called PetSmart, Inc., has introduced "Shareables"—snacks such as **peanut-butter-filled pretzels** that are nutritionally correct for both man and beast. No more worries about your toddler eating dog biscuits (or your dog getting into your Cheez-Its).

Mood collars for dogs will help insensitive owners discern when their pets are having a bad doggie day.

A DOGGIE IS FOREVER: A dog-and-cat-cloning project called Genetic Savings and Clone **banks the genes of your favorite critters** until the research is further along. Right now, **"Operation Copy Cat"** is working in tandem with a team at Texas A&M University. A dog named "Missy" (in a project named "Missyplicity") may be the first dog ever to be cloned. Missy's owners, wealthy folks from the San Francisco area, have funded the $2.3 million pro-

ject with the hope that soon there will be another Missy on the way to take the place of their beloved 13-year-old border collie–Siberian husky mix.

Once the research is developed, cloning your pet should become much cheaper—"under $20,000," according to Lou Hawthorne, CEO of Genetic Savings and Clone. **For more information, visit www.savingsandclone.com.**

■ **High-income, high-style pet lovers can now subscribe to** *Animal Fair* **(after** *Vanity Fair***), which features fashion spreads with faux-fur coats (for humans) and matching designer outfits for their dogs. Look for it at Petco, or on newsstands.**

GOOD DOGGIES: In Salt Lake City, Utah, dogs are now allowed into the public library—not so that they can sit and read *Animal Fair,* but because young children enjoy reading aloud to them. A sweet sight.

PET TO HAVE: The pet trend for 2001 is the "sugar glider"—a pocket-size marsupial from Australia.

The Difference Between Men and Women

SHOPPING: Women are more disciplined shoppers than are men, says Paco Underhill, the author of *Why We Buy: The Science of Shopping.* **Women are less apt than men to buy something solely because it's a good deal.** Fathers on a shopping trip are more easily manipulated by their kids into buying things than are mothers. The kid is out of

luck, though, if Dad can't easily find the object he's looking for in the store—he's likely to leave rather than ask for help.

AMAZING RACE: Men and women were tested by neurologists to see which sex is the better navigator. Men won—though it's still agreed that, when lost, they're less likely to ask for directions. Female study subjects were able to navigate out of a virtual maze in 3 minutes and 16 seconds; it took the males only 2 minutes and

(c o n t i n u e d)

22 seconds. German neurologist Dr. Matthias Riepe discovered that the brains of men and women are structured differently in the hippocampus, a banana-shaped area that is used in navigation.

GENDER ON THE ROAD: When female executives travel, only 20 percent of them bring along family photos, but 44 percent of males do.

Seventy percent of women say they get more pleasure from vacations than possessions, compared with 55 percent of men.

Here's to Your Health

"Web sites have already shaken up medicine by giving patients access to vast amounts of reference materials. Armed with facts—and sometimes fiction—gleaned from cyberspace, Net-savvy patients are taking charge of their own care. But the real revolution won't arrive until patients and doctors routinely interact with each other over the Net."

–Thomas E. Weber, columnist,
The Wall Street Journal

GOOD NEWS: Doctors at the University of Auckland (New Zealand) and Thomas Jefferson University in Philadelphia are developing a vaccine to lessen the damage caused by a stroke.

THE DOWNSIDE OF FLYING: What's worse than airplane food? "Airplane ear"—a newly named affliction that describes that screamingly awful pain some experience when an airplane ascends or descends rapidly. The pain comes if the eustachian tube in the ear can't regulate pressure quickly enough on either side of the eardrum. It causes a vacuum to form, which puts tension on the eardrum. Blood vessels can burst, or the eardrum can rupture.

There are some commonsense preventative measures: chewing gum or yawning can reduce the pressure. Travelers with ear problems, or colds or allergies, can start using a decongestant and small doses of nasal spray the day before (even healthy flyers can do this to shrink sinus and ear membranes, just in case). Earplanes, a new product, are $5 (per pair) plugs with slow-leaking valves to help regulate air flow.

■ **Exercise can help reduce gallstones,** reports *The New York Times*. So can drinking two or three cups of coffee a day.

SUN DOWN UNDER: Australians have more sun damage on the right side of their faces; Americans on their left. The reason? Driving (on opposite sides of the car).

(c o n t i n u e d)

FREE
CATALOG

for sizes 12 & up

Super Savings!

ROAMAN'S.

Discover the Best in Fashion, Fit and Value.

100% Guaranteed.

Best Selection in sportswear, dresses, coats, intimate apparel, shoes and accessories.
Bra cups B to II.
Shoe sizes 6 to 14, B to EEE.

Fall 2000

CALL today for your FREE catalog!

1-800-891-8100

Trends in Agriculture

"U.S. producers are farming organic in record numbers in order to capture high-value markets, lower input costs, boost farm income, and conserve resources."

–from www.usda.gov

■ The Worldwatch Institute predicts that farmers will be harvesting 25 percent **less genetically altered crops** this fall. The peak of the biotech trend may be past on American farms. Farmers who planted modified seeds hoped that they would lower costs and increase yields. They've found that it is not always the case. On the other hand, both government and industry could do better jobs of educating the public about the benefits of food biotechnology, says Iowa governor Tom Vilsack, a supporter of the high-tech crops.

CENTURY FARMS: There are now thousands of family farms in America that have been around for 100 years or more. To see a photo gallery and listing by state and county of some of these national gems, visit http://centuryfarms.fsa.usda.gov.

The Mood

"Long on cash and short on time, many Americans are focusing on a more intimate concern: making room in their lives for family and personal pursuits. They're looking for more efficient ways to volunteer; they're praying more—albeit sometimes online rather than at church; they're traveling with their kids more. Even sleep has become a priority, as successful people fight for more shut-eye and for more quality time when awake.

"Call it the triumph of time over money . . ."

–Wall Street Journal writers Edward Felsenthal and Amy Stevens

■ When it comes to choosing between more time and more money, American workers are increasingly choosing more time. **The shortening of workweeks,** especially among highly skilled workers, is starting to show up in government data. Employers, attempting to keep valuable employees, are offering shortened workweeks or time off for jobs well done—and finding their **sales and/or productivity increasing** as a result.

(c o n t i n u e d)

The Amazing Maize Maze®, a treasure-hunt

game show where you find mazemasters, music, map pieces, telestalks, kernels of knowledge . . . and YOURSELF.

"Survivors come out grinning from EAR to EAR." –CNN

"Think of this as a space where people are free to make discoveries about the world and each other . . . so sweet and so American." –*People*

As seen on *Today, Good Morning America,* CNN, and *Inside Edition.* **As heard on** NPR's *All Things Considered.* **As seen in** *USA Today* and *People* magazine.

Across America: Cherry Crest Farm, Paradise, PA, 717-687-6843; Howell Farm, Lambertville, NJ, 609-397-2555; Long Acre Farms, Macedon, NY, 315-986-9821; Pacific Earth Resources, Camarillo, CA, 805-495-LOST (5678); Carter Farms, Princeton, IA, 319-289-9999; Rural Hill Farm, Huntersville, NC, 704-875-3113; Mountain Creek Resort, Vernon, NJ, 973-209-3319.

Special programs for school groups, scout orienteering, birthday parties, and corporate team-building.

Log on: www.AmericanMaze.com
The official maze of The Old Farmer's Almanac

Seems the old adage, "I can do a year's worth of work in 11 months, but not 12," really holds true.

The desire for **more family and leisure time** has spawned a huge increase in services that will deliver to your home. Families are responding to the hectic pace of life by just staying home once they get there. Some personal trainers, masseuses, piano teachers, and even physicians are making house calls again. In some places, there is a Web-based service that will handle all your boring errands for a flat monthly fee. Streamline.com, for instance, delivers groceries, dry cleaning, repaired shoes, flowers, stamps, processed film, and prepared meals.

Downtown returns: The robust economy has trickled down to Main Street.

Empty stores are filling up; vacated warehouses are now crowded with high-technology firms and the services they spawn (programmers, after all, need coffee and lunch).

BLASTS FROM THE PAST

■ Raggedy Ann and Andy (their creators have cranked up production).

■ View-Masters (grown-ups want low-tech reminders of their childhoods).

■ Golf is cool.

■ Knitting is hot.

■ Stargazing is wildly popular.

■ Scrapbooks are big. So is genealogy, with the new help of the Internet.

So Long, Farewell, Adios

E-WHATEVER: We won't suddenly abandon buying and selling on the Internet, but watch for the disappearance of the "e" prefix to most things virtual in the next three to four years. By 2004, "e-commerce" will account for almost **two trillion dollars of economic activity**—almost a quarter of the U.S. economy. By then, it will cease to be a curiosity, shed its novelty and the cutting-edge "e," and become just plain old commerce. And maybe people will stop saying "dot com" all the time.

TRAVEL AGENTS: With the above-mentioned e-commerce (oops—commerce) and the rising comfort level of Americans with everything virtual, **travel plans will be made on-line** almost exclusively.

TYPEWRITERS: Several years ago, we forecast the end of the typewriter. Now we're saying **adios to the demise of the typewriter!** Surprise—despite the plethora of palm pilots, PCs, powerbooks, and pagers, the old clickety-clackety typewriter is holding its own. Sales have not risen, but neither have they dropped. **"The typewriter market is alive and well,"** states John Bermingham, CEO of Smith-Corona. The same goes for other products you'd think would be obsolete— Rolodexes and wall calendars. ☐☐

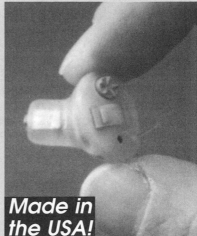
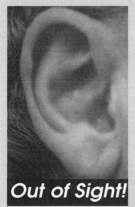

Our reason for being . . .

Probably the majority of North Americans think that this publication's primary mission is to forecast the weather. Not so. Of course, the weather forecasts are important, requiring the year-round efforts of solar scientist Dr. Richard Head and meteorologist Michael Steinberg. And, yes, except for 1938—when "averages" instead of forecasts were used—there have always been weather forecasts in this Almanac.

Many people think of us as a gardening book. A recent survey of our 13.1 million readers revealed that 5.8 million of them are active gardeners. So, indeed, gardening represents a major portion of our editorial fare.

Food represents another. I wish all of you could have been here at our office in Dublin, New Hampshire, on the day last April when 50 cakes, all made from reader recipes, were brought in for the Almanac staff to taste. (See page 196 for the winners.)

And, some would ask, what about the "Consumer Tastes and Trends" section? For all its fun and information, its basic purpose is to show future generations what life was like here in North America during the year of publication. Like a time capsule. Is that what an almanac is all about?

The answer is that none of the above descriptions represent the core reason for this publication's existence. Rather, since 1792, the heart and soul of *The Old Farmer's Almanac* has been—and always will be—the 28-page section we call the "Calendar Pages" (58-85). These are the pages that truly make an almanac an almanac. In the ancient Arabic language, the word *almanac,* roughly translated, meant "a calendar of the heavens." That explains our reason for being.

Aside from the title page, the Calendar Pages are the only pages our founder, Robert B. Thomas, would recognize were he to rise from his grave in Sterling, Massachusetts, to peruse this edition. The Calendar Pages are what most profoundly link us to the past.

For three months this past winter, two of our editors worked almost full time on the Calendar Pages, meticulously filling in data and symbols by hand onto large blowups of each page—just as it has been done for 209 years. Randy Miller's responsibility was the *Left*-Hand Calendar Pages. These feature the Sun and Moon risings and settings and all manner of predictions—100 percent accurate—based on astronomy.

Yes, Randy has a computer and occasionally consults several databases on the Internet. But he obtains most of what he needs on five-foot-long printouts sent by our astronomer, Amherst College astronomy professor Dr. George Greenstein. Additional information comes from Bob Berman, director of the Overlook and the Storm King Observatories, both in New York State. Those who read the Almanac carefully may also notice, this year, an improvement in our method of calculating the length of day for any location (see page 40). We thank reader Jeffry D. Mueller of Eldersburg, Maryland, for his elegant suggestion.

The *Right*-Hand Calendar Pages—which include religious and historical dates, sayings, additional astronomical data, the New England weather forecasts in rhyme, the "Farmer's Calendar" essays, and so forth—were the responsibility of Debra Keller. Deb also uses a computer, but she can hardly be seen behind the tall stacks of reference material

Covered by your Medicare!

DIABETICS

Type I & Type II

If you have Medicare or Insurance you may be eligible to receive your Diabetic Supplies at little or No Cost. Medicare Patients are eligible to receive Glucose Monitors, Test Strips, Lancets, Lancing Devices and Control Solutions at no cost. Patients with private or Group Insurance are eligible to receive the above items and also Insulin and Syringes. Male Diabetics with Impotence Problems are now entitled to receive the Encore at no cost through Medicare. Medicare and/or your insurance will reimburse us directly for your Diabetics Supplies. For more information, please call us toll-free at **1-800-799-1477** or fill out and return this form below. Sorry, HMO Patients do not qualify.

RESPIRATORY PATIENTS

Asthma, Emphysema, etc.

If you have Medicare or Insurance you may be eligible to receive a Nebulizer and Respiratory Medications at little or No Cost:

- **Albuterol(Proventil, Ventolin)**
- **Metaproterenol(Alupent)**
- **Acetylcisteine(Mucosil)**
- **Cromolyn(Intal)**
And many more!

Medicare and/or your Insurance Company will reimburse us directly for your Respiratory Supplies.
For more information please call us toll-free at **1-800-870-6831** or fill out and return this form below. Sorry, HMO Patients do not qualify.

• NO UP-FRONT COSTS • NO CLAIM FORMS TO FILE
• NO WAITING FOR REIMBURSEMENT • NO DELIVERY AND HANDLING CHARGES • NO COMPLICATED ORDERING PROCEDURES
• ALL PRODUCTS SHIPPED PER PRIORITY MAIL

Please send me more Information on
Diabetic Supplies [ ]   Respiratory Supplies [ ]

Name:_____

Address:_____

City: _____

State:_____ Zip:_____ Phone: (____)_____-_____

Providing Quality Health Care Services to Medicare and Insurance Patients since 1989

PRESCRIPTION PLUS PHARMACY
12773 Forest Hill Blvd. West Palm Beach FL 33414

that surround her desk. Included in there somewhere—and referred to often—are the many notebooks handwritten by Robb Sagendorph (1900-1970), the man who purchased this Almanac in 1939 for his descendants and current owners, the Trowbridge-Kaupi-Hale families.

So who uses the Calendar Pages, and why? Well, there are those who want to start a trip at dawn, or photograph the rising or setting Sun or Moon, or set sail at high tide, or know the date of, say, Easter—and there are a hundred more uses. However, I think Robb Sagendorph most effectively touched on the essence of the Calendar Pages in an essay he wrote only days before he died. Here is the conclusion to the essay:

"Tides, sunsets, moonrises, holidays—as a maker of almanacs, I find all these timetables useful in guiding us to what I like to call the edges of creation. In arriving there, we must have plans and calculations and all manner of data, so much of which is compiled each year in the Calendar Pages of *The Old Farmer's Almanac*. But once there, the open sky, sea, canyon, mountain peak, or stillness of a pond takes over and regulates our lives and thoughts. In nature's own house, we suddenly feel not careworn . . . but cared for."

J.D.H. Sr., June 2000

However, it is by our works and not our words that we would be judged. These, we hope, will sustain us in the humble though proud station we have so long held in the name of

Your obedient servant,

THE 2001 EDITION OF

The Old Farmer's Almanac

Established in 1792 and published every year thereafter

Robert B. Thomas (1766-1846), *Founder*

EDITOR *(12th since 1792)*: Judson D. Hale Sr.
MANAGING EDITOR: Susan Peery
ART DIRECTOR: Margo Letourneau
COPY EDITOR: Ellen Bingham
ASSISTANT MANAGING EDITOR: Mare-Anne Jarvela
SENIOR ASSOCIATE EDITOR: Debra Keller
RESEARCH EDITOR: Randy Miller
SENIOR CONSULTING EDITOR: Mary Sheldon
INTERNET EDITOR: Christine Halvorson
ASTRONOMER: Dr. George Greenstein
SOLAR PROGNOSTICATOR: Dr. Richard Head
WEATHER PROGNOSTICATOR: Michael A. Steinberg
WEATHER GRAPHICS AND CONSULTATION: Accu-Weather, Inc.
CONTRIBUTING EDITORS: Bob Berman, *Astronomy;*
Castle Freeman Jr., *Farmer's Calendar*
PRODUCTION DIRECTOR: Susan Gross
PRODUCTION MANAGER: David Ziarnowski
SENIOR PRODUCTION ARTISTS: Lucille Rines,
Rachel Kipka, Nathaniel Stout
ADVERTISING PRODUCTION ARTIST: Janet Calhoun
PRODUCTION ARTIST: Jill Shaffer
CREATIVE DIRECTOR, ON-LINE: Stephen O. Muskie
INTERNET PRODUCTION ASSISTANT: Lisa Traffie

GROUP PUBLISHER: John Pierce
PUBLISHER *(23rd since 1792)*: Sherin Wight
ADVERTISING PRODUCTION/CLASSIFIED: Donna Stone
MAIL-ORDER MARKETING MANAGER: Susan Way
DIRECT SALES MANAGER: Cindy Schlosser

ADVERTISING MARKETING REPRESENTATIVES
General and Mail-Order Advertising
Northeast & West: Robert Bernbach
Phone: 914-769-0051 • Fax: 914-769-0691
Midwest & South: Dan Waxman
Phone: 207-871-9376 • Fax: 207-879-0453

NEWSSTAND CIRCULATION: P.S.C.S.
DISTRIBUTION: Curtis Circulation Company

EDITORIAL, ADVERTISING, AND PUBLISHING OFFICES
P.O. Box 520, Dublin, NH 03444
Phone: 603-563-8111 • Fax: 603-563-8252

Web site: www.almanac.com

YANKEE PUBLISHING INC., MAIN ST., DUBLIN, NH 03444
Jamie Trowbridge, *President;* Judson D. Hale Sr., John Pierce, *Senior Vice Presidents;* Jody Bugbee, Judson D. Hale Jr., Sherin Wight, *Vice Presidents;* Steve Brewer, *Treasurer.*

The Old Farmer's Almanac publications are available at special discounts for bulk purchases for sales promotions or premiums. Contact At-a-Glance Group, 800-333-1125.

The newsprint in this edition of *The Old Farmer's Almanac* consists of 23 percent recycled content. All printing inks used are soy-based. This product is recyclable. Consult local recycling regulations for the right way to do it.   Printed in U.S.A.

Amazing Diabetes Improvement

(SPECIAL) – Here's important news for anyone with diabetes. A remarkable doctor's book is now available that reveals a medically tested method that normalizes blood sugar naturally...and greatly improves the complications associated with diabetes. People report **better vision, more energy, faster healing, regained feeling in their feet**, as well as a reduction of various risk factors associated with other diseases.

It's called the *"Diabetes Improvement Program"* and it was researched, developed and written by a doctor. It shows you exactly how nature can activate your body's built-in healers once you start eating the right combination of foods. It works for both Type I and Type II diabetes and it can reduce, and in some cases even eliminate, the need to take insulin. It gives diabetics control of their lives and a feeling of satisfaction that comes from having normal blood sugar profiles.

The results speak for themselves. The *"Diabetes Improvement Program"* is based on research that is so new most doctors aren't aware of it yet. It tells you which delicious foods to eat and which to avoid. It also warns you of the potential danger of certain so-called "diabetes" diets. It's been proven amazingly effective time and time again...and works so fast you can begin to feel improvement in a matter of days. The *"Diabetes Improvement Program"* is based on documented scientific principles that can:

• **Eliminate ketones and give you more abundant energy**
• **Make blood sugar levels go from High Risk to Normal**
• **Stimulate scratches and scrapes to heal faster**
• **Improve eyesight**
• **Improve your balance**
• **Help numb feet regain a level of feeling**
• **Reverse neuropathy and resultant heel ulcers**

Improvement can be seen in other areas as well, such as **lower blood pressure, lower cholesterol** and **reduced triglyceride levels**. There has also been a reduction of other risk factors associated with: **heart attacks, stroke, retinopathy, kidney damage**.

What's more, it can help improve **short term memory** and make you feel **more alert** and **no longer chronically tired**.

Improvements and even total cures of **double vision** or *diplopia* may also be experienced.

If you or someone you know have diabetes, this could be the most important book you'll ever read. As part of a special introductory offer, right now you can order a special press run of the *"Diabetes Improvement Program"* for only $12.95 plus $2.00 shipping. It comes with a 90 day money back guarantee. If you are not 100% satisfied, simply return it for a full refund...no questions asked.

Order an extra copy for family or friend and SAVE. You can order 2 for only $20 total.

HERE'S HOW TO ORDER:
Simply PRINT your name and address and the words "Diabetes Improvement" on a piece of paper and mail it along with a check or money order to: THE LEADER CO., INC., Publishing Division, Dept. DB432, P.O. Box 8347, Canton, Ohio 44711. VISA or MasterCard send card number and expiration date. Act now. Orders are fulfilled on a first come, first served basis.

©2000 The Leader Co., Inc.

Celebrate the Millennium
with *The 2001 Old Farmer's Almanac*
Collector's Hardcover Edition Package

This special expanded issue of *The Old Farmer's Almanac* welcomes the new millennium with 304 pages of facts, fun, and a few surprises.

You will also receive THREE FREE GIFTS: Replicas of the historic 1901 and 1801 editions of the Almanac, plus The Old Farmer's Almanac 2001 Gardening Calendar.

In addition to our famous weather forecasts, puzzles, gardening charts, recipes, precise astronomical data, and charming anecdotes, you'll find some timely feature stories on the topics of:

Science/Astronomy
– from the eerie aurora borealis to our sister planet named for the goddess of love, and more!

Gardening/Home
– from old-time home remedies for plants to the latest research on consumer trends, and more!

Food
– from delicious cracker recipes to prizewinning layer cakes, piemaking secrets, and more!

History/Geography
– from the history of penmanship to the bloody Battle of the Little Bighorn, and more!

Plus memorable stories about cooking for your cat, preventing wrinkles, getting a good night's sleep, and more!

Lock in Savings!
We're sure that once you receive your first Collector's Hardcover Edition of *The Old Farmer's Almanac*, you will want to add to your collection each year. By placing your order for this special offer, you are guaranteed a reservation for all future editions at the lowest price available. The new hardcover edition plus all free gifts will be mailed to you each September for a 10-day trial review. We'll send you a postcard in August to remind you and give you the chance to tell us if you've changed your address or changed your mind. If you want to receive the new Almanac, you don't have to do a thing. We'll ship it automatically. If you are not completely satisfied, simply return the book and owe nothing. The free gifts are yours to keep. You may cancel this program at any time.

THREE WAYS TO ORDER
ORDER ON-LINE: www.almanac.com/almanac
CALL TOLL-FREE: 800-223-3166
BY MAIL: The Old Farmer's Almanac, P.O. Box 37370, Boone, IA 50037-0370

How to Use This Almanac
Anywhere in the U.S.A.

■ The calendar pages **(58-85)** are the heart of *The Old Farmer's Almanac*. They present astronomical data and sky sightings for the entire year and are what make this book a true almanac, a "calendar of the heavens." In essence, these pages are unchanged since 1792, when Robert B. Thomas published his first edition. The long columns of numbers and symbols reveal all of Nature's precision, rhythm, and glory —an astronomical look at the year 2001.

–Beth Krommes

Please note: All times given in this edition of the Almanac are for Boston, Massachusetts, and are in Eastern Standard Time (EST), except from 2:00 A.M., April 1, until 2:00 A.M., October 28, when Eastern Daylight Time (EDT) is given. Key Letters (A-E) are provided so that readers can calculate times for their own localities. The following four pages provide detailed explanations.

Seasons of the Year

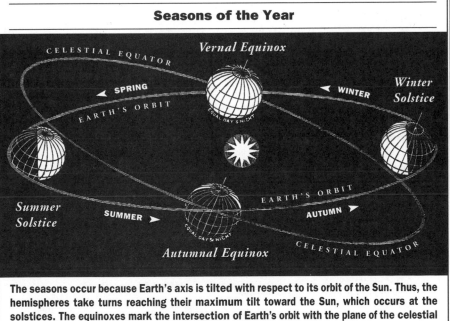

The seasons occur because Earth's axis is tilted with respect to its orbit of the Sun. Thus, the hemispheres take turns reaching their maximum tilt toward the Sun, which occurs at the solstices. The equinoxes mark the intersection of Earth's orbit with the plane of the celestial equator, when the hemispheres equally face the Sun.

■ The Web site for *The Old Farmer's Almanac,* **www.almanac.com,** has astronomical information for any location in the United States, as well as tide predictions for thousands of miles of coastline. Weather forecasts, history, advice, gardening tips, puzzles, and recipes are also available on-line. There's even a "black hole" in the corner of the home page.

(continued on next page)

The Left-Hand Calendar Pages

(Pages 58-84)

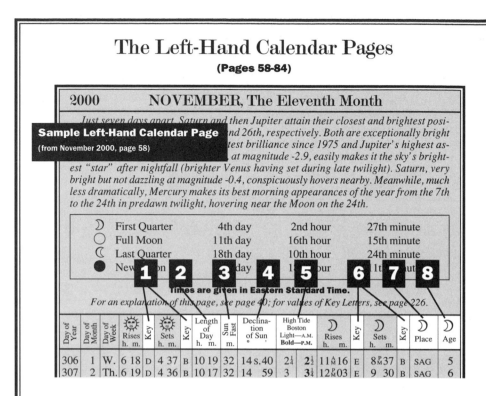

Sample Left-Hand Calendar Page
(from November 2000, page 58)

2000   NOVEMBER, The Eleventh Month

Just seven days apart, Saturn and then Jupiter attain their closest and brightest posi-
[...]nd 26th, respectively. Both are exceptionally bright
[...]test brilliance since 1975 and Jupiter's highest as-
[...]at magnitude -2.9, easily makes it the sky's bright-
est "star" after nightfall (brighter Venus having set during late twilight). Saturn, very
bright but not dazzling at magnitude -0.4, conspicuously hovers nearby. Meanwhile, much
less dramatically, Mercury makes its best morning appearances of the year from the 7th
to the 24th in predawn twilight, hovering near the Moon on the 24th.

☽ First Quarter	4th day	2nd hour	27th minute
○ Full Moon	11th day	16th hour	15th minute
☾ Last Quarter	18th day	10th hour	24th minute
● New [Moon]	[...]day	1[...]ur	1[...]ut

Times are given in Eastern Standard Time.

For an explanation of this page, see page 40; for values of Key Letters, see page 226.

Day of Year	Day of Month	Day of Week	☀ Rises h. m.	Key	☀ Sets h. m.	Key	Length of Day h. m.	Sun Fast m.	Declination of Sun ° '	High Tide Boston Light—A.M. **Bold**—P.M.	☽ Rises h. m.	Key	☽ Sets h. m.	Key	☽ Place	☽ Age
306	1	W.	6 18	D	4 37	B	10 19	32	14 s.40	2¼ / 2½	11⅚16	E	8⅗37	B	SAG	5
307	2	Th.	6 19	D	4 36	B	10 17	32	14 59	3 / 3¼	12⅜03	E	9 30	B	SAG	6

1 Use these two Key Letter columns to calculate the sunrise/sunset times for your locale. Each sunrise/sunset time is assigned a Key Letter whose value in minutes is given in the **Time Corrections table on page 226.** Find your city, or the city nearest you, in the table, and add or subtract those minutes to Boston's sunrise or sunset time.

E X A M P L E :

■ To find the time of sunrise in Denver, Colorado, on November 1, 2000:

Sunrise, Boston, with Key Letter D (above)	**6:18** A.M. EST
Value of Key Letter D for Denver (p. 227)	**+ 11 minutes**
Sunrise, Denver	**6:29** A.M. MST

2 This column shows how long the Sun is above the horizon in Boston. To determine your city's length of day, find the sunrise/sunset Key Letter values for your city **on page 226.** Add or subtract the sunset

value to Boston's length of day. Then simply *reverse* the sunrise sign (from minus to plus, or plus to minus) and add (or subtract) this value to the result of the first step.

E X A M P L E :

■ To find the length of day in Richmond, Virginia, on November 1, 2000:

Length of day, Boston (above)	**10:19**
Sunset Key Letter B (p. 229)	**+ 32 minutes**
	10:51
Reverse sunrise Key Letter D (p. 229, +17 to –17)	**– 17 minutes**
Length of day, Richmond (10 hr., 34 min.)	**10:34**

3 The Sun Fast column is designed to change sundial time to clock time in Boston. A sundial reads natural, or Sun, time, which is neither Standard nor Daylight time except by coincidence. From a sundial reading, subtract the minutes given in the Sun Fast column to get Boston clock time, and use Key Letter C in the table **on page 226** to convert the time to your city.

E X A M P L E :

■ To change sundial time into clock time in Boston, or Salem, Oregon, on November 1, 2000:

Sundial reading, Nov. 1 (Boston or Salem)	12:00 noon
Subtract Sun Fast (p. 40)	– 32 minutes
Clock time, Boston	11:28 A.M. EST
Use Key Letter C for Salem (p. 229)	+ 27 minutes
Clock time, Salem	11:55 A.M. PST

4 This column gives the degrees and minutes of the Sun from the celestial equator at noon EST or EDT.

5 The High Tide column gives the times of daily high tides in Boston. For example, on November 1, the first high tide occurs at 2:15 A.M. and the second occurs at 2:30 P.M. (A dash under High Tide indicates that high water occurs on or after midnight and so is recorded on the next day.) Figures for calculating high tide times and heights for localities other than Boston are given in the **Tide Corrections table on page 232.**

6 Use these two Key Letter columns to calculate the moonrise/moonset times for localities other than Boston. (A dash indicates that moonrise/moonset occurs on or after midnight and so is recorded on the next day.) Use the same procedure as explained in #1 for calculating your moonrise/moonset time, then factor in an additional correction based on longitude (see table below). For the longitude of your city, **see page 226.**

Longitude of city	Correction minutes
58° – 76°	0
77° – 89°	+1
90° – 102°	+2
103° – 115°	+3
116° – 127°	+4
128° – 141°	+5
142° – 155°	+6

E X A M P L E :

■ To determine the time of moonrise in Lansing, Michigan, on November 1, 2000:

Moonrise, Boston, with Key Letter E (p. 40)	11:16 A.M. EST
Value of Key Letter E for Lansing (p. 228)	+ 54 minutes
Correction for Lansing longitude 84° 33'	+ 1 minute
Moonrise, Lansing	12:11 P.M. EST

Use the same procedure to determine the time of moonset.

–Beth Krommes

7 The Moon's place is its *astronomical,* or *actual,* placement in the heavens. (This should not be confused with the Moon's *astrological* place in the zodiac, as explained **on page 180.**) All calculations in this Almanac are based on astronomy, not astrology, except for the information **on pages 180, 224, and 225.**

In addition to the 12 constellations of the astronomical zodiac, five other abbreviations may appear in this column: Auriga **(AUR),** a northern constellation between Perseus and Gemini; Cetus **(CET),** which lies south of the zodiac, just south of Pisces and Aries; Ophiuchus **(OPH),** a constellation primarily north of the zodiac but with a small corner between Scorpius and Sagittarius; Orion **(ORI),** a constellation whose northern limit first reaches the zodiac between Taurus and Gemini; and Sextans **(SEX),** which lies south of the zodiac except for a corner that just touches it near Leo.

8 The last column gives the Moon's age, which is the number of days since the previous new Moon. (The average length of the lunar month is 29.53 days.)

(c o n t i n u e d   o n   n e x t   p a g e)

The Right-Hand Calendar Pages

(Pages 59-85)

■ Throughout the Right-Hand Calendar Pages are groups of symbols that represent notable celestial events. The symbols and names of the principal planets and aspects are:

☉	**Sun**	♆	**Neptune**
○●☾	**Moon**	♇	**Pluto**
☿	**Mercury**	☌	**Conjunction (on the same celestial longitude)**
♀	**Venus**		
⊕	**Earth**		
♂	**Mars**	☊	**Ascending node**
♃	**Jupiter**	☋	**Descending node**
♄	**Saturn**	☍	**Opposition (180 degrees apart)**
⛢	**Uranus**		

For example, ☌ ♆ ☾ next to November 3, 2000 (see opposite page), means that a conjunction (☌) of Neptune (♆) and the Moon (☾) occurs on that date, when they are aligned along the same celestial longitude and appear to be closest together in the sky.

–Beth Krommes

The Seasons of 2000-2001

Fall 2000	**Sept. 22, 1:27 P.M. EDT**
Winter 2000	**Dec. 21, 8:37 A.M. EST**
Spring 2001	**Mar. 20, 8:31 A.M. EST**
Summer 2001	**June 21, 3:38 A.M. EDT**
Fall 2001	**Sept. 22, 7:04 P.M. EDT**
Winter 2001	**Dec. 21, 2:21 P.M. EST**

Earth at Perihelion and Aphelion 2001

■ Earth will be at perihelion on January 4, 2001, when it will be 91,402,145 miles from the Sun. Earth will be at aphelion on July 4, 2001, when it will be 94,502,872 miles from the Sun.

Movable Feasts and Fasts for 2001

Septuagesima Sunday	**Feb. 11**
Shrove Tuesday	**Feb. 27**
Ash Wednesday	**Feb. 28**
Palm Sunday	**Apr. 8**
Good Friday	**Apr. 13**
Easter Day	**Apr. 15**
Rogation Sunday	**May 20**
Ascension Day	**May 24**
Whitsunday-Pentecost	**June 3**
Trinity Sunday	**June 10**
Corpus Christi	**June 14**
First Sunday in Advent	**Dec. 2**

Chronological Cycles for 2001

Dominical Letter	**G**
Epact	**5**
Golden Number (Lunar Cycle)	**7**
Roman Indiction	**9**
Solar Cycle	**22**
Year of Julian Period	**6714**

Era	**Year**	**Begins**
Byzantine	**7510**	**Sept. 14**
Jewish (A.M.)*	**5762**	**Sept. 17**
Chinese (Lunar) [Year of the Snake]	**4699**	**Jan. 24**
Roman (A.U.C.)	**2754**	**Jan. 14**
Nabonassar	**2750**	**Apr. 23**
Japanese	**2661**	**Jan. 1**
Grecian (Seleucidae)	**2313**	**Sept. 14 (or Oct. 14)**
Indian (Saka)	**1923**	**Mar. 22**
Diocletian	**1718**	**Sept. 11**
Islamic (Hegira)*	**1422**	**Mar. 25**

***Year begins at sunset.**

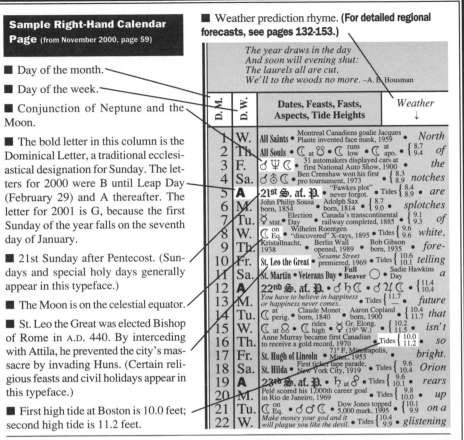

Sample Right-Hand Calendar Page (from November 2000, page 59)

■ Day of the month.

■ Day of the week.

■ Conjunction of Neptune and the Moon.

■ The bold letter in this column is the Dominical Letter, a traditional ecclesiastical designation for Sunday. The letters for 2000 were B until Leap Day (February 29) and A thereafter. The letter for 2001 is G, because the first Sunday of the year falls on the seventh day of January.

■ 21st Sunday after Pentecost. (Sundays and special holy days generally appear in this typeface.)

■ The Moon is on the celestial equator.

■ St. Leo the Great was elected Bishop of Rome in A.D. 440. By interceding with Attila, he prevented the city's massacre by invading Huns. (Certain religious feasts and civil holidays appear in this typeface.)

■ First high tide at Boston is 10.0 feet; second high tide is 11.2 feet.

■ Weather prediction rhyme. **(For detailed regional forecasts, see pages 132-153.)**

The year draws in the day
And soon will evening shut:
The laurels all are cut,
We'll to the woods no more. –A. E. Housman

D. M.	D. W.	Dates, Feasts, Fasts, Aspects, Tide Heights	Weather ↓
1	W.	**All Saints** • Montreal Canadiens goalie Jacques Plante invented face mask, 1959 •	*North*
2	Th.	**All Souls** • ☾ at ☋ • ☾ runs low • ☾ at apo. • {8.7 9.4	*of*
3	F.	☌♆☾ • 31 automakers displayed cars at first National Auto Show, 1900 •	*the*
4	Sa.	☌♅☾ • Ben Crenshaw won his first pro tournament, 1973 • {8.3 8.9	*notches*
5	**A**	**21st S. af. P.** • "Fawkes plot" never forgot. • Tides {8.4 8.9 •	*are*
6	M.	John Philip Sousa born, 1854 • Adolph Sax born, 1814 • {8.7 9.0 •	*splotches*
7	Tu.	☿ stat. • Election Day • Canada's transcontinental railway completed, 1885 • {9.1 9.3	*of*
8	W.	☾ on Eq. • Wilhelm Roentgen "discovered" X-rays, 1895 • Tides {9.6 9.6	*white,*
9	Th.	Kristallnacht, 1938 • Berlin Wall opened, 1989 • Bob Gibson born, 1935 •	*fore-*
10	Fr.	**St. Leo the Great** • *Sesame Street* premiered, 1969 • Tides {10.6 10.1	*telling*
11	Sa.	**St. Martin • Veterans Day** • Full Beaver ○ • Sadie Hawkins Day	*a*
12	**A**	**22nd S. af. P.** • ☌♄☾ • ☌♃☾ • {11.4 10.4	
13	M.	*You have to believe in happiness or happiness never comes.* • Tides {11.7 — •	*future*
14	Tu.	☾ at perig. • Claude Monet born, 1840 • Aaron Copland born, 1900 • {10.4 11.7	*that*
15	W.	☾ at ☊ • ☾ rides high • ☿ Gr. Elong. (19° W.) • {10.2 11.5 •	*isn't*
16	Th.	Anne Murray became first Canadian to receive a gold record, 1970 • Tides {10.0 11.2 •	*so*
17	Fr.	**St. Hugh of Lincoln** • 71° F, Minneapolis, Minn., 1953 •	*bright.*
18	Sa.	**St. Hilda** • First ticker tape parade, New York City, 1919 • Tides {9.6 10.4	*Orion*
19	**A**	**23rd S. af. P.** • ♄ at ☍ • Tides {9.6 10.1 •	*rears*
20	M.	Pelé scored his 1,000th career goal in Rio de Janeiro, 1969 • Tides {9.8 10.0 •	*up*
21	Tu.	☾ on Eq. • ☌♂☾ • Dow Jones topped 5,000 mark, 1995 • {10.1 9.9	*on a*
22	W.	*Make money your god and it will plague you like the devil.* • Tides {10.4 9.9 •	*glistening*

For a more complete explanation of terms used throughout the Almanac, see Glossary, page 46.

Predicting Earthquakes

■ Note the dates, in the **Right-Hand Calendar Pages,** when the Moon (☾) rides high or runs low. The date of the high begins the most likely five-day period of earthquakes in the Northern Hemisphere; the date of the low indicates a similar five-day period in the Southern Hemisphere. Also noted twice each month are the days when the Moon is on the celestial equator (☾ on Eq.), indicating likely two-day earthquake periods in both hemispheres.

–Beth Krommes

More Astronomical Data for 2001

Bright Stars .... page 54
Eclipses .... page 52
Full-Moon Dates 2001-2005........ page 52
Principal Meteor Showers .... page 52
The Twilight Zone .... page 234
The Visible Planets (Venus, Mars, Jupiter, Saturn, and Mercury).......... page 50

Holidays and Observances, 2001

A selected list of commemorative days, with federal holidays denoted by *.

Jan. 1 New Year's Day*
Jan. 15 Martin Luther King Jr.'s Birthday *(observed)**
Jan. 20 Inauguration Day *(D.C.)**
Feb. 2 Groundhog Day; Guadalupe-Hidalgo Treaty Day *(N.Mex.)*
Feb. 12 Abraham Lincoln's Birthday
Feb. 14 Valentine's Day
Feb. 15 Susan B. Anthony's Birthday *(Fla., Wis.)*
Feb. 19 George Washington's Birthday *(observed)**
Feb. 27 Mardi Gras *(Baldwin & Mobile Counties, Ala.; La.)*
Mar. 2 Texas Independence Day
Mar. 6 Town Meeting Day *(Vt.)*
Mar. 15 Andrew Jackson Day *(Tenn.)*
Mar. 17 St. Patrick's Day; Evacuation Day *(Suffolk Co., Mass.)*
Mar. 31 Cesar Chavez Day *(Calif.)*
Apr. 2 Pascua Florida Day
Apr. 13 Thomas Jefferson's Birthday
Apr. 16 Patriots Day *(Maine, Mass.)*
Apr. 27 National Arbor Day
May 1 May Day
May 8 Truman Day *(Mo.)*
May 13 Mother's Day
May 19 Armed Forces Day
May 21 Victoria Day *(Canada)*
May 28 Memorial Day *(observed)**
June 5 World Environment Day
June 11 King Kamehameha I Day *(Hawaii)*
June 14 Flag Day
June 17 Father's Day
June 18 Bunker Hill Day *(Suffolk Co., Mass.)*
June 19 Emancipation Day *(Tex.)*
June 20 West Virginia Day
July 1 Canada Day

July 4 Independence Day*
July 24 Pioneer Day *(Utah)*
Aug. 6 Colorado Day
Aug. 13 Victory Day *(R.I.)*
Aug. 16 Bennington Battle Day *(Vt.)*
Aug. 26 Women's Equality Day
Sept. 3 Labor Day*
Sept. 10 Admission Day *(Calif.)*
Oct. 8 Columbus Day *(observed)**; Thanksgiving Day *(Canada)*; Native Americans Day *(S.Dak.)*
Oct. 9 Leif Eriksson Day
Oct. 18 Alaska Day
Oct. 31 Halloween; Nevada Day
Nov. 4 Will Rogers Day *(Okla.)*
Nov. 6 Election Day
Nov. 11 Veterans Day*
Nov. 19 Discovery Day *(Puerto Rico)*
Nov. 22 Thanksgiving Day*
Nov. 23 Acadian Day *(La.)*
Dec. 25 Christmas Day*
Dec. 26 Boxing Day *(Canada)*

Religious Observances

Epiphany .... **Jan. 6**
Ash Wednesday .... **Feb. 28**
Islamic New Year .... **Mar. 26**
Palm Sunday .... **Apr. 8**
First day of Passover .... **Apr. 8**
Good Friday .... **Apr. 13**
Easter Day .... **Apr. 15**
Orthodox Easter .... **Apr. 15**
Whitsunday-Pentecost .... **June 3**
Rosh Hashanah .... **Sept. 18**
Yom Kippur .... **Sept. 27**
First day of Ramadan .... **Nov. 17**
First day of Chanukah .... **Dec. 10**
Christmas Day .... **Dec. 25**

How the Almanac Weather Forecasts Are Made

■ We derive our weather forecasts from a secret formula devised by the founder of this Almanac in 1792, enhanced by the most modern scientific calculations based on solar activity and current meteorological data. We believe that nothing in the universe occurs haphazardly but that there is a cause-and-effect pattern to all phenomena, thus making long-range weather forecasts possible. However, neither we nor anyone else has as yet gained sufficient insight into the mysteries of the universe to predict weather with anything resembling total accuracy.

Why wait ten months?

Now you can have rich, dark compost _in just 14 days!_

With the amazing Compos-Tumbler, you'll have bushels of crumbly, ready-to-use compost — _in just 14 days!_ (And, in the ten months it takes to make compost the old way, your ComposTumbler can produce _hundreds of pounds_ of rich food for your garden!)

Say good-bye to that messy, open compost pile (and to the flies, pests, and odors that come along with it!) Bid a happy farewell to the strain of trying to turn over heavy, wet piles with a pitchfork.

Compost the Better Way

Compost-making with the ComposTumbler is neat, quick and easy!

Gather up leaves, old weeds, kitchen scraps, lawn clippings, etc. and toss them into the roomy 18-bushel drum. Then, once each day, give the ComposTumbler's _gear-driven_ handle a few easy spins.

The ComposTumbler's Magic

Inside the ComposTumbler, carefully positioned mixing fins blend materials, pushing fresh mixture to the core where the temperatures are the hottest (up to 160°) and the composting bacteria most active.

After just 14 days, open the door, and you'll find an abundance of dark, sweet-smelling "garden gold" — ready to enrich and feed your garden!

NEW SMALLER SIZE!

Now there are 2 sizes. The 18-bushel original ComposTumbler and the NEW 9.5-bushel Compact ComposTumbler. Try either size risk-free for 1 year!

See for yourself! Try the ComposTumbler risk-free with our 1-Year Home Trial!

Glossary

Aphelion (Aph.): The point in a planet's orbit that is farthest from the Sun.

Apogee (Apo.): The point in the Moon's orbit that is farthest from Earth.

Celestial Sphere: An imaginary sphere projected into space that represents the entire sky, with an observer on Earth at its center. All celestial bodies other than Earth are imagined as being on its inside surface.

Conjunction: When two celestial bodies reach the same celestial longitude or right ascension, approximately corresponding to their closest apparent approach in the sky. (Dates for conjunction are given in the Right-Hand Calendar Pages 59-85; sky sightings of closely aligned bodies are given in the descriptive text at the top of the Left-Hand Calendar Pages 58-84.) **Inferior (Inf.):** A conjunction in which Mercury or Venus is between the Sun and Earth. **Superior (Sup.):** A conjunction in which the Sun is between a planet and Earth.

Declination: The celestial latitude of an object in the sky, measured in degrees north or south of the celestial equator; analogous to latitude on Earth. The Almanac gives the Sun's declination at noon EST or EDT.

Dominical Letter: Used to denote the Sundays in the ecclesiastical calendar in a given year, determined by the date on which the first Sunday of that year falls. If Jan. 1 is a Sunday, the letter is A; if Jan. 2 is a Sunday, the letter is B; and so on to G. In a leap year, the letter applies through February and then takes the preceding letter.

Eclipse, Lunar: The full Moon enters the shadow of Earth, which cuts off all or part of the Moon's light. **Total:** The Moon passes completely through the umbra (central dark part) of Earth's shadow. **Partial:** Only part of the Moon passes through the umbra. **Penumbral:** The Moon passes through only the penumbra (area of partial darkness surrounding the umbra).

Eclipse, Solar: Earth enters the shadow of the new Moon, which cuts off all or part of the Sun's light. **Total:** Earth passes through the umbra (central dark part) of the Moon's shadow, resulting in totality for observers within a narrow band on Earth. **Annular:** The Moon appears silhouetted against the Sun, with a ring of sunlight showing around it. **Partial:** The Moon blocks only part of the Sun.

Ecliptic: The apparent annual path of the Sun around the celestial sphere. The plane of the ecliptic is tipped 23½° from the celestial equator.

Elongation: The difference in degrees between the celestial longitudes of a planet and the Sun. **Greatest Elongation (Gr. Elong.):** The greatest apparent distance of a planet from the Sun, as seen from Earth.

Epact: A number from 1 to 30 that indicates the Moon's age on Jan. 1 at Greenwich, England; used for determining the date of Easter.

Equator, Celestial (Eq.): The circle around the celestial sphere that is halfway between the celestial poles. It can be thought of as the plane of Earth's equator projected out onto the sphere.

Equinox, Autumnal: The Sun appears to cross the celestial equator from north to south. **Vernal:** The Sun appears to cross the celestial equator from south to north.

Evening Star: A planet that is above the western horizon at sunset and less than 180° east of the Sun in right ascension.

Golden Number: A number in the 19-year cycle of the Moon, used for determining the date of Easter. (The Moon repeats its phases approximately every 19 solar years.) Add 1 to any given year and divide the result by 19; the remainder is the Golden Number. When there is no remainder, the Golden Number is 19.

Julian Period: A period of 7,980 years beginning Jan. 1, 4713 B.C. Devised in 1583 by Joseph Scaliger, it provides a chronological basis for the study of ancient history. To find the Julian year, add 4,713 to any year.

(continued on page 48)

Are you over 55?
"It's All Free for Seniors"

by Murry L Broach - Staff Writer

Washington DC (Special) An amazing new book reveals thousands of little-known Government giveaways for people over 55.

Each year, lots of these benefits are NOT given away simply because people don't know they're available... and the government doesn't advertise them.

Many of these fabulous freebies can be yours regardless of your income or assets. Entitled "Free for Seniors", the book tells you all about such goodies as how you can:

▶ Get free prescription drugs. (This one alone could save you thousands of dollars!)

▶ Get free dental care... for yourself AND for your grandkids.

▶ Get up to $800 for food.

▶ How you can get free legal help.

▶ How to get some help in paying your rent, wherever you live.

▶ How to get up to $15,000 free money to spruce up your home!

▶ Here's where to get $1,800 to keep you warm this winter.

▶ Access the very best research on our planet on how you can live longer.

▶ Are you becoming more forgetful? Here's valuable free information you should get now.

▶ Stop high blood pressure and cholesterol worries from ruling your life.

▶ Free help if you have arthritis of any type.

▶ Incontinence is not inevitable. These free facts could help you.

▶ Free eye treatment.

▶ Depression: Being down in the dumps is common, but it doesn't have to be a normal part of growing old.

▶ Free medical care from some of the very best doctors in the world for Alzheimer's, cataracts, or heart disease.

▶ New Cancer Cure? Maybe! Here's how to find out what's known about it to this point.

▶ Promising new developments for prostate cancer.

▶ Get paid $100 a day plus expenses to travel overseas!

▶ Up to $5,000 free to help you pay your bills.

▶ Free and confidential help with your sex life.

▶ Impotence? Get confidential help... Free therapies, treatments, implants, and much more.

▶ Hot Flashes? This new research could help you now!

▶ Find out if a medicine you're taking could be affecting your sex life.

There's more! Much, much more, and "Free for Seniors" comes with a solid no-nonsense guarantee. Send for your copy today and examine it at your leisure. Unless it makes or saves you AT LEAST ten times it's cost, simply return it for a full refund within 90 days.

To get your copy of "Free for Seniors", send your name and address along with a check or money-order for only $12.95 plus $2 postage and handling (total of $14.95) to: FREE FOR SENIORS, Dept. FS8287, 718 - 12th Street N.W., Box 24500, Canton, Ohio 44701.

To charge to your VISA or MasterCard, include your card number, expiration date, and signature. For even faster service, have your credit card handy and call toll-free 1-800-772-7285, Ext. FS8287.

Want to save even more? Do a favor for a friend or relative and order 2 books for only $20 postpaid. ©2000 TCO FS0130S03

http://www.trescoinc.com

Moon on Equator: The Moon is on the celestial equator.

Moon Rides High/Runs Low: The Moon is highest above or farthest below the celestial equator.

Moonrise/Moonset: The Moon's rising above or descending below the horizon.

Moon's Phases: The continually changing states in the Moon's appearance, caused by the different angles at which it is illuminated by the Sun. **First Quarter:** The right half of the Moon is illuminated, as seen from the Northern Hemisphere. **Full:** The Sun and the Moon are in opposition; the entire disk of the Moon is illuminated as viewed from Earth. **Last Quarter:** The left half of the Moon is illuminated, as seen from the Northern Hemisphere. **New:** The Sun and the Moon are in conjunction; the entire disk of the Moon is darkened as viewed from Earth.

Moon's Place, Astronomical: The actual position of the Moon within the constellations on the celestial sphere. **Astrological:** The position of the Moon within the astrological zodiac according to calculations made over 2,000 years ago. Because of precession of the equinoxes and other factors, this is not the Moon's actual position in the sky.

Morning Star: A planet that is above the eastern horizon at sunrise and less than 180° west of the Sun in right ascension.

Node, Ascending/Descending: Either of the two points where a body's orbit intersects the ecliptic. The body is moving from south to north of the ecliptic at the ascending node, and from north to south at the descending node. (An imaginary line through Earth that connects the Moon's nodes also aligns with an Earth-Sun line just twice a year, roughly six months apart; at these times, a new or full Moon that occurs when the Moon is at or near one of its nodes will result in an eclipse.)

Occultation (Occn.): The eclipse of a star or planet by the Moon or another planet.

Opposition: The Moon or a planet appears on the opposite side of the sky from the Sun (elongation 180°).

Perigee (Perig.): The point in the Moon's orbit that is closest to Earth.

Perihelion (Perih.): The point in a planet's orbit that is closest to the Sun.

Precession: The slowly changing position of the stars and equinoxes in the sky resulting from variations in the orientation of Earth's axis.

Right Ascension (R.A.): The celestial longitude of an object in the sky, measured eastward along the celestial equator in hours of time from the vernal equinox; analogous to longitude on Earth.

Roman Indiction: A number in a 15-year cycle, established Jan. 1, A.D. 313, as a fiscal term. Add 3 to any given year in the Christian era and divide by 15; the remainder is the Roman Indiction. When there is no remainder, the Roman Indiction is 15.

Solar Cycle: A period of 28 years in the Julian calendar, at the end of which the days of the month return to the same days of the week.

Solstice, Summer: The Sun reaches its greatest declination (23½°) north of the celestial equator. **Winter:** The Sun reaches its greatest declination (23½°) south of the celestial equator.

Stationary (Stat.): The apparent halted movement, as it reaches opposition, of a planet against the background of the stars, shortly before it appears to move backward (retrograde motion).

Sun Fast/Slow: The difference between a sundial reading and clock time.

Sunrise/Sunset: The visible rising and setting of the Sun's upper limb across the unobstructed horizon of an observer whose eyes are 15 feet above ground level.

Twilight: The period of time between full darkness (when the Sun is 18° below the horizon) and either sunrise or sunset. Twilight is classified as **astronomical,** when the Sun is between 18° and 12° below the horizon; **nautical,** when the Sun is between 12° and 6° below the horizon; and **civil,** when the Sun is less than 6° below the horizon.

The Visible Planets, 2001

■ Listed here for Boston are the times (EST/EDT) of the visible rising and setting of the planets Venus, Mars, Jupiter, and Saturn on the 1st, 11th, and 21st of each month. The approximate times of their visible rising and setting on other days can be found by interpolation. The capital letters that appear beside the times are Key Letters and are used to convert the times to other localities **(see pages 40 and 226)**. For definitions of morning and evening stars, see the **Glossary on page 46**.

Venus is a fine evening star for the first three months of 2001, dazzling on January 1 and growing brighter and rising higher through February (see feature on page 56). In April, it becomes a less impressive morning star for the rest of the year. In mid-July, Venus joins Saturn, the star Aldebaran, and the Moon; in early August, it meets Jupiter; and from October 28 to November 8, it is near Mercury. Venus is in conjunction with Mercury on April 6, with Saturn on July 15, and with Jupiter on August 5.

Mars enjoys a midyear opposition. This closest approach to Earth since 1988 keeps the planet bright all year, but it will move entirely in the low southerly sky for United States and Canadian observers. Thick horizon air should make the normally orange object a true "red planet." Its closest approach on June 21, the summer solstice, keeps Mars out all night now and for much of the summer, and makes it the very brightest "star" in the premidnight heavens from May through September.

	Boldface—P.M.				Lightface—A.M.				
Jan. 1.......	**set**	**8:13**	B	July 1 ...... rise	2:35	A	Jan. 1....... rise	1:55	D	July 1 ...... set	3:24	A
Jan. 11....	**set**	**8:31**	B	July 11 .... rise	2:30	A	Jan. 11..... rise	1:45	D	July 11 .... set	2:37	A
Jan. 21.....	**set**	**8:46**	B	July 21 .... rise	2:29	A	Jan. 21..... rise	1:35	D	July 21 .... set	1:55	A
Feb. 1	**set**	**8:57**	C	Aug. 1 ..... rise	2:34	A	Feb. 1 ...... rise	1:23	D	Aug. 1 ...... set	1:16	A
Feb. 11	**set**	**9:01**	D	Aug. 11 ... rise	2:44	A	Feb. 11 .... rise	1:11	D	Aug. 11 ... set 12:44		A
Feb. 21	**set**	**8:57**	D	Aug. 21 ... rise	2:59	A	Feb. 21 .... rise 12:58		E	Aug. 21 ... set 12:19		A
Mar. 1	**set**	**8:45**	D	Sept. 1 ..... rise	3:20	A	Mar. 1 ..... rise 12:47		E	Sept. 1 ...... **set** **11:57**		A
Mar. 11 ...	**set**	**8:13**	D	Sept. 11 ... rise	3:42	B	Mar. 11 ... rise 12:31		E	Sept. 11 ... **set** **11:41**		A
Mar. 21 ... rise		5:35	B	Sept. 21 ... rise	4:05	B	Mar. 21 ... rise 12:14		E	Sept. 21 ... **set** **11:29**		A
Apr. 1 ...... rise		5:41	B	Oct. 1 ...... rise	4:28	B	Apr. 1 ...... rise 12:50		E	Oct. 1 ...... **set** **11:19**		A
Apr. 11.... rise		5:00	B	Oct. 11 .... rise	4:52	B	Apr. 11.... rise 12:26		E	Oct. 11 .... **set** **11:12**		A
Apr. 21.... rise		4:28	B	Oct. 21 .... rise	5:16	C	Apr. 21.... rise 12:00		E	Oct. 21 .... **set** **11:08**		A
May 1...... rise		4:04	B	Nov. 1 ..... rise	4:43	D	May 1...... **rise** **11:30**		E	Nov. 1 ..... **set** **10:04**		A
May 11.... rise		3:44	B	Nov. 11 ... rise	5:08	D	May 11.... **rise** **10:55**		E	Nov. 11 ... **set** **10:02**		A
May 21.... rise		3:27	B	Nov. 21 ... rise	5:34	D	May 21.... **rise** **10:16**		E	Nov. 21 ... **set** **10:01**		A
June 1...... rise		3:10	B	Dec. 1...... rise	5:59	E	June 1...... **rise** 9:26		E	Dec. 1...... **set** **10:00**		B
June 11.... rise		2:56	B	Dec. 11 .... rise	6:24	E	June 11.... **rise** 8:36		E	Dec. 11 .... **set** 9:59		B
June 21.... rise		2:44	B	Dec. 21 .... rise	6:46	E	June 21.... set	4:17	A	Dec. 21 .... **set** 9:58		B
				Dec. 31 .... rise	7:03	E				Dec. 31 .... **set** 9:56		B

Mercury boasts four periods in 2001 when it is maximally high above the horizon and thus easily visible. A predawn opportunity lasts for a month starting on October 17 and includes a lingering meeting with Venus from October 28 to November 8. Mercury visits the western sky in deepening evening twilight from January 14 to February 8, from May 1 to June 5, and finally from December 26 into 2002. During these evening appearances, Mercury is brightest the first week.

DO NOT CONFUSE 1) Jupiter with Saturn, both visible in the constellation Taurus during the first four months or so of the year. Jupiter is ten times brighter. 2) Venus with Jupiter during their predawn meeting on August 5 and 6. Venus is much brighter. 3) Saturn with Taurus's star Aldebaran, all year. Saturn is brighter, and Aldebaran looks orange. 4) Saturn, Venus, and the star Aldebaran as they bunch together in the predawn eastern sky from July 11 to 15. Venus is the brightest by far, and Aldebaran the dimmest of the three.

Jupiter has a great year. In January, it is out all night, high and dominant, sharing Taurus with nearby Saturn. It remains brilliant through winter and much of spring, finally falling low into western twilight in May. Jupiter emerges in July in the morning sky but doesn't return to prominence until autumn, when it rises before midnight. In December, now rising at nightfall, it is at its brightest. Jupiter is in conjunction with Mercury on May 16 and July 12 and with Venus on August 5.

Saturn is better seen this year than at any time since the 1970s. Anchored high in northerly Taurus all year, Saturn keeps close company with brilliant Jupiter from January into May, then vanishes behind the Sun from mid-May to mid-June. At year's start and year's end, it is particularly prominent for much of the night, achieving an unusually bright magnitude of −0.4 from Thanksgiving to Christmas. Saturn is in conjunction with Mercury on May 7 and with Venus on July 15.

Boldface—P.M. Lightface—A.M.

Jupiter

Jan. 1	set	4:21	E	July 1	rise	4:19	A
Jan. 11	set	3:38	E	July 11	rise	3:50	A
Jan. 21	set	2:58	E	July 21	rise	3:20	A
Feb. 1	set	2:15	E	Aug. 1	rise	2:47	A
Feb. 11	set	1:38	E	Aug. 11	rise	2:17	A
Feb. 21	set	1:02	E	Aug. 21	rise	1:46	A
Mar. 1	set	12:35	E	Sept. 1	rise	1:12	A
Mar. 11	set	12:01	E	Sept. 11	rise	12:40	A
Mar. 21	**set**	**11:26**	E	Sept. 21	rise	12:07	A
Apr. 1	**set**	**11:52**	E	Oct. 1	**rise**	**11:29**	A
Apr. 11	**set**	**11:22**	E	Oct. 11	**rise**	**10:54**	A
Apr. 21	**set**	**10:53**	E	Oct. 21	**rise**	**10:17**	A
May 1	**set**	**10:24**	E	Nov. 1	**rise**	**8:35**	A
May 11	**set**	**9:55**	E	Nov. 11	**rise**	**7:54**	A
May 21	**set**	**9:26**	E	Nov. 21	**rise**	**7:13**	A
June 1	**set**	**8:55**	E	Dec. 1	**rise**	**6:30**	A
June 11	**set**	**8:26**	E	Dec. 11	**rise**	**5:45**	A
June 21	rise	4:49	A	Dec. 21	**rise**	**5:00**	A
				Dec. 31	**rise**	**4:14**	A

Saturn

Jan. 1	set	3:38	D	July 1	rise	3:15	A
Jan. 11	set	2:57	D	July 11	rise	2:40	A
Jan. 21	set	2:17	D	July 21	rise	2:04	A
Feb. 1	set	1:34	D	Aug. 1	rise	1:25	A
Feb. 11	set	12:56	D	Aug. 11	rise	12:49	A
Feb. 21	set	12:19	D	Aug. 21	rise	12:12	A
Mar. 1	**set**	**11:46**	D	Sept. 1	**rise**	**11:31**	A
Mar. 11	**set**	**11:11**	D	Sept. 11	**rise**	**10:53**	A
Mar. 21	**set**	**10:36**	D	Sept. 21	**rise**	**10:15**	A
Apr. 1	**set**	**10:58**	D	Oct. 1	**rise**	**9:32**	A
Apr. 11	**set**	**10:24**	D	Oct. 11	**rise**	**8:52**	A
Apr. 21	**set**	**9:51**	E	Oct. 21	**rise**	**8:11**	A
May 1	**set**	**9:18**	E	Nov. 1	**rise**	**6:26**	A
May 11	**set**	**8:45**	E	Nov. 11	**rise**	**5:44**	A
May 21	**set**	**8:12**	E	Nov. 21	**rise**	**5:02**	A
June 1	rise	5:00	A	Dec. 1	**rise**	**4:20**	A
June 11	rise	4:25	A	Dec. 11	set	6:23	E
June 21	rise	3:50	A	Dec. 21	set	5:40	E
				Dec. 31	set	4:58	E

Eclipses, 2001

■ There will be five eclipses in 2001, two of the Sun and three of the Moon. Solar eclipses are visible only in certain areas and require eye protection to be safely viewed. Lunar eclipses are technically visible from the entire night side of Earth, but during a penumbral eclipse, the dimming of the Moon's illumination is very slight.

1 Total eclipse of the Moon, January 9. The beginning of the umbral phase will be visible in northern Canada and most of Alaska. The end will be visible in northeastern North America. The Moon enters penumbra at 12:44 P.M. EST (9:44 A.M. PST); the umbral phase begins at 1:42 P.M. EST (10:42 A.M. PST); totality begins at 2:50 P.M. EST (11:50 A.M. PST) and ends at 3:52 P.M. EST (12:52 P.M. PST); the umbral phase ends at 4:59 P.M. EST (1:59 P.M. PST); the Moon leaves penumbra at 5:58 P.M. EST (2:58 P.M. PST).

2 Total eclipse of the Sun, June 21. This eclipse will not be visible in the United States or Canada.

3 Partial eclipse of the Moon, July 5. This eclipse will be visible only in Hawaii and the Aleutian Islands.

4 Annular eclipse of the Sun, December 14. The annular phase will not be visible in the United States or Canada. The partial phase will be visible in the central United States and Canada, beginning about 3:00 P.M. CST

and ending about 4:30 P.M. CST, and in coastal California, beginning about 12:00 P.M. PST and ending about 2:00 P.M. PST.

5 Penumbral Eclipse of the Moon, December 30. This eclipse will be visible in North America and Hawaii, except the end will not be visible along the eastern coast of North America. The Moon enters penumbra at 3:25 A.M. EST (12:25 A.M. PST) and leaves at 7:33 A.M. EST (4:33 A.M. PST).

Full-Moon Dates

	2001	2002	2003	2004	2005
Jan.	9	28	18	7	25
Feb.	8	27	16	6	23
Mar.	9	28	18	6	25
Apr.	7	26	16	5	24
May	7	26	15	4	23
June	5	24	14	3	22
July	5	24	13	2&31	21
Aug.	4	22	12	29	19
Sept.	2	21	10	28	17
Oct.	2	21	10	27	17
Nov.	1&30	19	8	26	15
Dec.	30	19	8	26	15

Principal Meteor Showers

Shower	Best Viewing	Point of Origin	Date of Maximum*	Peak Rate (/hr.)**	Associated Comet
Quadrantid	Predawn	N	Jan. 4	80	—
Lyrid	Predawn	S	Apr. 22	12	Thatcher
Eta Aquarid	Predawn	SE	May 4	20	Halley
Delta Aquarid	Predawn	S	July 30	10	—
Perseid	Predawn	NE	Aug. 11-13	75	Swift-Tuttle
Draconid	Late evening	NW	Oct. 9	6	Giacobini-Zinner
Orionid	Predawn	S	Oct. 21-22	25	Halley
Taurid	Midnight	S	Nov. 9	6	Encke
Leonid	Predawn	S	Nov. 18	20	Tempel-Tuttle
Andromedid	Late evening	S	Nov. 25-27	5	Biela
Geminid	All night	NE	Dec. 13-14	65	—
Ursid	Predawn	N	Dec. 22	12	Tuttle

* **Date of actual maximum occurrence may vary by one or two days in either direction.**
** **Approximate.**

Bright Stars, 2001

Transit Times

■ This table shows the time (EST or EDT) that a star transits the meridian (i.e., lies directly above the horizon's south point) at Boston, and the star's altitude above that point on the dates shown. The transit time on any other date differs from that of the nearest date listed by approximately four minutes for each day. To find the time of a star's transit for your location, convert its time at Boston using Key Letter C.*

Star	Constellation	Magnitude	Jan. 1	Mar. 1	May 1	July 1	Sept. 1	Nov. 1	Altitude (degrees)
Altair	Aquila	0.8	**12:48**	8:56	5:57	1:57	**9:49**	**4:49**	56.3
Deneb	Cygnus	1.3	**1:39**	9:47	6:47	2:48	**10:40**	**5:40**	92.8
Fomalhaut	Psc. Aus.	1.2	**3:54**	**12:02**	9:02	5:02	12:55	**7:55**	17.8
Algol	Perseus	2.2	**8:05**	**4:13**	**1:13**	9:13	5:09	12:09	88.5
Aldebaran	Taurus	0.9	**9:32**	**5:40**	**2:40**	10:40	6:37	1:37	64.1
Rigel	Orion	0.1	**10:10**	**6:18**	**3:18**	11:19	7:15	2:15	39.4
Capella	Auriga	0.1	**10:12**	**6:20**	**3:20**	11:20	7:17	2:17	93.6
Bellatrix	Orion	1.6	**10:21**	**6:29**	**3:29**	11:29	7:26	2:26	54.0
Betelgeuse	Orion	var. 0.4	**10:51**	**6:59**	**3:59**	11:59	7:56	2:56	55.0
Sirius	Can. Maj.	−1.4	**11:41**	7:49	4:49	**12:49**	8:45	3:45	31.0
Procyon	Can. Min.	0.4	12:38	8:43	5:43	**1:43**	9:39	4:39	52.9
Pollux	Gemini	1.2	12:44	8:49	5:49	**1:49**	9:45	4:45	75.7
Regulus	Leo	1.4	3:07	**11:12**	8:12	4:12	**12:08**	7:08	59.7
Spica	Virgo	var. 1.0	6:24	2:32	**11:28**	**7:28**	**3:24**	10:25	36.6
Arcturus	Bootes	−0.1	7:15	3:23	12:19	**8:19**	**4:15**	11:15	66.9
Antares	Scorpius	var. 0.9	9:27	5:35	2:36	**10:32**	6:28	**1:28**	21.3
Vega	Lyra	0.0	11:35	7:43	4:43	12:39	**8:35**	**3:36**	86.4

Time of Transit (EST/EDT) Boldface—P.M. Lightface—A.M.

Risings and Settings

■ To find the time of a star's rising at Boston on any date, subtract the interval shown at right from the star's transit time on that date; add the interval to find the star's setting time. To find the rising and setting times for your city, convert the Boston transit times above using the Key Letter shown at right before applying the interval.* The directions in which the stars rise and set, shown for Boston, are generally useful throughout the United States. Deneb, Algol, Capella, and Vega are circumpolar stars—they never set but appear to circle the celestial north pole.

Star	Interval (h. m.)	Rising Key	Dir.	Setting Key	Dir.
Altair	6:36	B	EbN	E	WbN
Fomalhaut	3:59	E	SE	D	SW
Aldebaran	7:06	B	ENE	D	WNW
Rigel	5:33	D	EbS	B	WbS
Bellatrix	6:27	B	EbN	D	WbN
Betelgeuse	6:31	B	EbN	D	WbN
Sirius	5:00	D	ESE	B	WSW
Procyon	6:23	B	EbN	D	WbN
Pollux	8:01	A	NE	E	NW
Regulus	6:49	B	EbN	D	WbN
Spica	5:23	D	EbS	B	WbS
Arcturus	7:19	A	ENE	E	WNW
Antares	4:17	E	SEbE	A	SWbW

* The values of Key Letters are given in the Time Corrections table (page 226).

−Beth Krommes

Checking Out

The Goddess of Love

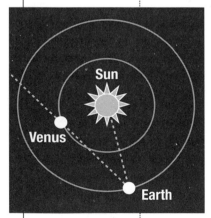

At greatest elonga-
tion, Venus and the
Sun are maximally
separated—by 47°.
This can allow the
evening star to be
seen several hours
after sunset against
a black night sky.

During the first months of 2001, North Americans will have their finest look at Venus in years. Like a UFO, it will grab the attention of and bewilder onlookers as it hovers with fantastic brilliance in the evening sky. When Venus reaches its greatest elongation (widest angle from the Sun) between January and March, the evening star is as high and prominent as possible. This optimal state of affairs occurred in 1993, and it happens again in 2001.

The eight-year interval is no fluke. Venus completes 13 orbits of the Sun in exactly the same time Earth makes 8. So after eight years, our sister planet returns like a meshed gear to the same observational situation.

The year 2001 starts with the evening star already prominent at dusk. As January progresses, Venus rises even higher, achieving its widest separation from the Sun—47 degrees—on the 17th, and then its greatest brilliancy a month later on February 21. But a lofty twilight perch and visibility for hours after sunset is only part of the majestic 2001 winter's tale.

Nearly as reflective as a mirror, Venus is the shiniest planet. Fully 76 percent of the sunlight striking its white sulfuric-acid clouds gets bounced away. Several factors now combine to make it even brighter. During the last week of February, Venus arrives at its closest point to the Sun, which floods it with the most intense possible lighting. At the same time, its increasing nearness to Earth brings it to a maximum brightness—"greatest brilliancy"—in our sky. Topping it all off, Earth, in its own elliptical path, is then just a few weeks past its yearly close approach to the nearly circular Venusian orbit, placing both worlds unusually close together. It all adds up to offer us an extraordinary visual treat, when Venus attains its high, prominent perch at a convenient early dinner hour.

And still the show's not over. From February to late March, Venus sinks lower at dusk as it prepares to pass between us and the Sun. During this time, steadily braced binoculars reveal a striking crescent. Any telescope, any magnification, makes it seem dreamlike, a strange featureless "moon" that appears larger and skinnier each March evening.

Then comes the kicker. On March 29, Venus passes between us and the Sun. (But not exactly between: *That* event will happen in June of 2004, a spectacular transit of Venus across the face of the Sun, which hasn't occurred since the 19th century.) This time around, Venus scoots far to the north of the Sun, granting more rewards to Northern Hemisphere inhabitants. Normally Venus is east or west of the Sun; now it's suddenly 10 degrees due north. This allows the planet to perform the seemingly impossible feat of setting after sunset but also coming up before sunrise.

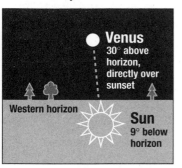

At greatest brilliancy in late February, Venus will shine luminously above the western horizon.

Because all these shenanigans involve the night's brightest "star," the dazzling show will be witnessed by billions of people. Most will not know that they are viewing our neighboring planet at its best.

It's touching that we named the most luminous "star" after the love goddess. It's sweet that the evening star's similar-to-Earth size suggests a sister world. But we'll never have a hands-on relationship. For all eternity, the nearest planet—that dazzling beacon in the west—will tantalize with a warning label: Look but don't touch.

➡ Spinning the Web: Go to www.almanac.com and click on Article Links 2001 for Web sites related to this article. –*The Editors*

A Few Sobering Facts About Venus

Few who gaze longingly at the glowing beacon in the western sky are aware of Venus's oddities.

■

For one thing, its day is longer than its year. Venus spins on its axis in 243 Earth-days but orbits the Sun in 225 Earth-days.

■

The Venusian surface is brightly lit despite being eternally overcast. With illumination that equals Earth's on a cloudy day, even inexpensive disposable cameras would take correctly exposed photos there, a situation encountered on no other planet.

■

No budding Ansel Adams is likely to go there. Ever. The planet's surface never budges from about 850°F, day and night. The air is suffocatingly dense, packed with 50 times greater pressure than a pressure cooker. Its atmosphere provides no oxygen whatsoever. Beneath clouds of concentrated acid droplets lies clear compressed air that distorts everything into funhouse-mirror images. Venus is more than weird; it's the most hellish planet in the known universe.

◻◻

2000   NOVEMBER, The Eleventh Month

Just seven days apart, Saturn and then Jupiter attain their closest and brightest positions to Earth this year, on the 19th and 26th, respectively. Both are exceptionally bright and high at midnight: Saturn's greatest brilliance since 1975 and Jupiter's highest ascent since 1989. Jupiter's brilliance, at magnitude -2.9, easily makes it the sky's brightest "star" after nightfall (brighter Venus having set during late twilight). Saturn, very bright but not dazzling at magnitude -0.4, conspicuously hovers nearby. Meanwhile, much less dramatically, Mercury makes its best morning appearances of the year from the 7th to the 24th in predawn twilight, hovering near the Moon on the 24th.

☽	First Quarter	4th day	2nd hour	27th minute
○	Full Moon	11th day	16th hour	15th minute
☾	Last Quarter	18th day	10th hour	24th minute
●	New Moon	25th day	18th hour	11th minute

Times are given in Eastern Standard Time.

For an explanation of this page, see page 40; for values of Key Letters, see page 226.

Day of Year	Day of Month	Day of Week	☀ Rises h. m.	Key	☀ Sets h. m.	Key	Length of Day h. m.	Sun Fast m.	Declination of Sun ° '	High Tide Boston Light—A.M. Bold—P.M.		☽ Rises h. m.	Key	☽ Sets h. m.	Key	Place	Age
306	1	W.	6 18	D	4 37	B	10 19	32	14 s.40	2¼	2½	11ᴹ16	E	8ᴾᴹ37	B	SAG	5
307	2	Th.	6 19	D	4 36	B	10 17	32	14 59	3	3¼	12ᴾᴹ03	E	9 30	B	SAG	6
308	3	Fr.	6 21	D	4 35	B	10 14	32	15 18	4	4	12 44	E	10 26	B	CAP	7
309	4	Sa.	6 22	D	4 33	B	10 11	32	15 36	5	5	1 20	E	11ᴾᴹ25	B	CAP	8
310	5	**A**	6 23	D	4 32	B	10 09	32	15 54	5¾	6	1 52	D	—	—	CAP	9
311	6	M.	6 24	D	4 31	B	10 07	32	16 12	6¾	7	2 21	D	12ᴬᴹ25	C	AQU	10
312	7	Tu.	6 26	D	4 30	A	10 04	32	16 30	7½	7¾	2 48	D	1 27	C	AQU	11
313	8	W.	6 27	D	4 29	A	10 02	32	16 48	8¼	8½	3 15	D	2 31	D	PSC	12
314	9	Th.	6 28	D	4 28	A	10 00	32	17 05	9	9¼	3 42	C	3 36	D	CET	13
315	10	Fr.	6 29	D	4 27	A	9 58	32	17 22	9¾	**10**	4 11	C	4 44	D	PSC	14
316	11	Sa.	6 31	D	4 26	A	9 55	32	17 38	10¼	10¾	4 44	B	5 54	E	CET	15
317	12	**A**	6 32	D	4 25	A	9 53	31	17 54	11	11½	5 22	B	7 06	E	TAU	16
318	13	M.	6 33	D	4 24	A	9 51	31	18 10	11¾	—	6 07	B	8 18	E	TAU	17
319	14	Tu.	6 34	D	4 23	A	9 49	31	18 25	12¼	12½	7 00	B	9 28	E	TAU	18
320	15	W.	6 35	D	4 22	A	9 47	31	18 40	1¼	1¼	8 01	B	10 32	E	GEM	19
321	16	Th.	6 37	D	4 21	A	9 44	31	18 55	2	2¼	9 09	B	11ᴹ28	E	GEM	20
322	17	Fr.	6 38	D	4 20	A	9 42	31	19 10	3	3¼	10 19	C	12ᴾᴹ15	E	CAN	21
323	18	Sa.	6 39	D	4 19	A	9 40	30	19 24	4	4¼	11ᴹ30	C	12 55	E	LEO	22
324	19	**A**	6 40	D	4 19	A	9 39	30	19 38	5¼	5½	—	—	1 29	D	LEO	23
325	20	M.	6 42	D	4 18	A	9 36	30	19 51	6¼	6½	12ᴬᴹ40	D	1 59	D	LEO	24
326	21	Tu.	6 43	D	4 17	A	9 34	30	20 05	7¼	7½	1 49	D	2 27	D	VIR	25
327	22	W.	6 44	D	4 17	A	9 33	30	20 17	8¼	8½	2 56	D	2 54	C	VIR	26
328	23	Th.	6 45	D	4 16	A	9 31	29	20 30	9	9½	4 02	E	3 22	B	VIR	27
329	24	Fr.	6 46	D	4 15	A	9 29	29	20 42	9¾	10¼	5 07	E	3 51	B	LIB	28
330	25	Sa.	6 48	D	4 15	A	9 27	29	20 53	10½	**11**	6 12	E	4 24	B	LIB	0
331	26	**A**	6 49	E	4 14	A	9 25	28	21 04	11¼	11¾	7 14	E	5 01	B	SCO	1
332	27	M.	6 50	E	4 14	A	9 24	28	21 15	11¾	—	8 14	E	5 42	A	OPH	2
333	28	Tu.	6 51	E	4 14	A	9 23	28	21 26	12½	12½	9 09	E	6 29	A	SAG	3
334	29	W.	6 52	E	4 13	A	9 21	27	21 36	1	1¼	9 58	E	7 20	B	SAG	4
335	30	Th.	6 53	E	4 13	A	9 20	27	21 s.46	1¾	2	10ᴬᴹ41	E	8ᴾᴹ15	B	SAG	5

NOVEMBER hath 30 days. 2000

The year draws in the day
And soon will evening shut:
The laurels all are cut,
We'll to the woods no more. –A. E. Housman

D. M.	D. W.	Dates, Feasts, Fasts, Aspects, Tide Heights	*Weather* ↓
1	W.	**All Saints** • Montreal Canadiens goalie Jacques Plante invented face mask, 1959 •	*North*
2	Th.	**All Souls** • ☾ at ☋ • ☾ runs low • ☾ at apo. • {8.7 / 9.4	*of*
3	F.	☌ ♆ ☾ • 31 automakers displayed cars at first National Auto Show, 1900 •	*the*
4	Sa.	☌ ♅ ☾ • Ben Crenshaw won his first pro tournament, 1973 • {8.3 / 8.9	*notches*
5	**A**	**21st S. af. P.** • "Fawkes plot" never forgot. • Tides {8.4 / 8.9 •	*are*
6	M.	John Philip Sousa born, 1854 • Adolph Sax born, 1814 • {8.7 / 9.0 •	*splotches*
7	Tu.	☿ stat. • Election Day • Canada's transcontinental railway completed, 1885 • {9.1 / 9.3	*of*
8	W.	☾ on Eq. • Wilhelm Roentgen "discovered" X-rays, 1895 • Tides {9.6 / 9.6	*white,*
9	Th.	Kristallnacht, 1938 • Berlin Wall opened, 1989 • Bob Gibson born, 1935 •	*fore-*
10	Fr.	**St. Leo the Great** • *Sesame Street* premiered, 1969 • Tides {10.6 / 10.1	*telling*
11	Sa.	**St. Martin** • **Veterans Day** • **Full Beaver** ○ • Sadie Hawkins Day	*a*
12	**A**	**22nd S. af. P.** • ☌ ♄ ☾ • ☌ ♃ ☾ • {11.4 / 10.4	
13	M.	*You have to believe in happiness or happiness never comes.* • Tides {11.7 / — •	*future*
14	Tu.	☾ at perig. • Claude Monet born, 1840 • Aaron Copland born, 1900 • {10.4 / 11.7	*that*
15	W.	☾ at ☊ • ☾ rides high • ☿ Gr. Elong. (19° W.) • {10.2 / 11.5 •	*isn't*
16	Th.	Anne Murray became first Canadian to receive a gold record, 1970 • Tides {10.0 / 11.2 •	*so*
17	Fr.	**St. Hugh of Lincoln** • 71°F, Minneapolis, Minn., 1953 •	*bright.*
18	Sa.	**St. Hilda** • First ticker tape parade, New York City, 1919 • Tides {9.6 / 10.4	*Orion*
19	**A**	**23rd S. af. P.** • ♄ at ☍ • Tides {9.6 / 10.1 •	*rears*
20	M.	Pelé scored his 1,000th career goal in Rio de Janeiro, 1969 • Tides {9.8 / 10.0 •	*up*
21	Tu.	☾ on Eq. • ☌ ♂ ☾ • Dow Jones topped 5,000 mark, 1995 • {10.1 / 9.9	*on a*
22	W.	*Make money your god and it will plague you like the devil.* • Tides {10.4 / 9.9 •	*glistening*
23	Th.	**St. Clement** • **Thanksgiving** • Boris Karloff born, 1887 • {10.7 / 9.9	*night,*
24	Fr.	☌ ☿ ☾ • Joseph F. Glidden patented barbed wire, 1874 • Tides {10.8 / 9.9 •	*to*
25	Sa.	New ● • Carry Nation born, 1846 • Joe DiMaggio born, 1914 • {10.9 / 9.8	*hunt*
26	**A**	**24th S. af. P.** • J. B. Sutherland patented refrigerated railroad car, 1867 •	*in a*
27	M.	♃ at ☍ • 76°F, St. Louis, Missouri, 1989 • 18 inches of snow, Galena, S.D., 1989	*forest*
28	Tu.	Berry Gordy Jr., founder of Motown Record Corp., born, 1929 • Tides {9.4 / 10.4 •	*of*
29	W.	☾ at ☋ • ☾ runs low • ☌ ♀ ☾ • {9.2 / 10.2	*crystalline*
30	Th.	**St. Andrew** • ☌ ♆ ☾ • ☾ at apo. • {8.9 / 9.8 •	*light.*

Our life is spent trying to find something to do with the time we have rushed through life trying to save. –Will Rogers

Farmer's Calendar

■ "Every man looks at his woodpile with a kind of affection," wrote Henry David Thoreau. He's right, too, isn't he? A simple woodpile has a familiar, reassuring presence. It's a satisfactory object in a way that's a little hard to account for, perhaps. We respond to the sight of a good woodpile with a level of contentment.

What is it that contents us? Not use, or not use alone. Today most of us know we do better to face the coming winter with a credit balance at the oil dealer's than with a big woodpile. Maybe we have an ancient, inherited memory of years when that woodpile was what stood between our forebears and the cold; but that kind of memory would lead us to look at our woodpile with anxiety rather than affection—the way we might, these days, look at our bank account.

It's not as fuel that a woodpile makes its particular appeal. It's as a symbol. We are cheered and comforted by our woodpile today because a woodpile is one of the stations of the year and expresses the essential ambiguity of all seasonal work. It represents a job that we know we can do well enough but that we also know will never finally be done. For woodpiles are built up that they may be torn down. Massive as they are, they're ephemeral. You'll have to build another next year, which you will then once more throw down. The woodpile reminds us of the fix we're in just by being alive on Earth. It connects us with the year, and so it connects us with one another. We may as well look at our woodpile with affection, then, for it makes us be philosophers.

DECEMBER, The Twelfth Month

Jupiter and Saturn dominate the heavens all night long throughout the month, retaining nearly their full brilliance. Both are fabulous through any telescope, whose users might also look toward Venus on the 11th, now more than 10 degrees above the horizon when darkness falls (the little bluish body to its right is Neptune). On the 24th and 25th, it's green Uranus that hovers to the right of dazzling Venus—an easy though rarely observed event for binocular users. In the early morning sky of the 20th, the Moon meets orange Mars and the blue star Spica. The winter solstice occurs on the 21st, at 8:37 A.M. EST. Although this date represents the year's longest night, the earliest sunset happened two weeks ago.

☽	First Quarter	3rd day	22nd hour	55th minute
○	Full Moon	11th day	4th hour	3rd minute
☾	Last Quarter	17th day	19th hour	41st minute
●	New Moon	25th day	12th hour	22nd minute

Times are given in Eastern Standard Time.

For an explanation of this page, see page 40; for values of Key Letters, see page 226.

Day of Year	Day of Month	Day of Week	☼ Rises h. m.	Key	☼ Sets h. m.	Key	Length of Day h. m.	Sun Fast m.	Declination of Sun ° '	High Tide Boston Light—A.M.	Bold—P.M.	☽ Rises h. m.	Key	☽ Sets h. m.	Key	☽ Place	☽ Age
336	1	Fr.	6 54	E	4 12	A	9 18	27	21s.55	2½	**2¾**	11 A.M. 19	E	9 P.M. 13	B	CAP	6
337	2	Sa.	6 55	E	4 12	A	9 17	26	22 04	3¼	**3½**	11 A.M. 52	E	10 12	B	CAP	7
338	3	**A**	6 56	E	4 12	A	9 16	26	22 12	4¼	**4¼**	12 P.M. 22	D	11 P.M. 12	C	AQU	8
339	4	M.	6 57	E	4 12	A	9 15	25	22 20	5	**5¼**	12 49	D	—	–	AQU	9
340	5	Tu.	6 58	E	4 12	A	9 14	25	22 27	6	**6¼**	1 15	D	12 A.M. 13	C	PSC	10
341	6	W.	6 59	E	4 12	A	9 13	25	22 34	6¾	**7**	1 41	C	1 16	D	CET	11
342	7	Th.	7 00	E	4 12	A	9 12	24	22 41	7½	**8**	2 09	C	2 21	D	PSC	12
343	8	Fr.	7 01	E	4 12	A	9 11	24	22 47	8¼	**8¾**	2 39	B	3 29	E	CET	13
344	9	Sa.	7 02	E	4 12	A	9 10	23	22 53	9	**9½**	3 14	B	4 40	E	ARI	14
345	10	**A**	7 03	E	4 12	A	9 09	23	22 58	9¾	**10½**	3 55	B	5 54	E	TAU	15
346	11	M.	7 04	E	4 12	A	9 08	22	23 03	10½	**11¼**	4 45	B	7 07	E	TAU	16
347	12	Tu.	7 04	E	4 12	A	9 08	22	23 07	11½	—	5 45	B	8 16	E	GEM	17
348	13	W.	7 05	E	4 12	A	9 07	21	23 11	12	**12¼**	6 53	B	9 19	E	GEM	18
349	14	Th.	7 06	E	4 12	A	9 06	21	23 15	1	**1**	8 05	B	10 11	E	CAN	19
350	15	Fr.	7 06	E	4 12	A	9 06	21	23 18	1¾	**2**	9 19	B	10 55	E	LEO	20
351	16	Sa.	7 07	E	4 13	A	9 06	20	23 21	2¾	**3**	10 31	C	11 A.M. 32	D	LEO	21
352	17	**A**	7 08	E	4 13	A	9 05	20	23 23	3¾	**4**	11 P.M. 41	C	12 P.M. 03	D	LEO	22
353	18	M.	7 09	E	4 14	A	9 05	19	23 24	4¾	**5¼**	—	–	12 32	C	VIR	23
354	19	Tu.	7 09	E	4 14	A	9 05	19	23 25	5¾	**6¼**	12 A.M. 48	D	12 59	C	VIR	24
355	20	W.	7 10	E	4 14	A	9 04	18	23 26	6¾	**7¼**	1 54	E	1 26	C	VIR	25
356	21	Th.	7 11	E	4 15	A	9 04	18	23 26	7¾	**8¼**	2 59	E	1 54	B	LIB	26
357	22	Fr.	7 11	E	4 15	A	9 04	17	23 26	8½	**9¼**	4 03	E	2 25	B	LIB	27
358	23	Sa.	7 11	E	4 16	A	9 05	17	23 25	9½	**10**	5 05	E	3 00	B	SCO	28
359	24	**A**	7 12	E	4 17	A	9 05	16	23 24	10	**10¾**	6 05	E	3 39	B	OPH	29
360	25	M.	7 12	E	4 17	A	9 05	16	23 22	10¾	**11½**	7 02	E	4 23	B	SAG	0
361	26	Tu.	7 12	E	4 18	A	9 06	15	23 20	11½	—	7 53	E	5 13	A	SAG	1
362	27	W.	7 13	E	4 19	A	9 06	15	23 17	12	**12**	8 39	E	6 07	B	SAG	2
363	28	Th.	7 13	E	4 19	A	9 06	14	23 14	12¾	**12¾**	9 19	E	7 04	B	CAP	3
364	29	Fr.	7 13	E	4 20	A	9 07	14	23 10	1½	**1½**	9 54	E	8 02	B	CAP	4
365	30	Sa.	7 13	E	4 21	A	9 08	13	23 06	2	**2¼**	10 24	E	9 02	C	AQU	5
366	31	**A**	7 13	E	4 22	A	9 09	13	23s.02	2¾	**3**	10 A.M. 52	D	10 P.M. 02	C	AQU	6

DECEMBER hath 31 days. 2000

He prayeth best, who loveth best
All things both great and small;
For the dear God who loveth us,
He made and loveth all. –Samuel Taylor Coleridge

D. M.	D. W.	Dates, Feasts, Fasts, Aspects, Tide Heights	*Weather* ↓
1	Fr.	☌ ♅ ☾ • 36.4 inches of snow, Marquette, Michigan, 1985 •	*Winter's*
2	Sa.	*Always leave something to wish for; otherwise you will be miserable from your very happiness.* •	*coming*
3	**A**	**1st S. in Advent** • Illinois became 21st state, 1818 • { 8.5 9.0 •	*fast*
4	M.	☌ ♇ ☉ • FDR ordered dissolution of the WPA, 1942 • Tides { 8.6 8.8	*and*
5	Tu.	Montgomery bus boycott began, 1955 • Martin Van Buren born, 1782 •	*furious,*
6	W.	St. Nicholas • ☾ on Eq. • Ira Gershwin born, 1896 • { 9.2 9.0 •	*Arctic*
7	Th.	St. Ambrose • Pearl Harbor attacked, 1941 • Tides { 9.7 9.2 •	*blast*
8	Fr.	Red Berenson born, 1941 • Sammy Davis Jr. born, 1925 • Tides { 10.3 9.6 •	*and*
9	Sa.	☌ ♄ ☾ • Clarence Birdseye born, 1886 • { 10.9 9.9	*snowflakes*
10	**A**	**2nd S. in Advent** • ☌ ♃ ☾ •	*flurrious.*
11	M.	Full Cold ○ • ☌ ♀ ♆ • Fiorello La Guardia born, 1882 •	*Your*
12	Tu.	☾ at ☊ • ☾ at perig. • Ed Koch born, 1924 • { 12.0 — •	*parka*
13	W.	St. Lucy • ☾ rides high • Mary Todd Lincoln born, 1818 • { 10.4 12.1	*better*
14	Th.	Halcyon Days • *The secret of contentment is the realization that life is a gift, not a right.* •	*have*
15	Fr.	Alexandre Eiffel born, 1832 • Sitting Bull died, 1890 • Tides { 10.3 11.5 •	*tight*
16	Sa.	Boston Tea Party, 1773 • Margaret Mead born, 1901 • { 10.1 11.0 •	*strings.*
17	**A**	**3rd S. in Advent** • Arthur Fiedler born, 1894 •	*Hark! a*
18	M.	☾ on Eq. • Su-Lin, first giant panda sent from China to U.S., arrived, 1936 •	*herald*
19	Tu.	*People who make music together cannot be enemies, at least while the music lasts.* • { 10.0 9.5	*angel*
20	W.	☌ ♂ ☾ • Ember Day • Harvey S. Firestone born, 1868 •	*sings!*
21	Th.	St. Thomas • **Winter Solstice** • Beware the Pogonip. • { 10.2 9.2 •	*Glory*
22	Fr.	First day of Chanukah • Ember Day • E. A. Robinson born, 1869 • { 10.3 9.2	*to*
23	Sa.	☌ ♀ ♅ • Ember Day • -50°F at Williston, N.D., 1983 • { 10.4 9.2	*the*
24	**A**	**4th S. in Advent** • Tides { 10.4 9.2 •	*newborn*
25	M.	**Christmas Day** • **New** ● • **Eclipse** ☉ • ☿ in sup. ☌	
26	Tu.	St. Stephen • **Boxing Day (Canada)** • ☾ at ☋ • ☾ runs low •	*son!*
27	W.	St. John • Radio City Music Hall opened in New York City, 1932 • { 9.1 10.3	*Glory*
28	Th.	Holy Innocents • ☌ ♆ ☾ • ☾ at apo. • Tides { 9.0 10.1	*to*
29	Fr.	☌ ♅ ☾ • ☌ ♀ ☾ • U.S. branch of YMCA organized, 1851 •	*two*
30	Sa.	Sandy Koufax born, 1935 • Rudyard Kipling born, 1865 • { 8.9 9.7 •	*thousand*
31	**A**	*Each day that Fortune gives you, be it what it may, set down for gain.* –Horace • { 8.8 9.4	*one!*

Farmer's Calendar

■ It was a couple of years ago, around this time, that we in this section realized we might be into an endless autumn. Winter simply failed to arrive. Through December, the days held sunny and warm in the sixties and seventies, the skies held clear, and the Weather Bureau saw no winter in sight. Snow and ice were not merely put off; they seemed to have been dropped from the program.

The queer thing about this prolonged spell of fine weather was not the weather itself but how uneasy it made everybody. You would think that being able to work comfortably outdoors in your shirt in the middle of December would be a matter for glee and gratitude. Not at all. The mild days filled us with foreboding. We glanced nervously at the soft blue skies, we shook our heads. We told one another: "We'll pay for this."

We'll pay for this. What an odd idea! As though warm weeks in December were borrowed, or bought on the installment plan, to be paid for later, with interest and at an inconvenient time. People seemed to feel that to go ahead and enjoy the strange sunny season was not permitted; that to do so would increase the cost of the inevitable payment. And observe the important thing about this idea: It's not so. A warm, bright December is not a loan. It's a gift. No December will be required of us again, ever, not the cold ones, not the warm ones. An easy winter, when we've had it, is gone past retrieval. We know this to our sorrow, let us remember it to our joy. Let us learn to take the gift.

2001 JANUARY, The First Month

The year begins brilliantly, with all five naked-eye planets prominent. Mercury pops out of the Sun's glare around the 14th to linger low in the southwest, and hovers near Uranus on the 22nd. Mars is an orange medium-bright "star" between Virgo and Libra, rising about 2:00 A.M. and climbing well up by dawn. Dazzling Jupiter and bright Saturn keep close company in Taurus; both are high at dusk and prominent most of the night. Venus, spectacular in the west at nightfall, reaches its greatest angular separation from the Sun (47 degrees) on the 17th. Earth is at perihelion (closest to the Sun) on the 4th. The end of a total lunar eclipse on the 9th is visible in northeastern North America.

☽	First Quarter	2nd day	17th hour	31st minute
○	Full Moon	9th day	15th hour	24th minute
☾	Last Quarter	16th day	7th hour	35th minute
●	New Moon	24th day	8th hour	7th minute

Times are given in Eastern Standard Time.

For an explanation of this page, see page 40; for values of Key Letters, see page 226.

Day of Year	Day of Month	Day of Week	☼ Rises h. m.	Key	☼ Sets h. m.	Key	Length of Day h. m.	Sun Fast m.	Declination of Sun ° '	High Tide Boston Light—A.M.	**Bold—P.M.**	☽ Rises h. m.	Key	☽ Sets h. m.	Key	☽ Place	☽ Age
1	1	M.	7 14	E	4 23	A	9 09	12	22s.57	3½	**3¾**	11 A.M. 17	D	11 P.M. 02	D	AQU	7
2	2	Tu.	7 14	E	4 23	A	9 09	12	22 51	4¼	**4½**	11 A.M. 43	D	—	–	PSC	8
3	3	W.	7 14	E	4 24	A	9 10	11	22 45	5	**5½**	12 P.M. 08	C	12 A.M. 05	D	CET	9
4	4	Th.	7 14	E	4 25	A	9 11	11	22 39	5¾	**6¼**	12 36	B	1 09	D	PSC	10
5	5	Fr.	7 14	E	4 26	A	9 12	10	22 33	6¾	**7¼**	1 07	B	2 16	E	ARI	11
6	6	Sa.	7 13	E	4 27	A	9 14	10	22 25	7½	**8¼**	1 44	B	3 27	E	TAU	12
7	7	**G**	7 13	E	4 28	A	9 15	9	22 18	8½	**9¼**	2 29	B	4 39	E	TAU	13
8	8	M.	7 13	E	4 29	A	9 16	9	22 09	9¼	**10**	3 23	B	5 51	E	TAU	14
9	9	Tu.	7 13	E	4 30	A	9 17	9	22 01	10¼	**11**	4 28	B	6 58	E	GEM	15
10	10	W.	7 13	E	4 31	A	9 18	8	21 52	11¼	**11¾**	5 40	B	7 57	E	GEM	16
11	11	Th.	7 12	E	4 33	A	9 21	8	21 42	**12**	—	6 56	C	8 47	E	CAN	17
12	12	Fr.	7 12	E	4 34	A	9 22	7	21 32	12¾	**1**	8 13	C	9 28	E	LEO	18
13	13	Sa.	7 12	E	4 35	A	9 23	7	21 22	1½	**1¾**	9 27	D	10 03	D	LEO	19
14	14	**G**	7 11	E	4 36	A	9 25	7	21 12	2½	**2¾**	10 37	D	10 34	D	VIR	20
15	15	M.	7 11	E	4 37	A	9 26	6	21 01	3½	**3¾**	11 P.M. 45	D	11 02	C	VIR	21
16	16	Tu.	7 10	E	4 38	A	9 28	6	20 49	4¼	**4¾**	—	–	11 30	C	VIR	22
17	17	W.	7 10	E	4 39	A	9 29	6	20 37	5¼	**5¾**	12 A.M. 51	E	11 A.M. 58	B	VIR	23
18	18	Th.	7 09	E	4 41	A	9 32	5	20 25	6¼	**7**	1 56	E	12 P.M. 28	B	LIB	24
19	19	Fr.	7 09	E	4 42	A	9 33	5	20 12	7¼	**8**	2 58	E	1 01	B	SCO	25
20	20	Sa.	7 08	E	4 43	A	9 35	5	19 59	8¼	**8¾**	3 59	E	1 38	B	OPH	26
21	21	**G**	7 07	E	4 44	A	9 37	4	19 46	9	**9¾**	4 56	E	2 21	A	SAG	27
22	22	M.	7 07	E	4 46	A	9 39	4	19 33	9¾	**10½**	5 49	E	3 08	B	SAG	28
23	23	Tu.	7 06	D	4 47	A	9 41	4	19 18	10½	**11**	6 37	E	4 01	B	SAG	29
24	24	W.	7 05	D	4 48	A	9 43	4	19 04	11	**11¾**	7 18	E	4 57	B	CAP	0
25	25	Th.	7 04	D	4 49	A	9 45	3	18 49	11¾	—	7 55	E	5 55	B	CAP	1
26	26	Fr.	7 04	D	4 51	A	9 47	3	18 34	12¼	**12¼**	8 27	E	6 54	C	AQU	2
27	27	Sa.	7 03	D	4 52	A	9 49	3	18 18	1	**1**	8 55	D	7 54	C	AQU	3
28	28	**G**	7 02	D	4 53	A	9 51	3	18 02	1½	**1¾**	9 21	D	8 54	D	AQU	4
29	29	M.	7 01	D	4 55	A	9 54	3	17 46	2¼	**2¼**	9 46	D	9 55	D	PSC	5
30	30	Tu.	7 00	D	4 56	A	9 56	2	17 29	2¾	**3**	10 11	C	10 P.M. 57	D	CET	6
31	31	W.	6 59	D	4 57	A	9 58	2	17s.12	3½	**4**	10 A.M. 37	C	—	–	PSC	7

JANUARY hath 31 days. 2001

Keen gleams the wind, and all the ground
Is bare and chapped with bitter cold.
The ruts are iron; the fish are found
Encased in ice as in a mold. –Charles De Kay

D. M.	D. W.	Dates, Feasts, Fasts, Aspects, Tide Heights	*Weather* ↓
1	M.	New Year's Day • Circumcision • { 8.7 / 9.0	*Breezin'*
2	Tu.	☾ on Eq. • First radio broadcast of religious services, KDKA, Pittsburgh, Pa., 1921 •	*but*
3	W.	Marvin Stone of Washington, D.C., patented a drinking straw, 1888 • { 9.0 / 8.7 •	*barely*
4	Th.	St. Elizabeth Seton • ⊕ at perihelion • { 9.3 / 8.7	*freezin'.*
5	Fr.	☌ ♄ ☾ • Twelfth Night • George Washington Carver died, 1943 • { 9.7 / 8.8	*Wet*
6	Sa.	Epiphany • ☌ ♃ ☾ • Kahlil Gibran born, 1883 • { 10.2 / 9.1	*as it*
7	G	1st S. af. Ep. • St. Distaff's Day • Charles Addams born, 1912	• *can*
8	M.	Plough Monday • Physicist Jean Foucault demonstrated that Earth rotates on its axis, 1851 •	*get!*
9	Tu.	Full Wolf ○ • Eclipse ☾ • ☾ rides high • ☾ at ☊ • { 11.8 / 10.2	
10	W.	☾ at perig. • The United States and Vatican City established diplomatic relations, 1984	*Mercury*
11	Th.	Baseball's American League established designated hitter rule, 1973 • { 12.1 / —	*lower:*
12	Fr.	John Singer Sargent born, 1856 • Jack London born, 1876 • Tides { 10.6 / 12.0	*Fire*
13	Sa.	St. Hilary • ☌ ☿ ♆ • NASA selected its first women astronauts, 1978 •	*up*
14	G	2nd S. af. Ep. • Propitious day for birth of women. • { 10.5 / 11.0 •	*the*
15	M.	Martin Luther King Jr.'s Birthday • ☾ on Eq. •	*snow*
16	Tu.	*We make more enemies by what we say than friends by what we do.* • { 10.1 / 9.6 •	*blower!*
17	W.	♀ Gr. Elong. (47° E.) • ☌ ♂ ☾ • Benjamin Franklin born, 1706	*Pity the*
18	Th.	Robert Clifton Weaver became first black U.S. cabinet member, 1966 • { 9.8 / 8.8 •	*ploddin'*
19	Fr.	Tokyo Rose pardoned by President Ford, 1977 • Tides { 9.7 / 8.6	*meter man—*
20	Sa.	St. Fabian • Inauguration Day • Favorable day for birth of men. • { 9.8 / 8.6	*his*
21	G	3rd S. af. Ep. • Record-setting -22°F, Akron, Ohio, 1985 • { 9.8 / 8.6	*boots*
22	M.	St. Vincent • ☾ at ☋ • ☾ runs low • ☌ ☿ ♅ •	*are*
23	Tu.	Leonard Thompson, age 14, became first diabetic to receive insulin injections, Toronto, 1922	*sodden,*
24	W.	New ● • ☾ at apo. • Chinese New Year • Tides { 10.1 / 8.9 •	*his*
25	Th.	Conversion of Paul • ♃ stat. • ♄ stat. • ☌ ☿ ☾ • { 10.1 / —	
26	Fr.	Sts. Timothy & Titus • George F. Green patented electric dental drill, 1875 •	*mien*
27	Sa.	Fire broke out on *Apollo I* spacecraft, killing three American astronauts, 1967 • { 9.1 / 9.9 •	*wan.*
28	G	4th S. af. Ep. • ☿ Gr. Elong. (18° E.) • ☌ ♀ ☾ • { 9.1 / 9.7 •	
29	M.	St. Thomas Aquinas • ☾ on Eq. • Tides { 9.1 / 9.5 •	*Shovel*
30	Tu.	*There is something about a closet that makes a skeleton restless.* • Tides { 9.2 / 9.2 •	*his*
31	W.	Jackie Robinson born, 1919 • Richard Drew of 3M Co. developed Scotch tape, 1928 •	*path!*

Farmer's Calendar

■ You would think that the weather of late years was complex and uncertain enough on its own without our adding to the difficulty. Especially in the last, say, ten years in my section, the seasons have seemed to mingle and interpenetrate in a way they haven't before. We have summers that push their way deep into the fall, falls that last half the winter, and springs that bulge over into their neighboring seasons at both ends like a bather who has had some bad advice from whoever sold her swimsuit to her. We no longer pretend to know what's going on. We shake our heads.

Even in the middle of our confusion about where our weather is going, however, we have at least had a settled vocabulary in which to question and debate. Now even that frail stop against doubt seems shaky. An example is in the demise of the *snow flurry*. You remember the flurry, of course: a light fall of snow, quick to start, quick to stop, and unlikely to accumulate. "Flurries in the higher elevations" was a common part of the weatherman's terminology at this time of year.

No longer. Flurries are now called *snow showers*. A perfectly good noun, *flurry*, is being replaced. Now we hear of "snow showers in the higher elevations." Why? Have we here another melancholy example of America's will to euphemism? Does a snow shower sound somehow easier to endure than a flurry, in the way a *corrections facility* is, ostensibly, a jollier place than a *prison*? Are snow showers supposed to make us feel better? And do they?

The month belongs to Venus (see feature on page 56). The evening star continues to brighten, achieving greatest brilliancy on the 21st while also standing high in fading evening twilight, an unusually dazzling combination. Saturn and Jupiter remain close and conspicuous before midnight; on the 2nd, both float alongside the gibbous Ground-hog-Day Moon. Steadily fading Mercury drops back into solar glare after the first week of this month. Mars brightens as it speeds through dim Libra and enters the splendid constellation Scorpius near month's end. The winter Milky Way is now at its best, optimally seen during the dark-sky stretch from the 20th to the 25th, near the time of the new Moon.

☽ First Quarter	1st day	9th hour	2nd minute
○ Full Moon	8th day	2nd hour	12th minute
☾ Last Quarter	14th day	22nd hour	23rd minute
● New Moon	23rd day	3rd hour	21st minute

Times are given in Eastern Standard Time.

For an explanation of this page, see page 40; for values of Key Letters, see page 226.

Day of Year	Day of Month	Day of Week	☀ Rises h. m.	Key	☀ Sets h. m.	Key	Length of Day h. m.	Sun Fast m.	Declination of Sun ° '	High Tide Boston Light—A.M. Bold—P.M.		☽ Rises h. m.	Key	☽ Sets h. m.	Key	Place	Age
32	1	Th.	6 58	D	4 59	A	10 01	2	16 s. 55	4¼	**4¾**	11ᴬ05	B	12ᴹ01	E	CET	8
33	2	Fr.	6 57	D	5 00	A	10 03	2	16 38	5¼	**5¾**	11ᴹ38	B	1 08	E	TAU	9
34	3	Sa.	6 56	D	5 01	A	10 05	2	16 21	6	**6¾**	12ᴾᴹ17	B	2 17	E	TAU	10
35	4	**G**	6 54	D	5 02	A	10 08	2	16 03	7	**7¾**	1 05	B	3 27	E	TAU	11
36	5	M.	6 53	D	5 04	A	10 11	2	15 45	8	**8¾**	2 03	B	4 35	E	GEM	12
37	6	Tu.	6 52	D	5 05	A	10 13	2	15 26	9	**9¾**	3 10	B	5 37	E	GEM	13
38	7	W.	6 51	D	5 06	A	10 15	1	15 07	10	**10¾**	4 25	B	6 32	E	CAN	14
39	8	Th.	6 50	D	5 08	B	10 18	1	14 48	11	**11½**	5 44	B	7 18	E	LEO	15
40	9	Fr.	6 48	D	5 09	B	10 21	1	14 29	11¾	—	7 01	C	7 57	E	LEO	16
41	10	Sa.	6 47	D	5 10	B	10 23	1	14 09	12¼	**12¾**	8 16	D	8 31	D	LEO	17
42	11	**G**	6 46	D	5 12	B	10 26	1	13 49	1¼	**1½**	9 28	D	9 01	D	VIR	18
43	12	M.	6 45	D	5 13	B	10 28	1	13 29	2	**2½**	10 38	E	9 30	C	VIR	19
44	13	Tu.	6 43	D	5 14	B	10 31	1	13 09	3	**3¼**	11ᴾᴹ45	E	9 59	B	VIR	20
45	14	W.	6 42	D	5 15	B	10 33	1	12 49	3¾	**4¼**	—	—	10 29	B	LIB	21
46	15	Th.	6 41	D	5 17	B	10 36	1	12 29	4¾	**5¼**	12ᴹ50	E	11 01	B	LIB	22
47	16	Fr.	6 39	D	5 18	B	10 39	2	12 08	5¾	**6¼**	1 52	E	11ᴬ38	B	OPH	23
48	17	Sa.	6 38	D	5 19	B	10 41	2	11 47	6¾	**7½**	2 51	E	12ᴾᴹ19	A	OPH	24
49	18	**G**	6 36	D	5 21	B	10 45	2	11 26	7¾	**8½**	3 45	E	1 04	B	SAG	25
50	19	M.	6 35	D	5 22	B	10 47	2	11 04	8½	**9¼**	4 35	E	1 55	B	SAG	26
51	20	Tu.	6 33	D	5 23	B	10 50	2	10 43	9¼	**10**	5 18	E	2 50	B	SAG	27
52	21	W.	6 32	D	5 24	B	10 52	2	10 21	10	**10¾**	5 56	E	3 48	B	CAP	28
53	22	Th.	6 30	D	5 26	B	10 56	2	9 59	10¾	**11¼**	6 29	E	4 47	C	CAP	29
54	23	Fr.	6 29	D	5 27	B	10 58	2	9 37	11¼	**11¾**	6 58	E	5 47	C	AQU	0
55	24	Sa.	6 27	D	5 28	B	11 01	2	9 15	**12**	—	7 25	D	6 48	D	AQU	1
56	25	**G**	6 26	D	5 29	B	11 03	2	8 52	12½	**12½**	7 50	D	7 49	D	PSC	2
57	26	M.	6 24	D	5 31	B	11 07	3	8 30	1	**1¼**	8 15	C	8 51	D	CET	3
58	27	Tu.	6 23	D	5 32	B	11 09	3	8 07	1½	**2**	8 40	C	9 54	E	PSC	4
59	28	W.	6 21	D	5 33	B	11 12	3	7 s. 45	2¼	**2½**	9ᴬᴹ07	C	10ᴹ59	E	CET	5

FEBRUARY hath 28 days. 2001

"How is your trade, Aquarius,
This frosty night?"
"Complaints is many and various
And my feet are cold," says Aquarius. –Robert Graves

D. M.	D. W.	Dates, Feasts, Fasts, Aspects, Tide Heights	Weather ↓
1	Th.	St. Brigid • First car insurance issued, 1898 • {9.3 8.7	*Groundhogs*
2	Fr.	Candlemas • Groundhog Day • ☌ ♄ ☾ • ☌ ♃ ☾ •	
3	Sa.	☿ stat. • Endangered Species Act, 1973 • Tides {9.8 8.7 •	*sleep in,*
4	G	5th S. af. Ep. • Auspicious day for marriage and repair of ships. •	*but*
5	M.	St. Agatha • ☾ at ☊ • First "Don't Walk" sign, New York City, 1952 •	*the*
6	Tu.	☾ rides high • Elizabeth II ascended to British throne, 1952 • {11.2 9.8	*plowman's*
7	W.	☾ at perig. • *You might as well fall flat on your face as lean over too far backward.* • {11.7 10.3	*up*
8	Th.	Full Snow ○ • First Colonial opera performed, Charleston, S.C., 1735 •	*early;*
9	Fr.	☌ ♅ ☉ • Record-setting -66°F, Yellowstone Park, 1933 • {12.1 —	*tossed,*
10	Sa.	RCA Victor awarded the first gold record—to Glenn Miller, 1942 • {11.0 11.9 •	*almost*
11	G	Septuagesima • ☾ on Eq. • Yalta agreement signed, 1945 •	*lost,*
12	M.	Abraham Lincoln born, 1809 • ☿ in inf. ☌ • Tides {10.9 10.9 •	*in a*
13	Tu.	*I care not for a man's religion whose dog or cat are not the better for it.* –Abraham Lincoln •	*storm's*
14	W.	St. Valentine • Sts. Cyril & Methodius • {10.2 9.4 •	*hurly-burly.*
15	Th.	☌ ♂ ☾ • Winter's back breaks. • Cyrus McCormick born, 1809 •	*Rainy*
16	Fr.	NBC broadcast the first daily newsreel, 1948 • Tides {9.5 8.4 •	*and mild*
17	Sa.	National premiere of "A Prairie Home Companion" on NPR, 1979 • Tides {9.3 8.2	*with*
18	G	Sexagesima • ☾ at ☋ • {9.3 8.2 •	*occasional*
19	M.	George Washington's Birthday (observed) • ☾ runs low • {9.4 8.4	
20	Tu.	☾ at apo. • ☌ ♆ ☾ • Ansel Adams born, 1902 • {9.6 8.6	*shivers.*
21	W.	☌ ☿ ☾ • ♀ Gr. Bril. • First issue of *The New Yorker* published, 1925 •	*Hark*
22	Th.	George Washington born, 1732 • Julius "Dr. J" Erving born, 1950 • {10.0 9.1 •	*to*
23	Fr.	New ● • Allied ground war against Iraq began, 1991 • Tides {10.1 9.3	*the*
24	Sa.	St. Matthias • ☿ stat. • Honus Wagner born, 1874 • {10.1 — •	*music*
25	G	Quinquagesima • First National Bank of U.S. chartered, 1791 • {9.5 10.0	*of*
26	M.	Pure Monday • ☾ on Eq. • ☌ ♀ ☾ • Levi Strauss born, 1829 •	*high-*
27	Tu.	Shrove Tuesday • Henry Wadsworth Longfellow born, 1807 •	*riding*
28	W.	Ash Wednesday • Mary Lyon born, 1797 • {9.7 9.4 •	*rivers!*

He who cannot rest, cannot work; he who cannot let go, cannot hold on; he who cannot find footing, cannot go forward. –Harry Emerson Fosdick

Farmer's Calendar

■ Every midwinter morning when it isn't snowing—and often when it is—a flock of goldfinches arrives here between 10:00 and 10:15. There are 25 or 30 of them, and they come for the bird feeder. They are tiny birds, but they're full of pepper. They appear in a body, scrapping, bickering, chasing one another, like a kindergarten class on an outing. They tear into the feeder as if they hadn't seen a thistle seed in a week. They consume half the seed in five minutes flat and scatter the rest over the ground. Then they abruptly fly off, all at once. The next day, they will be back, at the same hour—precisely the same hour. Not the least remarkable thing about the goldfinches is their iron regularity.

It is said of the German philosopher Kant that he was a man of such settled habits that the churchwarden in his town, Konigsberg, would time the town clock by his daily appearance as he took his constitutional. If the clock said it was 9:00 and Kant hadn't yet come into view, the warden would stop the works until the philosopher had made his appearance. In the author of the *Critique of Pure Reason*, such constancy is hardly surprising, perhaps. But in a goldfinch, a little ball of feathers that would almost fit into a teaspoon and that bounces about on the breeze like a scrap of fluff, it may be unexpected. Here is one of the light creatures of the air, scarcely bound to the earth at all, as free, physically, as any material thing can be—and it goes its daily round like the rest of us.

MARCH, The Third Month

Mars passes north of the star Antares during the first two weeks of March. Similar in brightness and color to the red planet, Antares means "rival of Mars." Venus drops lower throughout the month but is increasingly spectacular viewed through binoculars. Starting around the 20th, but optimally on the 27th, Venus is both an evening and a morning star and can be glimpsed low in the west after sunset and also in the east before sunrise. It is in inferior conjunction with the Sun on the 29th. Mercury is low and difficult to see before dawn, but the Moon has an eye-catching meeting with Jupiter and Saturn on the 1st and again on the 29th. The vernal equinox occurs at 8:31 A.M. EST on the 20th.

☽	First Quarter	2nd day	21st hour	3rd minute
○	Full Moon	9th day	12th hour	23rd minute
☾	Last Quarter	16th day	15th hour	45th minute
●	New Moon	24th day	20th hour	21st minute

Times are given in Eastern Standard Time.

For an explanation of this page, see page 40; for values of Key Letters, see page 226.

Day of Year	Day of Month	Day of Week	☼ Rises h. m.	Key	☼ Sets h. m.	Key	Length of Day h. m.	Sun Fast m.	Declination of Sun ° '	High Tide Boston Light—A.M.	Bold—P.M.	☽ Rises h. m.	Key	☽ Sets h. m.	Key	☽ Place	☽ Age
60	1	Th.	6 19	D	5 34	B	11 15	3	7 s. 22	3	**3½**	9 A.M. 38	B	—	–	ARI	6
61	2	Fr.	6 18	D	5 35	B	11 17	3	6 59	3¾	**4¼**	10 13	B	12 A.M. 05	E	TAU	7
62	3	Sa.	6 16	D	5 37	B	11 21	4	6 36	4½	**5¼**	10 56	B	1 13	E	TAU	8
63	4	**G**	6 15	D	5 38	B	11 23	4	6 13	5½	**6¼**	11 A.M. 47	B	2 19	E	GEM	9
64	5	M.	6 13	D	5 39	B	11 26	4	5 50	6¾	**7½**	12 P.M. 48	B	3 22	E	GEM	10
65	6	Tu.	6 11	D	5 40	B	11 29	4	5 26	7¾	**8½**	1 58	B	4 18	E	CAN	11
66	7	W.	6 10	D	5 41	B	11 31	4	5 03	8¾	**9½**	3 13	C	5 07	E	CAN	12
67	8	Th.	6 08	D	5 43	B	11 35	5	4 40	9¾	**10¼**	4 31	C	5 48	E	LEO	13
68	9	Fr.	6 06	D	5 44	B	11 38	5	4 16	10¾	**11¼**	5 48	D	6 24	D	LEO	14
69	10	Sa.	6 05	D	5 45	B	11 40	5	3 52	11½	—	7 03	D	6 56	D	VIR	15
70	11	**G**	6 03	D	5 46	B	11 43	5	3 29	12	**12¼**	8 16	D	7 26	C	VIR	16
71	12	M.	6 01	C	5 47	B	11 46	6	3 06	12¾	**1¼**	9 26	E	7 56	C	VIR	17
72	13	Tu.	5 59	C	5 49	B	11 50	6	2 42	1½	**2**	10 35	E	8 26	B	LIB	18
73	14	W.	5 58	C	5 50	B	11 52	6	2 19	2¼	**3**	11 P.M. 40	E	8 58	B	LIB	19
74	15	Th.	5 56	C	5 51	B	11 55	7	1 55	3¼	**3¾**	—	–	9 34	B	SCO	20
75	16	Fr.	5 54	C	5 52	B	11 58	7	1 31	4	**4¾**	12 A.M. 42	E	10 14	A	OPH	21
76	17	Sa.	5 53	C	5 53	B	12 00	7	1 07	5	**5¾**	1 39	E	10 59	A	SAG	22
77	18	**G**	5 51	C	5 54	B	12 03	7	0 44	6	**6¾**	2 31	E	11 A.M. 48	B	SAG	23
78	19	M.	5 49	C	5 55	B	12 06	8	0 s. 20	7	**7¾**	3 17	E	12 P.M. 42	B	SAG	24
79	20	Tu.	5 47	C	5 57	C	12 10	8	0 n. 03	8	**8¾**	3 56	E	1 39	B	CAP	25
80	21	W.	5 46	C	5 58	C	12 12	8	0 27	8¾	**9½**	4 31	E	2 38	B	CAP	26
81	22	Th.	5 44	C	5 59	C	12 15	9	0 51	9½	**10**	5 01	E	3 39	C	AQU	27
82	23	Fr.	5 42	C	6 00	C	12 18	9	1 14	10¼	**10¾**	5 29	D	4 39	C	AQU	28
83	24	Sa.	5 40	C	6 01	C	12 21	9	1 38	11	**11¼**	5 54	D	5 41	D	PSC	0
84	25	**G**	5 39	C	6 02	C	12 23	10	2 01	11½	**11¾**	6 19	D	6 43	D	CET	1
85	26	M.	5 37	C	6 03	C	12 26	10	2 25	**12¼**	—	6 44	C	7 47	E	PSC	2
86	27	Tu.	5 35	C	6 05	C	12 30	10	2 48	12½	**12¾**	7 11	B	8 52	E	CET	3
87	28	W.	5 33	C	6 06	C	12 33	10	3 12	1	**1½**	7 40	B	9 59	E	ARI	4
88	29	Th.	5 32	C	6 07	C	12 35	11	3 35	1¾	**2¼**	8 13	B	11 P.M. 06	E	TAU	5
89	30	Fr.	5 30	C	6 08	C	12 38	11	3 59	2½	**3**	8 53	B	—	–	TAU	6
90	31	Sa.	5 28	C	6 09	C	12 41	11	4 n. 22	3¼	**4**	9 A.M. 41	A	12 A.M. 12	E	TAU	7

MARCH hath 31 days. 2001

For glad spring has begun,
And to the ardent sun
The earth, long time so bleak,
Turns a frost-bitten cheek. –Celia Thaxter

D. M.	D. W.	Dates, Feasts, Fasts, Aspects, Tide Heights	*Weather* ↓
1	Th.	St. David • ☌ ♄ ☾ • Deke Slayton born, 1924 • { 9.8 / 9.1	*Winter's*
2	F.	St. Chad • ☌ ♃ ☾ • Battle of Bismarck Sea began, 1943 •	*encore*
3	Sa.	Norman Bethune born, 1890 • *The deed is everything, the glory naught.* • { 9.8 / 8.6	*with*
4	G	1st S. in Lent • Sunday of Orthodoxy •	*leonine*
5	M.	St. Piran • ☾ at ☊ • ☾ rides high • Tides { 10.2 / 9.0	*roar.*
6	Tu.	Elizabeth Barrett Browning born, 1806 • Alan Greenspan born, 1926 • { 10.6 / 9.4	*The*
7	W.	St. Perpetua • ♀ stat. • Ember Day • Luther Burbank born, 1849 •	*time*
8	Th.	☾ at perig. • IBM released PC-DOS version 2.0, 1983 • Tides { 11.5 / 10.6	*is out*
9	Fr.	Full Sap ○ • Ember Day • Fire destroyed Olds Motor Works in Detroit, 1901 • { 11.8 / 11.1	*of*
10	Sa.	☌ ☿ ♅ • Ember Day • Skunks mate now. • Tides { 11.9 / —	*joint:*
11	G	2nd S. in Lent • ☾ on Eq. • ☿ Gr. Elong. (27° W.) •	*O*
12	M.	St. Gregory • Charles Cunningham Boycott born, 1832 • { 11.4 / 11.2 •	*cursed*
13	Tu.	*He too serves a certain purpose who only stands and cheers.* • Tides { 11.1 / 10.6 •	*white!*
14	W.	Albert Einstein born, 1879 • First town meeting held in Faneuil Hall, Boston, 1743 • { 10.8 / 9.9	*We*
15	Th.	☌ ♂ ☾ • Beware the Ides of March. • Ruth Bader Ginsburg born, 1933 •	*get*
16	Fr.	Congress authorized the establishment of U.S. Military Academy at West Point, New York, 1802 •	*a*
17	Sa.	St. Patrick • Golda Meir became prime minister of Israel, 1969 • Tides { 9.3 / 8.2	*few*
18	G	3rd S. in Lent • ☾ at ☋ • ☾ runs low • ♇ stat. •	
19	M.	St. Joseph • Swallows return to San Juan Capistrano • { 9.0 / 8.2	*more*
20	Tu.	☌ ♆ ☾ • ☾ at apo. • **Vernal Equinox** • Tides { 9.1 / 8.4	*inches*
21	W.	☌ ♅ ☾ • Rocking-chair marathons were the rage in Quebec, Canada, 1955 •	*every*
22	Th.	☌ ☿ ☾ • British Parliament passed the Stamp Act, 1765 • { 9.6 / 9.1	*night!*
23	Fr.	*The winds of the daytime wrestle and fight longer and stronger than those of the night.* • { 9.9 / 9.5 •	*All*
24	Sa.	New ● • The *Exxon Valdez* ran aground, spilling 11 million gallons of oil, 1989 •	*this*
25	G	4th S. in Lent • ☾ on Eq. • Tides { 10.1 / 10.0 •	*snow*
26	M.	Annunciation • Robert Frost born, 1874 • { 10.1 / —	*accumulating*
27	Tu.	Alaskan earthquake of 8.4 on Richter scale was strongest in North American history, 1964 • { 10.2 / 10.0	*we*
28	W.	☌ ♄ ☾ • Barnum and Bailey combined their circuses, 1881 • { 10.3 / 9.8	*find*
29	Th.	☌ ♃ ☾ • ♀ in inf. ☌ • Pearl Bailey born, 1918 •	*deeply*
30	Fr.	Assassination attempt on President Ronald Reagan, 1981 • { 10.3 / 9.2 •	*aggra-*
31	Sa.	*March comes in with adders' heads and goes out with peacocks' tails.* • { 10.2 / 9.0 •	*vating!*

Farmer's Calendar

■ It was Roger Tory Peterson who, going on 70 years ago, brought into wide use a way of identifying birds in nature by means of *field marks:* conspicuous colors, bars, stripes, or spots peculiar to each species that allow its members to be distinguished unmistakably on the wing or in the bush. By publishing, in his *Field Guide to the Birds* (first edition, 1934), a simple, workable system of field marks, Peterson served not only naturalists but also the birds themselves. His work was essential to establishing the modern ethic of conservation. By helping millions of his readers to recognize the birds they saw, he led them to seek out more, and so to understand that birds and their habitats were to be cherished and protected. Peterson made the birds easy to love by making them easy to know.

Too easy, perhaps. No one would wish any part of Peterson's work undone, but in a way, he worked too well. For the efficient, rational method of identifying birds that he gave us plays into a kind of human laziness we might call the Fallacy of Identification. This is the idea that once we have confidently given a name to a seen bird, we've finished with it and can go on to another. You see a sparrow at the feeder: brown, barred wings, striped head, streaked back. Does it have a white throat? If so, it's a white-throated sparrow; if not, a white-crowned. Field marks get you that far. The Fallacy of Identification tempts you to go no further, when in fact you have learned the least interesting thing about your bird: its name. In knowing the birds so well, we may stop seeing them.

2001 APRIL, The Fourth Month

Jupiter and Saturn enjoy their final month of dual visibility. Both planets are now descending lower in the western sky at nightfall, and on the 25th and 26th, the pair hovers near the young crescent Moon. Mars, still steadily brightening, crosses into the constellation Sagittarius and starts rising in the southeast soon after midnight. Venus emerges in the predawn east to become a not-very-prominent apparition as a morning star for the remainder of the year. Mercury finishes its own poor performance as a morning star and will be missed by no one. Daylight Saving Time begins at 2:00 A.M. on the 1st.

☽ First Quarter	1st day	6th hour	49th minute
○ Full Moon	7th day	23rd hour	22nd minute
☾ Last Quarter	15th day	11th hour	31st minute
● New Moon	23rd day	11th hour	26th minute
☽ First Quarter	30th day	13th hour	8th minute

After 2:00 A.M. on April 1, Eastern Daylight Time (EDT) is given.

For an explanation of this page, see page 40; for values of Key Letters, see page 226.

Day of Year	Day of Month	Day of Week	☼ Rises h. m.	Key	☼ Sets h. m.	Key	Length of Day h. m.	Sun Fast m.	Declination of Sun ° '	High Tide Boston Light—A.M. Bold—P.M.	☽ Rises h. m.	Key	☽ Sets h. m.	Key	☽ Place	☽ Age
91	1	**G**	6 27	B	7 10	C	12 43	12	4 N.45	5¼ **6**	11ᴬм37	B	2ᴹ15	E	GEM	8
92	2	M.	6 25	B	7 11	C	12 46	12	5 08	6¼ **7**	12ᴾм42	B	3 12	E	GEM	9
93	3	Tu.	6 23	B	7 12	C	12 49	12	5 31	7½ **8¼**	1 53	B	4 02	E	CAN	10
94	4	W.	6 21	B	7 14	C	12 53	13	5 54	8½ **9¼**	3 08	C	4 44	E	LEO	11
95	5	Th.	6 20	B	7 15	D	12 55	13	6 17	9½ **10**	4 23	C	5 21	D	LEO	12
96	6	Fr.	6 18	B	7 16	D	12 58	13	6 39	10½ **11**	5 38	D	5 53	D	VIR	13
97	7	Sa.	6 16	B	7 17	D	13 01	13	7 02	11½ **11¾**	6 51	D	6 23	D	VIR	14
98	8	**G**	6 15	B	7 18	D	13 03	14	7 24	**12¼** —	8 03	E	6 52	C	VIR	15
99	9	M.	6 13	B	7 19	D	13 06	14	7 46	12½ **1**	9 14	E	7 22	B	VIR	16
100	10	Tu.	6 11	B	7 20	D	13 09	14	8 08	1¼ **1¾**	10 22	E	7 53	B	LIB	17
101	11	W.	6 10	B	7 21	D	13 11	14	8 30	2 **2¾**	11ᴾм28	E	8 28	B	SCO	18
102	12	Th.	6 08	B	7 23	D	13 15	15	8 52	2¾ **3½**	—	—	9 06	B	OPH	19
103	13	Fr.	6 06	B	7 24	D	13 18	15	9 14	3¾ **4¼**	12ᴬм29	E	9 50	B	SAG	20
104	14	Sa.	6 05	B	7 25	D	13 20	15	9 36	4½ **5¼**	1 24	E	10 39	B	SAG	21
105	15	**G**	6 03	B	7 26	D	13 23	15	9 57	5¼ **6¼**	2 13	E	11ᴬм32	B	SAG	22
106	16	M.	6 01	B	7 27	D	13 26	16	10 18	6¼ **7**	2 55	E	12ᴾм28	B	CAP	23
107	17	Tu.	6 00	B	7 28	D	13 28	16	10 39	7¼ **8**	3 32	E	1 27	B	CAP	24
108	18	W.	5 58	B	7 29	D	13 31	16	11 00	8¼ **9**	4 03	E	2 27	C	AQU	25
109	19	Th.	5 57	B	7 30	D	13 33	16	11 21	9¼ **9¾**	4 31	D	3 28	C	AQU	26
110	20	Fr.	5 55	B	7 32	D	13 37	17	11 42	10 **10½**	4 57	D	4 29	D	AQU	27
111	21	Sa.	5 54	B	7 33	D	13 39	17	12 02	10¾ **11**	5 22	D	5 31	D	PSC	28
112	22	**G**	5 52	B	7 34	D	13 42	17	12 23	11½ **11¾**	5 47	C	6 35	D	CET	29
113	23	M.	5 51	B	7 35	D	13 44	17	12 43	**12** —	6 13	C	7 41	E	PSC	0
114	24	Tu.	5 49	B	7 36	D	13 47	17	13 02	12¼ **12¾**	6 41	B	8 48	E	ARI	1
115	25	W.	5 48	B	7 37	D	13 49	18	13 22	1 **1½**	7 13	B	9 57	E	TAU	2
116	26	Th.	5 46	B	7 38	D	13 52	18	13 41	1½ **2¼**	7 52	B	11ᴬм06	E	TAU	3
117	27	Fr.	5 45	B	7 39	D	13 54	18	14 00	2¼ **3**	8 37	B	—	—	TAU	4
118	28	Sa.	5 43	B	7 41	D	13 58	18	14 19	3 **3¾**	9 31	B	12ᴬм11	E	GEM	5
119	29	**G**	5 42	B	7 42	D	14 00	18	14 37	4 **4¾**	10 34	B	1 10	E	GEM	6
120	30	M.	5 41	B	7 43	D	14 02	18	14 N.56	5 **5¾**	11ᴬм42	B	2ᴬм01	E	CAN	7

APRIL hath 30 days. 2001

Oh, how fresh the wind is blowing!
See! the sky is bright and clear,
Oh, how green the grass is growing!
April! April! are you here? –Dora R. Goodale

D. M.	D. W.	Dates, Feasts, Fasts, Aspects, Tide Heights	Weather ↓
1	**G**	**5th S. in Lent** • **All Fools** • **Daylight Saving Time begins, 2:00 A.M.** •	
2	M.	*To be a fool at the right time is also an art.* • Tides {10.1 9.0 •	*Fools*
3	Tu.	**St. Richard of Chichester** • Jane Goodall born, 1934 • {10.2 9.3	*mush*
4	W.	C. C. King isolated Vitamin C at the Univ. of Pittsburgh, 1932 • Muddy Waters born, 1915 •	*in.*
5	Th.	☾ at perig. • Booker T. Washington born, 1856 • Tides {10.9 10.4	*Here*
6	Fr.	☌ ☿ ♀ • First U.S. credit union opened in Manchester, N.H., 1909 •	*comes*
7	Sa.	☾ on Eq. • **Full Egg** ○ • Henry Ford died, 1947 • {11.3 11.3	*sunshine.*
8	**G**	**Palm Sunday** • **First day of Passover** • {11.3 —	*Oh,*
9	M.	*Music is the child of prayer, the companion of religion.* • Tides {11.5 11.1 •	*be*
10	Tu.	Buchenwald concentration camp liberated, 1945 • Francis Perkins born, 1880 •	*joyful.*
11	W.	Harold Washington became first black mayor of Chicago, 1983 • Tides {11.2 10.2 •	*Now*
12	Th.	☌ ♂ ☾ • FDR died, 1945 • Salk polio vaccine announced, 1955 • {10.7 9.6	*it's*
13	Fr.	**Good Friday** • Thomas Jefferson born, 1743 • {10.2 9.1 •	*cold*
14	Sa.	☾ at ☋ • ☾ runs low • *Grapes of Wrath* published, 1939 • {9.7 8.6 •	*and*
15	**G**	**Easter** • **Orthodox Easter** • *The Sun dances on Easter morn.* •	*wet*
16	M.	☌ ♆ ☾ • Shea Municipal Stadium in New York City dedicated, 1964 • {9.0 8.2	*and*
17	Tu.	☾ at apo. • ♀ stat. • ☌ ♅ ☾ • Tides {8.9 8.3 •	*oyful.*
18	W.	Opening day at the new Yankee Stadium, New York City, 1923 • {9.0 8.6 •	*A dash*
19	Th.	Battle of Lexington and Concord, 1775 • Grace Kelly married Prince Rainier III, 1956 •	*of*
20	Fr.	☌ ♀ ☾ • Over 15 inches of snow fell, Akron, Ohio, 1901 • {9.4 9.4	*snow,*
21	Sa.	☾ on Eq. • *Who soweth in rain, he shall reap it with tears.* • Tides {9.7 9.8 •	*a*
22	**G**	**1st S. af. Easter** • J. Robert Oppenheimer born, 1904 •	*flash*
23	M.	**St. George** • ☿ in sup. ☌ • **New** ● • {10.0 — •	*of*
24	Tu.	Robert B. Thomas born, 1766 • Robert Penn Warren born, 1905 •	*lightning.*
25	W.	**St. Mark** • ☌ ♄ ☾ • Ella Fitzgerald born, 1917 • {10.7 10.0	*Say a*
26	Th.	☌ ♃ ☾ • U.S. Holocaust Museum opened, 1993 • {10.9 9.9	*prayer*
27	Fr.	*After learning the tricks of the trade, many of us think we know the trade.* • Tides {10.9 9.7	*for*
28	Sa.	☾ at ☊ • ☾ rides high • Benito Mussolini executed, 1945 • {10.8 9.5 •	*air*
29	**G**	**2nd S. af. Easter** • Zubin Mehta born, 1936 • {10.6 9.3	*that's*
30	M.	George Washington was inaugurated as first U.S. president, 1789 •	*brightening.*

Let us be thankful for the fools. But for them the rest of us could not succeed . . . –Mark Twain

Farmer's Calendar

■ So the Tourist from Down Country—that pathetic butt of a thousand jokes—is driving the byways of rural Vermont. He's lost. He spots an Old-Timer on the road and asks him, "Say, Mister, can you tell me how to get to East Raspberry?" The Old-Timer thinks, then says, "If I were going to East Raspberry, I wouldn't start from here." You say you've heard that one? I'm not surprised. Here's another: Tourist from Down Country is visiting the homestead of Old-Timer. Tourist looks appreciatively around the trig little farm. "Nice place you've got here," says Tourist to Old-Timer. "Lived here all your life?" Old-Timer gives it one beat, then replies, "Not yet."

And on and on and on. The classic New England joke pits a stranger against an elder of the community who humbles the former with a sly stroke of wit. I have often wondered about these ancient jokes. Why is the hero always old? For that is the invariable convention. The local who triumphs over the visitor is a man of many years. Why? What is there in either of the foregoing jokes that requires a protagonist of any particular age? Can't the young be droll?

I think the insistence on the Old-Timer in these stories is a clue that they aren't quite what they seem. Their subject isn't really the confusing geography or the laconic humor of the New England countryside. Their subject is mortality. The Old-Timer is at the end of his life. He knows the road to East Raspberry, but he knows more. He knows it doesn't matter which road you take. They all go to the same place.

2001   MAY, The Fifth Month

Venus achieves its greatest brilliancy as a morning star on the 4th, a dazzling low-elevation beacon in the eastern sky before dawn. The cloudy inner planet meets the crescent Moon on the 19th. Saturn vanishes into solar glare. Jupiter falls closer to the western horizon each evening at dusk and meets Mercury on the 15th and 16th. Mercury is especially bright during the first half of the month and now achieves its highest-in-the-sky evening appearance of the year. It is near the young crescent Moon on the 24th. Mars brightens dramatically to become an eye-catching "star" rising in the southeast by 11:00 P.M. EDT and remaining in the south throughout the night.

○ Full Moon	7th day	9th hour	52nd minute
☾ Last Quarter	15th day	6th hour	11th minute
● New Moon	22nd day	22nd hour	46th minute
☽ First Quarter	29th day	18th hour	9th minute

Times are given in Eastern Daylight Time.

For an explanation of this page, see page 40; for values of Key Letters, see page 226.

Day of Year	Day of Month	Day of Week	☼ Rises h. m.	Key	☼ Sets h. m.	Key	Length of Day h. m.	Sun Fast m.	Declination of Sun ° '	High Tide Boston Light—A.M. Bold—P.M.	☽ Rises h. m.	Key	☽ Sets h. m.	Key	☽ Place	☽ Age
121	1	Tu.	5 39	B	7 44	D	14 05	18	15 N.14	6 — 6¾	12ᴾ_M54	C	2ᴬ_M45	E	LEO	8
122	2	W.	5 38	B	7 45	D	14 07	19	15 32	7¼ — **8**	2 08	C	3 22	E	LEO	9
123	3	Th.	5 37	B	7 46	D	14 09	19	15 50	8¼ — 8¾	3 20	D	3 54	D	LEO	10
124	4	Fr.	5 35	A	7 47	D	14 12	19	16 07	9¼ — 9¾	4 32	D	4 24	D	VIR	11
125	5	Sa.	5 34	A	7 48	D	14 14	19	16 24	10¼ — 10¾	5 43	D	4 52	C	VIR	12
126	6	**G**	5 33	A	7 49	D	14 16	19	16 41	11 — 11½	6 54	E	5 20	C	VIR	13
127	7	M.	5 32	A	7 51	D	14 19	19	16 58	**12** —	8 03	E	5 50	B	LIB	14
128	8	Tu.	5 30	A	7 52	D	14 22	19	17 14	12¼ — 12¾	9 11	E	6 23	B	LIB	15
129	9	W.	5 29	A	7 53	D	14 24	19	17 30	1 — 1½	10 15	E	6 59	B	OPH	16
130	10	Th.	5 28	A	7 54	D	14 26	19	17 45	1¾ — 2¼	11ᴾ_M14	E	7 41	A	OPH	17
131	11	Fr.	5 27	A	7 55	D	14 28	19	18 01	2¼ — **3**	—	–	8 28	B	SAG	18
132	12	Sa.	5 26	A	7 56	D	14 30	19	18 16	3 — 3¾	12ᴬ_M06	E	9 20	B	SAG	19
133	13	**G**	5 25	A	7 57	D	14 32	19	18 30	4 — 4¾	12 52	E	10 16	B	CAP	20
134	14	M.	5 24	A	7 58	D	14 34	19	18 45	4¾ — 5½	1 31	E	11ᴬ_M14	B	CAP	21
135	15	Tu.	5 23	A	7 59	E	14 36	19	18 59	5¾ — 6½	2 04	E	12ᴾ_M14	B	CAP	22
136	16	W.	5 22	A	8 00	E	14 38	19	19 13	6½ — 7¼	2 33	D	1 14	C	AQU	23
137	17	Th.	5 21	A	8 01	E	14 40	19	19 26	7½ — **8**	3 00	D	2 15	C	AQU	24
138	18	Fr.	5 20	A	8 02	E	14 42	19	19 40	8½ — **9**	3 25	D	3 16	D	PSC	25
139	19	Sa.	5 19	A	8 03	E	14 44	19	19 53	9¼ — 9¾	3 49	C	4 19	D	CET	26
140	20	**G**	5 18	A	8 04	E	14 46	19	20 05	10 — 10¼	4 14	C	5 24	E	PSC	27
141	21	M.	5 17	A	8 05	E	14 48	19	20 17	10¾ — **11**	4 41	B	6 32	E	CET	28
142	22	Tu.	5 16	A	8 06	E	14 50	19	20 29	11½ — 11¾	5 12	B	7 42	E	ARI	0
143	23	W.	5 15	A	8 07	E	14 52	19	20 40	**12¼** —	5 48	B	8 52	E	TAU	1
144	24	Th.	5 15	A	8 08	E	14 53	19	20 51	12½ — **1**	6 31	B	10 01	E	TAU	2
145	25	Fr.	5 14	A	8 09	E	14 55	19	21 02	1¼ — **2**	7 23	B	11 04	E	GEM	3
146	26	Sa.	5 13	A	8 10	E	14 57	19	21 13	2 — 2¾	8 24	B	11ᴾ_M59	E	GEM	4
147	27	**G**	5 13	A	8 11	E	14 58	19	21 23	2¾ — 3½	9 32	B	—	–	CAN	5
148	28	M.	5 12	A	8 11	E	14 59	18	21 33	3¾ — 4½	10 45	B	12ᴬ_M46	E	CAN	6
149	29	Tu.	5 11	A	8 12	E	15 01	18	21 42	4¾ — 5½	11ᴬ_M58	C	1 25	E	LEO	7
150	30	W.	5 11	A	8 13	E	15 02	18	21 51	5¾ — 6½	1ᴬ_M10	D	1 59	D	LEO	8
151	31	Th.	5 10	A	8 14	E	15 04	18	21 N.59	7 — 7½	2ᴾ_M21	D	2ᴬ_M28	D	VIR	9

MAY hath 31 days. 2001

The earth is waking at the voice of May,
The new grass brightens by the trodden way,
The woods wave welcome to the sweet spring day,
And the sea is growing summer blue. –Elizabeth A. Allen

D. M.	D. W.	Dates, Feasts, Fasts, Aspects, Tide Heights	Weather ↓
1	Tu.	Sts. Philip & James • May Day • Tides {10.3 / 9.4 •	*Mayday!*
2	W.	☾ at perig. • Gen. Stonewall Jackson fatally wounded, 1863 • {10.3 / 9.8	*Here's*
3	Th.	**Invention of the Cross** • Nellie Tayloe Ross became first woman director of U.S. Mint, 1933 •	*our*
4	Fr.	☾ on Eq. • ♀ Gr. Bril. • Haymarket Square Riot, Chicago, 1886 •	*SOS:*
5	Sa.	Cinco de Mayo: Battle of Puebla, 1862 • Karl Marx born, 1818 • {10.6 / 11.1 •	*Could*
6	**G**	**3rd 𝕾. af. Easter** • Chrysler introduced the DeSoto, 1928 • {10.7 / 11.3	*it*
7	M.	**Full Milk** ○ • ☌☿♄ • Tchaikovsky born, 1840 • Tides {10.6 / —	*rain*
8	Tu.	Julian of Norwich • Mount Pelée on Martinique erupted, 1902 •	*a little*
9	W.	St. Gregory of Nazianzus • Pancho Gonzales born, 1928 • {11.2 / 10.1	*less?*
10	Th.	☌♂☾ • ♆ stat. • Ara Parseghian born, 1923 • {11.0 / 9.7	*Could*
11	Fr.	☾ at ☋ • ♂ stat. • Minnesota statehood, 1858 • **Three** • {10.6 / 9.4	*it*
12	Sa.	☾ runs low • *Shear your sheep in May, And shear them all away.* • **Chilly** • {10.1 / 9.0	*get*
13	**G**	**4th 𝕾. af. Easter** • ☌♆☾ • **Saints** • {9.7 / 8.7	*a*
14	M.	☾ at apo. • "The Stars and Stripes Forever" first performed in public, Philadelphia, 1897 •	*little*
15	Tu.	**Census Day (Canada)** • ☌♅☾ • L. Frank Baum born, 1856 •	*warmer?*
16	W.	☌☿♃ • Olga Korbut born, 1955 • Henry Fonda born, 1905 • {8.9 / 8.6 •	*Yes*
17	Th.	*An hour of play discovers more than a year of conversation.* • Mia Hamm born, 1972 • {8.9 / 8.9 •	*to*
18	Fr.	Gertrude Belle Elion became first woman inducted into National Inventors Hall of Fame, 1991	*latter,*
19	Sa.	St. Dunstan • ☾ on Eq. • ☌♀☾ • Nellie Melba born, 1861 •	*no*
20	**G**	**Rogation 𝕾.** • 10 inches of snow, Stafford, Vt., 1892 • Tides {9.4 / 10.2	*to*
21	M.	**Victoria Day (Canada)** • D. A. Buck patented a low-cost watch, 1878 • {9.6 / 10.6	*former.*
22	Tu.	☿ Gr. Elong. (22° E.) • **New** ● • Mary Cassatt born, 1844 •	*There's*
23	W.	*Look upon life as a thing that is lent you, and use it accordingly.* • Tides {9.9 / — •	*a*
24	Th.	Ascension • Orthodox Ascension • ☌♃☾ • ☌☿☾ •	
25	Fr.	St. Bede • ☌♄☉ • Miles Davis born, 1926 • {11.4 / 10.0	*smatter-*
26	Sa.	St. Augustine of Canterbury • ☾ at ☊ • ☾ rides high •	*ing*
27	**G**	**1st 𝕾. af. Asc.** • ☾ at perig. • Tides {11.3 / 9.8 •	*of*
28	M.	Memorial Day • Shavuot • Sierra Club founded, 1892 •	*shatter-*
29	Tu.	♅ stat. • Edmund Hillary and Tensing Norgay reached summit of Mt. Everest, 1953 •	*ing*
30	W.	*Friends may come and go, but enemies accumulate.* • Tides {10.4 / 10.0 •	*thunder-*
31	Th.	Visit. of Mary • First U.S. copyright law signed, 1790 • {10.2 / 10.2	*stormers!*

Farmer's Calendar

■ "Lo, the winter is past, the rain is over and gone; the flowers appear on the earth; the time of the singing of birds is come, and the voice of the turtle is heard in our land." So it is written in the Old Testament, in what has always seemed to me to be the supreme evocation of spring in the North. How a Hebrew king writing in a desert country 3,000 years ago managed to get May in the New England uplands on the page with such emotional accuracy is beyond me, but I think I know where the power of his image lies: It's in the odd perfection of that line about the voice of the turtle.

The voice of the turtle. It's an expression of the simple relief, the gratitude of all life in these parts for the new heat of the spring Sun and for the softening and quickening of the earth. The writer's idea is that even the turtle, on climbing out of the mud where it has been imprisoned all winter under the frozen pond—even the turtle, which has no voice, feels the spring and stretches its lean and leathery throat to produce a grateful peep.

Or so I read the Bible for a matter of 40 years. Recently it has occurred to me that I have been all my life misunderstanding King Solomon. He wasn't saying the *turtle*—a shelled reptile—gives voice in the spring. He was talking about the *turtle dove,* a common bird. Boy, was I off! But I don't care. I still like my turtle better than Sol's. Corrected, the reading of the line is accurate, but accurate is all it is. Uncorrected, the reading is wrong—but the line is poetry. The best poem is the one you write yourself, even when it's somebody else's.

2001   JUNE, The Sixth Month

Jupiter is lost behind the Sun throughout June, while Saturn remains low and obscure in morning twilight. The month belongs to Mars and Venus, occupying opposite sides of the heavens. Venus, the dazzling morning star, achieves maximum Sun-separation on the 8th but is not high. Mars is brilliant as it sits close to the bright waning Moon on the 6th, reaches opposition with the Sun on the 13th, and achieves its closest approach to Earth since 1988 on the 21st. The summer solstice occurs on the 21st, at 3:38 A.M. EDT. With the Sun now at its annual high point, Mars' opposition means that it lurks in the zodiac's lowest zone. Thick horizon air will make the brilliant planet look red.

○ Full Moon	5th day	21st hour	39th minute
☾ Last Quarter	13th day	23rd hour	28th minute
● New Moon	21st day	7th hour	58th minute
☽ First Quarter	27th day	23rd hour	19th minute

Times are given in Eastern Daylight Time.

For an explanation of this page, see page 40; for values of Key Letters, see page 226.

Day of Year	Day of Month	Day of Week	☀ Rises h. m.	Key	☀ Sets h. m.	Key	Length of Day h. m.	Sun Fast m.	Declination of Sun ° '	High Tide Boston Light—A.M. Bold—P.M.		☽ Rises h. m.	Key	☽ Sets h. m.	Key	☽ Place	☽ Age
152	1	Fr.	5 10	A	8 15	E	15 05	18	22N.07	8	8½	3ᴾM31	D	2ᴬM56	C	VIR	10
153	2	Sa.	5 09	A	8 15	E	15 06	18	22 15	9	9½	4 40	E	3 23	C	VIR	11
154	3	**G**	5 09	A	8 16	E	15 07	18	22 22	10	10¼	5 49	E	3 51	B	LIB	12
155	4	M.	5 09	A	8 17	E	15 08	17	22 29	10¾	11	6 56	E	4 22	B	LIB	13
156	5	Tu.	5 08	A	8 17	E	15 09	17	22 36	11¾	11¾	8 01	E	4 56	B	SCO	14
157	6	W.	5 08	A	8 18	E	15 10	17	22 42	12½	—	9 02	E	5 35	A	OPH	15
158	7	Th.	5 08	A	8 19	E	15 11	17	22 48	12½	1¼	9 58	E	6 20	A	SAG	16
159	8	Fr.	5 07	A	8 19	E	15 12	17	22 53	1¼	2	10 47	E	7 10	B	SAG	17
160	9	Sa.	5 07	A	8 20	E	15 13	16	22 58	2	2½	11ᴾM29	E	8 05	B	SAG	18
161	10	**G**	5 07	A	8 20	E	15 13	16	23 02	2¾	3¼	—	—	9 03	B	CAP	19
162	11	M.	5 07	A	8 21	E	15 14	16	23 06	3½	4	12ᴬM04	E	10 02	B	CAP	20
163	12	Tu.	5 07	A	8 22	E	15 15	16	23 10	4¼	4¾	12 35	E	11ᴬM02	B	AQU	21
164	13	W.	5 07	A	8 22	E	15 15	16	23 14	5	5¾	1 02	D	12ᴾM02	C	AQU	22
165	14	Th.	5 07	A	8 22	E	15 15	15	23 17	6	6½	1 27	D	1 02	D	PSC	23
166	15	Fr.	5 07	A	8 23	E	15 16	15	23 19	6¾	7¼	1 51	D	2 03	D	CET	24
167	16	Sa.	5 07	A	8 23	E	15 16	15	23 21	7¾	8	2 15	C	3 06	D	PSC	25
168	17	**G**	5 07	A	8 24	E	15 17	15	23 23	8½	8¾	2 41	B	4 12	E	CET	26
169	18	M.	5 07	A	8 24	E	15 17	15	23 24	9½	9¾	3 09	B	5 20	E	ARI	27
170	19	Tu.	5 07	A	8 24	E	15 17	14	23 26	10¼	10½	3 42	B	6 31	E	TAU	28
171	20	W.	5 07	A	8 24	E	15 17	14	23 26	11	11¼	4 22	B	7 42	E	TAU	29
172	21	Th.	5 07	A	8 25	E	15 18	14	23 26	12	—	5 10	B	8 49	E	TAU	0
173	22	Fr.	5 08	A	8 25	E	15 17	14	23 26	12	12¾	6 09	B	9 50	E	GEM	1
174	23	Sa.	5 08	A	8 25	E	15 17	14	23 25	12¾	1½	7 17	B	10 42	E	GEM	2
175	24	**G**	5 08	A	8 25	E	15 17	13	23 24	1¾	2½	8 30	B	11ᴿM25	E	CAN	3
176	25	M.	5 09	A	8 25	E	15 16	13	23 22	2¾	3¼	9 46	C	—	—	LEO	4
177	26	Tu.	5 09	A	8 25	E	15 16	13	23 20	3½	4¼	11ᴬM00	C	12ᴬM01	E	LEO	5
178	27	W.	5 09	A	8 25	E	15 16	13	23 17	4½	5¼	12ᴿM13	D	12 32	D	VIR	6
179	28	Th.	5 10	A	8 25	E	15 15	12	23 14	5½	6¼	1 23	D	1 01	D	VIR	7
180	29	Fr.	5 10	A	8 25	E	15 15	12	23 11	6¾	7¼	2 32	D	1 28	C	VIR	8
181	30	Sa.	5 11	A	8 25	E	15 14	12	23N.08	7¾	8¼	3ᴹM39	E	1ᴬM55	C	VIR	9

JUNE hath 30 days. 2001

In June 'tis good to lie beneath a tree
While the blithe season comforts every sense,
Steeps all the brain in rest, and heals the heart,
Brimming it o'er with sweetness unawares. –J. R. Lowell

D. M.	D. W.	Dates, Feasts, Fasts, Aspects, Tide Heights	Weather ↓
1	Fr.	☾ on Eq. • First recorded U.S. earthquake, Plymouth, Mass., 1638 • { 10.0 10.5	*Awful*
2	Sa.	*Good judgment comes from experience, and experience comes from bad judgment.* • { 10.0 10.8	*wet*
3	**G**	**Whit S. • Pentecost • Orthodox Pentecost** • { 9.9 11.0	
4	M.	☿ stat. • ♇ at ☍ • First Pulitzer prizes awarded, 1917 • { 9.9 11.0 •	*for*
5	Tu.	**St. Boniface** • **Full Strawberry** ○ • { 9.8 11.0 •	*backyard*
6	W.	☌ ♂ ☾ • Ember Day • Nathan Hale born, 1755 •	*puttering—*
7	Th.	☾ at ☋ • First prime-time TV big-money show, "The $64,000 Question," premiered, 1955	*you*
8	Fr.	☾ runs low • ♀ Gr. Elong. (46° W.) • Ember Day • Tides { 10.7 9.3 •	*can*
9	Sa.	Ember Day • Congress authorized income tax withholding, 1943 • { 10.4 9.1	*count*
10	**G**	**Trinity** • **Orthodox All Saints** • ☌ ♆ ☾ • { 10.1 9.0	*on*
11	M.	**St. Barnabas** • ☌ ♅ ☾ • ☾ at apo. • { 9.8 8.8	*thunder*
12	Tu.	Chicago Bulls won their first NBA title, 1991 • Tides { 9.5 8.8 •	*muttering.*
13	W.	♂ at ☍ • The Yukon Territory became part of Canada, 1898 • { 9.2 8.8	*Bright*
14	Th.	**Corpus Christi** • ☌ ♃ ☉ • Burl Ives born, 1909 • { 9.0 8.9 •	*but*
15	Fr.	☾ on Eq. • 4 inches of snow fell at Mt. Mansfield, Stowe, Vt., 1959 • { 8.9 9.2	*brisky,*
16	Sa.	☿ in inf. ☌ • *The nail that sticks up gets hammered down.* • { 8.9 9.5	*showers*
17	**G**	**2nd S. af. P.** • ☌ ♀ ☾ • { 8.9 9.9 •	*bubble.*
18	M.	United States declared war on Great Britain, 1812 • Tides { 9.1 10.4 •	*Time*
19	Tu.	☌ ♄ ☾ • The Statue of Liberty arrived in New York Harbor, 1885 • { 9.4 10.8 •	*for*
20	W.	Chicago Bulls became first team in 27 years to win 3 NBA championships in a row, 1993 •	*whiskey*
21	Th.	**Summer Solstice** • **New** ● • ☾ at ☊ • ♂ closest approach • Eclipse ☉	
22	Fr.	☾ rides high • Congress created the U.S. Dept. of Justice, 1870 • { 11.6 10.0 •	*sours*
23	Sa.	**Midsummer Eve** • ☾ at perig. • Tides { 11.8 10.2 •	*(double).*
24	**G**	**3rd S. af. P.** • John Cabot sighted coast of Canada, 1497 •	*You'll*
25	M.	**Nativ. John the Baptist** • Custer's Last Stand, 1876 • { 11.6 10.3	*need a*
26	Tu.	*You have freedom when you're easy in your harness.* • Tides { 11.3 10.3 •	*sense of*
27	W.	Thurgood Marshall announced his resignation from the Supreme Court, 1991 •	*humid—*
28	Th.	**St. Irenaeus** • ☾ on Eq. • ☿ stat. • { 10.4 10.4 •	*raging*
29	Fr.	**Sts. Peter & Paul** • William James Mayo born, 1861 •	*rainstorms*
30	Sa.	National Organization for Women founded, 1966 • Tides { 9.7 10.5 •	*rumored.*

I don't know the key to success, but the key to failure is trying to please everybody. –Bill Cosby

Farmer's Calendar

■ *June 1.* Time to plant the beans—a good job to have ahead of you, provided your bean operation is on a trifling, quite unprofitable scale, as mine always is. Planting beans is a comparatively complex and laborious business; if you go into it for more than a couple of rows, it will break first your back, then your heart. But as long as you're a duffer, it's pure fun.

In some planting, you can simply scratch the dirt up a little and toss the seeds in the right general direction. But to get a green bean properly into the ground, you must put it to bed and tuck it in. I lay out the bean row with string, dress it carefully with compost, and dig it and rake it and till it until the soil is as smooth and uniform as ground coffee. Then I fling myself down beside the row and crawl along it, poking my right forefinger into the lush, brown earth every couple of inches to make the holes where the beans will repose, each one "a rich jewel in an Ethiop's ear."

The beans themselves I now shake out of their envelope. They are such pretty things: a shiny, buffed brown like mahogany or some other rare tropical wood. It seems a pity to bury them in the ground. I do so, however, dropping a bean into each dark hole. Then I go along the row patting the holes closed, patting the soil down firm. Somehow, that patting down is the most satisfactory part of the whole job, rounding it, giving it a finish, a completeness, following which the germination, growth, and eventual harvest of the beans would seem almost an anticlimax.

2001 JULY, The Seventh Month

Earth is at aphelion (farthest from the Sun) on the 4th. Although brilliant Mars is visible all night in the southerly constellation Ophiuchus, Venus and Mercury, joined by Saturn and Jupiter, have shifted entirely to the eastern predawn sky. The ringed world stubbornly remains in Taurus, but Jupiter moves into Gemini, its new home for the rest of the year. Look for beautiful gatherings in the middle of morning twilight: Dazzling Venus meets dimmer Saturn and the orange star Aldebaran from the 11th to the 15th, with the crescent Moon joining them on the 17th; lower in the east during this same five-day period, Jupiter and Mercury hover side by side, joined by the Moon on the 19th.

○	Full Moon	5th day	11th hour	4th minute
☾	Last Quarter	13th day	14th hour	45th minute
●	New Moon	20th day	15th hour	44th minute
☽	First Quarter	27th day	6th hour	8th minute

Times are given in Eastern Daylight Time.

For an explanation of this page, see page 40; for values of Key Letters, see page 226.

Day of Year	Day of Month	Day of Week	☼ Rises h. m.	Key	☼ Sets h. m.	Key	Length of Day h. m.	Sun Fast m.	Declination of Sun ° '	High Tide Boston Light—A.M.	**Bold—P.M.**	☽ Rises h. m.	Key	☽ Sets h. m.	Key	☽ Place	☽ Age
182	1	**G**	5 11	A	8 25	E	15 14	12	23N.04	8¾	**9**	4 P.M. 46	E	2 A.M. 24	B	LIB	10
183	2	M.	5 12	A	8 25	E	15 13	12	22 59	9¾	**10**	5 51	E	2 57	B	SCO	11
184	3	Tu.	5 12	A	8 24	E	15 12	11	22 54	10½	**10¾**	6 53	E	3 33	B	OPH	12
185	4	W.	5 13	A	8 24	E	15 11	11	22 49	11½	**11½**	7 51	E	4 15	B	SAG	13
186	5	Th.	5 13	A	8 24	E	15 11	11	22 43	**12¼**	—	8 42	E	5 03	A	SAG	14
187	6	Fr.	5 14	A	8 24	E	15 10	11	22 37	12¼	**12¾**	9 26	E	5 56	B	SAG	15
188	7	Sa.	5 14	A	8 23	E	15 09	11	22 31	12¾	**1½**	10 04	E	6 53	B	CAP	16
189	8	**G**	5 15	A	8 23	E	15 08	11	22 24	1½	**2¼**	10 36	E	7 52	B	CAP	17
190	9	M.	5 16	A	8 22	E	15 06	10	22 17	2¼	**2¾**	11 05	D	8 52	B	AQU	18
191	10	Tu.	5 17	A	8 22	E	15 05	10	22 09	3	**3½**	11 30	D	9 52	C	AQU	19
192	11	W.	5 17	A	8 21	E	15 04	10	22 01	3¾	**4¼**	11 P.M. 54	D	10 51	C	AQU	20
193	12	Th.	5 18	A	8 21	E	15 03	10	21 53	4½	**5**	—	–	11 A.M. 51	D	PSC	21
194	13	Fr.	5 19	A	8 20	E	15 01	10	21 44	5¼	**5¾**	12 A.M. 17	C	12 P.M. 52	D	CET	22
195	14	Sa.	5 20	A	8 20	E	15 00	10	21 35	6	**6½**	12 41	C	1 55	E	PSC	23
196	15	**G**	5 21	A	8 19	E	14 58	10	21 25	7	**7¼**	1 08	B	3 01	E	ARI	24
197	16	M.	5 22	A	8 18	E	14 56	10	21 15	7¾	**8¼**	1 38	B	4 09	E	TAU	25
198	17	Tu.	5 23	A	8 18	E	14 55	10	21 05	8¾	**9**	2 13	B	5 19	E	TAU	26
199	18	W.	5 23	A	8 17	E	14 54	9	20 55	9¾	**10**	2 57	B	6 28	E	TAU	27
200	19	Th.	5 24	A	8 16	E	14 52	9	20 44	10½	**10¾**	3 50	B	7 33	E	GEM	28
201	20	Fr.	5 25	A	8 15	E	14 50	9	20 33	11½	**11¾**	4 54	B	8 30	E	GEM	0
202	21	Sa.	5 26	A	8 15	E	14 49	9	20 21	**12½**	—	6 07	B	9 18	E	CAN	1
203	22	**G**	5 27	A	8 14	E	14 47	9	20 09	12½	**1¼**	7 24	B	9 58	E	LEO	2
204	23	M.	5 28	A	8 13	E	14 45	9	19 57	1½	**2¼**	8 42	C	10 33	D	LEO	3
205	24	Tu.	5 29	A	8 12	E	14 43	9	19 44	2½	**3**	9 58	D	11 03	D	LEO	4
206	25	W.	5 30	A	8 11	E	14 41	9	19 31	3¼	**4**	11 A.M. 11	D	11 31	C	VIR	5
207	26	Th.	5 31	A	8 10	D	14 39	9	19 18	4¼	**4¾**	12 P.M. 22	D	11 P.M. 59	B	VIR	6
208	27	Fr.	5 32	A	8 09	D	14 37	9	19 05	5¼	**5¾**	1 31	E	—	–	VIR	7
209	28	Sa.	5 33	A	8 08	D	14 35	9	18 51	6¼	**6¾**	2 39	E	12 A.M. 28	A	LIB	8
210	29	**G**	5 34	A	8 07	D	14 33	9	18 37	7¼	**7¾**	3 44	E	12 59	A	LIB	9
211	30	M.	5 35	A	8 06	D	14 31	9	18 22	8½	**8¾**	4 47	E	1 34	B	OPH	10
212	31	Tu.	5 36	A	8 05	D	14 29	9	18N.07	9¼	**9½**	5 P.M. 46	E	2 A.M. 14	B	SAG	11

JULY hath 31 days. 2001

Black bees on the clover-heads drowsily clinging,
Where tall feathered grasses and buttercups sway;
And all through the fields a white sprinkle of daisies,
Open-eyed at the setting of day. –Abba Woolson

D. M.	D. W.	Dates, Feasts, Fasts, Aspects, Tide Heights	*Weather* ↓
1	G	4th S. af. P. • Canada Day • Tides { 9.4 / 10.6	*These*
2	M.	Record-setting 107°F at Portland, Oregon, 1942 • Nostradamus died, 1566 • { 9.3 / 10.6 •	*are*
3	Tu.	☌ ♂ ☾ • Dog Days begin. • *Dog Days bright and clear, indicate a happy year.*	*the*
4	W.	Independence Day • ☾ at ☋ • ⊕ at aphelion • { 9.2 / 10.6 •	
5	Th.	☾ runs low • Full Thunder ○ • Eclipse ☾ • { 9.2 / —	*climes*
6	Fr.	First female students admitted to U.S. Naval Academy at Annapolis, Md., 1976 •	*to play*
7	Sa.	☌ ♆ ☾ • Sandra Day O'Connor nominated for U.S. Supreme Court, 1981 • { 10.4 / 9.1	*nine*
8	G	5th S. af. P. • ☌ ♅ ☾ • Tides { 10.2 / 9.1 •	*holes.*
9	M.	☾ at apo. • ☿ Gr. Elong. (21° W.) • 115°F at Ft. Scott, Kansas, 1860 •	*Stockpile*
10	Tu.	Miguel Vazquez performed first public quadruple somersault on trapeze, 1982 • { 9.8 / 9.1	*pickles,*
11	W.	Sir Wilfrid Laurier became first French Canadian Prime Minister of Canada, 1896 • { 9.6 / 9.1 •	*hot*
12	Th.	☾ on Eq. • ☌ ☿ ♃ • Buckminster Fuller born, 1895 • { 9.3 / 9.1	*dog*
13	Fr.	First World Cup soccer competition, Montevideo, Uruguay, 1930 • Tides { 9.0 / 9.2	*rolls.*
14	Sa.	Bastille Day • *It is not a revolt, it is a revolution.* –Duc de Liancourt to Louis XVI, 1789 •	*For*
15	G	6th S. af. P. • ☌ ♀ ♄ • Tom Thumb died, 1883 • { 8.8 / 9.7	*a*
16	M.	St. Swithin • *Apollo 11* was launched from Cape Canaveral, Fla., 1969 • { 8.8 / 10.1	*while*
17	Tu.	☌ ♄ ☾ • ☌ ♀ ☾ • Donald Sutherland born, 1934 • { 9.0 / 10.5	*it's*
18	W.	☌ ♃ ☾ • Hume Cronyn born, 1911 • Cornscateous air is everywhere. • { 9.2 / 11.0	*hot*
19	Th.	Occn. ☿ ☾ • ♂ stat. • ☾ at ☊ • Tides { 9.6 / 11.5 •	*as*
20	Fr.	☾ rides high • New ● • First Special Olympics held, Chicago, Ill., 1968 •	*hell:*
21	Sa.	☾ at perig. • National Women's Hall of Fame founded at Seneca Falls, N.Y., 1979 •	*kick*
22	G	7th S. af. P. • Sir Alexander Mackenzie reached Canadian Pacific coast, 1793 • { 12.0 / 10.6	
23	M.	St. Mary Magdalene • Pee Wee Reese born, 1918 •	*your shoes*
24	Tu.	Brigham Young and his Mormon followers reached the Great Salt Lake Valley, 1847 • { 11.8 / 10.8	*off,*
25	W.	St. James • ☾ on Eq. • *Coincidences are spiritual puns.* • { 11.4 / 10.8	*sweat*
26	Th.	St. Ann • Federal Bureau of Investigation established, 1908 • { 10.8 / 10.7 •	*a*
27	Fr.	Congress established Dept. of Foreign Affairs (later changed to Dept. of State), 1789 •	*spell.*
28	Sa.	First singing telegram delivered, 1933 • Beatrix Potter born, 1866 • { 9.7 / 10.4	*Ahh—*
29	G	8th S. af. P. • NASA established, 1958 • { 9.2 / 10.3	*ain't*
30	M.	♆ at ☍ • ☌ ♂ ☾ • Casey Stengel born, 1890 • Tides { 9.0 / 10.2	*life*
31	Tu.	Cornerstone laid for first U.S. government building, the Philadelphia Mint, 1792 • { 8.9 / 10.2	*swell?*

Farmer's Calendar

■ "Nothing," wrote Francis Bacon four hundred years ago, "is more pleasant to the eye than green grass kept finely shorn." No doubt he is right—hence, perhaps, a large part of the otherwise inexplicable charm of the game of golf. Hence, too, the need most householders evidently feel to keep their grass mown, and the effort and expense they devote to that job. It may seem that mowing the lawn is no more than one of the tiresome, repetitive duties we perform to keep time and nature conveniently in check, like washing the windows, raking the leaves, shoveling the snow—a purely negative endeavor. But is it? Bacon's remark suggests a different view.

After all, what are we afraid of from an unmown lawn? It's only grass. You can walk right over it. It won't hold you back, it won't grow up and attack you while you sleep. It is not the abode of fierce tigers and serpents (or if it is, you might think about moving to a different part of the country). If the grass gets in your way, you can simply whack it down a couple of times a year. You can even pave it over and forget it was ever there. If grass cutting was something we had to do for the practical purposes of everyday living, there would be no need of the weekly ritual of mowing. No, the conclusion is plain: Grass cutting is a human gesture; it belongs not to life, but to art. We mow, and mow again all summer long and on into the fall, because we like to look over that green grass finely shorn—we also like to smell it. Mowing is making beauty.

2001 AUGUST, The Eighth Month

Look for increasing numbers of "shooting stars" from the 6th through the 12th, even though the Perseid meteors of the 11th to the 13th could be ruined by a waning gibbous Moon. Meanwhile, eye-catching conjunctions spangle the predawn heavens. Venus and Jupiter, the night's two brightest "stars," pass just a degree apart on the 5th and 6th. The Moon skims past Saturn on the 14th, Jupiter on the 15th, and Venus on the 16th. Uranus, in Capricornus, is at opposition on the 15th. At magnitude 6.0, the giant green world is faintly visible to the naked eye under moonless conditions, which prevail around the 18th. Mars, although fading from its June glory, remains bright in the south.

○	Full Moon	4th day	1st hour	56th minute
☾	Last Quarter	12th day	3rd hour	53rd minute
●	New Moon	18th day	22nd hour	55th minute
☽	First Quarter	25th day	15th hour	55th minute

Times are given in Eastern Daylight Time.

For an explanation of this page, see page 40; for values of Key Letters, see page 226.

Day of Year	Day of Month	Day of Week	☼ Rises h. m.	Key	☼ Sets h. m.	Key	Length of Day h. m.	Sun Fast m.	Declination of Sun ° ′	High Tide Boston Light—A.M.	Bold—P.M.	☽ Rises h. m.	Key	☽ Sets h. m.	Key	☽ Place	☽ Age
213	1	W.	5 37	A	8 04	D	14 27	9	17N.52	10¼	**10½**	6 P.M. 38	E	2 A.M. 59	B	SAG	12
214	2	Th.	5 38	A	8 02	D	14 24	9	17 36	11	**11¼**	7 24	E	3 50	B	SAG	13
215	3	Fr.	5 39	A	8 01	D	14 22	9	17 21	11¾	**11¾**	8 04	E	4 46	B	CAP	14
216	4	Sa.	5 40	A	8 00	D	14 20	9	17 05	**12½**	—	8 38	E	5 44	B	CAP	15
217	5	**G**	5 41	A	7 59	D	14 18	10	16 48	12½	**1**	9 07	E	6 44	B	CAP	16
218	6	M.	5 42	A	7 57	D	14 15	10	16 32	1¼	**1¾**	9 34	D	7 44	B	AQU	17
219	7	Tu.	5 43	A	7 56	D	14 13	10	16 15	1¾	**2¼**	9 58	D	8 43	C	AQU	18
220	8	W.	5 44	A	7 55	D	14 11	10	15 58	2½	**3**	10 21	D	9 43	D	PSC	19
221	9	Th.	5 45	A	7 53	D	14 08	10	15 41	3¼	**3½**	10 44	C	10 43	D	CET	20
222	10	Fr.	5 46	A	7 52	D	14 06	10	15 23	3¾	**4¼**	11 09	C	11 A.M. 44	D	PSC	21
223	11	Sa.	5 47	A	7 51	D	14 04	10	15 06	4½	**5**	11 P.M. 36	B	12 P.M. 47	E	CET	22
224	12	**G**	5 48	A	7 49	D	14 01	11	14 48	5½	**5¾**	—	–	1 52	E	ARI	23
225	13	M.	5 49	A	7 48	D	13 59	11	14 29	6¼	**6¾**	12 A.M. 08	B	3 00	E	TAU	24
226	14	Tu.	5 50	A	7 46	D	13 56	11	14 11	7¼	**7½**	12 47	B	4 08	E	TAU	25
227	15	W.	5 51	B	7 45	D	13 54	11	13 52	8¼	**8½**	1 34	B	5 13	E	GEM	26
228	16	Th.	5 53	B	7 44	D	13 51	11	13 33	9¼	**9½**	2 32	B	6 14	E	GEM	27
229	17	Fr.	5 54	B	7 42	D	13 48	11	13 14	10¼	**10½**	3 40	B	7 06	E	CAN	28
230	18	Sa.	5 55	B	7 41	D	13 46	12	12 54	11¼	**11½**	4 56	B	7 50	E	CAN	0
231	19	**G**	5 56	B	7 39	D	13 43	12	12 35	**12**	—	6 15	C	8 28	D	LEO	1
232	20	M.	5 57	B	7 37	D	13 40	12	12 15	12¼	**1**	7 34	C	9 00	D	LEO	2
233	21	Tu.	5 58	B	7 36	D	13 38	12	11 55	1¼	**1¾**	8 51	D	9 30	D	VIR	3
234	22	W.	5 59	B	7 34	D	13 35	13	11 35	2	**2½**	10 06	D	9 59	C	VIR	4
235	23	Th.	6 00	B	7 33	D	13 33	13	11 15	3	**3½**	11 A.M. 18	E	10 28	B	VIR	5
236	24	Fr.	6 01	B	7 31	D	13 30	13	10 54	4	**4¼**	12 P.M. 28	E	10 59	B	LIB	6
237	25	Sa.	6 02	B	7 30	D	13 28	13	10 34	5	**5¼**	1 36	E	11 P.M. 34	B	LIB	7
238	26	**G**	6 03	B	7 28	D	13 25	14	10 13	6	**6¼**	2 41	E	—	–	OPH	8
239	27	M.	6 04	B	7 26	D	13 22	14	9 52	7	**7¼**	3 41	E	12 A.M. 12	A	OPH	9
240	28	Tu.	6 05	B	7 25	D	13 20	14	9 31	8	**8¼**	4 36	E	12 56	A	SAG	10
241	29	W.	6 06	B	7 23	D	13 17	15	9 09	9	**9¼**	5 23	E	1 46	B	SAG	11
242	30	Th.	6 07	B	7 21	D	13 14	15	8 48	10	**10**	6 05	E	2 40	B	SAG	12
243	31	Fr.	6 08	B	7 20	D	13 12	15	8N.26	10¾	**10¾**	6 P.M. 40	E	3 A.M. 38	B	CAP	13

AUGUST hath 31 days. 2001

The slow soft toads out of damp corners creep;
And evening's breath, wandering here and there
Over the quivering surface of the stream,
Wakes not one ripple from its summer dream. –P. B. Shelley

D. M.	D. W.	Dates, Feasts, Fasts, Aspects, Tide Heights	Weather ↓
1	W.	**Lammas Day** • ☾ at ☋ • Calamity Jane died, 1903 • {8.9 / 10.2	*It's a*
2	Th.	☾ runs low • Montgomery Ward announced the closing of its catalog business, 1985 •	*peach—*
3	Fr.	☌ ♆ ☾ • *Consistency requires you to be as ignorant today as you were a year ago.* •	*hit*
4	Sa.	Full Green Corn ○ • ☌ ♅ ☾ • "Rocket" Richard born, 1921 • {9.1 / —	
5	**G**	**9th S. af. P.** • ☾ at apo. • ☿ in sup. ☌ • ☌ ♀ ♃ •	
6	M.	**Transfiguration** • Lucille Ball born, 1911 • {10.2 / 9.3 •	*the beach!*
7	Tu.	**Name of Jesus** • Garrison Keillor born, 1942 • {10.0 / 9.3 •	*Torrider*
8	W.	**St. Dominic** • Snow and slush 6 inches deep fell on a ship on Lake Michigan, 1882 •	*than*
9	Th.	☾ on Eq. • Webster-Ashburton Treaty set eastern Canada-U.S. border, 1842 •	*Florider.*
10	Fr.	**St. Laurence** • "Candid Camera" TV premiere, 1948 • {9.3 / 9.4 •	*Mercy*
11	Sa.	**St. Clare** • Dog Days end. • First federal prisoners arrived at Alcatraz, 1934 •	*drops*
12	**G**	**10th S. af. P.** • Christy Mathewson born, 1880 • {8.8 / 9.6 •	*like*
13	M.	☌ ♄ ☾ • Berlin Wall (initially a barbed wire fence) erected, 1961 • {8.7 / 9.8	*rain,*
14	Tu.	*No man can think clearly when his fists are clenched.* • Tides {8.7 / 10.2 •	*quoth*
15	W.	**Assumption** • ☾ at ☊ • ♅ at ☍ • ☌ ♃ ☾ • {8.9 / 10.6	
16	Th.	☾ rides high • ☌ ♀ ☾ • Menachem Begin born, 1913 •	*Portia—*
17	Fr.	Cat Nights begin. • First successful transatlantic balloon trip, 1978 • {9.7 / 11.6	*now*
18	Sa.	New ● • Birth control pills marketed by G. D. Searle Co., 1960 • Tides {10.2 / 11.9	*it's*
19	**G**	**11th S. af. P.** • ☾ at perig. • {10.7 / —	*parched*
20	M.	Oliver Hazard Perry born, 1785 • *We have met the enemy and they are ours.* –Perry •	*and*
21	Tu.	☾ on Eq. • American Bar Association founded, Saratoga, N.Y., 1878 • {12.1 / 11.3	*what a*
22	W.	Pittsburgh Pirates owner Barney Dreyfuss suggested a baseball World Series, 1903 •	*scorcher!*
23	Th.	Fannie Farmer opened her School of Cookery, Boston, 1902 • {11.3 / 11.2	*Lightning*
24	Fr.	**St. Bartholomew** • British forces invaded Washington, D.C., 1814 •	*flickers,*
25	Sa.	♇ stat. • Leonard Bernstein born, 1918 • Tides {9.9 / 10.5	*thunder*
26	**G**	**12th S. af. P.** • Lee De Forest born, 1873 • {9.3 / 10.1	*clatters;*
27	M.	☌ ♂ ☾ • *Snobs talk as if they had begotten their own ancestors.* • {8.9 / 9.9	*apple*
28	Tu.	**St. Augustine of Hippo** • ☾ at ☋ • Tides {8.7 / 9.7	*pickers*
29	W.	☾ runs low • New England cold wave: 25°F, Vermont; 2.5" snow, Mt. Washington, N.H., 1965	*leave*
30	Th.	☌ ♆ ☾ • "Hotline" between White House and Kremlin, 1963 • {8.7 / 9.8 •	*their*
31	Fr.	William Saroyan born, 1908 • Itzhak Perlman born, 1945 • {8.9 / 10.0 •	*ladders.*

Farmer's Calendar

■ Sometimes it seems as though we experience the changes of the seasons in our minds more than through our senses. Put another way, the seasons change in us as well as in nature.

A couple of summers ago, August brought a string of cold, wet days to this vicinity—nowhere near frost, but raw and gray. When normally I would have been sitting around outside wondering why no useful work was getting done, now I found it more comfortable to speculate indoors.

The weather passed, the Sun came out, the temperature went back up. In general, the height of summer resumed—and it didn't. In the outside world, it was summer again. The grass was still green, no leaves had even thought of turning, the pumpkins showed no color at all, the asters along the roadsides had only begun to bloom. In the external world, I'm saying, it was still summer. But for me, somehow, summer was over. I neglected the garden, ignored the lawn, moved on to autumn attitudes. One day, I happened to pass our patch of blueberries and was surprised to find them full of fruit. Before the cold spell, I had grazed among the high bushes every evening, like a deer. Now I'd forgotten the blueberries. Those few nasty, cold days had clicked over the switch in my heart that turns the mind of summer to the mind of fall; the summer was over, even though it wasn't, nowhere near.

It's funny how that works: We are creatures of habit, of reaction and response, as much as—more than—we are creatures of experience. The seasons of our lives we make ourselves.

2001   SEPTEMBER, The Ninth Month

Striking late-summer conjunctions continue, as the Moon's tilted path keeps carrying it within a single degree of a series of planets. It closely meets Saturn (now rising before midnight) on the 10th, skims past Jupiter on the 12th, and passes 3 degrees north of Venus on the 15th. Venus, losing some of its earlier luster, stands just half a degree from Leo's blue star, Regulus, on the 20th. Autumn begins with the equinox on the 22nd, at 7:04 P.M. EDT, marking the Sun's transit of Earth's equator. Mars, crossing back into Sagittarius, keeps fading as Earth pulls ahead, leaving the red planet behind in the dust (or, more accurately, directly in front of the dusty center of our galaxy).

○ Full Moon	2nd day	17th hour	43rd minute
☾ Last Quarter	10th day	14th hour	59th minute
● New Moon	17th day	6th hour	27th minute
☽ First Quarter	24th day	5th hour	31st minute

Times are given in Eastern Daylight Time.

For an explanation of this page, see page 40; for values of Key Letters, see page 226.

Day of Year	Day of Month	Day of Week	Rises h. m.	Key	Sets h. m.	Key	Length of Day h. m.	Sun Fast m.	Declination of Sun ° '	High Tide Boston Light—A.M. **Bold—P.M.**		☽ Rises h. m.	Key	☽ Sets h. m.	Key	☽ Place	☽ Age
244	1	Sa.	6 09	B	7 18	D	13 09	15	8 N.04	11¼	**11½**	7ᴹ11	E	4ᴹ37	B	CAP	14
245	2	**G**	6 11	B	7 16	D	13 05	16	7 42	**12**	—	7 38	D	5 37	B	AQU	15
246	3	M.	6 12	B	7 15	D	13 03	16	7 20	12	12½	8 02	D	6 37	C	AQU	16
247	4	Tu.	6 13	B	7 13	D	13 00	16	6 58	12¾	1¼	8 26	D	7 37	C	PSC	17
248	5	W.	6 14	B	7 11	D	12 57	17	6 36	1¼	1¾	8 49	C	8 37	D	CET	18
249	6	Th.	6 15	B	7 09	D	12 54	17	6 13	2	2¼	9 12	C	9 38	D	PSC	19
250	7	Fr.	6 16	B	7 08	D	12 52	17	5 51	2¾	3	9 38	B	10 40	E	CET	20
251	8	Sa.	6 17	B	7 06	D	12 49	18	5 28	3¼	3¾	10 08	B	11ᴹ43	E	ARI	21
252	9	**G**	6 18	B	7 04	C	12 46	18	5 06	4	4½	10 43	B	12ᴹ49	E	TAU	22
253	10	M.	6 19	B	7 02	C	12 43	18	4 43	5	5¼	11ᴹ25	B	1 55	E	TAU	23
254	11	Tu.	6 20	B	7 01	C	12 41	19	4 20	6	6¼	—	–	2 59	E	TAU	24
255	12	W.	6 21	B	6 59	C	12 38	19	3 57	7	7¼	12ᴹ17	B	4 00	E	GEM	25
256	13	Th.	6 22	B	6 57	C	12 35	20	3 34	8	8¼	1 18	B	4 54	E	GEM	26
257	14	Fr.	6 23	B	6 55	C	12 32	20	3 11	9	9¼	2 29	B	5 41	E	CAN	27
258	15	Sa.	6 24	B	6 54	C	12 30	20	2 48	10	10¼	3 45	B	6 21	E	LEO	28
259	16	**G**	6 25	B	6 52	C	12 27	21	2 25	10¾	11	5 04	C	6 55	D	LEO	29
260	17	M.	6 26	B	6 50	C	12 24	21	2 02	11¾	—	6 23	D	7 26	D	VIR	0
261	18	Tu.	6 27	B	6 48	C	12 21	21	1 39	12	12½	7 40	D	7 56	C	VIR	1
262	19	W.	6 28	B	6 47	C	12 19	22	1 15	1	1¼	8 56	D	8 25	C	VIR	2
263	20	Th.	6 30	C	6 45	C	12 15	22	0 52	1¾	2¼	10 09	E	8 56	B	VIR	3
264	21	Fr.	6 31	C	6 43	C	12 12	22	0 29	2¾	3	11ᴹ21	E	9 30	B	LIB	4
265	22	Sa.	6 32	C	6 41	C	12 09	23	0 N.05	3½	3¾	12ᴹ29	E	10 08	B	SCO	5
266	23	**G**	6 33	C	6 39	C	12 06	23	0 S.17	4½	4¾	1 33	E	10 51	A	OPH	6
267	24	M.	6 34	C	6 38	C	12 04	23	0 41	5½	5¾	2 31	E	11ᴹ40	A	SAG	7
268	25	Tu.	6 35	C	6 36	C	12 01	24	1 04	6½	6¾	3 22	E	—	–	SAG	8
269	26	W.	6 36	C	6 34	C	11 58	24	1 27	7½	7¾	4 05	E	12ᴹ33	A	SAG	9
270	27	Th.	6 37	C	6 32	C	11 55	24	1 51	8½	8¾	4 42	E	1 30	B	CAP	10
271	28	Fr.	6 38	C	6 31	B	11 53	25	2 14	9¼	9½	5 14	E	2 29	B	CAP	11
272	29	Sa.	6 39	C	6 29	B	11 50	25	2 37	10	10¼	5 42	D	3 29	B	AQU	12
273	30	**G**	6 40	C	6 27	B	11 47	25	3 S.00	10¾	11	6ᴹ07	D	4ᴹ29	C	AQU	13

SEPTEMBER hath 30 days. 2001

A shadow rests upon the fields
As earlier suns are setting;
The corn has reached the tasseled age,
Its silken tresses netting. –Stephen H. Thayer

D. M.	D. W.	Dates, Feasts, Fasts, Aspects, Tide Heights	*Weather* ↓
1	Sa.	☌ ♅ ☾ • ☾ at apo. • Jacques Cartier died, 1557 • { 9.1 / 10.1	*Splishes,*
2	G	13th S. af. P. • Full Barley ○ • { 9.3 / —	*sploshes,*
3	M.	Labor Day • Sweden switched from driving on the left to the right, 1967 • { 10.1 / 9.5	*then*
4	Tu.	CBS demonstrated color TV on station WXAB, 1940 • Paul Harvey born, 1918 • { 10.1 / 9.6 •	*it's*
5	W.	☾ on Eq. • Sam Houston elected first president of Republic of Texas, 1836 •	*cool—*
6	Th.	*It's best to learn as we go, not go as we have learned.* • Tides { 9.8 / 9.8 •	*wear*
7	Fr.	Buddy Holly born, 1936 • Boulder Dam (renamed Hoover Dam) began operating, 1936	*galoshes*
8	Sa.	Second U.S. coast-to-coast railroad, Northern Pacific, completed, 1883 • Tides { 9.3 / 9.8	*back*
9	G	14th S. af. P. • Colonel Harland Sanders born, 1890 • { 9.1 / 9.8	*to*
10	M.	Occn. ♄ ☾ • Arnold Palmer born, 1929 • Tides { 8.8 / 9.8 •	*school.*
11	Tu.	☾ at ☊ • Battle of Brandywine, 1777 • Tides { 8.7 / 10.0 •	*Cold*
12	W.	☾ rides high • Occn. ♃ ☾ • H. L. Mencken born, 1880 • { 8.8 / 10.2	*and*
13	Th.	Battle of Quebec, 1759 • Walter Reed born, 1851 • { 9.0 / 10.6	*miserable;*
14	Fr.	Holy Cross • First solo balloon crossing of the Atlantic, 1984 • { 9.5 / 11.0	*rain*
15	Sa.	☌ ♀ ☾ • Roy Acuff born, 1903 • Gaylord Perry born, 1938 • { 10.1 / 11.5 •	*so*
16	G	15th S. af. P. • ☾ at perig. • Lauren Bacall born, 1924 •	*thick*
17	M.	New ● • 20.5 inches of snow, Lander, Wy., 1965 • Tides { 11.2 / — •	*it's*
18	Tu.	Rosh Hashanah • ☾ on Eq. • ☿ Gr. Elong. (27° E.) • ☌ ☿ ☾ •	
19	W.	Ember Day • *Listen or thy tongue will keep thee deaf.* • { 11.8 / 11.7	*scissorable!*
20	Th.	First meeting of National Research Council, 1916 • Financial panic of 1873 • { 11.5 / 11.6	*Chilly*
21	Fr.	St. Matthew • Ember Day • H. G. Wells born, 1866 • { 10.9 / 11.3	*for the*
22	Sa.	Autumnal Equinox • Ember Day • Tommy Lasorda born, 1927 • { 10.3 / 10.8	*equi-*
23	G	16th S. af. P. • Walter Pidgeon born, 1897 • { 9.6 / 10.3 •	*nox:*
24	M.	☾ at ☋ • ☌ ♂ ☾ • Faneuil Hall, Boston, opened to public, 1742 •	*better*
25	Tu.	☾ runs low • Ford Motor Co. established 8-hour workday and 5-day week, 1926 • { 8.7 / 9.5	*buy*
26	W.	♄ stat. • *Abbey Road,* the last album the Beatles made together, released, 1969 • { 8.5 / 9.3	*a*
27	Th.	Yom Kippur • ☌ ♆ ☾ • "The Tonight Show" TV premiere, 1954 •	*box*
28	Fr.	☌ ♅ ☾ • *The school of hard knocks is an accelerated curriculum.* • Tides { 8.7 / 9.5	*of*
29	Sa.	St. Michael • ☾ at apo. • VFW est., 1899 • Tides { 9.0 / 9.7	*extra*
30	G	17th S. af. P. • Babe Ruth hit 60th home run of season, 1927 •	*socks!*

A ship in port is safe, but that is not what ships are for.
Sail out to sea and do new things. –Rear Adm. Grace Hopper

Farmer's Calendar

■ Who are Flora, Camille, Fifi, Gilbert, Hugo, and Andrew? Your cousins? The others who work in your department, who live on your street? No, they are not neighbors, not colleagues. They are nobody's friends. They're storms: six of the bigger, more destructive Atlantic hurricanes of the past 30 years or so. Their cheery, ordinary names take on a kind of ominous power.

Hurricanes' names are given each year by the World Meteorological Organization. Since 1953, the WMO has used people's names for storms. Before that, hurricanes were known informally by the names of places they had famously attacked, as with the Great New England Hurricane of 1938. A less casual system was needed to distinguish the successive storms of a season so they could be watched and reported on—not only for the sake of weather science, but more, to let civil defense workers warn and evacuate threatened communities. Beginning in 1950, storm names followed the U.S. military's well-known alphabetic titles: Able, Baker, Charlie, Dog, etc. But this system gave the same names to storms of different years. There had to be a way of naming storms that allowed more variation and specificity. Giving each storm as it developed the name of a person, from an alphabetical list, did that.

As for the subtle suggestion of menace in hurricanes' names, the WMO has thought of that, too. When a really bad storm comes along, the policy is to retire its name. Flora, Fifi, Hugo, and the rest won't be back.

OCTOBER, The Tenth Month

Venus and Mercury, low in the east in predawn twilight, are on display in an unusually long-lasting meeting from October 28 to November 8. Mars, well up at dusk, keeps fading as it crosses into Capricornus in late October. Jupiter and Saturn both rise before midnight; Jupiter, now in Gemini, is higher in our sky than it has been since 1990. This month, the Milky Way is at its best at nightfall during the relatively moonless period from the 9th to the 17th. The galaxy's center is marked by a glow in Sagittarius just to the right of where Mars presently hovers. The mediocre Orionid meteors peak on the 22nd after the crescent Moon sets. Daylight Saving Time ends at 2:00 A.M. on the 28th.

○	Full Moon	2nd day	9th hour	49th minute
☾	Last Quarter	10th day	0 hour	20th minute
●	New Moon	16th day	15th hour	23rd minute
☽	First Quarter	23rd day	22nd hour	58th minute

After 2:00 A.M. on October 28, Eastern Standard Time (EST) is given.

For an explanation of this page, see page 40; for values of Key Letters, see page 226.

Day of Year	Day of Month	Day of Week	☀ Rises h. m.	Key	☀ Sets h. m.	Key	Length of Day h. m.	Sun Fast m.	Declination of Sun ° '	High Tide Boston Light—A.M. Bold—P.M.	☽ Rises h. m.	Key	☽ Sets h. m.	Key	☽ Place	☽ Age
274	1	M.	6 41	C	6 25	B	11 44	26	3 s.24	11½ **11¾**	6ᴘ30	D	5ᴀ29	D	AQU	14
275	2	Tu.	6 43	C	6 24	B	11 41	26	3 47	**12** —	6 53	C	6 30	D	CET	15
276	3	W.	6 44	C	6 22	B	11 38	26	4 10	12¼ **12½**	7 17	C	7 31	D	PSC	16
277	4	Th.	6 45	C	6 20	B	11 35	27	4 33	1 **1¼**	7 42	B	8 33	E	PSC	17
278	5	Fr.	6 46	C	6 19	B	11 33	27	4 56	1½ **1¾**	8 10	B	9 37	E	ARI	18
279	6	Sa.	6 47	C	6 17	B	11 30	27	5 19	2¼ **2½**	8 43	B	10 42	E	TAU	19
280	7	**G**	6 48	C	6 15	B	11 27	28	5 42	3 **3**	9 22	B	11ᴀ48	E	TAU	20
281	8	M.	6 49	C	6 13	B	11 24	28	6 05	3¾ **4**	10 09	B	12ᴘ52	E	TAU	21
282	9	Tu.	6 50	C	6 12	B	11 22	28	6 28	4½ **4¾**	11ᴍ06	A	1 53	E	GEM	22
283	10	W.	6 51	C	6 10	B	11 19	28	6 51	5½ **5¾**	—	–	2 48	E	GEM	23
284	11	Th.	6 53	C	6 08	B	11 15	29	7 13	6½ **6¾**	12ᴀ11	B	3 36	E	CAN	24
285	12	Fr.	6 54	C	6 07	B	11 13	29	7 36	7½ **8**	1 23	B	4 17	E	CAN	25
286	13	Sa.	6 55	C	6 05	B	11 10	29	7 58	8½ **9**	2 39	C	4 52	D	LEO	26
287	14	**G**	6 56	D	6 04	B	11 08	29	8 20	9½ **10**	3 56	C	5 23	D	LEO	27
288	15	M.	6 57	D	6 02	B	11 05	30	8 43	10½ **10¾**	5 12	D	5 53	C	VIR	28
289	16	Tu.	6 58	D	6 00	B	11 02	30	9 05	11¼ **11¾**	6 28	D	6 21	C	VIR	0
290	17	W.	7 00	D	5 59	B	10 59	30	9 27	**12** —	7 44	E	6 51	B	VIR	1
291	18	Th.	7 01	D	5 57	B	10 56	30	9 48	12½ **1**	8 58	E	7 24	B	LIB	2
292	19	Fr.	7 02	D	5 56	B	10 54	31	10 10	1½ **1¾**	10 10	E	8 01	B	LIB	3
293	20	Sa.	7 03	D	5 54	B	10 51	31	10 31	2¼ **2½**	11ᴀ18	E	8 42	A	OPH	4
294	21	**G**	7 04	D	5 53	B	10 49	31	10 53	3 **3¼**	12ᴘ21	F	9 30	A	SAG	5
295	22	M.	7 05	D	5 51	B	10 46	31	11 14	4 **4¼**	1 16	E	10 22	A	SAG	6
296	23	Tu.	7 07	D	5 50	B	10 43	31	11 35	5 **5**	2 03	E	11ᴘ19	B	SAG	7
297	24	W.	7 08	D	5 48	B	10 40	31	11 56	6 **6**	2 43	E	—	–	CAP	8
298	25	Th.	7 09	D	5 47	B	10 38	31	12 17	7 **7**	3 16	E	12ᴀ18	B	CAP	9
299	26	Fr.	7 10	D	5 45	B	10 35	32	12 37	7¾ **8**	3 45	E	1 19	B	AQU	10
300	27	Sa.	7 12	D	5 44	B	10 32	32	12 58	8¾ **9**	4 11	D	2 19	B	AQU	11
301	28	**G**	6 13	D	4 43	B	10 30	32	13 18	8½ **8¾**	3 35	D	2 19	C	AQU	12
302	29	M.	6 14	D	4 41	B	10 27	32	13 38	9¼ **9½**	3 57	D	3 20	D	PSC	13
303	30	Tu.	6 15	D	4 40	B	10 25	32	13 57	9¾ **10¼**	4 21	C	4 21	D	CET	14
304	31	W.	6 16	D	4 39	B	10 23	32	14 s.17	10½ **10¾**	4ᴍ45	B	5ᴀ23	E	PSC	15

OCTOBER hath 31 days. 2001

A birdnote sounding here and there,
A bloom, where leaves are brown and sober,
Warm noons, and nights with frosty air,
And loaded wagons say,—October. –Thomas S. Collier

D. M.	D. W.	Dates, Feasts, Fasts, Aspects, Tide Heights	*Weather* ↓
1	M.	**St. Remigius** • ☿ stat. • Jimmy Carter born, 1924 •	*Sopping,*
2	Tu.	**Succoth** • ☾ on Eq. • **Full Harvest** ○ • Tides {9.8 — •	*and*
3	W.	Johns Hopkins Univ. opened in Baltimore, Md., 1876 • James Herriot born, 1916 •	*the*
4	Th.	**St. Francis of Assisi** • Tides {9.9 10.1 •	*temperature's*
5	Fr.	First televised speech from White House, 1947 • Tides {9.8 10.2 •	*dropping.*
6	Sa.	George Westinghouse born, 1846 • The "Orient Express" completed first run, 1883 •	*Praise*
7	G	**18th S. af. P.** • ☌ ♄ ☾ • Tides {9.3 10.2 •	*these*
8	M.	☾ at ☊ • First group of WAVES started naval training, 1942 • {9.1 10.1	*days*
9	Tu.	☌ ♃ ☾ • Joshua C. Stoddard patented first calliope, 1855 • Tides {8.9 10.0	*of*
10	W.	☾ rides high • Helen Hayes born, 1900 • *Porgy and Bess* opened, NYC, 1935 •	*heat*
11	Th.	**Columbus Day** • **Thanksgiving Day (Canada)** • Tides {9.0 10.2 •	*and*
12	Fr.	Khrushchev pounded his shoe on his desk at the U.N. General Assembly, 1960 • {9.3 10.5	*haze.*
13	Sa.	☿ in inf. ☌ • *An intellectual is a person whose mind watches itself.* • {9.8 10.8	*Praise*
14	G	**19th S. af. P.** • ☾ at perig. • ☌ ♀ ☾ • {10.4 11.1	*the*
15	M.	☾ on Eq. • Final Lincoln-Douglas debate, 1858 • {11.0 11.4 •	*hillsides*
16	Tu.	New ● • Grand opening of the Tremont House in Boston, 1829 • {11.5 11.4	*all*
17	W.	**St. Ignatius of Antioch** • ♆ stat. • Tides {11.8 —	*ablaze.*
18	Th.	**St. Luke** • Pierre Trudeau born, 1919 • Chuck Berry born, 1926 • {11.3 11.8	*Praise*
19	Fr.	St. Luke's Little Summer • "The Star-Spangled Banner" sung for first time, Baltimore, Md., 1814 •	*the*
20	Sa.	Jackie Kennedy married Aristotle Onassis, 1968 • Mickey Mantle born, 1931 • {10.4 11.2	*rain*
21	G	**20th S. af. P.** • ☾ at ☋ • Tides {9.9 10.6 •	*that*
22	M.	☾ runs low • ☿ stat. • 104°F, San Diego, Calif., 1965 • {9.3 10.0	*strips*
23	Tu.	☌ ♂ ☾ • *If you think education is expensive, try ignorance.* • Tides {8.8 9.5	*the*
24	W.	☌ ♆ ☾ • Annie Taylor went over Niagara Falls in a barrel, 1901 •	*trees,*
25	Th.	**St. Crispin** • ☌ ⛢ ☾ • Charge of the Light Brigade, 1854 • {8.4 9.0	*and*
26	Fr.	☾ at apo. • Shoot-out at the O.K. Corral, 1881 • Tides {8.5 9.1 •	*carpets*
27	Sa.	*The greatest obstacle to discovery is not ignorance—it is the illusion of knowledge.* • {8.8 9.2 •	*all*
28	G	**21st S. af. P.** • **Daylight Saving Time ends, 2:00 A.M.** • {9.1 9.4 •	*the*
29	M.	**Sts. Simon & Jude** • ☾ on Eq. • ☿ Gr. Elong (19° W.) • {9.5 9.5	*land*
30	Tu.	⛢ stat. • John Adams born, 1735 • Ezra Pound born, 1885 • Tides {9.8 9.7	*with*
31	W.	**All Hallows Eve** • Earl Lloyd became first black to play in NBA game, 1950 •	*leaves.*

Farmer's Calendar

■ Deep in the southern woodlands, the magnificent Franklinia blooms in the late fall—or does it? The answer is a mystery. This species is something like the Amelia Earhart of North American botany: famous, admired, vanished.

It was John Bartram (1699-1777), a Philadelphia plant collector who was our first major native-born naturalist, who discovered *Franklinia alatamaha* and named it for his friend and fellow townsman, Benjamin Franklin. Bartram's son William also knew the species, having found it on a botanizing expedition with his father about 1765. The younger Bartram described Franklinia at greater length some years later in his *Travels* (1791). According to William Bartram, Franklinia is a flowering tree, 15 to 20 feet tall, with large white blossoms resembling the camellia; oblong, toothed, alternate leaves; and a fruit like a large, woody apple. Most uncommonly, he found it to bloom in the late fall. The Bartrams discovered Franklinia growing abundantly over an area of two or three acres along the banks of the Altamaha River in Georgia. "We never saw it grow in any other place," wrote William, "nor have I ever since seen it growing wild, in all my travels, from Pennsylvania to . . . the banks of the Mississippi."

Both Bartrams were trained scientific observers. They did not invent Franklinia, nor did they hallucinate it. Nevertheless, after their early encounter with the species in Georgia, the tree was never found in the wild again.

The Moon passes close to Jupiter on the 6th. Mercury displays its best morning-star appearance of the year as it hovers next to Venus during the first week of November. Saturn now rises at nightfall, and much brighter Jupiter rises by 10:00 P.M. EST, dominating the heavens for the remainder of the night. The Leonid meteors will keep observers awake on the night of the 17th-18th. Mars, the only bright "star" low in the south at nightfall, offers the year's best chance to locate dim Uranus when it floats just below the seventh planet on the 26th. A Moon-Saturn conjunction occurs on the 30th.

○	Full Moon	1st day	0 hour	41st minute
☾	Last Quarter	8th day	7th hour	21st minute
●	New Moon	15th day	1st hour	40th minute
☽	First Quarter	22nd day	18th hour	21st minute
○	Full Moon	30th day	15th hour	49th minute

Times are given in Eastern Standard Time.

For an explanation of this page, see page 40; for values of Key Letters, see page 226.

Day of Year	Day of Month	Day of Week	☼ Rises h. m.	Key	☼ Sets h. m.	Key	Length of Day h. m.	Sun Fast m.	Declination of Sun ° '	High Tide Boston Light—A.M. Bold—P.M.		☽ Rises h. m.	Key	☽ Sets h. m.	Key	☽ Place	☽ Age
305	1	Th.	6 18	D	4 37	B	10 19	32	14s.36	11	11½	5ᴘM12	B	6ᴍ27	E	ARI	16
306	2	Fr.	6 19	D	4 36	B	10 17	32	14 55	11½	—	5 44	B	7 33	E	TAU	17
307	3	Sa.	6 20	D	4 35	B	10 15	32	15 13	12¼	12¼	6 21	A	8 40	E	TAU	18
308	4	**G**	6 21	D	4 34	B	10 13	32	15 32	12¾	1	7 06	A	9 47	E	TAU	19
309	5	M.	6 23	D	4 32	B	10 09	32	15 50	1½	1¾	8 00	B	10 49	E	GEM	20
310	6	Tu.	6 24	D	4 31	B	10 07	32	16 08	2½	2½	9 02	B	11ᴍ46	E	GEM	21
311	7	W.	6 25	D	4 30	B	10 05	32	16 26	3¼	3½	10 11	B	12ᴍ35	E	CAN	22
312	8	Th.	6 26	D	4 29	A	10 03	32	16 43	4¼	4½	11ᴘM24	B	1 17	E	CAN	23
313	9	Fr.	6 28	D	4 28	A	10 00	32	17 01	5¼	5½	—	–	1 53	E	LEO	24
314	10	Sa.	6 29	D	4 27	A	9 58	32	17 18	6¼	6¾	12ᴍ38	C	2 24	D	LEO	25
315	11	**G**	6 30	D	4 26	A	9 56	32	17 34	7¼	7¾	1 52	D	2 53	D	VIR	26
316	12	M.	6 31	D	4 25	A	9 54	31	17 50	8¼	8¾	3 06	D	3 20	C	VIR	27
317	13	Tu.	6 33	D	4 24	A	9 51	31	18 06	9	9½	4 20	E	3 49	C	VIR	28
318	14	W.	6 34	D	4 23	A	9 49	31	18 22	10	10½	5 34	E	4 19	B	LIB	29
319	15	Th.	6 35	D	4 22	A	9 47	31	18 37	10¾	11¼	6 47	E	4 53	B	LIB	0
320	16	Fr.	6 36	D	4 21	A	9 45	31	18 52	11½	—	7 58	E	5 33	B	OPH	1
321	17	Sa.	6 38	D	4 20	A	9 42	31	19 06	12	12¼	9 04	E	6 18	A	OPH	2
322	18	**G**	6 39	D	4 20	A	9 41	30	19 20	1	1	10 05	E	7 09	A	SAG	3
323	19	M.	6 40	D	4 19	A	9 39	30	19 34	1¾	1¾	10 56	E	8 06	A	SAG	4
324	20	Tu.	6 41	D	4 18	A	9 37	30	19 48	2½	2¾	11ᴍ40	E	9 05	B	SAG	5
325	21	W.	6 43	D	4 17	A	9 34	30	20 02	3½	3½	12ᴘM17	E	10 06	B	CAP	6
326	22	Th.	6 44	D	4 17	A	9 33	30	20 15	4¼	4½	12 47	E	11ᴍ06	B	CAP	7
327	23	Fr.	6 45	D	4 16	A	9 31	29	20 27	5¼	5¼	1 14	D	—	–	AQU	8
328	24	Sa.	6 46	D	4 16	A	9 30	29	20 39	6	6¼	1 38	D	12ᴀ07	C	AQU	9
329	25	**G**	6 47	D	4 15	A	9 28	29	20 51	7	7¼	2 01	D	1 07	D	PSC	10
330	26	M.	6 48	D	4 15	A	9 27	28	21 02	7¾	8	2 23	C	2 07	D	CET	11
331	27	Tu.	6 50	E	4 14	A	9 24	28	21 13	8½	8¾	2 47	B	3 09	D	PSC	12
332	28	W.	6 51	E	4 14	A	9 23	28	21 24	9	9½	3 13	B	4 12	E	CET	13
333	29	Th.	6 52	E	4 13	A	9 21	27	21 34	9¾	10¼	3 42	B	5 18	E	ARI	14
334	30	Fr.	6 53	E	4 13	A	9 20	27	21s.44	10½	11	4ᴘM18	B	6ᴍ26	E	TAU	15

NOVEMBER hath 30 days. 2001

When the tree bares, the music of it changes:
Hard and keen is the sound, long and mournful;
Pale are the poplar boughs in the evening light
Above my house, against a slate-cold cloud. –Conrad Aiken

D. M.	D. W.	Dates, Feasts, Fasts, Aspects, Tide Heights	Weather ↓
1	Th.	All Saints • Full Beaver ○ • Stephen Crane born, 1871 • {10.4 9.7	*Damp*
2	Fr.	All Souls • ♃ stat. • James Thurber died, 1961 • Tides {10.6 —	*and*
3	Sa.	☌ ♄ ☾ • 96°F in Los Angeles, 1890; record high for November for 76 years •	*dismal,*
4	G	22nd S. af. P. • ☾ at ☊ • ☌ ♂ ♆ • {9.6 10.7	
5	M.	George B. Selden received first U.S. patent for automobile, 1895 • {9.4 10.6 •	*turning*
6	Tu.	☾ rides high • ☌ ♃ ☾ • Election Day • {9.2 10.5	*colder,*
7	W.	*If voting changed anything, they'd make it illegal.* • Tides {9.1 10.3 •	*then*
8	Th.	First U.S. college for women, Mt. Holyoke, founded, 1837 • Astronomer Edmund Halley born, 1656 •	*a*
9	Fr.	Carl Sagan born, 1934 • J. William Fulbright born, 1905 • {9.3 10.1 •	*warm*
10	Sa.	St. Leo the Great • Sadie Hawkins Day • {9.6 10.2 •	*hiatus;*
11	G	23rd S. af. P. • Veterans Day • ☾ at perig. •	*rain*
12	M.	St. Martin • ☾ on Eq. • 105°F, Craftonville, Calif., 1906 • {10.7 10.6	*and*
13	Tu.	Holland Tunnel, connecting New York City and Jersey City, N.J., opened, 1927 • {11.2 10.7	*snow*
14	W.	First streetcar, drawn by horses, began operating in New York City, 1832 • {11.5 10.7	*that's*
15	Th.	New ● • *One person with belief is equal to a force of 99 who have only interests.* • {11.7 10.5	*so*
16	Fr.	Arturo Toscanini made U.S. conducting debut at the Met., 1908 • {11.6 —	*abysmal*
17	Sa.	St. Hugh of Lincoln • ☾ at ☋ • Tides {10.2 11.3	*comes*
18	G	24th S. af. P. • Margaret Atwood born, 1939 • {9.9 10.9 •	*to*
19	M.	☾ runs low • Roy Campanella born, 1921 • James Garfield born, 1831 •	*irritate*
20	Tu.	☌ ♆ ☾ • Hubble space telescope photographed the Eagle Nebula, 1995 •	*us!*
21	W.	☌ ♂ ☾ • ☌ ♅ ☾ • Stan Musial born, 1920 • {8.8 9.4	*Thanks*
22	Th.	Thanksgiving • *Gratitude is the memory of the heart.* • {8.5 9.1 •	*for*
23	Fr.	St. Clement • ☾ at apo. • Franklin Pierce born, 1804 • {8.5 8.8 •	*our*
24	Sa.	Congress passed Brady handgun-control bill, 1993 • {8.6 8.80	*abundant*
25	G	25th S. af. P. • Carry Nation born, 1846 • {8.8 8.8	*blessings!*
26	M.	☾ on Eq. • ☌ ♂ ♅ • Sojourner Truth died, 1883 • {9.2 8.9	*Sunny*
27	Tu.	Savings and loan bailout: Congress authorized additional $70 billion for FDIC, 1991 •	*days*
28	W.	20°F, Tallahassee, Fla., 1950, matched previous November record • Tides {9.9 9.3	*and*
29	Th.	Louisa May Alcott born, 1832 • Busby Berkeley born, 1895 • {10.3 9.4	*onion*
30	Fr.	St. Andrew • Full Frost ○ • Occn. ♄ ☾ •	*dressing!*

Do not condemn the judgment of another because it differs from your own. You may both be wrong. –Dandemis

Farmer's Calendar

■ Some years ago in a little town in Maine, the kids arrived at their school one Monday morning around this time of year to find a bear sleeping in the playground. The playground had one of those tunnels made of a half-buried steel culvert. The children at play were meant to creep through it. None did so that morning, you may be sure, for the bear had chosen their tunnel as its winter den. I don't recall exactly how the episode ended; one of the teachers told the bear to hibernate someplace else, I guess. Teachers put up with a lot these days.

All over the North, the bears are going into their dens. The sexes den differently, it seems. Male bears flop down about anywhere—hence, no doubt, the playground bear above. Females prepare a proper den, a protected hole, a hollow log, or a tree cavity that they improve with leaves and other insulation. A female bear may give birth in her den, so she's more deliberate than her mate in choosing a place for hibernation.

In fact, *hibernation* is a misnomer in the bear. Unlike woodchucks, bats, and some mice, bears don't exhibit true hibernation. Their essential physical processes don't slow down as much, or as uniformly, as the real hibernators do. Still, bears *do* sleep, deeply, in the den. And whatever you call their wintering, it sounds like a good deal. There is something comforting about the idea of hibernation, a kind of vicarious solace for us all. When the days get short, dark, and cold, and the snow begins to fly—you check out. Maybe scientists don't call that hibernation, but the bears do.

2001 DECEMBER, The Twelfth Month

Saturn, close to the nearly full Moon as December opens (and again on the 27th), reaches opposition on the 3rd, rising at sunset. At magnitude -0.4, it is outshone only by the Dog Star, Sirius, and dazzling Jupiter. With Mars fading and sinking lower in the southwest, and Mercury and Venus low and unimpressive, Jupiter and Saturn are the year-end celebrities. Look for the splendid Geminid meteors on the 13th and 14th. A partial solar eclipse can be seen from the central United States and Canada on the 14th. The winter solstice occurs on the 21st, at 2:21 P.M. EST. Jupiter is closest to Earth on the 30th and brightest on New Year's Eve, rising brilliantly in the northeast at nightfall.

☾	Last Quarter	7th day	14th hour	52nd minute
●	New Moon	14th day	15th hour	47th minute
☽	First Quarter	22nd day	15th hour	56th minute
○	Full Moon	30th day	5th hour	40th minute

Times are given in Eastern Standard Time.

For an explanation of this page, see page 40; for values of Key Letters, see page 226.

Day of Year	Day of Month	Day of Week	☼ Rises h. m.	Key	☼ Sets h. m.	Key	Length of Day h. m.	Sun Fast m.	Declination of Sun ° '	High Tide Boston Light—A.M.	**Bold—P.M.**	☽ Rises h. m.	Key	☽ Sets h. m.	Key	☽ Place	☽ Age
335	1	Sa.	6 54	E	4 13	A	9 19	27	21s.53	11	**11¾**	5 P.M. 00	B	7 A.M. 34	E	TAU	16
336	2	**G**	6 55	E	4 12	A	9 17	26	22 02	11¾	—	5 52	B	8 41	E	TAU	17
337	3	M.	6 56	E	4 12	A	9 16	26	22 10	12½	**12½**	6 53	B	9 41	E	GEM	18
338	4	Tu.	6 57	E	4 12	A	9 15	26	22 18	1¼	**1½**	8 02	B	10 34	E	GEM	19
339	5	W.	6 58	E	4 12	A	9 14	25	22 25	2	**2¼**	9 14	B	11 19	E	CAN	20
340	6	Th.	6 59	E	4 12	A	9 13	25	22 32	3	**3¼**	10 28	C	11 A.M. 56	E	LEO	21
341	7	Fr.	7 00	E	4 12	A	9 12	24	22 39	4	**4¼**	11 P.M. 41	C	12 P.M. 28	D	LEO	22
342	8	Sa.	7 00	E	4 11	A	9 11	24	22 46	5	**5¼**	—	–	12 57	D	VIR	23
343	9	**G**	7 01	E	4 11	A	9 10	23	22 52	6	**6½**	12 A.M. 54	D	1 24	C	VIR	24
344	10	M.	7 03	E	4 12	A	9 09	23	22 57	7	**7½**	2 05	D	1 51	C	VIR	25
345	11	Tu.	7 03	E	4 12	A	9 09	23	23 02	8	**8½**	3 17	E	2 19	B	VIR	26
346	12	W.	7 04	E	4 12	A	9 08	22	23 06	8¾	**9½**	4 28	E	2 51	B	LIB	27
347	13	Th.	7 05	E	4 12	A	9 07	22	23 10	9¾	**10¼**	5 39	E	3 27	A	LIB	28
348	14	Fr.	7 06	E	4 12	A	9 06	21	23 14	10½	**11**	6 47	E	4 09	A	OPH	0
349	15	Sa.	7 07	E	4 12	A	9 05	21	23 17	11¼	**11¾**	7 50	E	4 57	A	SAG	1
350	16	**G**	7 08	E	4 13	A	9 05	20	23 20	**12**	—	8 46	E	5 52	A	SAG	2
351	17	M.	7 08	E	4 13	A	9 05	20	23 22	12½	**12¾**	9 34	E	6 51	B	SAG	3
352	18	Tu.	7 09	E	4 13	A	9 04	19	23 23	1¼	**1¼**	10 14	E	7 51	B	CAP	4
353	19	W.	7 10	E	4 14	A	9 04	19	23 25	2	**2**	10 47	E	8 53	B	CAP	5
354	20	Th.	7 10	E	4 14	A	9 04	18	23 26	2¾	**3**	11 16	E	9 53	C	AQU	6
355	21	Fr.	7 11	E	4 15	A	9 04	18	23 26	3½	**3¾**	11 A.M. 41	D	10 53	C	AQU	7
356	22	Sa.	7 11	E	4 15	A	9 04	17	23 26	4¼	**4½**	12 P.M. 04	D	11 P.M. 53	C	AQU	8
357	23	**G**	7 12	E	4 16	A	9 04	17	23 25	5¼	**5½**	12 26	C	—	–	CET	9
358	24	M.	7 12	E	4 16	A	9 04	16	23 24	6	**6½**	12 49	C	12 A.M. 53	D	PSC	10
359	25	Tu.	7 12	E	4 17	A	9 05	16	23 22	6¾	**7¼**	1 13	B	1 55	E	PSC	11
360	26	W.	7 12	E	4 18	A	9 06	15	23 20	7¾	**8¼**	1 40	B	2 59	E	ARI	12
361	27	Th.	7 12	E	4 18	A	9 06	15	23 17	8½	**9**	2 12	B	4 05	E	TAU	13
362	28	Fr.	7 13	E	4 19	A	9 06	14	23 14	9¼	**9¾**	2 51	B	5 14	E	TAU	14
363	29	Sa.	7 13	E	4 20	A	9 07	14	23 11	10	**10½**	3 40	A	6 22	E	TAU	15
364	30	**G**	7 13	E	4 21	A	9 08	13	23 07	10¾	**11¼**	4 38	A	7 27	E	GEM	16
365	31	M.	7 13	E	4 21	A	9 08	13	23s.03	11½	—	5 P.M. 46	A	8 A.M. 25	E	GEM	17

DECEMBER hath 31 days. 2001

Ring out false pride in place and blood,
The civic slander and the spite;
Ring in the love of truth and right,
Ring in the common love of good. –Alfred, Lord Tennyson

D. M.	D. W.	Dates, Feasts, Fasts, Aspects, Tide Heights	Weather ↓
1	Sa.	Marilyn Monroe appeared in first issue of *Playboy*, 1953 • Tides {10.9 9.6 •	*Bright*
2	G	1st S. in Advent • ☾ at ☊ • Monroe Doctrine, 1823 •	*out,*
3	M.	☾ rides high • ☌ ♃ ☾ • ♄ at ☍ • Tides {9.6 11.1	*then*
4	Tu.	☿ in sup. ☌ • Record highs in the Northeast: 70°F, Boston; 65°F, Burlington, Vt., 1982 •	*a*
5	W.	The AFL and the CIO labor groups merged, 1955 • Tides {9.5 10.8	*whiteout!*
6	Th.	St. Nicholas • ☾ at perig. • ☌ ♇ ☉ • {9.5 10.5	*Cloudy*
7	Fr.	St. Ambrose • **National Pearl Harbor Remembrance Day** • Tides {9.6 10.2	*with*
8	Sa.	*Using your imagination is the one time in life you can really go anywhere.* • {9.7 10.0	*a*
9	G	2nd S. in Advent • ☾ on Eq. • {10.0 9.8 •	*chance*
10	M.	First day of Chanukah • First recorded sighting of Aurora Borealis in New England, 1719 •	*of*
11	Tu.	Nitrous oxide (laughing gas) first used in dentistry, Hartford, Conn., 1844 • {10.7 9.8 •	*glop;*
12	W.	Beethoven paid Haydn 19¢ for his first music lesson, Vienna, 1792 • Tides {11.0 9.9	*shop*
13	Th.	St. Lucy • Abel Tasman discovered New Zealand, 1642 • Grandma Moses died, 1961 •	*'til*
14	Fr.	☾ at ☋ • New ● • Eclipse ☉ • Tides {11.2 9.8	*you*
15	Sa.	Halcyon Days • *Visits always give pleasure—if not the arrival, the departure.* • {11.1 9.6	*drop.*
16	G	3rd S. in Advent • ☾ runs low • {10.9 —	*Season's*
17	M.	Aztec calendar stone discovered in Mexico City, 1790 • {9.4 10.6 •	*greetings*
18	Tu.	☌ ♆ ☾ • Antonio Stradivari died, 1737 • Tides {9.2 10.3	*might*
19	W.	☌ ♅ ☾ • Ember Day • Albert L. Jones patented corrugated paper, 1871 •	*bring*
20	Th.	☌ ♂ ☾ • Branch Rickey born, 1881 • Tides {8.8 9.5	*sleetings.*
21	Fr.	St. Thomas • ☾ at apo. • **Winter Solstice** • Ember Day •	*Here's*
22	Sa.	Ember Day • First gorilla born in captivity, Columbus, Ohio, 1956 • Tides {8.6 8.8	*a*
23	G	4th S. in Advent • ☾ on Eq. • Beware the Pogonip. •	*year*
24	M.	For the first time since Lenin's death, the bells of St. Basil's Cathedral, Moscow, rang, 1990 • {8.8 8.4	*you*
25	Tu.	Christmas Day • *Music is well said to be the speech of angels.* •	*might*
26	W.	St. Stephen • **Boxing Day (Canada)** • Henry Miller born, 1891 • {9.5 8.6 •	*find*
27	Th.	St. John • Johannes Kepler, the "father of modern astronomy" born, 1571 •	*comic—*
28	Fr.	Holy Innocents • Occn. ♄ ☾ • Tides {10.3 9.1 •	*2002*
29	Sa.	☾ at ☊ • American Meteorological Society founded, St. Louis, Mo., 1919 • {10.7 9.4	*is*
30	G	1st S. af. Ch. • ☾ rides high • Eclipse ☾ • **Full Long Nights** ○	
31	M.	*Happiness is a form of courage.* • Tides {11.4 — •	*palindromic!*

Farmer's Calendar

■ It occurs to me that I have seen snow, in greater or lesser quantities, in every winter of my life except possibly the first. I happened to be born well to the south of snow country and so must have missed out at the very beginning. Since then, though, I have never lived through a winter in which no snow at all fell on my head—or if I have, such winters have been no more than one or two.

I am 55. You would think that anyone who has shoveled, scraped, and waded his way through that many winters' snow might be getting the hang of the stuff at last. Snow ought to hold nothing new for one who has served it for more than half a century. Alas, it's not so. Snow can still surprise me, not by its depth, certainly not by its sublime intractability, but, even now, by its stealth.

Each year in this season, for a moment, snow puzzles me. Spring, summer, and autumn have taken away my memory. I'll be outdoors, tending to some task of doubtful necessity, when I become aware of . . . *stuff* . . . *matter* that seems to be falling from the sky. Not much of it, a piece here, another there. It's solid but slight, it settles softly, almost like ash. Is it ash? Is the chimney on fire? Are the neighbors burning brush? Is it a kind of out-of-season bud- or flower-fall that's coming from the trees? Is it manna from heaven, as in the Bible? Is it flying gnats? A little more falls. It's pale in color, and when it lands, it disappears. Not manna, then. Oddly cold to the touch, too, almost wet. Hold on! I know this stuff. It was here last winter.

A FINE YEAR FOR THE

Aurora Borealis

A glow on the northern horizon may mean that nature is staging one of its splashiest shows—the pulsating, ephemeral beauty of the aurora borealis, or northern lights.

BY BOB BERMAN

–photo by Dick Hutchinson

THE AURORA BOREALIS—LARGEST AND eeriest of nature's light shows—chooses its admirers. If you live in a big city, you can see neon lights but not THE lights. If your home is ringed by year-round greenery, you've probably never glimpsed the green sky-curtains. Like most classy spectacles, the aurora does not make itself promiscuously available.

Until this year, that is. Every 11 years or so, the Sun boils over with violent, dark storms—sunspots and solar flares—that spray Earth with shotgun blasts of subatomic pellets. The solar invaders are not electrically neutral atoms but broken fragments bristling with charge. They inflame our planet's protective magnetic field.

Throw charged particles across a magnetic field and you generate big-time electricity. We're not talking ordinary nuclear power-plant stuff, or even lightning-level jolts. Here, in the upper atmosphere, the Sun's detritus produces a hundred trillion watts. A million amps. The real thing.

This kind of power is more than enough to goose oxygen electrons to leap into higher orbits. As they fall back to where they're more comfortable, they emit colored photons of light: the aurora borealis.

People imagine correctly that the aurora occurs over the North Pole. But *which* North Pole? There are two. There's the Pole of rotation (or geographic Pole) at latitude 90 degrees north, the one to which explorers try to trek. And there's the other, quieter pole, the magnetic Pole to which compass needles point. The two are far apart, and it is the magnetic Pole that hosts the northern lights. Any aurora visible from your backyard is just a small piece of an immense glowing ring centered at the magnetic North Pole.

Here's where Canadians and Americans get lucky. The magnetic Pole sits in Canada at latitude 78 degrees, due north of Colorado and Saskatchewan. It's nearly a thousand miles closer than the geographic Pole. Conversely, for continental Europeans and Russians, the magnetic Pole lies over the far side of the geographic Pole. They'd have to travel all the way to the Arctic Circle to see the same number of auroras that residents of New York and Toronto do. That's why

Do You Hear What I Hear?

Are the northern lights noisy or silent? There are two contradictory answers, and both are weird. Most observers (this writer included) have never heard a sound. It's a big part of the ghostly experience. Imagine the sky aflame with shimmering streamers and pulsating patterns, all accompanied by the absence of the slightest whisper. But some level-headed observers insist they've been overwhelmed with hisses and crackles similar to noises periodically reported through the centuries. Perhaps some people can sense the huge electrical energies coursing along the ground under a major auroral display.

Watch Your Own Sunspots
(carefully)

It was Galileo who first demonstrated that sunspots actually rotate across the surface of the Sun. Amateur Galileos with *safe* (see guidelines below) solar-viewing equipment can monitor sunspots themselves to predict magnetic storms and auroras. A giant sunspot grouping that rotates into view and heads for the middle of the Sun can be the cannon that's about to blast our world with bits of charged atoms.

To see your own spots, purchase welder's goggles, shade number 12 or 14 (but *not* 10 or lower). Wear them to view the Sun. They can even be rigged to attach over binoculars. WARNING: The shade 12 or 14 welder's goggles *must* block the light *before* it enters the binoculars. Do not place the goggles between the eyepiece lenses and your eyes. The fitting must be tight and foolproof. Even a moment's glance at the direct Sun through binoculars can destroy vision. *If you're not 100 percent sure of your device, don't use it. Never let children handle such an arrangement.*

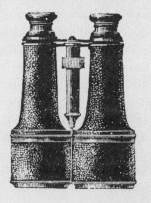

the northern lights are as rare in Paris as they are in Miami.

In mid-2000, the solar cycle peaked again, and for reasons not yet understood, auroral activity peaks about a year after sunspot maximum. So we can expect that auroral peak to occur around May of 2001. The last maximum brought auroral displays that people are still talking about. The one on March 13, 1989, lit the heavens all the way to Mexico and produced full-sky light shows over the entire United States and Canada from dusk 'til dawn. Huge electrical charges avalanched along the ground, surging so powerfully through power lines that parts of eastern Canada were thrown into a nightlong blackout. Automatic garage doors throughout North America kept opening and closing.

This year, people glancing up as they walk from car to house at night should pay attention to any unaccustomed glow in the north. If it evolves into motion or patterns, by George, you've got it—you're seeing the northern lights. You may simply notice ghostly pale-green or ruby-red blotches that come and go leisurely—or wildly. Sharp-edged rays may radiate from below the horizon or hang suspended in the northern sky. The lights may take the form of "curtains" that slowly rustle. Or, instead, the sky can host a series of rising arcs resembling a mad scientist's lab in a 1940s horror movie. The creative patterns are ever new.

OK, you're sold. How to see them? The high-probability route is to join a tour group going to Alaska, or visit those long-lost relatives in the Yukon. But, happily, people living in the United States (especially the northern half) or anywhere in Canada can expect to observe them from their own backyard. A few easy tips will quickly raise your odds:

- Avoid cities (the sky glow is too bright). Visit friends in the country.

- Avoid nights with bright moonlight, especially the five nights that center on each full Moon.

- Choose nights with crystal-clear skies for aurora watching.

- Check up on the Sun's "weather," now reported daily on the Web with reasonably accurate aurora predictions. (See right.)

From rural sites, auroras will be visible this year—you can count on it. The best displays can arrive unexpectedly, so any clear, moonless night deserves a quick northward check. You might even set up a northern lights alert, a telephone tree to notify friends, neighbors, and fellow sky-watchers.

1 General George
Armstrong Custer fin-
ished dead last in his
West Point class—34th
out of 34.

TEN THINGS *(or More)*

YOU MAY NOT KNOW ABOUT THE

BATTLE OF THE LITTLE

BIGHORN

*(plus a short
recap of the
most famous
fight in
American
history)*

O n Sunday, June 25, 1876, a
sweltering summer day, Lieutenant Colonel George Armstrong Custer and some 225
blue-shirted troopers split off from the rest of the
7th Cavalry and rode down a ravine toward the
cottonwood-tree-lined banks of the Little
Bighorn River in Montana Territory. The troopers were hoping to engage "hostiles," who refused to gather on the Great Sioux Reservation
for Indians. The 36-year-old Custer and his officers did not know how many Lakota Sioux and
Cheyenne lay ahead—he disbelieved Crow and
Arikara scouts who told him there were so many
that "it would take many days to kill them all"—
but it didn't matter to the "boy general." (Though
Custer's true rank was lieutenant colonel, he
had held a field promotion to general in the Civil
War.) A bold, surprise attack was a strategy that
had never failed to work for him during the Civil

2 Custer was known for his flowing blond hair, which, in his early years, he anointed with cinnamon oil. But he had his hair cut short just days before the battle along the Little Bighorn.

3 Neither Custer nor his men carried sabers with them during the battle. Custer, however, owned a sword that he had taken as a trophy during the Civil War. It was inscribed: *No me saques sin razon; no me envaines sin*

George Armstrong Custer favored a buckskin outfit for campaigning.

Everyone has heard of Custer's Last Stand, fought 125 years ago on a windswept prairie in Montana Territory. But certain details and mysteries continue to intrigue us.

by Jim Robbins

91

honor, or "Draw me not without reason, nor sheathe me without honor."

4 Custer was a strict disciplinarian with his men, sometimes ordering them to be punished for trivial offenses—yet he once walked the floor all night with a sick puppy.

5 Custer loved to go on campaign with the regimental band playing his favorite tunes, "Garry Owen" and "The Girl I Left Behind."

War and in other Indian battles, even against superior numbers. It would work here.

The buckskin-clad Custer had just divided the 625 men of the 7th Cavalry into three groups. He and Major Marcus Reno were to lead two battalions toward the village. Reno was to attack with his men from the south "and pitch into anything [he] might find." Captain Frederick Benteen took the rest, including packs of ammunition, and was ordered to ride toward the southwest of the main column to keep any Indians from escaping.

Left: John Martin. *Above:* Painting of the battle by White Bird, a Cheyenne Indian who took part in the fight at age 15.

6 Comanche, the 14-year-old gelding of Captain Myles Keogh, though seriously wounded, survived the battle. Nursed back to health but never again put to work, Comanche lived another 15 years, venerated as the 7th Cavalry's living battle memorial.

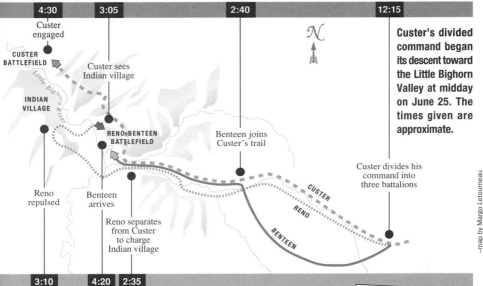

4:30 — Custer engaged

CUSTER BATTLEFIELD

3:05 — Custer sees Indian village

2:40

12:15

𝒩

INDIAN VILLAGE

Little Bighorn River

RENO-BENTEEN BATTLEFIELD

Benteen joins Custer's trail

Custer's divided command began its descent toward the Little Bighorn Valley at midday on June 25. The times given are approximate.

Custer divides his command into three battalions

CUSTER

RENO

BENTEEN

Reno repulsed

Benteen arrives

Reno separates from Custer to charge Indian village

—map by Margo Letourneau

3:10   4:20   2:35

As Custer and Reno trotted down a creek, they surprised a small band of Lakota Sioux, who galloped furiously back to the village to spread the alarm. Custer ordered Reno to charge the fleeing Indians and attack the village, indicating he would follow in support. Reno rode into the bottom of the valley and splashed across the Little Bighorn River to engage the tribes who had pitched tepees there.

Instead of following up on Reno's attack, Custer turned his battalion north, perhaps planning to skirt the village and attack it from a different direction. When Custer crested a bluff overlooking the river and saw the number of tepees in the valley, he was concerned, but not enough to rethink

William W. Cooke wrote out Custer's last order to Benteen for help. Benteen's version of the hastily scrawled note appears at the top.

his plan. Part of what drove Custer was opportunity. The trick in beating the Indians, he believed, was to surprise them. Custer issued a command for Benteen that Adjutant Cooke hastily scribbled down. "Benteen," it read, "Come on. Big village. Be quick. Bring packs. PS. bring packs." He handed it to a trumpeter, John Martin, who was ordered to ride at top speed for Benteen. Martin, an Italian immigrant who had recently anglicized his name from Giovanni Martini, was possibly the last man to see Custer and his men alive.

Fighting to protect their families and the village, an estimated 1,500 warriors grabbed rifles, war clubs, and bows and arrows to repel the invaders. It was among the largest number of battle-ready Indians ever assembled. "I

Left: Low Dog, an Oglala Sioux leader. The Indians had the numerical advantage but also used more-sophisticated rifles than did Custer's cavalry. *Top:* Frederick Benteen. *Above:* Marcus Reno.

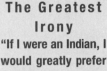

8 The Battle of the Little Bighorn has probably produced a greater volume of material than any other battle in U.S. history, including Gettysburg.

9 The number of people who claimed to be the lone survivor of the battle was

heard the alarm, but I did not believe it," said Low Dog, an Oglala Sioux war leader, several years after the battle. "I thought it was a false alarm. I did not think it possible that any white men would attack us, so strong as we were."

Custer and the men under his command were quickly overwhelmed. His battalion split into two groups, coming under severe attack, but regrouped on what is now called Last Stand Hill. Precisely what happened next is unknown— all the men who rode with Custer, including his younger brothers, Boston and Tom, and his nephew, Autie, were killed. Indian participants wouldn't talk about the battle for fear of retribution. Two Moons, a Northern Cheyenne, however, described the fight as a quick one, over "in the time it takes a hungry man to eat his dinner."

Meanwhile, Reno and Benteen, commanding the remainder of the 7th, were in trouble. Reno, without Custer's support, lost an estimated 40 men as he attacked the village and quickly retreated back across the river in total disarray under the withering enemy fire. Benteen's command joined him on the bluffs above the river, and together the 360 or so remaining soldiers and men guarding the pack train came under furious attack until nightfall. During the night, the men dug rifle pits with tin cups, mess plates, and knives and piled up saddles, wooden boxes, and dead horses around a shallow depression to make breastworks. A lone surgeon treated the wounded. Custer was somewhere to the north, they thought. At dawn, the Indians renewed their attack, pinning the soldiers down well into the afternoon. The Indians then set a grass fire so the smoke would obscure their movements, and that evening the entire village set out to the south in the direction of the Bighorn Mountains.

What, Reno and Benteen wondered, had happened to Custer? General Alfred Terry and his command, marching

The Greatest Irony

"If I were an Indian, I would greatly prefer to cast my lot among those of my people who adhered to the free, open plains rather than submit to the confined limits of a reservation, there to be the recipient of the blessed benefits of civilization, with vices thrown in without stint or measure."

George Armstrong Custer,
My Life on the Plains

greater than the number of men who were killed.

10 When Custer parted company with officers along the Yellowstone, Colonel John Gibbon called to him, "Now Custer, don't be greedy. Wait for us." Custer called back "No, I will not." Exactly what he meant is lost to history.

How Many Indians?

Estimates of Indian strength at the battle fluctuate wildly, from a low of 1,500 warriors to a mythical 12,000. National Park Service interpreters at the battlefield today use figures drawn from Dr. John S. Gray's 1976 book, *Centennial Campaign: The Sioux War of 1876,* which gives an exhaustive analysis of population statistics and other data. Gray's findings coincide with the first estimates by white observers, who at once began revising their estimates upward. For example, Captain Benteen's first guess, on June 27, was 1,500 to 1,800 warriors; by evening of that day, he called it 2,500; by July 4, it was up to 3,000; three years later, in 1879, the estimate had grown to 8,000 to 9,000. Gray's calculations: possibly as many as 2,000 Indian warriors, if older boys participated in the fighting.

Custer and Bloody Knife, 1874. Before the battle, Custer ignored the scout's warning.

south from the Yellowstone up the Bighorn River, were expecting to meet up with Custer. Terry reached Reno and Benteen on the morning of June 27. Before encountering the besieged command, however, Terry's troops came upon the Last Stand. At first, they thought they saw dead buffalo lying on the side of a hill. As they got closer, they realized it was Custer and his men, dead, with most of the 210 corpses stripped naked and mutilated. Some of the troopers' watches were still ticking. A burial party was formed and prairie soil was hastily scraped over many of the bodies.

The wounded of the 7th were carried 15 miles to the Bighorn River and laid on beds of prairie grass on the deck of the steamboat *Far West,* which took them downriver to the Yellowstone. The boat made the 710-mile trip to Fort Abraham Lincoln in Bismarck, Dakota Territory, in a record 54 hours, docking on July 5 with its decks draped in black in deference to the dead.

Newspaper reports reached easterners on July 6, and demands for retribution were swift. Though the tribes had won the Battle of the Little Bighorn, they had lost the war. By the summer of 1877, the Lakota and Cheyenne had dispersed, some surrendering, some crossing into Canada, and some returning to the reservation. Their way of life on the Plains was a thing of the past. □□

➡ Spinning the Web: Go to www.almanac.com and click on Article Links 2001 for Web sites related to this article. *–The Editors*

Do you sleep better if your head is pointed due north? Will eating raw onions cure insomnia? And how about counting sheep? Here's a look at some ancient and modern myths about sleep. (Don't doze off now . . .)

Putting Sleep Myths to Bed

by Victoria Doudera

What is sleep? Many a restless night has been spent pondering this age-old question. For nearly as long as humans have dozed, we've struggled with the elusive quality of slumber. The mysterious nature of sleep has led to superstitions, folklore, and dubious sleep aids and practices.

Antiquated ATTITUDES AND SLEEP SUPERSTITIONS

You'll live longer if you sleep with your head to the north.

■ A good many New Englanders were once in the habit of sleeping with their heads to the north, aligned with the magnetic pole. Contrary types, however, slept with their heads pointing east. They reasoned that because Earth turns in an easterly direction, it was healthier to go through space headfirst.

Sleep experts today believe that better health and a longer life are indeed influenced by good sleep habits. Just sleep in the position you find most comfortable. Not sure what that is? Many times it's the position you wake up in.

Sleep is caused by a collection of fatigue toxins.

■ What causes us to become drowsy? As late as the 1930s, many Americans believed that sleep was caused by a lack of blood to the brain. But the sleep/wake connection,

—illustrated by Lynn Jeffery

according to scientists, is actually a complex dance between two opposing systems, one pushing arousal and the other pushing sleep.

According to Dr. Peter Hauri, director of the Mayo Clinic Insomnia Program and coauthor of *No More Sleepless Nights,* both systems are active all the time. "Whether you sleep or not depends on which of the two is dominant at a certain time," he notes. Because the arousal system is the more powerful of the two, researchers suggest that sleep-seekers avoid "arousal toxins," such as caffeine and alcohol.

Newborn babies need 20 to 22 hours of sleep a day.

■ Dr. Nathaniel Kleitman, pioneer sleep researcher, and his colleagues found that newborns need less sleep than was once believed. The norm for newborns is about 15 hours of sleep a day—though rarely will they slumber for more than a few hours at a time.

Premidnight sleep is better than postmidnight sleep.

■ Once it was believed that the Moon and stars favored premidnight sleep. "An hour of sleep before midnight is worth two hours

Dr. Nathaniel Kleitman
AND THE SCIENCE OF SLEEP

■ **Known as the father of contemporary sleep research, Dr. Nathaniel Kleitman (1895-1999) sounded a wake-up call in 1939 with the publication of his studies, called *Sleep and Wakefulness.* He was the first to gather information on slumber and, with his students, to identify sleep's different stages. He also studied sleep deprivation, once going for 180 hours without sleep, and concluded that forcing someone to stay awake was a bona fide form of torture.**

–University of Chicago

In 1953, Dr. Kleitman and one of his students, Dr. Eugene Aserinsky, announced their discovery of regular periods of rapid eye movements, or REM, and its association with dreaming. In 1956, Dr. Kleitman and another student, Dr. William Dement, found that certain kinds of eye movements were associated with certain types of motion in dreams, and that the average person spends about two hours every night dreaming.

thereafter," goes an English proverb published in 1670. Here in America, our very own Benjamin Franklin extolled the maxim "Early to bed and early to rise, makes a man healthy, wealthy, and wise."

Through studies of shift workers, sleep researchers have shown that what matters in terms of restful sleep is regularity of hours, not specific times. Perhaps the only advantage to going to bed before midnight is the possibility of extra sack time. **(continued)**

Counting sheep cures insomnia.

■ The idea that repetitive counting could put you to sleep is appealing, but researchers now know that concentration of any kind—even on harmless

sheep—can actually inhibit slumber. Remember, the arousal system is stronger than the sleep system. If an exciting vision of sheep jumping over a fence is too stimulating, sleep will lose out.

Dreams last only a few seconds.

■ Sometimes they seem that brief, but studies by Dr. Kleitman reported that the average dream lasts 10 to 30 minutes. The final dream of the night is the longest and can last up to an hour. Dreams occur during REM sleep, which, for most people, happens about every 90 minutes throughout the night. For a six-hour-per-night sleeper, that translates to four dreams a night.

To sleep well is to sleep like a log.

■ This old saw comes from a French expression, "Dormir comme une taupe," or "To sleep like a mole." Moles have poor eyesight and live in the dark, so it was assumed that they slept pretty well. Incorrect pronunciation led to the confusing saying, "To sleep like a top." Because this made no sense, the word *log* was substituted.

Can you enjoy log-like sleep? Not really. Logs are motionless, but the average sleeper changes position 20 to 60 times per night.

Everyone is bright and cheery after a good night's sleep.

■ Dr. Kleitman and his students found that grogginess is normal upon waking. Sleep is a different state of consciousness. The transition from it to wakefulness is not always pretty.

(continued)

Grouchy folks are often said to have gotten up on the wrong side of the bed. Which is the "wrong" side? Some claim that it is the left, or "sinister," side. Others believe that you must exit the bed from the same side you entered it or a bad day will ensue.

Sleeping with Mexican hairless dogs will cure rheumatism.

■ This old Texas legend has not been disproved!

THE SAD TRUTH ABOUT SLEEP

■ Sleep has become a threatened species. Over the past two decades, Americans have added about 158 hours—almost a month—to their yearly work and commuting schedules. When we can't fit in activities during the day, we steal from the night. "You snooze, you lose" has become our mantra.

Over the last century, our average nightly total sleep time has shrunk by more than 20 percent. We're working more, resting less. Sleep specialists say this deprivation has led to a silent epidemic of daytime drowsiness.

Sleep myths aren't relics of the past. According to the National Sleep Foundation, most Americans have poor knowledge of sleep and subscribe to at least a few modern myths. When given the Foundation's "sleep IQ test," 83 percent of the adult public flunked.

HOW TO CURE INSOMNIA!

■ According to the National Sleep Foundation, 56 percent of adults in the United States report one or more symptoms of insomnia a few nights a week or more. Possible solutions:

■ **Make sure your room is neither too hot nor too cold.**

■ **Steer clear of caffeine. Say no to nightcaps: Alcohol may help you get to sleep quickly but may interfere with extended sleep. Avoid heavy meals before bed; a light snack is OK.**

■ **Don't exercise right before bed.**

■ **Try herbs: Chamomile tea is an old sleep-inducing favorite. The scent of lavender is relaxing. Smells of spiced apple and salty sea air are said to lower stress.**

■ **Invest in linen sheets. Researchers at the University of Milan report that**

- linen sheets help you to fall asleep faster.

- ■ Paint your room green (for peacefulness and to lower the heart rate); blue (to cause the brain to secrete tranquilizing hormones); violet and other purples (for calming the nerves); or pink (for calming high-strung or hot-tempered types).

- ■ Use the bedroom only for sleeping (or sex). Don't read, watch TV, knit, or (heaven forbid) pay bills in the bedroom.

How Much Sleep Do You Need?

Six hours' sleep for a man, seven for a woman, and eight for a fool. –English proverb

■ Actually, normal sleep times for adults range from five to ten hours per night, with the average working out to about 7.5 hours of shut-eye a night. One or two people in a hundred can get by with just five hours; another small minority needs ten.

MODERN MYTHS AND MISCONCEPTIONS

Losing a little sleep here and there doesn't really hurt.

■ Research has shown that small sleep losses, accumulated night after night, really do add up. "Like gamblers playing with borrowed money, many sleep-deprived persons live in the red of lost sleep, often compromising their responsibilities at their jobs, sometimes using drugs for temporary energy," writes Dr. Hauri. Sleep loss affects memory, making it difficult to learn new things or perform daily tasks. Sleep problems can cause premature aging and can prevent a speedy recovery from illness.

A sleep debt can become so overpowering that we succumb even in a potentially dangerous situation. Drowsiness and falling asleep at the wheel are leading causes of car accidents. The U.S. Department of Transportation estimates that each year, 100,000 drowsiness-related crashes claim more than 1,500 lives.

Teenagers require less sleep than adults and young children.

■ Most teens actually need more sleep—9 or 9½ hours a day—than most children half their age. As any parent who has tried to rouse a tired teen knows, adolescents like to burn the midnight oil and sleep late in the morning. But what frustrated adults see as a preference may actually be a natural rhythm. "Teens have a difficult time falling asleep," says New Hampshire sleep specialist Dr. David Brown. "Their normal rhythm is predisposed to staying up late and waking up later."

Older adults need less sleep than younger adults.

■ Experts say that our adult sleep requirements change very little with age. What fluctuates, however, are our sleep patterns. Older adults tend to fall asleep earlier and awaken earlier than younger adults. With age, the lighter stages of sleep increase and the deeper stages decrease. As a result, older adults tend to wake up more often during the night.

For optimal health, you need to catch up on all the sleep you miss.

■ Your sleep debt can be forgiven without making a total payback. If you went without sleep for ten days or so, you would probably sleep for 14 to 18 hours per day for about three days, then return to your normal sleep schedule. For those of us who cut our sleep short for several nights, that means getting a little extra sleep for a night or two, then resuming a schedule that gives us the sleep we need.

Are We Born to Nap?

■ The urge to take an afternoon siesta is nearly universal, even in people who've slept well. Our energy slumps because of a normal dip in body temperature that occurs about 12 hours after the midpoint of our nighttime sleep. Afternoon naps, made up of restful non-REM sleep, can wipe away fatigue, sharpen your memory, and improve your mood. But if you're having problems falling or staying asleep at night, keep your eyes open during the day. Relaxation exercises and meditation are better afternoon alternatives for insomniacs. □□

➡ Spinning the Web: Go to www.almanac.com and click on Article Links 2001 for Web sites related to this article. –*The Editors*

Life after Death

There is nothing more certain than death. But what is death? Are those who die really dead, or are they more alive than ever? If they are not dead, where are they? The Bible assures us that there is life beyond the grave for all, and that is the divine purpose to restore the dead to life in the resurrection.

Where will you be in the resurrection?

Will you see and know your loved ones who have died?

You will enjoy the Bible's answer to these questions in the free booklet:

"Life after Death"

Send today for your FREE copy:

The Bible Answers, Dept. F
Box 60, General Post Office
New York, NY 10116
1-800-234-DAWN
Visit us on the Web:
www.dawnbible.com

If the skin on your face looks more "mature" than you'd like it to, here are a few time-honored ways to smooth out those crow's-feet and squint lines.

Cover your face with raw egg white (with or without a few drops of lemon juice) before you brush your teeth each morning, and rinse it off as you shower. This tones the skin.

Using a small, soft paintbrush or cosmetic brush, paint your face with raw egg yolk, concentrating on wrinkles and lines. While the egg is drying, make a paste of 2 tablespoons mayonnaise, ½ teaspoon fuller's earth, and ½ teaspoon powdered kelp. Apply this over the egg yolk and rinse off after 10 minutes.

Twice a day, rub olive oil onto your clean face. Pat on fresh lemon juice, drop by drop, until your skin feels tacky. Then briskly rub sea salt or kosher salt over your face. (Now you know how a salad feels!) Rinse off with warm water and pat dry.

Blend 2 teaspoons yogurt with ½ teaspoon honey, ½ teaspoon lemon juice, and the contents of a 400 I.U. vitamin E capsule. Smooth over your face and let penetrate for 15 minutes, then rinse.

HOW TO

Prevent Wrinkles

AND GIVE

YOURSELF A

Face-Lift

Emergency Antiwrinkle Measures Before a Big Event

Make wrinkles disappear for a few hours: Stir a raw egg white with a fork, and carefully paint it onto each wrinkle with a fine camel's hair brush. Let dry, then apply makeup foundation with a light hand. Try not to get caught in the rain.

"Iron" your face: Smooth on a generous coating of petroleum jelly or vegetable oil. Heat a metal spoon in a cup of hot water. "Iron" lines and creases with the back of the spoon, reheating it as needed. Tissue off excess jelly or oil, and pat on skin freshener.

Calisthenics to Control Crevices Around the Mouth

Form an "O" with your mouth and tense the muscles for 6 seconds, then relax for 6 seconds. Repeat 5 times.

Open your mouth in a wide yawn, then stretch your lips over your teeth and smile. Hold for 6 seconds, then relax. Repeat 5 times.

Push your lips out as far as possible and suck in your cheeks. Hold for 6 seconds, then relax. Repeat 5 times.

A RECIPE FROM THE 1870S

Pomade de Ninon de l'Enclos

Take of oil of almonds, 4 ounces avoirdupois; hog's lard, 3 ounces; spermaceti, 1 ounce; melt, add of expressed juice of house-leek, 3 Imperial ounces, and stir until the mixture solidifies by cooling. A few drops of esprit de rose, or of eau de Cologne, or lavande, may be added to scent it at will. Used as a general skin-cosmetic; also for wrinkles or freckles. It is said to be very softening, cooling, and refreshing. ☐☐

These tips are taken from old books in the archives of The Old Farmer's Almanac and from *Mother Nature's Guide to Vibrant Beauty & Health,* by Myra Cameron (Prentice Hall, 1990).

SPEAKING of BEARS

They are the world's most powerful and ferocious omnivores; they are also the object of many a small child's affection. What is it about bears that inspires both fear and an irresistible desire to hug them?

Dan Ludington loaded his gun and walked out into the cold Alaskan air. A grizzly bear had been terrorizing the countryside, and Ludington intended to kill the beast.

"I was standing there, cold and undecided—my binoculars in one hand, my rifle in the other," he told Outdoor Life *magazine back in the 1940s, soon after the incident occurred, "when the sow exploded like a four-footed thunderclap from the line of brush not 30 feet away. Her deep-throated roar ripped through the silence on the ridge."*

Instinctively, Ludington swung his rifle toward the grizzly and pulled the trigger. "In the split second that should have preceded the blast," he said, *"I glimpsed the sow's crazy red eyes and the hair standing ramrod straight along her back. Then I experienced the sickest, most all-gone moment in my life."*

Ludington's gun refused to fire. "Desperately, I pumped another shell into the chamber just as 800 pounds of rock-hard, crazy-mad grizzly slammed me to the ground . . ."

In 1902, President Teddy Roosevelt, a great outdoorsman, went hunting in Mississippi. Presented with the opportunity to shoot a bear (depending on the version you believe, it was either a cub or a full-grown bear who'd been captured and roped to a tree so the president could take aim), Roosevelt refused, saying it would not be sporting. Clifford Berryman, a cartoonist for *The Washington Star*, drew a cartoon of the

Opposite page: *The grizzly bear, a subspecies of the brown bear.*

President Theodore Roosevelt, inspiration for our teddy bears.

BY JAMIE KAGELEIRY

hunt, showing Roosevelt with a gun in one hand, turning away from a little bear. Soon the cartoon was seen by all, and the president was a hero.

Morris Michtom, a toy-store owner in Brooklyn, New York, decided to capitalize on the little bear's popularity, so he had his wife sew a small brown stuffed bear with button eyes. Michtom put the little bear into his display window next to the *Star* cartoon, with a sign, "Teddy's Bear." You know the rest. Many of us still have our childhood teddy bear, an animal we fell asleep holding and took with us when we left home.

Mauling monster, savage species, loner, unpredictable, mad, red-eyed, crazy. Or cuddly, playful, wise, and loyal—Smokey, Yogi, Pooh, Paddington. And, of course, Teddy.

The sun bear.

WILL THE REAL BEAR PLEASE STAND UP?

Bears, like humans, are complicated creatures. And the diametrically opposed characteristics we accord them—cold-blooded ferocity and nurturing tenderness—can easily be contained in the same bear. Bears have bad days, too—an abscessed tooth, for example, can provoke a really foul mood, but a fresh mound of snow will inspire a grown grizzly bear to slide and frolic like a giant toddler. Coming up with the "typical bear" is difficult: Not even biologists agree on who exactly belongs in beardom. Some scientists contend that pandas, for instance, are not bears at all but are more like raccoons. And koalas, supermodels of the teddy-bear set, are definitely not bears but marsupials.

The bear is a mammal and is the world's

Though grizzly bears are the most feared, polar bears are actually the most dangerous—anything that moves is considered food.

The polar bear.

only large omnivore. Bears have five toes, except for those murky pandas, who have six in their forepaws; and like humans, they are plantigrade—that is, they walk on the sole of the foot and set the heel down. They are nearsighted but can detect form and movement from afar. There are eight species and many subspecies of bears.

The American black bear is the common bear we've all come to love—the one we picture snooping around national parks, the one who plays the clown in the circus. He is native to North America; has a small, straight nose; and hibernates. After the country was settled, this bear was heavily hunted, and millions of acres of his forest home were cleared for farming. Like other species of bears in modern times, the black bear has become scarce.

Brown bears are the big guys—the coastal browns have been measured at 2,500 pounds, though the average adult male is closer to 800 pounds. Grizzly bears, which are the inland brown bears, average about 650 pounds and measure between three and five feet high, paw to shoulder when standing on all four legs. They are often seen standing on their hind legs and can walk bipedally (on two feet) for several yards (and be trained to do it for much longer). A standing grizzly can reach up more than seven feet. They're shaggy and not uniform in color, leading to the "grizzly" label. The world's largest omnivores, brown bears are the ones with the big hump of muscle on their back, and the ones who, deservedly, can inspire the most fear in man.

The third North American bear is "Nanook," a nickname for the polar bear. Naturalist John Muir described this wandering "sea bear" as ". . . a noble-looking animal, and of enormous strength, living bravely and warm amid eternal ice." Except for pregnant sows, polar bears do not hibernate. Mature males typically weigh about 1,150 pounds and stand almost five-and-a-half feet tall from paw to shoulder. The largest polar bear ever measured weighed 2,210 pounds. Though grizzlies are the most feared, polar bears are actually the most dangerous—anything that moves is considered food.

(continued)

BEARS OF THE WORLD

- American black bear, *Ursus americanus,* North America

- Asiatic black bear, *Selenarctos thibetanus,* Southern Asia

- Brown bear, *Ursus arctos,* North America and Eurasia

- Giant panda, *Ailuropoda melanoleuca,* China

- Polar bear, *Ursus maritimus,* North America and Eurasia (Arctic Ocean)

- Sloth bear, *Melursus ursinus,* Eurasia

- Spectacled bear, *Tremarctos ornatus,* South America

- Sun bear, *Helarctos malayanus,* Southeast Asia (Malaysia)

The Asiatic black bear.

BEAR
POPULATIONS
IN THE
UNITED
STATES AND
CANADA

United States

■ Black bears: about 300,000, most of them in Alaska, California, Idaho, Maine, Montana, Oregon, and Washington, with smaller numbers in many other states. Even New Jersey claims about 300.

■ Grizzly bears: about 40,000 in Alaska, and another 1,000 mostly in Montana and Wyoming's Yellowstone National Park.

■ Polar bears: about 2,000, all in Alaska.

Canada

■ Black bears: about 350,000, spread among all provinces except Prince Edward Island, with the largest populations in Alberta, British Columbia, Ontario, and Quebec.

■ Grizzly bears: about 25,000, concentrated in British Columbia, the Yukon, and the Northwest Territories.

■ Polar bears: about 15,000 in the Far North.

Dan Ludington, the Alaskan homesteader:

"Luckily, my binoculars broke the force of the sow's first swipe at my chest, made with a right paw the size of a football. But her claws laid open my chest as neatly as a surgeon's knife.

"Then I was on the ground, and from my worm's-eye view, the bear looked as big as a mountain. Methodically, she began making mincemeat of my left arm, and when I yelled in pain, she snapped at my head . . ."

Much about bears is illusory: They appear slow and clumsy, perhaps because of their furry girth; in truth, they are agile and fast, able to outrun a pack of dogs and climb a limbless tree with ease. Grizzly and black bears can run at least 30 miles an hour, faster than the speediest Olympic sprinter. Bears are the most powerful animals of their size, able to kill a moose with a single blow, then carry the carcass for a great distance. And never confuse a mother bear with gentle Pooh. The wrath of a mother bear with cubs is legendary. From the minute she gives birth, writes Gary Brown in *The Great Bear Almanac* (Lyons & Burford, 1993), "her maternal behavior is paramount—she is 'cubbing' without fatherly assistance and will fiercely defend her cubs."

"In the years since," said bear-attack victim Ludington, "I've relived that moment a thousand times in my dreams.

"Without fail, the memory of the grating sound the sow's teeth made across my skull is enough to awaken me in a cold sweat. . . .

"While I kicked and screamed and cursed, I kept thinking what a lousy way this was to die. I thought of Maxine and the kids—Maxine with another baby on the way and me in hock up to my blood-soaked eyebrows. Then, as if annoyed at the time it was taking to put me away, the grizzly bit through my face from the center of my nose to my right temple. The blurred image of her oncoming fangs was the last thing I ever saw through my right eye.

"Annoyed at my incessant kicking, the sow . . .

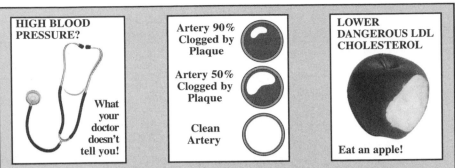

WHAT IS IT ABOUT PANDAS?
(Are they bears or not?)

■ Giant pandas, China's national treasure and the World Wildlife Fund's symbol of world conservation, have been the focus of a classification controversy among scientists, some of whom think they belong in the raccoon family. Pandas, though clearly bear-like in build, gait, and reproductive behavior, are not bear-like in many ways: They have six (instead of five) toes on their front feet, they have distinct black and white markings, and there's no heel pad on their hind feet, meaning they don't leave human-like tracks, as other bears do. Pandas don't even sound like bears—they bleat, more like sheep. After studies in the 1980s determined that pandas were more bear-like than raccoon-like, scientists decided that pandas, who descended from bears but split from the family Ursidae more than 20 million years ago, are "specialized bears."

—Weststock

transferred her attention from my head to my left leg. . . . In that single, redeeming instant, I pointed the rifle at her broad chest and pulled the trigger.

"I saw the hair blow straight up on the grizzly's back as 250 grains of lead crashed completely through her. Her death roar and that of the rifle sounded almost as one. She flopped on her belly at my feet—lifeless."

Ludington not only lived to tell the tale of his encounter with the angry mother grizzly—he slept every night thereafter with the bear itself, skinned and used as a rug in his bedroom.

There are no other animals we anthropomorphize more than we do bears. Bears are like us: We're both mammals; we both stand up on our hind legs. They walk like us, and they sit down like us—often leaning back against something and crossing one leg over the other. They like sweets, eat with their hands, snore, nurse, and discipline their young (they even spank them). Some Native American legends go so far as to say that the grizzly is the ancestor of the human race.

In *The Great Bear Almanac,* author Brown quotes writers Paul Shepard and Barry Sanders: "The combination of overall awareness and seeming nonchalance is among the bear's most man-like capacities: a taciturn, calculating mixture of knowing and blasé sophistication that can be unnerving to human observers."

It has often been said that bears walking around in the wild look like humans dressed up in bear suits. You see something so familiar, so similar, and something in you feels as if you could almost predict just what it's thinking, and just what it might do next.

Almost. □□

➤ **Spinning the Web: Go to www.almanac.com and click on Article Links 2001 for Web sites related to this article.** *–The Editors*

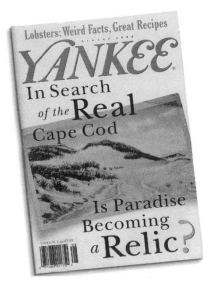

"In all ages Men have been Self-Tormentors," noted chronicler John Brand in 1813. ". . . the bad Omens fill a catalogue infinitely more extensive than that of the good." Most of us are awestruck at coincidences and freakish occurrences, and many of us still believe these things predict our destiny, usually for the worse. We may think of the medieval age as the highwater mark of belief in superstition, yet centuries later, we still hedge our bets by knocking on wood at the corporate meeting, by avoiding row 13 on the commuter plane, by throwing spilled salt over our shoulder at the cyberspace café.

Old rituals continue to calm us with a sense of control in an otherwise chaotic world. Computers have only made them more accessible. Will the groundhog see his shadow? Watch his winter prediction on the Web. Is a passing comet a sure sign of doom? Join (or not) the Web browsers who believe.

If your foot itches,
you will tread strange ground.

What? Me Superstitious?

Who's a Believer?

When it comes right down to it, there's a whole lot of wood-knocking going on. A recent Gallup poll concerning superstitions turned up the following statistics:

- A little superstitious **28%**
- Somewhat or very superstitious **27%**
- Don't miss a chance to knock on wood **25%**
- Nervous about a black cat crossing the path . . **13%**
- Never risk walking under a ladder **12%**
- Fear the number 13 . . . . **11%**
- Believe something bad will occur **9%**
  when a mirror breaks
- Think that lucky clothing can help **2%**
- Believe in picking up lucky pennies **1%**

(c o n t i n u e d)

B Y   C H R I S T I N E   S C H U L T Z

Is It Good Luck to Be Superstitious?

■ "We derive tremendous comfort from thinking we can either avoid an undesirable result or bring about a desired result. In this way, superstition is an extremely useful tool," says Terence Sandbek, a clinical psychologist in Sacramento, California, who has studied the subject. "Superstitions are like alcohol. A little may actually be constructive. More than a little might impair the ability to function."

Or maybe luck is independent of belief. Upon winning the Nobel prize for quantum theory in 1918, physicist Max Planck's laboratory was overrun by curious journalists. A reporter immediately spotted the horseshoe that Max kept hanging above his doorway. "You don't believe in such outmoded superstitions, do you?" said the reporter.

"Surely not," the learned physicist replied. "However, I'm told a horseshoe will bring you good luck whether you believe it or not."

Tracking Down Offtrack Beliefs

■ Though scientific evidence shows that other ocean areas have more plane crashes than the Bermuda Triangle, people continue to be superstitious about flying over it. Why? Perhaps we notice only the things we're already looking for. "It's the same sort of logic— 'I wouldn't have seen it if I hadn't believed it'— at work in conspiracy theories," says Michael Shermer, author of *Why People Believe Weird Things: Pseudoscience, Superstition, and Other Confusions of Our Time*. But worse than the Bermuda Triangle, says Shermer, is the belief in Bigfoot. "We've seen enough tracks," he says. "Find the body already."

THE STORY BEHIND
Seven Superstitions

1   Why hanging a horseshoe brings good luck.

■ Iron was once considered a sacred metal that could protect humans because Mars (the god of iron) was the enemy of Saturn (the god of witches). What's more, the horseshoe shape resembled the crescent Moon, which had long hung as a safeguard on church doors. What most people don't know is that not all horseshoes do the trick. To work good magic, the shoe must be lost by a horse and found by you with the open end pointing your way. Then you must spit between the prongs and throw the shoe over your shoulder, or nail it above your front door with the two ends facing up so that the luck will not spill out.

 Why walking under a ladder brings bad luck.

■ In the days before the gallows, criminals were hung from the highest rung of a ladder, beneath which their ghosts were later said to linger. Others believed that a ladder resting against a building formed a sacred triangle inhabited by spirits. Passing through the triangle disrupted that sacred life, opening the path for evil.

 Why breaking a mirror brings bad luck.

■ Our ancestors believed that the image we see in a mirror is our very soul. A broken mirror, therefore, meant that a soul had been set adrift in the world. The trick to counteracting such misfortune is to wait seven hours before picking up the pieces, or bury them at midnight in a cemetery on a moonless, starless night.

 Why you should throw spilled salt over your shoulder.

■ Salt was once a rare and precious commodity believed by the ancients to have magical properties. Spilling some was considered a calamity that foretold a family quarrel. To fix matters, simply throw a pinch of spilled salt over your left shoulder and say, "With this case, may ill luck pass."

 Why knocking on wood holds off harm.

■ In ancient times, certain trees were believed to house deities, who could be invoked by touching the tree (later, by just touching wood). Other reasons:

During the medieval period, sinners found safety when their knuckles rapped on the sanctuary of a wooden church door; or the custom may be some kind of lingering veneration for the cross on which Jesus was crucified.

 ## *Why you should never let a black cat cross your path.*

■ With their glow-in-the-dark eyes, cats have long been considered supernatural. But 5,000 years ago, Egyptians  revered them, and royalty mummified their cats and had them buried beside them. It wasn't until the witch hunts of the Middle Ages that black cats were thought to be connected with the devil and, therefore, were carriers of bad luck.

-H. Armstrong Roberts

 ## *Why it's good luck to carry a rabbit's foot.*

■ Because they burrow underground and are such fertile creatures, rabbits are believed to ward off bad luck and bring on good luck. But you must obtain one in the following manner: With a silver bullet, shoot a rabbit during a full Moon, then cut off its left hind foot and dunk it in the rainwater of a hollow stump. Carry the foot in your left back pocket or around your neck until it has become old and dried out, at which point it will be at its most potent.

 ## *The Numbers Game*

■ **Can you say triskaidekaphobia 13 times fast?**

People (including horror writer Stephen King) who fear the number 13 and who especially dread Friday the 13th, are triskaidekaphobiacs. Experts say that the fear got its start in Biblical times when Jesus invited 12 disciples (including Judas the trai-

Is it bad luck to break a mirror? Not necessarily. Just wait seven hours before picking up the pieces, or bury them at midnight in a cemetery on a moonless, starless night.

 ## *Superstitions Around the House*

The Oldest of House-Building Superstitions

■ Long ago, it was thought that an earth god ruled the soil, so anyone who wanted to use a piece of his land to build a house on had to place a coin or a lucky object inside a corner wall.

The Latest in House-Selling Superstitions

■ As real estate prices skyrocketed and house sales dwindled at the end of

tor) to the Last Supper, making an unlucky 13 for dinner. Because the worst of fates—crucifixion—befell him that Friday, we have held onto our fear of Fridays and 13 ever since. The fear is still so prevalent, in fact, that many tall buildings lack a 13th floor, and many airplanes conveniently skip row 13. Maybe it's for the best—the *British Medical Journal* reports that studies show "significantly more road traffic accidents on Friday the 13th than on Friday the 6th."

you leave, and pass it through a window when you arrive, and butter its paws so that it stays put.

"And do not take your pig trough. And do not move on Friday."

–from Cross Your Fingers, Spit in Your Hat: Superstitions and Other Beliefs, *collected by Alvin Schwartz*

The Luck of the Birds and the Bees

■ **If a bird flies through the house, it means important news will come. But if the bird can't get back out, the news is death.**

■ **If a woodpecker knocks at your house, the news is bad.**

the 20th century, sales of statues of St. Joseph, the patron saint of home and family, rose dramatically. It seems that frazzled house-sellers were burying the figurines in their yards in the magical manner prescribed—whatever that might be. Some believed that St. Joseph had to be planted head up, others said head down. Some maintained that he must face the house, others said he must face away.

And Don't Forget to Butter Fluffy's Paws

■ If you must leave your old house and move to a new one, do not take your broom with you.

"And do not take your cat unless you wave it at some friends when

–H. Armstrong Roberts

■ **If a wren nests near your house, the news is good. But better yet is the tiny hummingbird, which brings the most good luck of all the birds.**

■ **Make a wish on a swift before it flies out of sight— or on the first robin you see in the spring—and your wish will come true.**

■ **If a swift nests in the chimney, bedbugs are sure to nest in your bed.**

■ **To some Native Americans, if a hawk passed overhead as they made battle plans, it meant surefire victory.**

(c o n t i n u e d)

■ New Englanders and Europeans once believed that bees were just as smart as people, so they kept their bees up-to-date on the latest news. If a family wedding took place, someone would hang a white ribbon on the hive or bring a piece of cake for the bees. When someone died, the beekeeper would stand before the hive and make a formal announcement to his bees. If he neglected to tell them, it was said, the bees would die or leave.

. . . and the Groundhog

■ Every year since 1888, German tradition has held that on February 2 (the Christian holiday of Candlemas), someone should watch and see if the groundhog sees its shadow. If it does, there will be six more weeks of winter. That such a prediction could take hold is intriguing enough, but that it would continue gaining steam into the 21st century is even more amazing.

These days, a groundhog named Punxsutawney Phil is an international celebrity who lives in a heated hutch at the public library in Punxsutawney, north of Pittsburgh, Pennsylvania. In 1999, his actions were broadcast live for the first time on the World Wide Web. The governor announced that Phil's Internet prediction was part of a new campaign to market Pennsylvania as a "high-tech business hub"—and so it was that one old superstition came to be considered cutting edge.

–photo courtesy Punxsutawney Area Chamber of Commerce

Baguette Etiquette and Other Travel Tips

■ If you turn your baguette bottomside-up in France, your waiter will avoid you and doom will not.

■ In Sweden, placing your keys onto a table opens the door to bad luck, as surely as setting a hat onto a bed does in the United States.

■ Do not shake hands with a Russian while standing in a doorway, or you and your acquaintance will soon be shaking hands with bad luck.

■ In Thailand, keep an eye out for an elephant passing in the streets—it brings great

Irrit ble Bowel?

If you suffer problems such as constipation, bloating, diarrhea, gas, stomach cramps, heartburn, pain and discomfort associated with foods, you should know about a new book, *The Irritable Bowel Syndrome & Gastrointestinal Solutions Handbook*.

The book contains the latest up-to-date information on the bowel—how it functions, what can go wrong, how it can best be treated, and how to protect yourself from irritable bowel problems. The book gives you specific facts on the latest natural and alternative remedies that can bring prompt and lasting relief without the use of dangerous drugs. You'll learn all about these new remedies and find out how and why they work.

You'll discover what you can do to avoid irritable bowel and stomach problems, what foods actually promote healing, and what to avoid at all costs. The book even explains a simple treatment that has helped thousands rid themselves of irritable bowel problems, yet is little-known to most people—even doctors.

The book also explains how the gastrointestinal system works, how food is digested, how specific foods affect the bowel, why certain foods and activities cause problems, why over 20 million people suffer irritable bowel problems—and how people are now able to overcome their problems.

Many Americans are putting up with troublesome irritable bowel and stomach problems because they are unaware of new natural treatments and the welcome relief that is now available.

Get all the facts. Order this book today. The book is being made available for only $12.95 *(plus $3 P&H)*. To order, send name and address with payment to United Research Publishers, Dept. FAS-7; PMB 5; 103 North Coast Highway 101; Encinitas CA 92024. For MasterCard or VISA send card number and expiration date. You may return the book within 90 days for a refund if not satisfied.

SCIATICA RELIEF!

If you have ever suffered Sciatica symptoms such as pain in the buttocks and lower back, or pain and numbness in your legs and feet, you should get a copy of a new book called *The Sciatica Relief Handbook*. The book shows you how to prevent Sciatica flare-ups, and how to stop pain if you now have a Sciatica problem.

The book contains the latest up-to-date information on Sciatica—what causes painful symptoms, how to best treat them, and how to protect yourself from Sciatica problems. The book gives you specific facts on the latest natural, alternative and medical treatments that can bring prompt and lasting relief—without the use of dangerous drugs or surgery. You'll learn all about these remedies and learn how and why they work to bring dramatic relief.

You'll discover what to immediately do if Sciatica symptoms start and what to avoid at all costs to prevent possible serious problems. You'll even discover a simple treatment that has helped thousands get relief, yet is little known to most people—even doctors.

The book explains all about the Sciatic nerve, the various ways it may become inflamed and cause pain, how to find out what specifically causes distress (you may be surprised), what to do and what not to do—and why over 165 million people experience Sciatica and lower back pain.

Many people are putting up with Sciatica pain—or have had Sciatica pain in the past and are at risk of a recurrence—because they do not know about new prevention and relief measures that are now available.

Get all the facts. The book is available for only $12.95 *(plus $3 P&H)*. To order, simply send your name and address with payment to United Research Publishers, Dept. FAK-3; PMB 5; 103 North Coast Highway 101; Encinitas CA 92024. For VISA or MasterCard send card number and expiration date. You may return the book within 90 days for a refund if not completely satisfied. ∎

luck. What's more, if you pay the fee, you can walk beneath its belly for bonus benevolence (with extra points if you are pregnant).

■ If you are in a group photo in the Philippines and there are only three of you, never stand in the middle. Superstition says that you'll get sick or die. You must switch places (this is hard if the other two share the superstition), or better yet, get a fourth to join you.

How to Ensure a Merry Christmas

■ For health throughout the year, eat an apple on Christmas Eve.

■ For strength, eat a raw egg first thing Christmas morning.

■ So as not to lose a friend, eat plum pudding on Christmas Day.

■ Pair the family shoes side by side on Christmas Eve, according to Scandinavian belief, and you will sidestep quarrels in the coming year. Should you get new shoes for Christmas, do not wear them that first day, or, say the Rhinelanders, you're sure to step in bad luck.

–photo: H. Armstrong Roberts

... and Have a Happy New Year

■ To get rich in the coming year, let the Moon shine into your empty purse on New Year's Eve, or eat hog jowls and black-eyed peas on New Year's Day. But whatever you do, don't eat both ends of a bread loaf before eating the middle.

■ At midnight, open a window and shoo out the year's backlogged bad luck, then welcome in the good luck with open arms.

■ Carry nothing from the house on New Year's Day. Break nothing, lend nothing, and do no washing (or you'll wash your luck away). Also, be sure to act nice, for your behavior on January 1 sets the pattern for the whole year.

What Not to Do in the Theater

■ Don't quote *Macbeth* during rehearsals.

■ Don't whistle backstage, or you'll forget your lines or fall on your face onstage.

■ Don't wear yellow.

■ Don't wish someone good luck before a performance, or the person will have bad luck.

■ Don't carry a makeup box or let your shoes squeak.

(continued)

Christmas at the Almanac Music Hall

$\mathcal{S}$leigh bells, a rousing fiddle, chimes, a swinging cornet, and an old upright piano. Featuring Peter Ecklund and the Howard Fishman Quartet, this collection of Christmas music is pure of heart and as timeless as Christmas itself.

13 selections, including ...
Sleigh Ride 🎄 Have Yourself a Merry Little Christmas 🎄 It Came upon a Midnight Clear 🎄 I'll Be Home for Christmas 🎄 Winter Wonderland 🎄 The Christmas Waltz 🎄 Frosty the Snowman 🎄 White Christmas 🎄 *and more ...*

Hear RealAudio clips on
www.almanac.com/business/music.xmas.html

Available in CD, Cassette Tape, or LP Album! *Only $14.95**

🎄 For Compact Disc, order
　Item: OFNDCDC Key:NDMCOFAB
🎄 For Cassette Tape, order
　Item: OFNDCSC Key: NDMCOFAB
🎄 For LP 33-1/3 RPM Album, order
　Item: OFNDLPC Key: NDMOFAB
　* Please add $3.95 PER ORDER for s&h.

THREE WAYS TO ORDER:
1) On-line: www.almanac.com/holiday
2) Toll-free: 800-223-3166
3) Mail: The Old Farmer's Almanac
　　P.O. Box 37370
　　Boone, IA 50037-0370

TERMS: Payment, including shipping and handling, must be received with your order. We accept Visa, MasterCard, American Express, and Discover cards. Personal check or money order also accepted in U.S. funds drawn on a U.S. bank.

🎄 🎄 🎄 🎄 🎄 🎄 🎄

Seafaring Superstitions

The list of sailing superstitions is as long as the ocean is wide. Here are just a few:

When at sea, don't ever say the words *church, egg, knife, minister,* or *pig.*

Don't ever bring a dog, a dead body, a woman in a white apron, a suitcase, a banana, a rabbit, a sewing pin, or a clergyman onboard. Bring a cat instead.

Don't change the name of your boat or end its name with the letter *a.*

If you see a dolphin swimming north, the weather will be good. If one is swimming south, the weather will be stormy.

Three seagulls flying together, or a shark following your boat, means death.

■ Wearing a plain gold earring will protect you from drowning and evil spirits.

■ Whatever you do, do not whistle in the wheelhouse, drop a mop or bucket overboard, leave port on a Friday, look back at home as you leave, have your mother wash your clothes on the day you set sail, cut your fingernails or hair in calm seas, look at the new Moon through glass, or flip the hatch covers upside down.

"If you care to ignore these words of caution, you do so at your own risk," reports *National Fisherman.* "If you follow them religiously, well, it will probably have no bearing whatsoever on the outcome of your trip or your safety on the water. But that doesn't really matter; most fishermen will adhere to at least a few of them anyway.... Maybe it's because there's such a need for calm on the water.... Or maybe, as some fishermen will attest, it's because they have met a sinister minister on the way to the dock, left on a Friday, or had a crewman who whistled on watch, and they paid the price."

The Roundabout Rituals of Romance

Love is a crazy, complicated affair made trickier by the tangle of superstitions that go along with it. According to the book *Cross Your Fingers, Spit in Your Hat,* you must pull a hair from the head of the one you love to make him or her love you deeply. Or offer your love a glass of lemonade in which you have soaked your toenail clippings, or add three drops of your blood to a bowl of soup.

(c o n t i n u e d)

-H. Armstrong Roberts

The Old Farmer's Almanac
DON'T MISS AN ISSUE!

3-Year Subscription Only $14 Including Shipping!

Tired of searching for a copy of *The Old Farmer's Almanac* every year? Now you can have it delivered to your home each September for three years for only $14. Shipping is included and it's tax free! Subscribe to the regional issue that is adapted to where you live.

Once your sweetheart has devoured one of these concoctions, he or she will love you always.

The readers of *Canadian Living* have their own stories. One said her mother always told her, "Don't lick your plate clean or your husband will be bald." Another Canadian reader said that she was late for her own wedding because her mother is superstitious about being the third car to leave anywhere. Following the first two cars in the wedding party would have meant a funeral would follow, she said. While they waited, the bride remembered that they had forgotten the groom's ring, but because it is also bad luck to double back, her mother would not let her return to get it, so the tardy bride was forced to wing it on the ring, as well.

Sports: It's Just Another Word for Superstition

■ What does it take to become an Olympic gold medalist? A pink hat, smelly socks, and maybe even a big roll of duct tape.

Volleyball player Karch Kiraly was forced to modify his lucky pink beach-volleyball hat to meet Olympic indoor regulations when his team went for the gold in 1984, so modify it he did. And sure enough, the pink brought him the gold—and again in 1988. He still wears the hat.

Decathlon gold-medal winner Bruce Jenner had a pair of lucky socks from his alma mater, Graceland College in Iowa, that he wore at every competition until they were nothing but threads. Even then, he would not chance losing his luck, so he taped them to his feet. Today his lucky socks are framed and hung in a place of honor in his home.

Superstitions of the Superstars

■ **Throughout his entire NBA career, Michael Jordan continued to wear, underneath his Bulls uniform, the same University of North Carolina gym shorts that had helped him win the national college basketball championship. All told, his lucky shorts brought him and the Chicago Bulls six championships.**

–photo courtesy University of North Carolina Sports Information Office

■ **Tiger Woods was wearing red when he won the prestigious Masters golf tournament in 1997, and so he now does as his mother says and continues to wear lucky red on Sundays.**

The Battiness of Baseball

■ Of all the people who use superstitious routines to fend off performance

anxiety, the most ritualistic are baseball players. Of those, Wade Boggs takes the chicken. After noticing a correlation between multiple hits and eating poultry for dinner back in his 1982 rookie season, Boggs, who retired in 1999, asked his wife to fix him chicken before every game. She went on to accumulate more than 40 recipes. But eating chicken is only one of more than 80 different rituals that Boggs undertook before and after every game. "Everyone has a routine," says Boggs. "Mine just took five hours."

His superstitions all served to wrap him in a cocoon of concentration, which may have its own merit, says Nancy Clark, director of Nutrition Services at Sports Medicine of Brookline: "There's something to be said for the power of the mind. If you believe it will make you a better athlete, it probably will."

But former umpire Ron Luciano takes a different view: "Wearing a hat in some silly way can't possibly bring good luck. The only things that really work are talent, hard work, and sitting with your right leg crossing your left knee with your arms folded across your chest."

The Hoodoo of Hockey

■ Next to baseball players, hockey players have got to be the most superstitious athletes. When New York Islander defenseman Ken Morrow grew a beard before the 1980 playoffs, his teammates copied him. They won the Stanley Cup, and thereafter started a trend among other NHL players.

Detroit Red Wings coach, Scotty Bowman, not only avoids floor 13 of hotels and

Morrow teammate Clark Gillies.

room numbers that add up to 13, but he believes that a 20-year-old comb has helped make him the winningest coach in NHL history.

"This all has to do with psychological comfort," says Matt Vukovich, a professor of health and physical education, who studies athletes' patterns. "They've probably had a good performance at one time, and they want to repeat it, so they try to replicate their training, diet, clothes, sleep patterns."

Don't Worry: Something Is Bound to Happen

■ "The saddest thing about the omens is their inconsistency," writes Brewton Berry in *You and Your Superstitions*. "They are as inharmonious as the Democratic Party. . . . What if your nose itches? You will have a visitor. You are going to be angry. You will see your true love before night. Someone is thinking of you. You will kiss a stranger. You are going to kiss a fool. Or, according to canny New Englanders, it means that you will either be kissed, cussed, or vexed. Can't miss." □□

General Weather Forecast
2 0 0 0 - 2 0 0 1

(For detailed regional forecasts, see pages 134-153.)

Most years in the past decade were, overall, much warmer than normal. Although the coming year is not expected to bring back memories of bone-chilling, thumb-numbing winters, it will bring temperatures pretty close to normal. Of more concern is the possibility of significant drought from the Desert Southwest across Texas, Oklahoma, and parts of the Deep South, and northward through the central Great Plains.

November through March will start relatively cold across much of the country, with only the nation's southeast quadrant and perhaps New England expected to be at or above normal. The pattern will shift in December, with warmer-than-normal temperatures in the western half of the nation and colder-than-normal temperatures in the East. In January, cold air will dominate from the northern Great Plains into the Southeast, and relatively mild temperatures will prevail in the Northeast and the Southwest. February will be relatively mild in most of the country, with colder-than-normal temperatures limited to the West Coast, the Rockies, and the northern Great Plains. The pattern will reverse again in March, with above-normal temperatures in Florida, Georgia, portions of the Great Lakes region, and most places west of the Mississippi.

Precipitation will be above normal in portions of New England, western New York, the Ohio Valley, and Arkansas, and well above normal in the Pacific Northwest. Precipitation will be below normal across the Desert Southwest, from Texas northward through the Great Plains, in much of the Deep South, and from New York City southward to Florida.

Snowfall will be greater than normal from New York City and New England westward through much of the Great Lakes region, the northernmost Great Plains, the northern Rockies, and the Pacific Northwest, and down the spine of the Sierras. Also expect a swath of above-normal snowfall from southwestern Texas into central Oklahoma. Folks in other areas prone to snow can expect below-normal snowfall.

April and May will be relatively cool everywhere except in Florida, Texas, the central Great Plains, and most of the Southwest. Rainfall will be below normal in the Middle Atlantic states, southern Florida, the Deep South, the central Great Plains, the Desert Southwest, and the Pacific Northwest. Above-normal rainfall will be the rule in eastern Georgia, northern Florida, and southern California; near Lakes Erie and Ontario; and along the Canadian border from the Rockies eastward to upper Michigan.

June through August will be hotter than normal from the Middle Atlantic and southeastern states westward to Texas and the central Great Plains. Expect cooler-than-normal temperatures from Maine into the Adirondacks and from upper Michigan westward to Washington and Oregon.

Rainfall will be below normal, with the threat of drought, from Maine to Florida; across the Ohio and Tennessee Valleys; and in Alabama, Texas, Oklahoma, the eastern Rockies, and the Desert Southwest. The Great Lakes and Mississippi Valley will be wet. Elsewhere, rainfall should be close to normal.

September through October will be drier than normal in the Desert Southwest, from Texas northward through the Plains states, in the western Ohio and Tennessee Valleys, and throughout the Great Lakes region. A tropical storm in mid-September will bring much-needed rains from the Florida panhandle to southern New England. Elsewhere, rainfall should be near normal. Temperatures will be cooler than normal in the Northeast and the Atlantic coastal states. Expect warmer-than-normal temperatures in most areas west of the Mississippi.

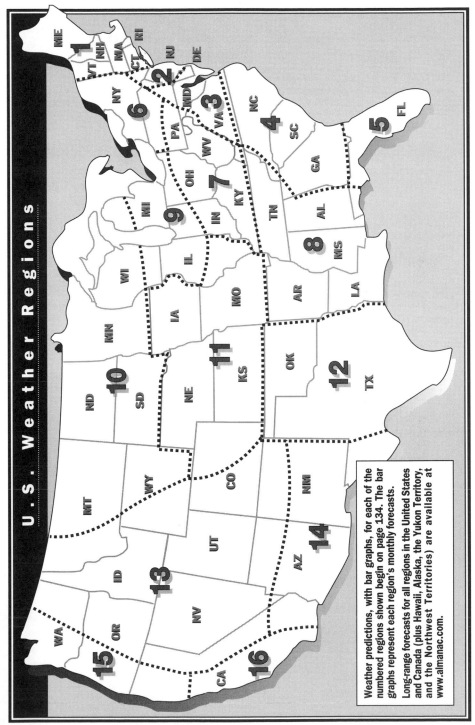

U.S. Weather Regions

ME

1

VT NH MA
CT RI

NJ DE

2

NY MD

6

3

NC

PA

VA

SC

4

WV

5

FL

OH

7

GA

MI

KY

TN

AL

9

IN

8

MS

IL

WI

AR

LA

MO

IA

MN

11

KS

OK

12

10

NE

TX

ND

SD

WY

CO

NM

MT

14

UT

AZ

13

ID

NV

15

WA

OR

16

CA

Weather predictions, with bar graphs, for each of the numbered regions shown begin on page 134. The bar graphs represent each region's monthly forecasts.

Long-range forecasts for all regions in the United States and Canada (plus Hawaii, Alaska, the Yukon Territory, and the Northwest Territories) are available at www.almanac.com.

New England

SUMMARY: If you're looking for an old-fashioned New England winter, with bone-chilling cold, frequent northeasters, and snow up to your windowsill, this isn't the winter for you. Rather, expect a winter with temperatures a bit above normal, precipitation near normal, and snow up to your knees. November and December will be colder than normal before a substantial January thaw. February will be warmer than normal before a cold March. The biggest snowstorms of the season are expected in mid-November, late January, mid-February, and mid-March. Expect record cold in mid-December, with another cold spell around New Year's and relatively cold weather in mid-March.

April and May will continue cool, with temperatures about three degrees below normal. Most places will see some snow in April. Precipitation will be near normal. May will be cool, with a warm spell in the last week.

The summer season will be pleasant. Temperatures from June through August will be close to normal across southern New England and cooler in the north. Watch for hot spells in the first and fourth weeks of June and in mid- to late August. Rainfall will be frequent enough in most spots to avoid any prolonged dry spells.

September will be wetter and cooler than normal. October will start with heavy rain, with another storm at midmonth, but otherwise, the month will be mostly dry and pleasant.

NOV. 2000: Temp. 43° (avg.); precip. 3" (1" below avg.). 1-5 Cool, rain; snow north. 6-11 Mild, then rain to snow. 12-16 Cold, periods of snow. 17-24 Brisk, chilly, flurries. 25-30 Mild, rain and snow showers.

DEC. 2000: Temp. 29° (2° below avg.); precip. 2.5" (1" below avg.; 2.5" below south). 1-8 Cold, sunny; flurries north. 9-12 Some sun, seasonable. 13-17 Blustery, bitter cold. 18-22 Sunny, mild, then cold. 23-27 Flurries, cold. 28-31 Snow, not as cold.

JAN. 2001: Temp. 28° (2° above avg.; 6° above north); precip. 4" (1" above avg.). 1-9 Windy, mild, frequent rain. 10-13 Cool; snow south. 14-18 Seasonable south; snow, mild north. 19-24 Seasonable, snow; rain south. 25-31 Periods of snow; rain, snow south.

FEB. 2001: Temp. 32° (5° above avg.); precip. 3.5" (0.5" above avg.). 1-6 Mild, rain south; snow north, some heavy. 7-13 Cold, snowstorm. 14-17 Sunny, cold. 18-22 Rain, mild, then cold and snow. 23-28 Mild, a few showers.

MAR. 2001: Temp. 35° (3° below avg.); precip. 5" (1.5" above avg.; avg. north). 1-3 Heavy rain, snow. 4-7 Seasonable. 8-13 Cold; heavy snow. 14-17 Sunny, cold. 18-22 Snowstorm, cold. 23-25 Snow. 26-31 Warm, a few showers.

APR. 2001: Temp. 46° (3° below avg.); precip. 3.5" (avg.). 1-6 Rain, snow, then sunny and cool. 7-12 Seasonable, sun, showers. 13-20 Chilly, periods of rain, snow. 21-23 Warm, thunderstorms. 24-30 Seasonable, rain.

MAY 2001: Temp. 54° (3° below avg.); precip. 3.5" (avg.). 1-9 Sunny, seasonable, a few showers. 10-14 Rain, chilly. 15-20 Rain, mild, then sunny days and chilly nights. 21-24 Rain, cool. 25-31 Warm, thunderstorms.

JUNE 2001: Temp. 65° (1° below avg. north; 1° above south); precip. 2" (1.5" below avg.). 1-5 Showers, cool. 6-10 Hot, humid, thunderstorms. 11-14 Sunny, cool. 15-22 Warm, a few thunderstorms. 23-26 Sunny, hot, humid. 27-30 Heavy rain, cool.

JULY 2001: Temp. 68° (3° below avg.); precip. 2.5" (1" below avg.). 1-10 Warm, sunny, a few thunderstorms. 11-14 Sunny. 15-19 Showers. 20-31 Sunny south; showers, cool north.

AUG. 2001: Temp. 72° (2° above avg.; 1° below north); precip. 3.5" (avg.). 1-7 Warm, sunny, a few showers. 8-12 Sunny, warm. 13-18 Cool, rain. 19-25 Hot, then cool and dry. 26-31 Warm, a few thunderstorms.

SEPT. 2001: Temp. 58° (5° below avg.); precip. 4" (1" above avg.). 1-5 Rain, then sunny and cool. 6-11 Mild, then rain and raw. 12-18 Chilly, periods of rain. 19-21 Sunny, cool. 22-30 Rain, cool.

OCT. 2001: Temp. 55° (1° above avg.); precip. 3.5" (1" below avg. north; 1" above south). 1-2 Heavy rain. 3-6 Sunny days, frosty nights. 7-11 Sunny, warm. 12-15 Sunny, seasonable. 16-23 Heavy rain, then sunny. 24-31 Showers, mild.

Caribou

Burlington

Boston

Hartford

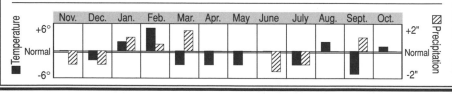

Greater New York–New Jersey

SUMMARY: Overall, November through March will be milder and drier than normal, with slightly above-normal snowfall. The winter season will start colder than in recent years, with below-normal temperatures in November and December and maybe a white Christmas. Then January and February will bring relatively mild temperatures, with occasional cold spells. Although March will come in like a wet lamb, there's the possibility of heavy snow around midmonth, with well below normal temperatures. In fact, March will be snowier than the months from November through February combined. The coldest weather will be in mid-December, with other cold spells coming at midmonth in November, January, February, and March.

Temperatures in April and May will be cooler than normal, despite an abundance of sunshine. Although rainfall will generally be below normal, enough is expected for an abundance of May flowers.

June through August will be drier than normal. Look for the first heat wave of the season in the first full week of June, with more hot weather a couple of weeks later. Although July will bring its usual hot weather, relatively cool temperatures will prevail through a good part of the month. August will be hot, especially in the first half of the month.

Watch for an early frost in the interior in September, as the month brings cool temperatures with near-normal rainfall. October will be wet, with frequent rains beginning in midmonth.

NOV. 2000: Temp. 44° (1° below avg.); precip. 2.5" (1" below avg.). 1-5 Rain arriving, cool. 6-10 Sunny, mild, then rain. 11-14 Cold, rain to snow. 15-21 Sunny, cool. 22-25 Showers, cold. 26-30 Mild, sprinkles.

DEC. 2000: Temp. 33° (2° below avg.); precip. 1.5" (2" below avg.). 1-11 Rain, snow, then sunny and cold. 12-16 Cold with occasional snow. 17-22 Cold, clear. 23-31 Flurries, then mild.

JAN. 2001: Temp. 30° (1° above avg.); precip. 3" (avg.). 1-7 Mild, rain. 8-14 Cold; light snow. 15-22 Sunny, cold. 23-31 Mild, periods of rain, some heavy.

FEB. 2001: Temp. 36° (5° above avg.); precip. 4" (0.5" above avg.). 1-9 Mild, sunny, a few showers. 10-13 Cold, rain, snow. 14-17 Sunny, cold. 18-22 Periods of rain, snow. 23-28 Mild, occasional rain.

MAR. 2001: Temp. 38° (2° below avg.); precip. 4.5" (1" above avg.). 1-5 Rain, mild. 6-9 Heavy rain, cold. 10-14 Snowstorm, cold. 15-18 Cold, flurries. 19-23 Snow, cold. 24-31 Mild, periods of rain.

APR. 2001: Temp. 47° (3° below avg.); precip. 4" (0.5" above avg.). 1-8 Rain, then sunny and cold. 9-15 Rain, continued cool. 16-20 Cool, rain, wet snow. 21-30 Warm, showers.

MAY 2001: Temp. 57° (3° below avg.); precip. 3.5" (0.5" below avg.). 1-5 Cool, dry. 6-9 Hot, thunderstorms. 10-14 Cool, occasional rain. 15-20 Cool, dry. 21-23 Rain, cool. 24-27 Hot, rain. 28-31 Sunny, comfortable.

JUNE 2001: Temp. 70.5° (0.5° above avg.); precip. 2.5" (1" below avg.). 1-5 Cool, a few thunderstorms. 6-9 Sunny, hot, humid. 10-14 Thunderstorms, then sunny and cool. 15-21 Warm, humid, a few thunderstorms. 22-26 Sunny, hot. 27-30 Heavy rain, cool.

JULY 2001: Temp. 72° (3° below avg.); precip. 3" (1" below avg.). 1-10 Warm, a few showers. 11-15 Cool; heavy rain. 16-22 Warm, humid, a few thunderstorms. 23-28 Sunny. 29-31 Rain.

AUG. 2001: Temp. 75° (2° above avg.); precip. 3" (1" below avg.). 1-5 Sunny, hot. 6-12 Hot, humid, a few thunderstorms. 13-20 Rain, then sunny and cool. 21-31 Warm, thunderstorms.

SEPT. 2001: Temp. 61° (5° below avg.); precip. 2.5" (1" below avg.). 1-5 Sunny, cool. 6-11 Periods of rain, seasonable. 12-16 Chilly; light rain. 17-22 Warm, rain, then cool. 23-30 Sunny, then rain.

OCT. 2001: Temp. 56° (1° above avg.); precip. 4" (1" above avg.). 1-7 Sunny, cool. 8-11 Sunny, warm. 12-17 Rainy intervals, seasonable. 18-23 Pleasant north; light rain south. 24-27 Rain, warm. 28-31 Cool, some sun.

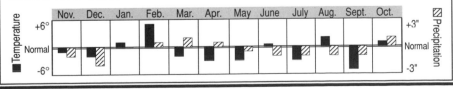

Middle Atlantic Coast

SUMMARY: The winter will be colder than in recent years, with temperatures from November through March averaging close to normal. Snowfall and precipitation will be below normal. The season will get off to a cold start in November and December. January will be near normal, followed by a mild February. Cold spells in March will be interrupted by days with springtime warmth. The snowiest periods will occur in mid-November and mid-January. The coldest spells will be in mid-December, mid-January, and mid-March. Stormiest periods are expected in late January and the first half of March.

April and May will be pleasant overall, with temperatures cooler than normal. Rainfall will be below normal in the north and near normal in the south. Expect the season's first hot weather in the first or second week of May.

Summer temperatures will be hotter than normal but mostly without prolonged extreme heat. Rainfall overall will be below normal, despite heavy rain in late June and mid-July. August, in particular, will be dry, with few thunderstorms.

September will be changeable. Rapidly moving weather systems and 30-degree temperature swings will be common. Watch for a heavy rainstorm late in the month, then above-normal rainfall in October.

NOV. 2000: Temp. 48° (1° below avg.); precip. 2" (1" below avg.). 1-4 Rain; snow west. 5-12 Sunny, warm, then showers. 13-18 Rain, snow, then sunny and seasonable. 19-25 Showers, then sunny and cold. 26-30 Flurries, then warm.

DEC. 2000: Temp. 37° (2° below avg.); precip. 1" (2" below avg.). 1-4 Periods of rain and snow. 5-11 Sunny, cold. 12-17 Showers, cold. 18-22 Warm, then sunny and cold. 23-31 Sprinkles, mild.

JAN. 2001: Temp. 34° (avg.); precip. 3.5" (0.5" above avg.). 1-6 Mild, some rain. 7-9 Sunny, pleasant. 10-14 Rain, snow. 15-18 Cold. 19-24 Some rain, snow, warm. 25-31 Rain; snow west.

FEB. 2001: Temp. 41° (4° above avg.); precip. 3" (avg.). 1-4 Sunny, warm. 5-14 Alternating showers and sun, mild. 15-19 Cold, then rain and mild. 20-22 Sprinkles, cool. 23-28 Showers, then sunny and warm.

MAR. 2001: Temp. 44° (2° below avg.); precip. 4" (0.5" above avg.). 1-4 Rain, then sun. 5-9 Heavy rain; snow north. 10-13 Cold, rain south; snow north. 14-17 Sunny, mild. 18-23 Chilly; light rain. 24-27 Sunny, mild. 28-31 Thunderstorms, warm.

APR. 2001: Temp. 54° (2° below avg.); precip. 2.5" (1" below avg.). 1-4 Rain, then pleasant. 5-12 Rain, cool. 13-17 Sunny, cool. 18-24 Showers, warm. 25-30 Rain, seasonable.

MAY 2001: Temp. 63° (2° below avg.); precip. 4" (1" below avg. north; 1" above south). 1-3 Sunny, cool. 4-8 Turning hot, humid. 9-12 Showers, cool. 13-17 Seasonable, a few thunderstorms. 18-27 Cool, rain. 28-31 Clear days, crisp nights.

JUNE 2001: Temp. 76° (2° above avg.); precip. 3.5" (0.5" above avg. east; 1" below west). 1-5 Dry, warm. 6-11 Hot, sunny. 12-15 Cool, showers. 16-21 Sunny, hot, a few thunderstorms. 22-24 Sunny, warm. 25-30 Hot, humid, then thunderstorms and cool.

JULY 2001: Temp. 76° (2° below avg.); precip. 4.5" (avg.). 1-8 A few thunderstorms, then pleasant. 9-18 Warm, thunderstorms. 19-23 Hot, thunderstorms. 24-26 Sunny, pleasant. 27-31 Cool, a few showers.

AUG. 2001: Temp. 78° (2° above avg.); precip. 2.5" (2" below avg.). 1-8 Hot, a few thunderstorms. 9-12 Sunny, hot. 13-15 Thunderstorms, cool. 16-19 Sunny, cool. 20-25 Hot, humid. 26-31 A few thunderstorms.

SEPT. 2001: Temp. 67° (3° below avg.); precip. 2.5" (1" below avg.; 1" above southwest). 1-4 Sunny days, chilly nights. 5-8 Sprinkles, warm. 9-15 Warm, thunderstorms, then cool. 16-19 Dry. 20-22 Chilly; heavy rain. 23-26 Pleasant. 27-30 Light rain.

OCT. 2001: Temp. 60° (1° above avg.); precip. 5" (2" above avg.). 1-7 Sunny, cool. 8-13 Warm, rain. 14-21 Frequent rain. 22-28 Warm, rain. 29-31 Cool.

Baltimore

Washington

Richmond

Roanoke

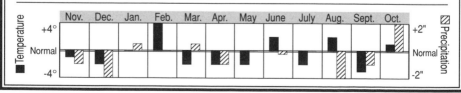

Black Listed Cancer Treatment Could Save Your Life

Baltimore, MD—As unbelievable as it seems the key to stopping many cancers has been around for over 30 years. Yet it has been banned. Blocked. And kept out of your medicine cabinet by the very agency designed to protect your health—the FDA.

In 1966, the senior oncologist at St. Vincent's Hospital in New York rocked the medical world when he developed a serum that **"shrank cancer tumors in 45 minutes!"** 90 minutes later they were gone... Headlines hit every major paper around the world. Scientists and researchers applauded. Time and again this life saving treatment worked miracles, but the FDA ignored the research and hope he brought and shut him down.

You read that right. He was not only shut down—but also forced out of the country where others benefited from his discovery. That was 32 years ago. How many other treatments have they been allowed to hide?

Decades ago, European research scientist Dr. Johanna Budwig, a six-time Nobel Award nominee, discovered a totally natural formula that not only protects against the development of cancer, but people all over the world who have been diagnosed with incurable cancer and sent home to die have actually benefited from her research—and now lead normal lives.

After 30 years of study, Dr. Budwig discovered that the blood of seriously ill cancer patients was deficient in certain substances and nutrients. Yet, healthy blood always contained these ingredients. It was the lack of these nutrients that allowed cancer cells to grow wild and out of control.

By simply eating a combination of two natural and delicious foods (found on page 134) not only can cancer be prevented—but in case after case it was actually healed! "Symptoms of cancer, liver dysfunction, and diabetes were completely alleviated." Remarkably, what Dr. Budwig discovered was a totally natural way for eradicating cancer.

However, when she went to publish these results so that everyone could benefit—**she was blocked by manufacturers with heavy financial stakes!** For over 10 years now her methods have proved effective—yet she is denied publication—blocked by the giants who don't want you to read her words.

What's more, the world is full of expert minds like Dr. Budwig who have pursued cancer remedies and come up with remarkable natural formulas and diets that work for hundreds and thousands of patients. *How to Fight Cancer and Win* author William Fischer has studied these methods and revealed their secrets for you—so that you or someone you love may be spared the horrors of conventional cancer treatments.

As early as 1947, Virginia Livingston, M.D., isolated a cancer-causing microbe. She noted that every cancer sample analyzed (whether human or other animal) contained it.

This microbe—a bacteria that is actually in each of us from birth to death—multiplies and promotes cancer when the immune system is weakened by disease, stress, or poor nutrition. Worst of all, the microbes secrete a special hormone protector that short-circuits our body's immune system—allowing the microbes to grow undetected for years. No wonder so many patients are riddled with cancer by the time it is detected. But there is hope even for them...

Turn to page 82 of *How to Fight Cancer and Win* for the delicious diet that can help stop the formation of cancer cells and shrink tumors.

They walked away from traditional cancer treatments... and were healed! Throughout the pages of *How to Fight Cancer and Win* you'll meet real people who were diagnosed with cancer—suffered through harsh conventional treatments—only to be miraculously healed by natural means! Here is just a sampling of what others have to say about the book.

"We purchased *How to Fight Cancer and Win*, and immediately my husband started following the recommended diet for his just diagnosed colon cancer. He refused the surgery that our doctors advised. Since following the regime recommended in the book he has had no problems at all, cancer-wise. If not cured, we believe the cancer has to be in remission."—*Thelma B.*

"I bought *How to Fight Cancer and Win* and this has to be the greatest book I've ever read. I have had astounding results from the easy to understand knowledge found in this book. My whole life has improved drastically and I have done so much for many others. The information goes far beyond the health thinking of today."—*Hugh M.*

"I can't find adequate words to describe my appreciation of your work in providing *How to Fight Cancer and Win*. You had to do an enormous amount of research to bring this vast and most important knowledge to your readers.

My doctor found two tumors on my prostate with a high P.S.A. He scheduled a time to surgically remove the prostate, but I canceled the appointment. Instead I went on the diet discussed in the book combined with another supplement. Over the months my P.S.A. has lowered until the last reading was one point two." —*Duncan M.*

"In my 55 years as a Country Family Physician, I have never read a more 'down to earth,' practical resume of cancer prevention and treatments, than in this book. It needs to be studied worldwide for the prevention of cancer by all researchers who are looking for a cure."—*Edward S., MD*

"As a cancer patient who has been battling lymphatic cancer on and off for almost three years now, I was very pleased to stumble across *How to fight Cancer and Win*. The book was inspiring, well-written and packed with useful information for any cancer patient looking to maximize his or her chances for recovery."—*Romany S.*

"I've been incorporating Dr. Budgwig's natural remedy into my diet and have told others about it. Your book is very informative and has information I've never heard about before (and I've read many books on the cancer and nutrition link). Thanks for the wonderful information."—*Molly G.*

Don't waste another minute. There are only a limited number of books in stock—and unless order volume is extraordinarily high we may not be able to print more life-saving copies. Claim your book today and you will be one of the lucky few who no longer have to wait for cures that get pushed "underground" by big business and money hungry giants.

To get your copy of *How to Fight Cancer and Win* call **1-888-821-3609 and ask for code 1897** to order by credit card. Or write "Fight Cancer—Dept. FCBK-1897F" on a plain piece of paper with your name, address, phone number (in case we have a question about your order) and a check for $19.95 plus $4.00 S&H (MD residents, add 5% sales tax) and mail to: **Agora Health Books, Dept. FCBK-1897F, P.O. Box 977, Frederick, MD 21705-9838.**

If you are not completely satisfied, return the book within one year for a complete and total refund—no questions asked. This will probably be the most important information you and your loved ones receive—so order today!

© 2000 Agora South Inc.

Piedmont and Southeast Coast

SUMMARY: November through March will bring near- to slightly above normal temperatures, with near-normal precipitation in the north and below-normal amounts in the south. Snowfall will be below normal, with the best chance for snow in mid-January in the northern interior. Watch for a severe freeze toward the end of November. Other cold spells will occur in early to mid-December and early to mid-January. The stormiest weather will occur in mid- and late January and the first half of March.

April and May will be cooler than normal, especially in the north. Rainfall will be near or below normal in the west and above normal in the east.

The summer season will be hotter than normal, with few, if any, prolonged heat waves. Rainfall will be less than normal, especially in the interior, where drought will threaten in August and the first half of September. The most widespread thunderstorms are expected from mid-June to mid-July, with few thunderstorms in August.

After a dry start to September, the remains of a tropical storm moving northeastward from the Gulf of Mexico will bring heavy rain. October will be pleasant, with more sunshine than normal for the month.

NOV. 2000: Temp. 55° (avg.); precip. 2.5" (0.5" below avg.). 1-4 Cool, rain. 5-10 Warm, dry. 11-13 Rain, cool. 14-16 Sunny, warm. 17-21 Seasonable, periods of rain. 22-25 Sunny, widespread freeze. 26-30 Warm, showers.

DEC. 2000: Temp. 46° (avg.); precip. 3" (1" below avg.). 1-11 Showers, then sunny and cold. 12-16 Rain, then sunny and cold. 17-20 Sunny, warm. 21-24 Cold, rain. 25-31 Mild west; rain coast.

JAN. 2001: Temp. 41° (1° below avg.); precip. 5" (1" above avg.). 1-6 Cold, sunny coast; sprinkles elsewhere. 7-11 Cold. 12-18 Rain; some snow inland. 19-25 Mild, a few showers. 26-31 Rain, warm.

FEB. 2001: Temp. 47° (3° above avg.); precip. 3.5" (avg.). 1-5 Mild; light rain. 6-9 Mild. 10-14 Warm, rain, thunderstorms. 15-17 Sunny, cool. 18-25 Showers, seasonable. 26-28 Warm.

MAR. 2001: Temp. 53.5° (2° below avg. north; 1° above south); precip. 4" (1" above avg. north; 2" below south). 1-6 Seasonable, showers. 7-10 Heavy rain, cool. 11-19 Sunny, cold. 20-22 Warm. 23-31 Warm, a few thunderstorms.

APR. 2001: Temp. 60.5° (1.5° below avg.); precip. 4.5" (1" above avg.). 1-5 Cool, rain. 6-10 Warm; heavy rain. 11-16 Sunny, cool days, cold nights. 17-23 Sunny, warm. 24-30 Warm, showers, thunderstorms.

MAY 2001: Temp. 69.5° (2° below avg. north; 1° above south); precip. 3.5" (2" below avg. west; 2" above east). 1-5 Rain, then pleasant. 6-9 Sunny, hot. 10-15 Sunny, warm. 16-20 Hot, thunderstorms, then sunny and cool. 21-25 Sunny, warm. 26-31 Thunderstorms, cool.

JUNE 2001: Temp. 77° (1° above avg.); precip. 4" (2" below avg. west; 2" above east). 1-6 Sunny, warm. 7-10 Warm, humid; thunderstorms west. 11-15 A few thunderstorms. 16-22 Hot, humid, a few thunderstorms. 23-30 Warm, a few thunderstorms.

JULY 2001: Temp. 80° (1° below avg. north; 1° above south); precip. 4.5" (avg.). 1-6 Heavy thunderstorms, then sunny and warm. 7-14 Hot, humid, thunderstorms. 15-20 Hazy sun, hot; thunderstorms west. 21-24 Hot, humid, thunderstorms. 25-29 Thunderstorms, cool. 30-31 Sunny, hot.

AUG. 2001: Temp. 79° (1° above avg.); precip. 1.5" (2" below avg.). 1-12 Hot, sunny, a few thunderstorms. 13-17 Thunderstorms, then sunny and cool. 18-31 Warm, humid, a few thunderstorms.

SEPT. 2001: Temp. 72° (2° below avg.); precip. 2.5" (1" below avg.; 3" above west). 1-6 Warm days, chilly nights. 7-10 Sunny, hot. 11-17 Thunderstorms, then pleasant. 18-21 Tropical rains, flooding possible. 22-25 Sunny, cool. 26-30 Warm, rain.

OCT. 2001: Temp. 64° (avg.); precip. 3" (avg.). 1-6 Sunny, cool. 7-9 Sunny, warm. 10-16 Rainy periods. 17-19 Some sun, warm. 20-24 Occasional rain. 25-31 A few showers.

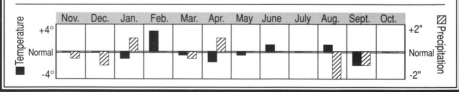

Florida

SUMMARY: November through March will have close-to-normal temperatures, with a relatively chilly December and January but generally mild weather in November and February. Expect some frost into central Florida in early January, but odds are against a severe freeze. Rainfall will be near normal from November through January, with dry weather being the rule in February and March. The rainiest periods will come in early November and mid-January. Some spots will see no rain at all in March.

Rainfall will pick up in April, although South Florida is expected to remain drier than normal until early May. Temperatures in April and May will be close to normal.

The summer season will be hotter and drier than normal. The most prolonged hot spell is expected from mid-July through the first ten days of August. Expect the heaviest rain in June across the north, with below-normal rainfall in much of the south. July thunderstorm activity will be less than usual across most of the state, with pockets of drought possible, especially across the south. Above-normal rainfall is expected in the south in August.

September and October will be one to two degrees cooler than normal, with below-normal rainfall in much of the state, despite the threat of two tropical storms. The first of these storms will bring heavy rain in mid-September, especially in the north. The second storm will threaten central and northern areas in the second week of October.

NOV. 2000: Temp. 69° (1° above avg.); precip. 3" (1" above avg.; 1" below south). 1-4 Rain. 5-12 Sunny, warm. 13-16 Showers, cool. 17-22 Sunny, warm, then showers. 23-25 Sunny, chilly. 26-30 Warm, thunderstorms.

DEC. 2000: Temp. 62° (1° below avg.); precip. 2" (2" below avg. north; 1" above south). 1-9 Cool, a few showers. 10-13 Chilly; freeze north. 14-19 Sunny, cool north; seasonable south. 20-22 Showers. 23-31 Sunny, chilly.

JAN. 2001: Temp. 59° (2° below avg.); precip. 3.5" (0.5" above avg.). 1-9 Sunny, chilly; frost central. 10-13 A few showers. 14-18 Rain, chilly north; warm south. 19-22 Sunny, cool. 23-25 Warm. 26-31 Warm, a few thunderstorms.

FEB. 2001: Temp. 65° (2° above avg.); precip. 2" (1" below avg.). 1-5 Warm, a few thunderstorms. 6-8 Sunny, cool. 9-14 Sunny, warm; thunderstorms north. 15-18 Sunny, cool. 19-28 Sunny, warm; a few showers north.

MAR. 2001: Temp. 67° (avg.); precip. 1.5" (2" below avg.). 1-10 Sunny, warm, mainly dry. 11-21 Cool, sunny. 22-31 Sunny, becoming warm.

APR. 2001: Temp. 71.5° (0.5° below avg.); precip. 5" (2" above avg.; 2" below south). 1-4 Cool, rain. 5-9 Sunny, cool, then warm. 10-17 Showers, then sunny and cool. 18-26 Thunderstorms, warm. 27-30 Warm, a few thunderstorms.

MAY 2001: Temp. 76° (1° above avg.); precip. 4" (avg.). 1-5 Heavy rain south; cool north. 6-10 Sunny, warm. 11-17 Sunny, warm north; thunderstorms, then sunny south. 18-21 Warm, thunderstorms. 22-31 Warm, thunderstorms.

JUNE 2001: Temp. 79.5° (0.5° below avg.); precip. 6" (2" above avg. north, 2" below south). 1-8 Warm, dry. 9-17 Warm, a few thunderstorms. 18-30 Daily thunderstorms, hot.

JULY 2001: Temp. 83° (1° above avg.); precip. 3.5" (3.5" below avg.). 1-9 Thunderstorms, then sunny and hot. 10-21 Hot, humid, a few thunderstorms. 22-31 Hot, humid, thunderstorms.

AUG. 2001: Temp. 82.5° (0.5° above avg.); precip. 7.5" (1" below avg. north; 2" above south). 1-9 Hot, a few thunderstorms. 10-17 Warm, sunny; thunderstorms south and central. 18-21 Sunny, hot. 22-27 Hot, humid, thunderstorms. 28-31 Thunderstorms, warm.

SEPT. 2001: Temp. 78° (2° below avg.); precip. 4" (2" below avg.). 1-8 Thunderstorms, then cool north; showers south. 9-13 Warm, thunderstorms. 14-20 Tropical storm possible. 21-23 Cool north; thunderstorms south. 24-30 Pleasant, then thunderstorms.

OCT. 2001: Temp. 74° (1° below avg.); precip. 7" (4" above avg. north; 2" below south). 1-3 Sunny, warm. 4-7 Seasonable, rain. 8-11 Tropical storm possible. 12-20 Sunny, then thunderstorms. 21-27 Sunny. 28-31 Thunderstorms.

Jacksonville

Tampa

Orlando

Miami

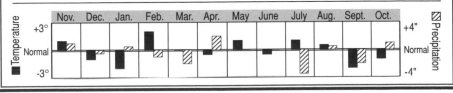

Upstate New York

SUMMARY: The winter will bring temperatures near or slightly colder than normal, with near-normal precipitation but above-normal snowfall. November and December will have frequent cold spells, with heavy lake snows. Snowstorms outside the snow belts will occur toward mid-November and in mid-December. Watch for the coldest temperatures of the season in mid- and late December. Expect a battle between cold and mild air masses in January, before a relatively mild February. March will be on the cold side, with a major snowstorm in the second week and a couple more snow events in the second half of the month.

Watch for an April Fool's snowstorm, with more snow in midmonth, followed by the first warm weather of the spring. It won't last long, though, as April and May will be two to three degrees cooler than normal. Expect abundant rainfall, with above-normal precipitation in most of the region.

June through August will bring near-normal temperatures and above-normal rainfall in most spots, although the southeast will be cooler and drier than normal. The hottest spells will come in early and late June and in mid- to late August. June will be a pleasant month, with below-normal rainfall. July will see temperatures relatively cool for what is normally the hottest month of the year. That honor will go to August, which will also be the wettest month of the summer.

September will be much cooler than normal, followed by a relatively mild October. Rainfall will be below normal.

NOV. 2000: Temp. 37° (2° below avg.); precip. 3.5" (1" below avg. east; 1" above west). 1-5 Chilly, sprinkles, flurries. 6-10 Mild, rain. 11-15 Snow, windy, cold. 16-21 Cold, rain and snow showers. 22-26 Windy, cold; heavy lake snows. 27-30 Mild, rain, then flurries and colder.

DEC. 2000: Temp. 26° (1° below avg.); precip. 1.5" (1.5" below avg.). 1-12 Cold, lake squalls. 13-17 Bitter cold, snow. 18-27 Thaw, then cold with lake snows. 28-31 Mild, flurries.

JAN. 2001: Temp. 21° (avg.); precip. 2.5" (avg.). 1-6 Flurries, then mild with showers. 7-9 Seasonable. 10-20 Flurries, cold. 21-23 Mild. 24-26 Snow north; rain south. 27-31 Flurries, then rain and mild.

FEB. 2001: Temp. 27° (4° above avg.); precip. 3" (0.5" above avg.). 1-9 Mild, rain; snow north. 10-14 Seasonable, rain, snow. 15-19 Cold, snow, then warm and rain. 20-23 Cold, snow. 24-28 Mild, showers.

MAR. 2001: Temp. 31° (2° below avg.); precip. 3.5" (0.5" above avg.). 1-4 Rain, then cold. 5-7 Mild, then flurries. 8-13 Heavy snow, cold. 14-16 Sunny, cold. 17-20 Snow, cold. 21-22 Sunny, cold. 23-25 Rain, snow. 26-31 Warm, showers.

APR. 2001: Temp. 42° (3° below avg.); precip. 4" (1" above avg.). 1-8 Snowstorm, then sunny days and cold nights. 9-12 Rain. 13-18 Chilly, rain, snow. 19-23 Warm, thunderstorms. 24-30 Cool, rain.

MAY 2001: Temp. 54° (2° below avg.); precip. 4" (2" above avg. northwest; 1" below southeast). 1-8 Sunny, warm, a few thunderstorms. 9-14 Cool, showers. 15-17 Warm, thunderstorms. 18-21 Cool, rain. 22-25 Warm, thunderstorms. 26-31 Rain, cool, then pleasant.

JUNE 2001: Temp. 66° (2° above avg. west; avg. east); precip. 2.5" (1" below avg.). 1-9 Hot, a few thunderstorms. 10-14 Sunny, cool. 15-19 Warm, a few thunderstorms. 20-23 Thunderstorms, then sunny and cool. 24-26 Hot, thunderstorms. 27-30 Damp, cool.

JULY 2001: Temp. 68° (3° below avg.); precip. 4" (2" above avg. west; 1" below east). 1-8 Cool, thunderstorms. 9-13 Sunny; cool nights. 14-21 Warm, showers. 22-28 Sunny; cool nights. 29-31 Humid, showers.

AUG. 2001: Temp. 69° (1° above avg.); precip. 4" (avg.; 3" above north). 1-7 Warm, a few showers. 8-11 Sunny, warm. 12-17 Showers, cool. 18-21 Clouds, sun. 22-26 Hot, humid; heavy thunderstorms. 27-31 Warm, thunderstorms.

SEPT. 2001: Temp. 56° (5° below avg.); precip. 3" (0.5" below avg.). 1-4 Chilly. 5-7 Sunny, warm. 8-17 Cool, rain. 18-21 Sunny, cool. 22-30 Showers, cool.

OCT. 2001: Temp. 53° (3° above avg.); precip. 1.5" (1.5" below avg.). 1-6 Sunny; cold nights. 7-11 Sunny, warm. 12-15 Cool. 16-21 Showers, then cool. 22-26 Warm. 27-31 Showers, cool.

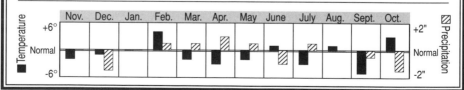

Indiana Firm Discovers:

Special *New* cream for arthritis

(SPECIAL)–A small company in central Indiana has developed a special cream that relieves arthritis pain in minutes, even chronic arthritis pain—deep in the joints. The product which is called **PAIN-BUST-R-II,** is one of the fastest acting therapeutic formulas ever developed in the fight against arthritis. Immediately upon application it goes to work by penetrating deep to the areas most affected—the joints themselves, bringing fast relief where relief is needed most. Men and women who have suffered arthritis pain for years are reporting incredible results with this product. Even a single application seems to work remarkably well in relieving pain and bringing comfort to cramped, knotted joints. ***PAIN-BUST-R-II** was researched and formulated to be absorbed directly into the joints and muscles—where the pain originates. Long-time arthritis sufferers will be glad to know that this formula will help put an end to agonizing days and sleepless nights. It is highly recommended by users who have resumed daily activities and are enjoying life again.

Read what our users have to say:

"I use **PAIN BUST** because I suffer from tension in my back and shoulders. I can't praise your product enough, I've used other ointments, but they don't seem to work as fast nor last as long. Thank you. Thank you...Thank you!" *C.K.F.*

"Last night when I went to sleep I rubbed some **PAIN BUST** on my sore aching knee. 15 minutes later I fell sound asleep and woke 8 hours later with absolutely no pain. I wish I knew about **PAIN BUST** long ago." *B.M.S.*

NO-RISK FREE TRIAL
We Trust You — Send No Money!

TO ORDER: Just write **"PAIN BUST•RII"** on a sheet of paper and send it along with your name, address and the number of tubes you wish to order. We will promptly ship you 1 large tube for $7.95, 2 large tubes for $13.90 or 3 large tubes for only $19.35 *(SAVES $4.50)*. Prices include all shipping and handling. We will enclose an invoice and if for any reason you wish to cancel your order, simply mark Cancel on the invoice and there will be no charge to you. You don't even have to bother returning the merchandise. Send for your <u>NO-RISK FREE TRIAL ORDER</u> today to: Continental Quest/Research Corp. 220 W. Carmel Dr. - Dept. OFA-01 Carmel, IN 46032.

Greater Ohio Valley

SUMMARY: Temperatures from November through March will be near or above normal, with above-normal precipitation. Snowfall will be below normal in most spots, with above-normal snowfall mostly in the north. Snowstorms will occur in mid-November, mid-January, and the second week of March. The coldest periods of the season will be in late November, the second and third weeks of December, and mid- to late January. November will begin with thunderstorms, followed by the season's first snowfall. Mild and cold periods will alternate in November, with mostly cold weather in the first half of December, then alternating mild and cold spells again. The first two-thirds of January will be cold, with milder temperatures being the rule from late January to early March. After snowy periods in mid-March, the rest of the month will be mild.

April will start with a touch of snow, and the month as a whole will be cool. May will be warmer, although still below normal, with heavy rain in the second half of the month.

June will be hot, but overall, the summer will bring temperatures close to normal. Expect the hottest temperatures in the first and last weeks of June and in late July. Rainfall will be close to normal, averaged across the region.

September will be cooler and October milder than normal. Expect wet weather in the southeast.

NOV. 2000: Temp. 44° (1° below avg.); precip. 4.5" (1" above avg.; 1" below southeast). 1-4 Cold. 5-10 Warm, thunderstorms. 11-14 Cold, snow. 15-20 Warm, thunderstorms, then cold. 21-25 Cold, snow. 26-30 Rain, warm, then cold.

DEC. 2000: Temp. 35° (avg.; 3° below southeast); precip. 0.5" (2.5" below avg.). 1-7 Cold, a few flurries. 8-15 Cold, snow showers. 16-19 Warm, cloudy. 20-24 Cold, sprinkles, flurries. 25-31 Mild, dry.

JAN. 2001: Temp. 29° (avg.); precip. 3" (0.5" above avg.). 1-8 Cold, then flurries. 9-15 Cold, snow. 16-20 Cold, snow. 21-25 Mild, rain to snow, then cold. 26-31 Mild, rain; heavy east.

FEB. 2001: Temp. 36° (4° above avg.); precip. 5" (2" above avg.). 1-6 Mild, showers. 7-12 Rain, mild. 13-17 Cold, flurries. 18-23 Warm, thunderstorms, then cold. 24-28 Windy, showers, warming.

MAR. 2001: Temp. 42° (1° below avg.); precip. 6" (2" above avg.). 1-6 Heavy rain, then dry. 7-13 Snowstorm. 14-19 Cool, light rain and snow. 20-22 Rain. 23-25 Sunny, chilly. 26-31 Warm; heavy rain.

APR. 2001: Temp. 50° (3° below avg.); precip. 3" (1" below avg.). 1-7 Flurries, cold, then pleasant. 8-15 Showers; cold, flurries east. 16-23 Cool, then warm with showers. 24-30 Seasonable, a few thunderstorms.

MAY 2001: Temp. 61° (2° below avg.); precip. 5" (1" above avg.). 1-7 Sunny, warm. 8-11 Showers, chilly. 12-14 Sunny days, chilly nights. 15-17 Warm, thunderstorms. 18-25 Sunny, warm, then rain and thunderstorms. 26-31 Cool; rain east, then sunny.

JUNE 2001: Temp. 74° (2° above avg.); precip. 4.5" (1" above avg.; 1" below east). 1-8 Sunny, hot. 9-20 Warm, a few thunderstorms. 21-23 Sunny. 24-30 Thunderstorms, hot.

JULY 2001: Temp. 74° (2° below avg.); precip. 4.5" (3" above avg. northeast; 2" below southwest). 1-5 Thunderstorms, warm. 6-17 Comfortable, a few thunderstorms. 18-22 Thunderstorms east; hot west. 23-25 Cool. 26-31 Hot, thunderstorms.

AUG. 2001: Temp. 74° (avg.; 2° above east); precip. 2.5" (1" below avg.). 1-8 Hot, a few thunderstorms. 9-11 Sunny, warm. 12-18 Showers, then sunny and cool. 19-22 Sunny, hot. 23-26 Hot, thunderstorms. 27-31 Pleasant.

SEPT. 2001: Temp. 65° (3° below avg.); precip. 3" (2" above avg. southeast; 2" below northwest). 1-5 Sunny, cool. 6-11 Hot, thunderstorms. 12-15 Chilly, showers. 16-21 Cool. 22-25 Pleasant. 26-30 Rain, seasonable.

OCT. 2001: Temp. 59° (3° above avg.); precip. 1.5" (1" below avg.). 1-5 Sunny days, chilly nights. 6-12 Sunny, warm. 13-19 Warm, showers. 20-22 Rain, cool. 23-26 Sunny, warm. 27-31 Showers, cold.

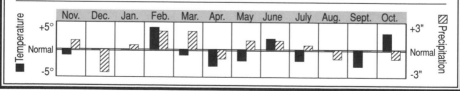

Deep South

SUMMARY: November through March will be milder than normal, with below-normal snowfall across the north and no snow in the south. Expect less rain than usual in the south, with above-normal rain in the north. Dry weather will be the rule in November, despite heavy rain late in the month. December will be unusually dry. Expect above-normal rainfall in the north in January, February, and March, but less in the south. The most significant snow in the north is expected toward mid-January. Heavy rain from mid-January to early February will bring flooding, especially in the north. In the south, drought will occur in many areas.

Rainfall in April and May will be less than normal throughout the region, as drought intensifies across the south. Temperatures will be a bit cooler than normal.

June through August will have the usual number of thunderstorms, but they will be spread out more than usual in the east. Temperatures will be hotter than usual, with a major heat wave from late July to mid-August. The extra heat will make the drought even worse.

A tropical storm after mid-September will end the drought and provide much-needed rainfall in the south and east. October will see temperatures and rainfall both near normal.

NOV. 2000: Temp. 54° (1° above avg. south; 1° below north); precip. 3" (1" below avg.). 1-4 Cool, showers. 5-9 Warm, humid, thunderstorms. 10-13 Cool; rain north. 14-16 Sunny, warm. 17-21 Thunderstorms, cool. 22-24 Sunny, cold. 25-30 Warm; heavy rain, then cool.

DEC. 2000: Temp. 45° (avg.); precip. 2" (3" below avg.). 1-7 Sunny, cold. 8-11 Sprinkles; flurries north. 12-16 Showers, cold. 17-24 Warm, showers. 25-31 Sunny, cold, then warm.

JAN. 2001: Temp. 37° (2° below avg.); precip. 5.5" (3" above avg. north; 1" below south). 1-9 Sunny, cold. 10-17 Cold, rain; snow north. 18-21 Dry, mild. 22-24 Warm, rain; heavy north. 25-31 Rain, local flooding.

FEB. 2001: Temp. 47° (4° above avg.); precip. 7.5" (3" above avg.; avg. east). 1-4 Rain. 5-7 Seasonable. 8-11 Warm, thunderstorms. 12-14 Warm south; rain north. 15-21 Mild, thunderstorms. 22-25 Sunny, then showers. 26-28 Warm.

MAR. 2001: Temp. 52° (1° below avg.); precip. 5" (1" above avg.; 2" below south). 1-4 Thunderstorms, cool. 5-10 Rain, chilly. 11-14 Sunny, cool. 15-20 Warm. 21-24 Thunderstorms, cool. 25-31 Warm, a few thunderstorms.

APR. 2001: Temp. 61° (2° below avg.); precip. 3.5" (1" below avg.). 1-5 Cool, thunderstorms. 6-8 Sunny, warm. 9-15 Thunderstorms, cool.

16-22 Showers, warm. 23-26 Thunderstorms, cool. 27-30 Warm, thunderstorms.

MAY 2001: Temp. 72° (1° above avg.; 1° below northeast); precip. 2" (2.5" below avg.). 1-7 Sunny, hot. 8-10 Rain, cool. 11-17 Hot. 18-20 Cool, showers. 21-24 Hot; Gulf thunderstorms. 25-31 Thunderstorms, cool.

JUNE 2001: Temp. 79° (1° above avg.); precip. 4" (2" above avg. west; 1" below east). 1-5 Sunny, hot. 6-15 Warm, a few thunderstorms. 16-18 Sunny, hot. 19-30 Hot, humid, a few thunderstorms.

JULY 2001: Temp. 81° (1° above avg.); precip. 5.5" (2" above avg.). 1-4 Heavy thunderstorms. 5-9 Hot; thunderstorms east. 10-18 Warm, a few thunderstorms. 19-24 Hot, a few thunderstorms. 25-27 Cool. 28-31 Hot, humid.

AUG. 2001: Temp. 80.5° (0.5° above avg.); precip. 1" (2" below avg.). 1-12 Hot; widely scattered thunderstorms. 13-17 Thunderstorms, cool. 18-20 Hot. 21-25 Hot, a few thunderstorms. 26-31 Warm, a few thunderstorms.

SEPT. 2001: Temp. 73° (1° below avg.); precip. 5.5" (6" above avg. southeast; 2" below northwest). 1-5 Sunny, cool. 6-10 Sunny, hot. 11-15 Thunderstorms, cool. 16-19 Possible hurricane. 20-23 Warm. 24-26 Heavy rain. 27-30 Warm.

OCT. 2001: Temp. 65° (1° above avg.); precip. 3" (avg.). 1-12 Sunny. 13-16 Rain. 17-22 Warm, dry. 23-27 Rain. 28-31 Breezy, some sun.

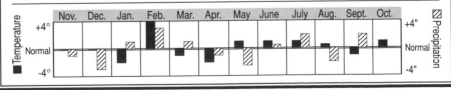

Chicago and Southern Great Lakes

SUMMARY: The winter season will not be particularly harsh, but compared with recent winters, it may seem to be. Expect temperatures to average only a bit above normal from November through March, with near-normal precipitation. Expect above-normal snowfall in much of the area, but less snow than normal in the west. The best chances for major snowstorms are mid-November, late January, and the second week of March. Mild temperatures just before Christmas make a white Christmas unlikely in most spots. The coldest spells are anticipated in the next to last week of November, toward mid-December, in mid-January, and in mid-February.

April and May temperatures will be cooler than normal overall. Expect the season's first hot weather toward the end of May. Much of the region will be drier than normal, except for a rainy spell in the east in late May.

June through August will be hotter than normal, with abundant rainfall. Look for an especially hot June, with record heat in the west late in the month.

September and October will be about as nice as they come, with above-normal amounts of sunshine, comfortable temperatures through mid-October, and little rainfall. However, winter will be here before you know it.

NOV. 2000: Temp. 38° (2° below avg.); precip. 3" (0.5" above avg.). 1-4 Cold, flurries. 5-9 Warm, thunderstorms. 10-14 Cold, snow. 15-17 Warm, showers. 18-20 Sunny, cool. 21-25 Cold, snow. 26-30 Showers, mild, then cold.

DEC. 2000: Temp. 28° (avg.); precip. 1" (1.5" below avg.). 1-8 Cold, lake snows. 9-15 Cold, flurries. 16-23 Some sun, mild. 24-31 Seasonable, light rain and snow.

JAN. 2001: Temp. 22° (avg.); precip. 0.5" (1" below avg.). 1-6 Mild west; rain, snow east. 7-12 Mild west; seasonable east. 13-15 Cold, periods of snow. 16-21 Cold, lake snows. 22-27 Snow. 28-31 Sunny, then mild with rain.

FEB. 2001: Temp. 29° (4° above avg.); precip. 2.5" (1" above avg.). 1-5 Cold, snow. 6-12 Mild, light rain and snow. 13-17 Sunny, cold. 18-23 Rain, mild, then cold. 24-28 Warm, rain.

MAR. 2001: Temp. 37° (avg.); precip. 3" (0.5" above avg.). 1-7 Cold, rain, snow. 8-12 Snow, cold. 13-22 Chilly, occasional rain and snow. 23-25 Sunny, cool. 26-31 Warm, thunderstorms.

APR. 2001: Temp. 46° (3° below avg.); precip. 4" (1" above avg.). 1-7 Rain, snow, then clear. 8-14 Thunderstorms, warm, then sunny and cool. 15-18 Dry, cool. 19-23 Thunderstorms. 24-30 Cool, occasional rain.

MAY 2001: Temp. 57° (2° below avg.); precip. 4" (2" above avg. east; 1" below west). 1-2 Sunny, cool. 3-7 Severe thunderstorms, warm. 8-14 Cool, showers, then sunny. 15-22 Thunderstorms, warm, then pleasant. 23-31 Thunderstorms, hot; then cool, rain east.

JUNE 2001: Temp. 74° (4° above avg.); precip. 4" (avg.). 1-3 Sunny. 4-8 Hot, sunny. 9-20 Sunny, warm, a few thunderstorms. 21-24 Sunny, warm. 25-30 Hot, showers.

JULY 2001: Temp. 72° (2° below avg.); precip. 5" (1" above avg.). 1-8 Warm, sunny, a few thunderstorms. 9-14 Occasional thunderstorms. 15-21 Warm, sunny. 22-26 Cool. 27-31 Hot, thunderstorms.

AUG. 2001: Temp. 73° (1° above avg.); precip. 4.5" (1" above avg.). 1-11 Hot, a few thunderstorms. 12-16 Sunny, cool. 17-20 Clouds, showers. 21-25 Thunderstorms, hot. 26-31 Sunny, warm.

SEPT. 2001: Temp. 61° (3° below avg.); precip. 1.5" (2" below avg.). 1-3 Sunny, cool. 4-8 Warm, showers. 9-12 Sunny, cold. 13-17 Warm, showers. 18-23 Clear days, cool nights. 24-30 Mostly clear, a few showers.

OCT. 2001: Temp. 57° (5° above avg.); precip. 1" (2" below avg.). 1-5 Sunny, chilly. 6-11 Sunny, warm. 12-21 Mild, sun and clouds. 22-27 A shower, then sunny and warm. 28-31 Cold.

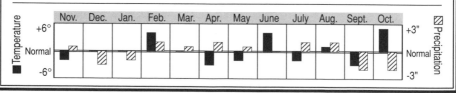

Flush Prostate Disorders Out Of Your Body!

...And *Trigger Rapid Healing Of Even The Most Enlarged Prostate!*

Thanks to a stunning new product developed by a San Diego company, if you suffer from prostate disorders, you can now get <u>rapid</u> and <u>dramatic</u> <u>relief!</u>

Yes it's true! There's a new, just released prostate supplement that is so incredibly <u>powerful</u>, it can actually <u>flush</u> <u>out</u> the dangerous toxins that scientists say cause prostate disorders for men over 45. This new supplement, is <u>so</u> <u>potent</u> experts believe it can...

Trigger Rapid Healing Of Prostate Disorders... Even If Other Treatments Have Failed You!

According to leading researcher Dr. Michael Ernest, this new supplement is so effective because "it helps rid the body of the <u>mutant hormone</u> <u>DHT</u> that attacks the prostate tissue and causes it to become diseased!"

The new product is called *Nature's Prostate Remedy™* and it is a scientifically formulated combination of <u>three</u> of the world's most powerful and <u>clinially</u> <u>documented</u> prostate healing herbs, plus seven other miracle nutrients, all shown to rejuvenate the prostate!

Here is a breakdown of the truly remarkable "prostate defenders" contained in *Nature's Prostate Remedy.*

Prostate Defender #1

The first healing herb is called *Pygeum africanum.* Dozens of clinical studies document that *Pygeum* is a safe, effective herb that <u>shrinks</u> <u>enlarged</u> <u>prostate</u> <u>tissue</u>, and relieves pain and swelling. This healing herb is so effective, that over 80% of all doctors' prescriptions for prostate enlargement in France contain *Pygeum* extract!

Prostate Defender #2

This second healing herb contained in *Nature's Prostate Remedy* is called *Urtica dioica* extract and studies show that when combined with *Pygeum*, this dynamic "healing-duo" is so profoundly effective that it creates a fortress around the <u>prostate that shields it from toxins</u> <u>and other cellular invaders!</u>

<u>**But wait, it gets better!**</u> The herb Saw Palmetto is one of the most highly effective natural prostate treatments available. In fact, over 20 clinical studies credit Saw Palmetto with as high as a...

90% Success Rate In Treating Men With An Enlarged Prostate!

Therefore, the formulators of *Nature's Prostate Rem-*

☑ **No More Frequent Middle-Of-The-Night Trips To The Bathroom!**

☑ **No More Sudden -- *Even Uncontrollable* -- Urges To Urinate!**

☑ **No More Dignity- Robbing Incontinence!**

☑ **No More Pain and Discomfort!**

☑ **No More Sexual Dysfunction!**

edy added...

Prostate Defender #3

Saw Palmetto extract, the third powerful healing herb contained in *Nature's Prostate Remedy*. Clinical studies show that Saw Palmetto plays a vital role in flushing out the dangerous hormone DHT.

Now, with *Nature's Prostate Remedy*, you can have the combined force of <u>all three of these scientifically documented healing herbs</u>... working simultaneously in your body to heal your prostate condition.

100% Satisfaction Guaranteed!

Take an entire <u>120 days</u> and <u>experience</u> <u>for yourself</u> the dramatic relief *Nature's Prostate Remedy* will bring to you... <u>without</u> <u>risking</u> <u>a single penny!</u> If you're not 100% satisfied, we'll promptly send you a full, no-questions asked refund!

Get A <u>FREE</u> 64 Page Health Book Just For Trying It!

It's called *Prostate Healing Miracles* (a $14.95 value) – and it's YOURS FREE with your order.

⌐ – –Priority Order Form– – ¬

Please rush me the following Nature's Prostate Remedy:

❏ **BEST VALUE – <u>YOU SAVE $24.95!</u>** 4 month supply for only $74.85 (plus $5 S&H: Total $79.85)

❏ **GREAT VALUE – <u>YOU SAVE $8.48!</u>** 2 month supply for only $41.42 (plus $5 S&H: Total $46.42)

❏ **GOOD VALUE** – 1 month supply for the low price of only $24.95 (plus $5 S&H: Total $29.95)

Name_____

Address_____

City_____ State_____

Zip_____ Phone (_____)_____

Make check payable and mail to:
Active Health Labs, Dept. 575
12526 High Bluff Dr., #300, San Diego, CA 92130
Order Over The Internet: www.activehealthlabs.com

Credit Card Orders Call 1-800-600-0612 (Dept. 575)

Northern Great Plains–Great Lakes

SUMMARY: From November through March, temperatures will be much colder than normal in the northeast but near normal in the southwest. Expect near-normal snowfall, with below-normal precipitation. Winter will get off to an early start in November, with frequent flurries, cold temperatures, and gusty winds. Many spots will see their heaviest snowfall toward the end of March. Temperatures will average colder than normal during each month of the season, although the southwest will be more moderate. Coldest temperatures are expected in mid-December and mid-January. Despite the general cold, there will be several mild periods and even a brief January thaw.

April will be much cooler than normal, with snow at the start of the month and again after midmonth. May will warm up dramatically, with a good amount of sunshine and many scattered thunderstorms.

The summer season will get off to a hot start in June, with cooler-than-normal temperatures in July and August. Watch for an early June heat wave, with temperatures in many spots topping the century mark. Rainfall will be below normal in the western half of the region but wetter than normal in the east. Most of the rain will be in the form of thunderstorms.

September and October will be warmer and drier than normal, with especially pleasant weather in mid-September. Of course, no matter how nice the weather is at this time of year, it's only a matter of weeks until winter returns.

NOV. 2000: Temp. 27° (5° below avg.); precip. 2" (0.5" above avg.). 1-4 Showers, mild. 5-10 Snow, windy, bitter cold. 11-13 Cold, flurries. 14-20 Occasional snow. 21-24 Cold. 25-30 Snow, cold.

DEC. 2000: Temp. 16° (3° below avg.; 3° above southwest); precip. 0.5" (0.5" below avg.). 1-5 Cold, flurries. 6-7 Mild. 8-13 Cold, flurries. 14-18 Moderating. 19-21 Flurries, cold. 25-31 Sunny, mild. 22-24 Snow, cold. 25-31 Sunny, mild.

JAN. 2001: Temp. 10° (2° below avg.; 1° above southwest); precip. 0.5" (0.5" below avg.). 1-7 Some sun, mild. 8-16 Snow, cold. 17-22 Mild; light snow. 23-27 Sunny, cold. 28-31 Sunny, mild.

FEB. 2001: Temp. 15° (1° below avg.); precip. 0.5" (0.5" below avg.). 1-6 Mild. 7-11 Flurries, cold. 12-16 Sunny, cold. 17-22 Snow, then sunny and cold. 23-28 Mild, sprinkles, flurries.

MAR. 2001: Temp. 28° (2° below avg. northeast; 2° above southwest); precip. 1.5" (avg.). 1-9 Cold; light snow. 10-14 Mild, some sun. 15-20 Sunny and warm south; flurries north. 21-23 Snow, cold. 24-31 Rain east; snow west.

APR. 2001: Temp. 39° (5° below avg.); precip. 1.5" (0.5" below avg.). 1-5 Cold; light snow. 6-8 Sunny, nice. 9-13 Sunny, cool. 14-20 Mild, then cool with showers. 21-24 Chilly; occasional snow. 25-30 Showers, cool.

MAY 2001: Temp. 59° (3° above avg.); precip. 2" (1" below avg.; 2" above north). 1-7 Changeable, a few showers. 8-17 Sunny, warm. 18-25 Warm, a few thunderstorms. 26-31 Warm; thunderstorms west.

JUNE 2001: Temp. 69° (4° above avg.); precip. 3.5" (0.5" below avg.). 1-7 Sunny, hot. 8-16 Warm, a few thunderstorms. 17-21 Seasonable, a few thunderstorms. 22-25 Hot, then thunderstorms and cool. 26-30 Thunderstorms, seasonable.

JULY 2001: Temp. 70° (3° below avg.); precip. 4.5" (1" below avg. west; 3" above east). 1-10 Warm, a few thunderstorms. 11-14 Thunderstorms, cool. 15-20 Sunny, hot. 21-27 Cool, thunderstorms. 28-31 Sunny, hot.

AUG. 2001: Temp. 68° (3° below avg.); precip. 3" (0.5" below avg.). 1-6 Thunderstorms, some sun; cool west. 7-10 Sunny, hot. 11-15 Cool, showers. 16-18 Sunny, warm. 19-22 Hot, thunderstorms. 23-31 Rain, cool.

SEPT. 2001: Temp. 61° (2° below avg. east; 6° above west); precip. 2" (1" below avg.). 1-5 Sunny, comfortable. 6-9 Cool; light rain. 10-17 Sunny, seasonable. 18-21 Sunny, warm. 22-25 Cool, showers. 26-30 Sunny, pleasant.

OCT. 2001: Temp. 50° (4° above avg.); precip. 1.5" (0.5" below avg.). 1-3 Sunny, cool. 4-6 Sunny, warm. 7-9 Thunderstorms, cool. 10-15 Sunny, warm. 16-24 Seasonable, a few showers. 25-31 Sunny, then cold with showers.

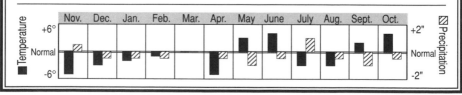

Central Great Plains

SUMMARY: Expect below-normal snowfall, with well below normal precipitation from November through March. Temperatures will be milder than normal in most of the region, though a bit colder than normal in much of Iowa. November will be colder and drier than normal despite several inches of snow in the foothills. December and January will remain cold in the northeast, with milder-than-normal temperatures in the west, especially in the latter half of December. January will have two or three snowy periods. February is expected to bring more precipitation than the other winter months, with the season's heaviest snowfall early in the month in the east and toward month's end in the west. Unusually warm temperatures in mid-March will mark the end of winter in all but the foothills.

April will be cool. May will be warmer than normal, with the season's first hot temperatures early in the month. After a relatively dry winter, below-normal rainfall in April and May will cause worry about drought.

The drought will intensify through June and early July, with much-needed thunderstorms few and far between. Heavy thunderstorms in late July will bring some relief before a dry August. Temperatures will be near or just above normal from June through August, with the most-prolonged heat waves in June and mid-August.

Dry, warm weather will be the rule in September and October, though temperatures will trend rapidly downward.

NOV. 2000: Temp. 38° (5° below avg. north; 1° below south); precip. 1" (1.5" below avg.). 1-3 Chilly east; snow west. 4-7 Warm east; flurries west. 8-12 Flurries, cold. 13-15 Warm. 16-20 Showers, cool. 21-24 Flurries, cold. 25-27 Snow, mild. 28-30 Cool.

DEC. 2000: Temp. 32° (8° above avg. southwest; 2° below northeast); precip. 1" (1" below avg.). 1-4 Cold, flurries. 5-7 Sunny, mild. 8-12 Sunny, cold. 13-15 Sunny, cold east; mild west. 16-22 Sunny, warm. 23-25 Sunny, cool. 26-31 Sunny, warm.

JAN. 2001: Temp. 23.5° (3° below avg. east; 2° above west); precip. 0.5" (0.5" below avg.). 1-4 Sunny, mild west; cold east. 5-8 Sunny, mild. 9-13 Cold; light snow. 14-19 Cold, flurries. 20-24 Snow. 25-31 Cold; light snow.

FEB. 2001: Temp. 34° (5° above avg.; 1° below west); precip. 1.5" (avg.). 1-3 Snow west; rain east. 4-6 Snow southeast. 7-11 Showers east; snow west. 12-17 Cold; warm west. 18-20 Mild; rain east. 21-22 Cold. 23-27 Warm. 28 Snow west.

MAR. 2001: Temp. 40° (avg.); precip. 1" (1" below avg.). 1-10 Snow, cold. 11-15 Warm, showers, flurries. 16-20 Sunny, warm. 21-24 Thunderstorms, cool. 25-27 Sunny, warm. 28-31 Warm east; chilly west.

APR. 2001: Temp. 48° (4° below avg.; 1° below southwest); precip. 2" (1" below avg.). 1-4 Snow west; rain east. 5-8 Sunny. 9-13 Sunny, cool. 14-15 Sunny, warm. 16-19 Chilly, rain. 20-23 Thunderstorms, then cool. 24-30 Cool, then thunderstorms.

MAY 2001: Temp. 67° (5° above avg.); precip. 3" (1" below avg.). 1-6 Thunderstorms, hot. 7-10 Cool; light rain. 11-15 Warm. 16-20 Seasonable, rain. 21-24 Warm, thunderstorms. 25-31 Warm.

JUNE 2001: Temp. 76° (4° above avg.; avg. southeast); precip. 3" (1" below avg.; 1" above southeast). 1-7 Sunny, hot. 8-11 A few thunderstorms, warm. 12-19 Hot, thunderstorms. 20-24 Sunny, hot. 25-30 Warm, thunderstorms.

JULY 2001: Temp. 78° (avg.); precip. 6.5" (3" above avg.). 1-5 Warm, thunderstorms. 6-11 Hot, thunderstorms. 12-17 Cool, thunderstorms. 18-21 Sunny, hot. 22-27 Warm; thunderstorms. 28-31 Sunny, hot.

AUG. 2001: Temp. 75° (avg.); precip. 1.5" (2" below avg.). 1-8 Warm, thunderstorms. 9-15 Hot, thunderstorms, then cool. 16-19 Warm. 20-25 Hot, thunderstorms. 26-31 Hot, then showers.

SEPT. 2001: Temp. 69° (6° above avg. west; avg. east); precip. 1" (2" below avg.). 1-7 Sunny, hot. 8-13 Showers, cool. 14-18 Hot, then cool. 19-23 Hot days, comfortable nights. 24-30 Showers.

OCT. 2001: Temp. 59° (4° above avg.); precip. 2" (1" below avg.). 1-6 Cool, then warm. 7-13 Thunderstorms, warm. 14-19 Mild, a few showers. 20-23 Sunny, cool, then warm. 24-31 Mild east; cold, snow west.

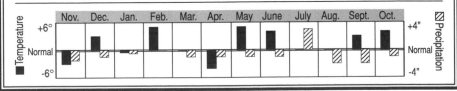

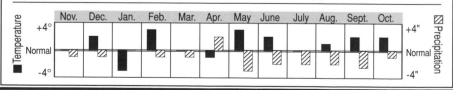

Texas–Oklahoma

SUMMARY: Precipitation will be well below normal from November through March, with temperatures near or just above normal. Expect a snowstorm in the Texas Panhandle and Oklahoma in late January, with light snow in November, and light snow and ice in mid-January and early March. Significant snow in the Metroplex will occur in mid-January. Coldest temperatures are expected in mid-December and mid- and late January, with many places experiencing unusually cold temperatures in early November and early March.

April will be the wettest month of the year in much of the region and will be the only month with widespread, above-normal rainfall. Thunderstorms late April will bring excessive downpours with local flooding. Much of the April rain will miss the north, but rainy weather will shift northward in May, with drought resuming in the south.

Summer will be hot, especially from San Antonio to the Metroplex, where temperatures from June through August will average two to three degrees above normal. Hot weather will be the rule almost every day from June through the first part of August. Rainfall will be dangerously low in much of the area.

Dry weather will continue through September and October, with warmer-than-normal temperatures.

NOV. 2000: Temp. 56° (avg.; 2° below north); precip. 1" (1" below avg.). 1-3 Rain south; snow northwest. 4-9 Sunny, warm. 10-14 Showers, cool. 15-17 Sunny, warm. 18-21 Thunderstorms, cool. 22-26 Rain; snow north. 27-30 Rain, cool.

DEC. 2000: Temp. 51° (2° above avg.); precip. 0.5" (1" below avg.). 1-4 Sunny, cool. 5-6 Light rain. 7-11 Sunny, cold. 12-14 Cool north; a few thunderstorms south. 15-19 Sunny, warm. 20-23 Sunny, mild. 24-31 A few showers, then sunny.

JAN. 2001: Temp. 41° (3° below avg.); precip. 1.5" (avg.). 1-7 Sunny, cool. 8-11 Sunny, mild. 12-14 Rain; snow north. 15-18 Rain; freezing drizzle north. 19-22 Warm. 23-31 Cold, rain south; snow north.

FEB. 2001: Temp. 53° (3° above avg.); precip. 0.5" (1" below avg.). 1-4 Cold, thunderstorms south; snow north. 5-12 Mild, a few thunderstorms. 13-18 Mild; rain south. 19-28 Warm.

MAR. 2001: Temp. 57° (avg.); precip. 1.5" (1" below avg.). 1-5 Cold. 6-9 Cold, rain south; freezing drizzle north. 10-15 Sunny, then showers. 16-21 Warm. 22-31 A few thunderstorms.

APR. 2001: Temp. 65° (1° below avg.); precip. 5" (2" above avg.; 1" below north). 1-4 Light rain; cool north. 5-7 Warm. 8-12 Thunderstorms, cool. 13-18 Periods of rain. 19-21 Sunny, warm. 22-26 Heavy thunderstorms, local flooding. 27-30 Sunny, warm.

MAY 2001: Temp. 75° (3° above avg.; 1° below south); precip. 1.5" (3" below avg.; 1" above north). 1-7 Hot. 8-11 Thunderstorms, cool. 12-16 Sunny, warm. 17-25 Seasonable; thunderstorms north. 26-31 Hot; a few thunderstorms north.

JUNE 2001: Temp. 82° (2° above avg.; 1° below south); precip. 1.5" (2" below avg.; 0.5" above south). 1-6 Warm; a few thunderstorms north. 7-13 Hot; occasional thunderstorms south. 14-22 Hot, a few thunderstorms. 23-30 Hot, dry.

JULY 2001: Temp. 84° (avg.; 3° above central); precip. 0.5" (2" below avg.; avg. north). 1-5 Hot, a few thunderstorms. 6-12 Thunderstorms north; hot elsewhere. 13-17 Hot, a few thunderstorms. 18-22 Hot; thunderstorms south. 23-31 Thunderstorms northwest; hot elsewhere.

AUG. 2001: Temp. 84° (1° above avg.); precip. 1" (2" below avg.). 1-10 Searing heat. 11-12 Thunderstorms. 13-24 Cool, then hot with thunderstorms. 25-31 Thunderstorms south; cool north.

SEPT. 2001: Temp. 78° (5° above avg. north; 1° below south); precip. 1.5" (2.5" below avg.). 1-7 Rain in the Valley, pleasant elsewhere. 8-11 Hot, thunderstorms. 12-16 Hot. 17-23 Thunderstorms north; hot. 24-30 Thunderstorms, warm.

OCT. 2001: Temp. 69° (2° above avg.); precip. 2" (1" below avg.). 1-5 Sunny, warm. 6-14 Cool, a few thunderstorms. 15-18 Sunny days, cool nights. 19-21 Sunny. 22-27 Showers south; sunny north. 28-31 Rainy periods.

Old Farmer's Almanac Calendars for 2001 ...

WALL CALENDARS

❖ Full color! Large grid with plenty of room to write
❖ Heavy stock that is easy to write on with pen or pencil

New

Item: OF01CGC $6.99 each

Item: OF01CAD $6.99 each

Item: OF01CWW $6.99 each

Order one or order many! Only $3.95 per order for shipping and handling.

EVERY DAY CALENDARS

❖ Handy page-per-day format
❖ Daily wit and wisdom based on each calendar's topic

Item: OF01CHR $10.99 each

Item: OF01CEW $10.99 each

Item: OF01CEV $10.99 each

TERMS:

Payment, including shipping and handling, must be received with your order. We accept Visa, MasterCard, American Express, and Discover cards. Personal check or money order also accepted in U.S. funds drawn on a U.S. bank.

THREE WAYS TO ORDER:

1) On-line: www.almanac.com/calendars
2) Toll-free: 800-223-3166
3) Mail: The Old Farmer's Almanac
   P.O. Box 37370, Boone, IA 50037-0370
PLEASE MENTION Key: CABOFAB when mailing or phoning in your order.

Rocky Mountains

SUMMARY: November through March will be unusually mild across the south, with near-normal temperatures across the north. Precipitation will be close to normal, with near- or above-normal snowfall. The season will start on the cold side, but December and January will be much milder than normal across much of the region. February and March will be close to normal in temperature. Expect the coldest weather in early to mid-November, late January, and mid-February. The most-widespread substantial snowfalls will occur in early to mid-November, mid-January, and mid-February.

April and May will be fairly typical, as winter's cold yields to summer's warmth. It will be a bit cooler and wetter than normal in the north, a bit warmer and drier than normal in the south.

The summer season will also be fairly typical, with near-normal heat, and rainfall near or a bit below normal. Thunderstorms will be frequent enough to avert a drought in most of the region, although drought conditions are likely in the south and east. Expect prolonged heat waves in mid- to late June and through much of July.

With September warmer and October cooler than normal, October nights will seem especially chilly. Precipitation will be close to normal overall, with the first significant snowfalls in the latter half of October.

NOV. 2000: Temp. 40° (2° below avg.); precip. 1" (avg.). 1-3 Sunny. 4-12 Cold, snow; rain south. 13-18 Rain and snow showers. 19-23 Mild; showers north. 24-30 Cold, rain and snow.

DEC. 2000: Temp. 32° (4° above avg.); precip. 0.5" (0.5" below avg.; 2" above west). 1-3 Cold, snow showers. 4-7 Sunny, seasonable. 8-11 Sunny south; rain, snow north. 12-21 Mild, sunny east; rain west. 22-25 Cold, snow showers north and west; sunny southeast. 26-31 Mild; showers north and west.

JAN. 2001: Temp. 29° (8° above avg. southeast; 2° below northwest); precip. 2" (1" above avg.; avg. southwest). 1-9 Mild south; rain, snow north. 10-18 Rain, mild south; snow, cold north. 19-21 Snow. 22-25 Cold; snow north and central. 26-31 Sunny, cold.

FEB. 2001: Temp. 30° (2° below avg.); precip. 0.5" (0.5" below avg.). 1-5 Flurries, then cold. 6-12 Mild, then cold with snow. 13-20 Snow, not as cold. 21-25 Mild. 26-28 Cold, snow showers.

MAR. 2001: Temp. 40° (1° above avg.); precip. 1" (1" below avg.). 1-8 Cold; snow showers north and central. 9-19 Sunny, unseasonably warm. 20-24 Showers, flurries, then cool. 25-31 Mild, then cool with rain and snow showers.

APR. 2001: Temp. 48.5° (2° above avg. northeast; 1° below southwest); precip. 2" (1" above avg. northwest; 1" below southeast). 1-4 Sunny, seasonable. 5-11 Showers; snow west. 12-19 Mild. 20-24 Cool; light rain. 25-30 Warm south; showers north.

MAY 2001: Temp. 57.5° (1° below avg. west; 2° above east); precip. 2" (0.5" above avg. north; avg. south). 1-8 Cool, occasional rain. 9-16 Sunny, warm. 17-23 Thunderstorms, cool. 24-28 Sunny, hot. 29-31 Thunderstorms, cool.

JUNE 2001: Temp. 66° (2° below avg. northwest; 2° above southeast); precip. 1" (0.5" below avg.). 1-7 Sunny, hot. 8-14 A few thunderstorms, not as hot. 15-22 Sunny, hot. 23-30 Thunderstorms, cool.

JULY 2001: Temp. 73° (1° below avg.; 1" above avg. west; 0.5" below east). 1-3 Sunny, hot. 4-8 A few thunderstorms. 9-12 Sunny, hot. 13-24 Hot, a few thunderstorms. 25-31 Sunny, cool.

AUG. 2001: Temp. 71° (1° below avg.); precip. 0.5" (0.5" below avg.). 1-4 Sunny, seasonable. 5-13 Sunny, a few thunderstorms. 14-19 Sunny, hot. 20-26 Thunderstorms, cool. 27-31 Hot.

SEPT. 2001: Temp. 66° (3° above avg.); precip. 0.5" (0.5" below avg.). 1-6 Sunny, hot, a few thunderstorms. 7-12 Sunny, hot. 13-17 Thunderstorms, cool. 18-25 Sunny, warm. 26-30 A few thunderstorms.

OCT. 2001: Temp. 51° (2° below avg. north; avg. south); precip. 1.5" (1" above avg. north; avg. south). 1-6 Warm south; chilly, rain north. 7-16 Seasonable. 17-19 Cold; snow north and central. 20-24 Sunny south; rain north. 25-31 Rain, snow.

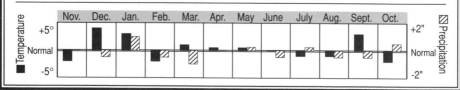

Desert Southwest

SUMMARY: November through March will be warmer and drier than normal. Expect near-normal snowfall in places that get snow, though much of the season's total will fall in a late-January blizzard. After near-normal temperatures in November, December and the first three weeks of January will be exceptionally mild, interrupted by only occasional cold spells. Temperatures in February and March will average near or just above normal. The winter will be generally dry, except in January.

The dry trend will continue in April and May, with thunderstorms few and far between. Temperatures will also continue to average warmer than normal, with hot weather in late April and mid- and late May.

Warm and dry weather will continue through June. Near-normal rainfall in July will not be enough to break the drought, and August will bring only half the normal rainfall. Temperatures in July and August will be seasonably hot but a bit below normal in the west.

September days will be hot, but nights will generally be cooler. Expect little, if any, rain. October will be much cooler, with temperatures close to normal. Record cold is anticipated in the last full week of the month.

NOV. 2000: Temp. 56° (1° below avg.); precip. 0.4" (0.2" below avg.). 1-4 Sunny days, cold nights. 5-6 Warm. 7-11 Showers. 12-15 Warm days, cool nights. 16-21 Pleasant. 22-30 Cool, a few showers; snow in higher elevations.

DEC. 2000: Temp. 54° (6° above avg.); precip. 0.3" (0.7" below avg.). 1-4 Cool, a few showers. 5-16 Mild days, chilly nights. 17-22 Warm. 23-31 Clouds, then mild.

JAN. 2001: Temp. 50° (3° above avg.); precip. 1.3" (0.7" above avg.). 1-6 Sunny, mild. 7-9 Warm, clouds and sun. 10-16 Cold, a few showers; snow in higher elevations. 17-21 Warm; high clouds. 22-25 Cool, showers. 26-31 Blizzard north and east; showers southwest.

FEB. 2001: Temp. 52.5° (0.5° above avg.); precip. 0.3" (0.3" below avg.). 1-3 Cold, rain, snow. 4-8 Sunny, mild. 9-12 Windy, cool, a few showers. 13-17 Sunny, mild. 18-21 Windy, cold, dust storm. 22-28 Warm, sun and clouds.

MAR. 2001: Temp. 59° (1° above avg.); precip. 0.1" (0.5" below avg.). 1-5 Sunny, cool, then warm. 6-10 Sunny, cool. 11-20 Sunny, warm. 21-23 Windy, cool. 24-25 Sunny, warm. 26-31 Cool, a few showers, then sunny.

APR. 2001: Temp. 67° (1° above avg.); precip. 0.0" (0.4" below avg.). 1-7 Sunny. 8-14 Sun and clouds, a few thunderstorms. 15-20 Sunny, warm. 21-23 Cool. 24-30 Sunny, hot.

MAY 2001: Temp. 77° (3° above avg.); precip. 0.0" (0.3" below avg.). 1-9 Sunny, comfortable.

10-14 Sunny, hot. 15-19 Hot; thunderstorms north. 20-25 Sunny, hot. 26-31 Sunny, hot, a few thunderstorms.

JUNE 2001: Temp. 86° (2° above avg.); precip. 0.2" (0.1" below avg.). 1-8 Hot, sunny, a few thunderstorms. 9-14 Not as hot, widely separated thunderstorms. 15-21 Sunny, hot days, warm nights. 22-30 Sunny, a few thunderstorms, less hot.

JULY 2001: Temp. 87° (1° below avg.); precip. 1.2" (0.2" above avg.; 0.2" below east). 1-3 Sunny, hot. 4-17 Hot, a few thunderstorms. 18-20 Windy, a few thunderstorms, less hot. 21-27 Cool, a few thunderstorms. 28-31 Sunny, hot.

AUG. 2001: Temp. 87° (1° below avg. west; 1° above east); precip. 0.8" (0.7" below avg.). 1-5 Sunny, hot. 6-15 Clouds and sun, a few thunderstorms. 16-22 Sunny, a few thunderstorms, hot. 23-31 Sunny, hot.

SEPT. 2001: Temp. 84° (3° above avg.); precip. 0.2" (0.8" below avg.). 1-5 Sunny, hot west; cool east. 6-14 Sunny, hot. 15-25 Sunny, a few thunderstorms, hot south; cool north. 26-30 Sunny, hot.

OCT. 2001: Temp. 71° (avg.); precip. 0.4" (0.4" below avg.). 1-9 Sunny, warm. 10-12 Showers east. 13-16 Sunny, warm. 17-20 Cool, showers. 21-22 Sunny, warm. 23-25 Windy, cold, blowing dust, a few showers. 26-31 Cold.

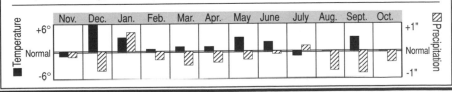

Pacific Northwest

SUMMARY: If you like cold winters with plenty of rain and snow, your wish will come true. November through March will feature temperatures averaging about two degrees colder than normal, rain as much as a foot more than normal, and well above normal snowfall. Most of the rain will come in the first half of the period. Prepare for two or three major snowfalls, with heavy snow likely in the first half of November, mid-December, mid- to late January, and early to mid-February. Watch for record cold in early November, with other cold spells in late January and early to mid-February.

April and May will be typical for this time of year, with slightly above normal temperatures and slightly below normal rainfall. Expect prolonged stretches of pleasant weather in each month.

June through August will also be close to normal. June will be cool, but otherwise, temperatures and precipitation will average close to normal. The hottest weather will occur toward mid-July.

As we move into autumn, rainfall will increase. September will be relatively dry, but October will be much wetter than normal. Expect rain nearly every day, with the heaviest rainfall occurring around midmonth and toward month's end.

NOV. 2000: Temp. 42° (4° below avg.); precip. 9" (3" above avg.). 1-4 Mild; light rain. 5-8 Snow, record cold. 9-11 Snowstorm. 12-14 Heavy rain. 15-21 Stormy; heavy rain. 22-26 Seasonable, rain. 27-30 Sunny, then rain.

DEC. 2000: Temp. 42° (avg.; 3° above south); precip. 14" (8" above avg.). 1-5 Rain, heavy at times. 6-11 Sunny, then rain. 12-20 Snow, then windy and warm with heavy rain. 21-25 Sunny, cold. 26-31 Heavy rain.

JAN. 2001: Temp. 41° (avg.); precip. 6.5" (1" below avg. north; 2" above south). 1-7 Mild; light rain. 8-10 Heavy rain. 11-17 Rain, mild. 18-22 Sunny, then a snowstorm. 23-28 Sunny, cold. 29-31 Mild; light rain.

FEB. 2001: Temp. 39° (5° below avg.); precip. 4.5" (avg.). 1-6 Dry, chilly, then mild. 7-11 Snowstorm, cold. 12-16 Rain; heavy south. 17-23 Snow, then occasional rain. 24-28 Rain turning to snow.

MAR. 2001: Temp. 47° (avg.; 4° below north); precip. 3" (1" above avg. north; 2" below south). 1-6 Cold, rain, snow. 7-13 Sunny, mild. 14-24 Seasonable, some rain. 25-31 Cool, sprinkles.

APR. 2001: Temp. 51° (1° above avg.); precip. 1.5" (1" below avg.). 1-5 Clouds and sun, some rain. 6-11 Dry, seasonable. 12-16 Mild, sunny. 17-26 Dry, some sun. 27-30 Rain.

MAY 2001: Temp. 56° (avg.); precip. 2" (avg.). 1-6 Occasional rain, cool. 7-12 Sunny, warm. 13-19 Seasonable, clouds and sun. 20-24 Warm, rain. 25-31 Cool; light rain.

JUNE 2001: Temp. 60° (3° below avg.); precip. 1.5" (1" above avg. north; 1" below south). 1-13 Cool, rain. 14-18 Cloudy, cool. 19-21 Sunny, warm. 22-27 Cool, clouds and sun. 28-30 Occasional rain, mainly north.

JULY 2001: Temp. 68° (avg.); precip. 1" (avg.). 1-6 Sunny, warm. 7-9 Cool, a few showers. 10-14 Sunny, hot. 15-19 Sunny, warm. 20-25 Sunny, warm days, cool nights. 26-31 Cool, rain, then sun.

AUG. 2001: Temp. 69° (avg.); precip. 1" (avg.). 1-6 Sunny, warm. 7-10 Cool, a few thunderstorms. 11-16 Sunny, warm. 17-21 Cool, rain. 22-31 Sunny, pleasant.

SEPT. 2001: Temp. 64° (1° below avg. north; 1° above south); precip. 1" (1" below avg.; 1" above north). 1-5 Occasional rain. 6-13 Seasonable, morning fog, afternoon sun. 14-23 Rainy intervals north; sun and showers south. 24-30 Showers north; sunny south.

OCT. 2001: Temp. 54° (2° below avg.); precip. 7.5" (4" above avg.). 1-6 Occasional rain. 7-9 Rain north; dry south. 10-20 Frequent rain, some heavy. 21-26 Cool, rain. 27-31 Stormy; heavy rain.

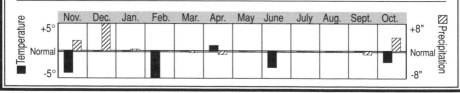

California

SUMMARY: Expect frequent heavy rainfall in the north from November through mid-January, with above-normal amounts everywhere except in the southeast. From late January through March, rainfall will be well below normal. Temperatures will follow a similar pattern, with above-normal temperatures in the first half of the winter season, then cooler-than-normal temperatures in the second half. Stormiest periods will be in early to mid-November, mid- to late December, and early and mid-January. Expect above-normal snowfall in the mountains.

April and May will bring a bit more rain than normal, with seasonable temperatures on average. Watch for a touch of summer in early to mid-May, when temperatures reach record highs.

The summer season will be a bit warmer than normal near the coast but cooler than normal in the Valley. Expect less-than-usual amounts of coastal fog and clouds, with abundant sunshine the rule from June through August. Hottest temperatures will occur in mid- to late June throughout the region, mid-July in the Valley, mid-July and mid-September in the Bay area, and early to mid-September in the south.

September and October will see rainfall a bit above normal in most of the area, but the weather will be relatively dry in the south. September will have hot spells, but October will be cool, especially in the second half.

NOV. 2000: Temp. 55° (1° below avg.); precip. 4.5" (2" above avg.). 1-4 Sunny, warm. 5-6 Cool, coastal clouds. 7-11 Heavy rain, chilly. 12-13 Sunny, mild. 14-17 Rain, cool. 18-21 Pleasant. 22-24 Low clouds, fog. 25-30 Damp.

DEC. 2000: Temp. 53° (3° above avg.); precip. 4.5" (6" above avg. north; 2" below south). 1-5 Rain, then sunny. 6-8 Cloudy north; sunny south. 9-11 Cloudy. 12-15 Stormy north; sunny south. 16-21 Heavy rain. 22-31 Rain north; sunny south.

JAN. 2001: Temp. 50° (1° above avg.); precip. 6" (5" above avg. west; 1" above east). 1-9 Rain north; clouds south. 10-13 Rain north; sunny south. 14-21 Stormy; heavy rain. 22-25 Sunny north; light rain south. 26-31 Cool.

FEB. 2001: Temp. 49° (3° below avg.); precip. 2" (1° below avg.). 1-7 Sunny, seasonable. 8-11 Sunny, cold. 12-15 Rain north; sunny south. 16-20 Rain. 21-28 Light rain north; pleasant south.

MAR. 2001: Temp. 55.5° (1° below avg. west; 2° above east); precip. 0.5" (2" below avg.). 1-7 Sunny, cool. 8-12 Sunny, warm. 13-23 Sunny, mild. 24-31 Rain, cool, then sunny and warm.

APR. 2001: Temp. 58° (avg.); precip. 2" (0.5" above avg.). 1-3 Sunny. 4-8 Rain, chilly. 9-18 Seasonable, dry. 19-21 Rain. 22-26 Seasonable. 27-30 Occasional rain.

MAY 2001: Temp. 62.5° (1° above avg. west; 2° below east); precip. 0.8" (0.2" above avg.). 1-5 Rain, cool. 6-10 Sunny, hot. 11-14 Showers, then cool. 15-20 Seasonable. 21-31 Cool.

JUNE 2001: Temp. 67° (2° above avg. west; 2° below east); precip. 0.0" (0.1" below avg.). 1-7 Sunny; hot inland. 8-10 Sunny, cool. 11-19 Sunny, coastal clouds, seasonable. 20-23 Sunny, hot. 24-30 Sunny, comfortable.

JULY 2001: Temp. 69° (1° above avg. west; 3° below east); precip. 0.0" (avg.). 1-6 Sprinkles northwest; sunny elsewhere. 7-11 Sunny. 12-21 Sunny, warm; hot in the Valley. 22-25 Sunny. 26-31 Mist northwest; cool in the Valley.

AUG. 2001: Temp. 70° (1° above avg. west; 1° below east); precip. 0.0" (avg.). 1-5 Seasonable. 6-11 Seasonable; cool in the Valley. 12-15 Clouds north; seasonable elsewhere. 16-19 Sunny, warm. 20-24 Seasonable. 25-31 Hot in the Valley; seasonable elsewhere.

SEPT. 2001: Temp. 69° (2° above avg.); precip. 0.5" (0.2" below avg.). 1-4 Hot south; seasonable elsewhere. 5-9 Sunny, seasonable. 10-12 Thunderstorms north; hot south. 13-14 Sunny, cool. 15-22 Hot north; then hot south. 23-30 Warm, a few thunderstorms.

OCT. 2001: Temp. 61° (1° below avg.); precip. 1.1" (0.3" above avg.; 0.3" below south). 1-4 Clouds; showers north. 5-9 Pleasant. 10-15 Seasonable. 16-17 Showers. 18-24 Rain north; cold central and south. 25-31 Rain, chilly.

San Francisco

Fresno

Los Angeles

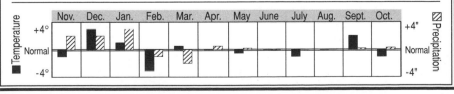

SCHWABE, HALE, GLEISSBERG, AND WILLETT*

AND THE

SEARCH FOR THE SOLAR-CLIMATE CONNECTION

Every 11 years or so, sunspots—intense magnetic storms on the surface of the Sun—reach a maximum intensity.
For centuries, observers have mapped and tracked this cycle and tried to link it with our weather. With sunspot activity having peaked in 2000, you can bet that climatologists are studying the Sun and crunching the numbers.

BY CLIFFORD NIELSEN

* Hint: They're not a bunch of small-town lawyers.

One misty morning near Mount Lycabettus in Greece, about 400 B.C., a man named Meton was observing the Sun as he sought to determine predictable changes in the location of sunrise and moonrise. The mist made blemishes on the Sun stand out with unusual clarity, and acting on a hunch, Meton looked back through 20 years of his notes. He concluded that weather tended to be rainier when spots appeared on the Sun. This is the first known discovery of the solar-climate link.

It was another 2,000 years before anyone in Europe noted sunspots again. In the early 1600s, five astronomers, including Galileo, "discovered" them almost simultaneously. In 1801, Sir William Herschel, most famous for his discovery of infrared radiation, announced that he had found a direct correlation between sunspot activity and the price of grain in London. Unfortunately, the tendency reversed itself almost before the ink on his essay had dried, and the connection showed up only sporadically through the remainder of the 19th century.

–HAO/NCAR Archives

Heinrich Schwabe

Half a century later, in 1851, German apothecary Heinrich Schwabe's notes were published, proving periodicity in sunspot cycles, an average of 11.3 years during which sunspot count increased to a peak and then decreased. When Schwabe announced his discovery, the rush to connect the sunspot cycle to virtually all natural phenomena rivaled the California gold rush. Supposed connections were made between the 11-year cycles and salmon populations, grain harvests, mood swings, illness, the Indian monsoon, and even volcanoes and earthquakes. The "success" of these forecasts universally rivaled that of Herschel's—sporadic correlations at best.

(c o n t i n u e d)

SOLAR CYCLES BY DURATION		
One Schwabe	=	11 years (average)
Two Schwabes	=	One Hale (22 years average)
Four Hales	=	One Gleissberg (88 years average)

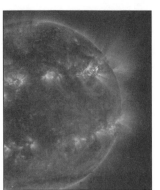

Active regions of sunspots, flares, and coronal mass ejections appear as white areas in this 1998 photo of the Sun.

In the 20th century, meteorologists began looking for consistent atmospheric changes that could be associated with changes in the sunspot count. In 1951, Hurd Curtis Willett, professor of meteorology at MIT, rocked the meteorological world by publishing an article in the *Journal of the American Meteorological Society*. In "An Extrapolation of Sunspot-Climate Connection," Willett contended that large-scale weather patterns, drought trends, heavy rainfall trends, and hurricane activity could be generally predicted well in advance based on the progression of two sunspot cycles. One is the Hale, or double-sunspot, cycle; the other is the Gleissberg cycle.

A Hale cycle is simply two of Schwabe's 11-year cycles linked together. The Sun changes polarity every 11 years or so, in close synchrony with the low period in sunspots, so it takes roughly 22 years to come full circle. (This was first observed by George Ellery Hale in 1912.) The Sun's northern hemisphere has a positive charge during the first 11-year cycle, a negative charge during the second.

A Gleissberg cycle (named for German astronomer Wolfgang Gleissberg) is four Hale cycles linked together, or roughly 88 years. The Gleissberg cycle is shorter—about 80 years—when the Sun is unusually active, as it was during the 20th century. When the Sun is less active, the Gleissberg cycle can stretch to 100 years or more.

Hurd Willett also defined three discrete and different circulation patterns in Earth's atmosphere. A "stressed" pattern, found during high sunspot activity, is one in which the atmosphere is dominated by strong troughs of low pressure and ridges of high pressure; highly variable and often violent weather, including an unusual number of tornadoes and hurricanes; and long periods of drought in various parts of the world. The years 1934, 1955, 1976, and 1998 through 2000 have been typical of the stressed-circulation pattern.

A second circulation pattern, called high-latitude zonal circulation, is also associated with highly active sunspot activity, particularly during the middle of Gleissberg cycles. The circulation becomes more steadily west to east, but the jet stream and the storm tracks have a northerly displacement. Drought is common in the tropics,

Dr. Hurd Curtis Willett

and the lack of rainfall in the African Sahel results in a decrease in Atlantic tropical cyclone activity (hurricanes), as was the instance between 1970 and 1994.

In a third circulation pattern, low-latitude zonal, the storm tracks slip south, and dry conditions prevail in northerly latitudes. Significant rainfall penetrates into northern Africa, and midlatitudes are relatively cool and moist. This pattern would be prevalent, Willett said, were there no sunspot peaks at all.

Willett's ideas were controversial when he first presented them in 1951, but they later received vindication. After three destructive hurricanes made landfall in the Northeast in 1954, insurance companies asked Willett what to expect next. After two more hurricanes struck in 1955, Willett predicted that the worst was over. Beginning in 1960, hurricane activity would remain low for at least 30 years, he said. The forecast also predicted that cooler and wetter weather would prevail for the next three decades, and advised that the Great Salt Lake would reach its largest historical size near the end of the century.

All of this was picked up by the *Saturday Evening Post* on March 17, 1956. The forecast worked out, in Willett's words, "pretty well." Tropical cyclones decreased in number; wetter and cooler conditions became so predominant that by the mid-1970s, warnings were being issued about the onset of a new Ice Age; and the Great Salt Lake reached its greatest historical size in 1987.

The research into the link between sunspots and the weather is ongoing. Charles Perry of the U.S. Geological Survey has noted that a sunspot peak is often accompanied by drought throughout the country and particularly in the western United States. The winter of 1999-2000 fell in such a period, and although there was some precipitation, the entire country was drier than normal.

Dr. Richard Head, one of the foremost solar-cycle forecasters and the solar prognosticator for *The Old Farmer's Almanac,* notes that the current Hale cycle will end around 2008. He believes that sunspot activity will then tail off and that

the coming Gleissberg cycle will be relatively quiet. Consequently, this century may witness low-latitude zonal flow and cooler and wetter conditions in the midlatitudes of the Northern Hemisphere. So don't throw out those umbrellas just yet.

■

THE SCHWABE CYCLE

This cycle has been observed and studied for more than 150 years, and its duration can range from about 9 to 14 years. Its weather effects are not fully understood. At the peak of the cycle, many of the Sun's signals increase, including irradiance and solar winds.

■

THE HALE DOUBLE-SUNSPOT CYCLE

Because the Sun's irradiance output follows 11-year cycles rather than 22-year cycles, the influence of the Hale cycles is most likely found in the effects of the magnetic signature of solar wind particles. When the Sun's northern hemisphere is positively charged, solar wind particles are negatively charged, and vice versa. Solar wind bombardment at the highest levels of Earth's atmosphere, particularly in the Northern Hemisphere, may result in dramatic circulation changes.

■

THE GLEISSBERG CYCLE

This, like the 22-year cycle, is clear in the sunspot record and can range from about 80 to 100 years. It also shows up in meteorological records. One curiosity of the Gleissberg (sometimes called the "secular" cycle), is that it tends to reverse itself in terms of weather effects in the subsequent cycle. □□

For more on sunspots, see our article on the aurora borealis, page 86.

➡ **Spinning the Web: Go to www.almanac.com and click on Article Links 2001 for Web sites related to this article. –*The Editors***

"We're looking for people

IF YOU WANT TO WRITE AND SEE YOUR WORK PUBLISHED, there's no better way to do it than writing books and stories for children and teenagers. Ideas flow naturally, right out of your own life. And while it's still a challenge, the odds of getting that first, unforgettable check from a children's publisher are better than they are from any other kind of publisher.

Your words will never sound as sweet as they do from the lips of a child reading your books and stories. And the joy of creating books and stories that truly reach young people is an experience you won't find anywhere else.

A surprisingly big market

But, that's not all. The financial rewards go far beyond most people's expectations, because there's a surprisingly big market out there for writers who are trained to tap it. More than $1.5 *billion* worth of children's books are purchased annually, and almost 500 publishers of books and 600 publishers of magazines related to children and teenagers buy freelance writing. That means that *there are thousands of manuscripts being purchased every month of the year!*

Yet two big questions bedevil nearly every would-be writer…"Am I really qualified?" and "How can I get started?"

"Am I really qualified?"

At the Institute of Children's Literature®, this is our definition of a "qualified person": someone with an aptitude for writing who can take constructive criticism, learn from it, and turn it into a professional performance.

To help us spot potential authors, we've developed a reliable test for writing aptitude based upon our 30 years of experience. It's free, and we don't charge for our evaluation. Those who pass are eligible to enroll and receive our promise:

You will complete at least one manuscript for submission to an editor or publisher by the time you finish the course.

You learn by corresponding with your own personal instructor—a nationally published writer or professional editor—in the privacy and comfort of your own home.

One-on-one training with your own instructor

Each relationship is tailored to the individual student's needs, yet every instructor works more or less the same way:

• When you're ready—at your own time and your own pace—you mail back each completed assignment.

• Your instructor reads it and rereads it to get everything out of it that you've put into it.

• Then he or she edits your assignment just the way a publishing house editor might—if he or she had the time.

• Your instructor mails it back to you

Writing for Children and Teenagers is recommended for college credits by the Connecticut Board for State Academic Awards and approved by the Connecticut Commissioner of Higher Education.

The students' statements in this ad were provided voluntarily by them, without remuneration, from 1994 to 1999.

to write children's books"

with a detailed letter explaining his or her edits and tells you what your strong points and weaknesses are, and what you can do to improve.

It's a matter of push and pull. You push and your instructor pulls, and between you both, you learn how to write and how to market your writing.

"I hit pay dirt"

This method really works. The proof of the pudding is offered by our students.

"My first two attempts met with rejection, and on the third, I hit pay dirt with *Listen Magazine,*" says Marjorie Kashdin, East Northport, NY. "My instructor was invaluable…It's not everyone who has his own 'guardian editor!'"

"I was attracted by the fact that you require an aptitude test," says Nikki Arko, Raton, NM. "Other schools sign you up as long as you have the money to pay, regardless of talent or potential."

"…a little bird…has just been given…freedom"

"The course has helped me more than I can say," writes Jody Drueding, Boston, MA. "It's as if a little bird that was locked up inside of me has just been given the freedom of the garden."

Romy Squeri, Havertown, PA, says, "I met two of your students in my critique group and realized that they were the best writers there."

"I'd take the course again in a heartbeat!"

"I'd take the course again in a heartbeat!" says Tonya Tingey, Woodruff, UT. "It made my dream a reality."

"…it is comforting to know that there are still people out there who deliver what they promise," writes Meline Knago, Midland, TX. "The Institute is everything it says it is—and maybe even more."

Of course, not everyone gets pub-

lished; we simply promise you the best training available.

FREE—Writing Aptitude Test and illustrated brochure

We offer a free Writing Aptitude Test to people who are interested in writing for children and teenagers, and we don't charge for our professional evaluation of it.

We also offer a free, illustrated brochure describing our course, *Writing for Children and Teenagers,* and introducing you to 64 of our instructors.

If your test reveals a true aptitude for writing, you'll be eligible to enroll. But that's up to you.

There is no obligation.

Get both free

Institute of Children's Literature
93 Long Ridge Road
West Redding, CT 06896-0812

Yes, please send me your free Writing Aptitude Test and illustrated brochure. I understand I'm under no obligation, and no salesperson will visit me.

Please circle one and print name clearly:

Mr.   Mrs.   Ms.   Miss   D8313

Name _____

Street _____

City _____

State _____ Zip _____

—COPYRIGHT © ICL 2000, A DIVISION OF THE INSTITUTE, INC.

COOKING for Your CAT

Does your cat look bored when you rattle the bag of dry kibble or reach for the can opener? Try your talents at homemade cat food—your popularity is guaranteed!

BY PAIGE B. GRIGLUN

Cats are carnivores. Their bodies crave vitamin A, taurine, and animal fats found in meats. A feline digestive system also needs plant fiber, such as grass or other "veggies." Unfortunately, most commercial cat foods contain minimal amounts of meat and nary a single vegetable. Though most cats will continue to eat the same store-bought diet day after day, year after year, they welcome new food with gusto.

On average, cats eat between 10 and 20 small meals (just the size of a tasty mouse) a day. Because the feline nose is four times as keen as ours, cats will often reject food that's been left uncovered for too long.

The meals and snacks below do not call for long hours in the kitchen—just a bit of shopping for special ingredients to keep on hand. To appeal to a cat's finicky tastes, prepare a whole recipe and divide it into small, tightly wrapped portions to keep in the refrigerator or freezer.

At the first sound of a hungry meow, heat food to room temperature and serve lovingly. If your furry friend snubs tuna, try mackerel; if he ignores carrots, go for cauliflower. Experiment! And always check with your veterinarian if your cat has special dietary needs. The recipes we offer here are meant to supplement kitty's regular diet, not replace it.

CRUNCHY TREATS

Find food-quality bonemeal, a good source of protein, at natural-food supermarkets or pet stores.

1/2 cup whole-wheat flour
1/2 cup nonfat dry milk
1/4 cup wheat germ
1/4 cup bonemeal
1/2 teaspoon brewer's yeast
pinch of catnip (optional)
1/2 beaten egg
1 teaspoon vegetable oil or cod liver oil
1/2 cup chicken stock
5 ounces boneless mackerel or canned tuna, packed in oil; or chopped cooked chicken

Mix dry ingredients and catnip, if using, in a large bowl and add egg, oil, and chicken stock. Mash fish or meat with a fork and add to mixture in bowl. Blend well. Shape into dime-size balls. Place onto a lightly greased baking sheet and press to flatten. Bake at 350°F for about 8 minutes, until golden, turning once. Let treats cool before serving. Store in an airtight container in the refrigerator for up to a week, or wrap in foil in packets of 10 and store in the freezer.

Makes about 60 treats.

"SPARROW" SOUP

juices from a medium-size roasted chicken or small turkey
2 to 3 cups water
pinch of garlic powder, to taste

After roasting a chicken or turkey, save the juices at the bottom of the pan. Skim off fat. Add water and garlic powder. Stir to blend. Serve lukewarm. Store leftover soup in the refrigerator for up to 5 days, or freeze.

CAT'S CANAPES

1 egg, beaten
1/4 cup grated cheddar cheese
1-1/2 slices whole-wheat bread, crumbled
1/4 cup finely chopped broccoli or string beans, or grated carrots
1 teaspoon brewer's yeast
pinch of catnip (optional)

Mix all ingredients well, mashing with a fork or your fingers. Drop by teaspoonfuls onto a lightly greased baking sheet. Bake at 350°F for 8 minutes. Cool. Break treats in half before serving. Store in an airtight container for up to 10 days, or freeze.

Makes about 36 treats.

BETTER-THAN-GRASS SALAD

1 small carrot, peeled and grated
1/4 cup peeled and grated zucchini
1/2 cup chopped alfalfa sprouts
1 teaspoon chopped fresh parsley
1/8 cup chicken stock
1/4 teaspoon dried or fresh catnip (optional)

Combine vegetables in a medium bowl. Add chicken stock and toss. Sprinkle with catnip and serve at room temperature. Store leftovers in the refrigerator for up to 3 days (do not freeze). **Makes 1 to 2 cups.**

HAMBURGER OR CHICKEN LOAF

2 eggs
1 cup milk
1 tablespoon vegetable oil
1 teaspoon bonemeal
1 tablespoon finely chopped cooked vegetable (corn, green beans, or broccoli)
1 pound raw lean hamburger meat or ground chicken
4 slices whole-wheat bread, crumbled

Mix eggs, milk, oil, bonemeal, and chopped vegetable. Add meat and bread pieces; stir. Do not overmix. Press into a greased 9x5-inch loaf pan and bake at 350°F for 50 minutes. Pour off excess juices. Let loaf set for 20 minutes before serving. Store leftovers in the refrigerator for up to 5 days, or wrap in foil in serving portions and freeze. □□

➡ Spinning the Web: Go to www.almanac.com and click on Article Links 2001 for Web sites related to this article. –*The Editors*

POETIC LICENSE

One hundred years of automobile license plates have taken us from simple initials to JST PUSH to INUDAT1! And collectors love them all. ■ **by Martha White**

–illustrated by Eldon Doty

■ The invention of the automobile was still centuries away when Martha "Mother" Shipton (1488-1561) offered this prophecy: "Carriages without horses shall go, And accidents fill the world with woe." Sure enough, in 1900, there were 8,000 "horseless carriages" nationwide, and as Mother Shipton had predicted, these newfangled inventions were wreaking havoc, running into each other, scaring horses and pedestrians, damaging property, and generally running amok.

New York State finally decided that it needed more control, so 100 years ago, on April 25, 1901, vehicle owners were required to pay $1 to register their names, addresses, and a description of their machine with the secretary of state. In return, each owner was issued a license plate.

These first, simple license plates were about three inches high and featured the owner's initials (precursors to today's

–photo below: H. Armstrong Roberts

vanity, or prestige, plates). The state of New York issued 954 of them in 1901. That same year, Connecticut passed the first speeding law, prohibiting drivers from exceeding 12 miles per hour on country highways and 8 miles per hour within city limits. In 1905, the U.S. Automobile Association was formed. Its primary purpose was to provide "scouts" to advise motorists of police "traps" along the highways and byways. The quick popularity of the automobile had spurred state governments into a kind of Keystone Kops chase to keep the peace.

"But Officer, a goat ate it!"

Before long, all the states and Canadian provinces required license plates, and they came in a variety of materials and designs. Porcelain was common; in fact, in Delaware, it was not discontinued until 1942. Steel,

–license plate photos courtesy Drew Steitz, *PL8S Magazine* editor

From the top: Eisenhower-Nixon inaugural plate (1957); Alaska's topsy-turvy plate (1976); Pennsylvania's brass-on-leather plate (1904-05); and New York's hand-painted wooden plate (c. 1902).

galvanized steel, tin, aluminum, and even copper (in Arizona) were other choices. Ontario's inaugural plates, in 1908, were made of leather. Because of metal shortages during World War II, New Brunswick used wood for motorcycle and trailer plates. For the same reason, Wyoming and other states used soybean-based fiberboard—briefly. In his book *License Plates of the United States,* Jim Fox notes that the soybean-based plates were especially popular with goats.

Over time, the three-inch plates expanded in length and width; owners' initials changed to numbers or code letters. Metal plates with their numbers stamped in paint (called "flats") gave way, by the 1920s, to embossed metal plates. Lately, all sorts of fancy graphics, from lobsters to sunsets, have appeared on the plates. Dates, tags, stickers, mottoes, and special designations add to the clutter. Eventually, many barns and garages sported an outdated license plate or two tacked to the wall—mementos of earlier times. As the plate variations mounted, those barn wall collections expanded, as well. Hobbyists and traders started scouring secondhand shops and flea markets for old plates. Junkyards, rural dumps, auto scrap yards, and even local Department of Motor Vehicles offices became collectors' paradises. Today, conventions, swap meets, and Internet Web sites have expanded the trading. Rare or vintage plates occasionally sell for thousands of dollars at auctions, but $10 to $20 covers an average sale.

EXPLORE CANADA'S ARCTIC
9999
NORTHWEST TERRITORIES

–plate above courtesy Ralph Oeckinghaus, www.ralph.at

WYOMING
1936 0 1

FEB — AGRICULTURE
VAM 3 RW-054
KEEPS FLORIDA GREEN

19
Georgia 98
5559
1996 Paralympic

MAY VIRGINIA 97
4343WD
WILDLIFE CONSERVATIONIST

From the top: Polar bears for Arctic cars; the Wyoming governor's own plate (1936); Florida's farm plate; Georgia's Paralympics plate (1996); and Virginia's special wildlife issue (1997).

Making a Case for Vanity, or RUSQTSI
("ARE YOU AS CUTE AS I?")

■ In 100 years, some things have not changed. Many vehicle owners still identify themselves by having their initials on their license plates. On the other hand, specialized vanity plates today can cost many dollars extra. "New-age" environmental vanity plates, sporting a loon or

Honk If You're from Oiho

The Automobile License Plate Collectors Association (ALPCA), formed in 1954, has grown to be the world's largest club of license plate collectors, with over 3,000 active members in 19 countries. Through ALPCA's Web site (www.alpca.org) and other license plate collectors' links, you can discover, for instance, that Pope John Paul II has his own vanity plate (a pontiff's miter, of course).

With so many license plates on the market and so many collectors, specialization is key. New collectors may specify a "run" they hope to complete, such as a collection of every state's plate for their birth year. Some people collect only truck plates, dealer plates, environmental plates, or motorcycle plates.

Costs can become prohibitive, especially if you collect rare plates, such as those printed with errors. Some Ohio and South Carolina plates, for example, were issued as OIHO and SOUTH CAROLNIA before the errors were caught. Rumor has it that the OIHO plates were used for years before anyone complained! Possibly, drivers even preferred them—it looks right in a rearview mirror, after all.

Cracking the Code

With a little training, you can learn to read more from a license plate than just the state motto. Some states, for example, have letter or number codes that indicate

Alberta's Smithson International Truck Museum—well worth the drive for license-plate lovers.

Plate Collectors' Paradise

■ To tour the world's largest public plate display, go to Rimbey, Alberta, Canada, where you'll find the Smithson International Truck Museum in Pas Ka Poo Park. Here, over 2,200 plates from 55 countries are on display in the John Roberts License Plate Collection. The museum also houses 19 fully restored International Harvester half-ton trucks, one for each year of production up through 1974. For more information, call 403-843-2004.

—courtesy Rob Gilgan / Rimbey Review

other kind of wildlife, offer a donation toward certain nonprofit protective agencies.

Each state must exercise its own department of censure, to ensure that offensive plates are not issued. Screening for tastelessness can be difficult, however, unless you know how to crack the codes.

Can you read these actual plates?

PB4UGO	Pee before you go
GO4THNX	Go forth and multiply
LVUBYBY	Love you, bye bye
IRIGHTI	Right between the eyes
GDSGIFT	God's gift
6A LDY	Sexy lady
INUDAT1	I knew that one

Imaginary Vanities

■ In October 1995, *Atlantic Monthly* magazine ran a contest on their Online Wordgame Web site, where avid puzzlers submitted fictitious vanity plates for historic figures. Submissions had to contain no more than seven capital letters or digits, and the famous person had to have lived before the advent of the automobile. Some submissions for King Henry VIII, for example, included 6WIVES, XWIVES, HEADSUP, HEDSOFF, NEXT, and NECKST. Copernicus got ITROT8S ("it rotates"); Christopher Columbus was tagged ITS RND, NOTFLAT, and LANDHO; and Oedipus was awarded ILUVMOM. Nathaniel Hawthorne, author of *The Scarlet Letter,* rated an A PLUS. Our favorites were the philosophers: Plato, with Y; Socrates, with Y NOT; and Aristotle, with Y ASK Y.

in what county a car is registered. Author Jim Fox recalls that the president of the United States used to have the number 100 on his Washington, D.C., plate, until it was considered too big a security risk in the late 1960s. Plate reading in the Washington, D.C., area can still offer plenty of information, however, as you begin to decode the licenses for various political delegations from all over the world.

Vanity plates offer still more information, perhaps giving personal initials (was there ever an FDR, perhaps, or a JFK?), business names (TVDNR1 for a frozen-foods tycoon), or occupations (DR2B for a medical student, 2THDOC for a dentist, or XNAVY for a retired Navy member). You can even get ad-

vice, as with this plate from Illinois: JST PUSH, which we're told means "Just pray until something happens."

Dictionary of Commonly Used "Words"

■ To help you get started with designing your own vanity plate, we offer this brief dictionary.

B4	before	R	are
D	the	S	as, yes
F	if	U	you
GR8	great, grate	XTC	ecstasy
L	hell	Y	why
M	am, I'm	YFS	wife's
M8	mate	6	sex
N	an, and, in	6A or 6E	sexy
QT	cute		☐☐

➡ Spinning the Web: Go to www.almanac.com and click on Article Links 2001 for Web sites related to this article. –*The Editors*

"I Know Impotence...
Let me help you feel like a young man again."

After heart surgery and medications left me impotent, I worked with urologists to design safe and effective products that any man can successfully use to regain sexual potency. Since 1989, Vet-Co has become a leading world-class manufacturer of quality medical impotence products. Vet-Co products are FDA registered and covered by Medicare.

Our products are prescribed by impotence specialists around the world. All products are discreetly shipped to your door. **Why wait another day to live your life to the fullest?** Call one of my customer service professionals today and learn more. I am so confident that you'll find my products useful, we offer an **unconditional, risk-free, 30-day money-back guarantee.**

Sincerely,

Sol Shapiro

Sol Shapiro
President Vet-Co, Inc.

You deserve the best! Great for...
- Men who want immediate results.
- Men who want a safe and reliable form of treatment.
- Men unsuccessful with prescription medications for impotence.
- Men wanting a natural, non-invasive option.

is a division of:

WE'LL FILE YOUR MEDICARE. VC FA 01

A *Rose* FOR *Daddy Frank*

Robbie Tucker was just a neophyte rose grower when he decided to hybridize a new rose to honor his grandfather. Using his guest-room closet as a greenhouse, he created national award-winning miniature roses. But he's still on a quest for that perfect red rose.

by Christine Schultz

YOU PROBABLY NEVER HEARD OF DADDY FRANK KONCZAK, who raised parakeets, ran a paper route, and fixed neighbors' lawn mowers in his garage in small-town Clyde, Texas, but someday you might. Someday you might open a rose catalog and see a brilliant-red hybrid tea named 'Daddy Frank', a rose that suggests his wild flash of color and form. For though Daddy Frank was never a wealthy man, he always wore a hat and looked as sharp as a movie star or maybe a gangster—flamboyant and full of bull, as his grandson Robbie Tucker will tell you.

Robbie grew up a mile down the road from Daddy Frank and spent many a 4 A.M. rolling newspapers with his grand-dad, many an afternoon cleaning flyways for the thousands of birds he raised, and many a day listening to his granddad's stories. When Daddy Frank passed away in 1987, he left a hole in his grandson's heart. "I was sitting around missing him one day," says Robbie, "and I thought, here's going to be my goal: To come up with an awesome red hybrid tea named in his honor."

Robbie was living in Houston, Texas, and had befriended Mary Fulgham, a fellow rose grower who created a rose to honor her cousin Steve Silverthorn, who had

–illustrated by Renée Quintal Daily   –photos courtesy Robbie Tucker

Looking sharp in this 1926 photograph is Frank Konczak, Robbie Tucker's grandfather and hero. Robbie's dream is to honor Frank with a perfect red rose.

Robbie's first attempt at rose hybridizing created 'Miss Flippins'—winner of the National Mini Queen competition in 1997.

I can remember breaking a taproot and feeling so awful, thinking I might just have killed the 'Daddy Frank' rose."

lost his battle to Hodgkin's disease. Mary showed Robbie how to cross roses. Once he'd made up his mind to do it, Robbie couldn't get enough. He joined the Rose Hybridizers Association, ordered every newsletter ever printed, and read every word.

What he learned about hybridizing was that anyone could do it. As a manager for ALCOA Industrial Chemicals, he had had no experience with roses until two years earlier, when he and his wife and two children moved into their house in Houston. Only one scrawny rose bloomed in his whole barren yard. Robbie did exactly the wrong thing and moved it into the shade. Despite his mistake, the rose lived. The next year, he put in four more bushes. They got black spot.

He called local rose expert Patsy Williams, who not only diagnosed his rose problem over the phone while doing dishes, but also persuaded the Tuckers to join the Houston Rose Society to learn more.

With Patsy as guru, Robbie caught the rose-growing fever. By the following year, he had 125 bushes in his yard and a passion for roses in his heart. Though ideally you would hybridize in a greenhouse to avoid bees and bad weather, Robbie didn't have that option. On July 2, 1993, his grandfather's birthday, he made his first crosses in his garden in Franklin, Tennessee, where his family had moved.

To understand how hybridizing works, Robbie explains, you must know that a rose has both male and female anatomy. The anthers (male) form pollen that fertilizes the pistils (female). When the bloom chosen to be the female was between half and three-quarters open, Robbie removed the petals, then removed the anthers so that the rose could not self-pollinate. That same night, he collected pollen from the rose variety that he wanted to use as the father. To do this, he removed the petals, then cut off the top neck (peduncle) of each rose from the last leaf up to the bloom. The cut left what looked like a little paintbrush. He set that onto a white piece of paper in the house to dry overnight.

In the morning, he gently tapped the little paintbrush, and golden pollen fell onto the paper. He took the peduncle outside. Overnight, the pistils of the female rose had formed the sticky secretion needed to break open the pollen capsules so that the sperm could fertilize the plant. He carefully painted the pollen onto the pistils. They carried the sperm down into the ovaries, where seeds would form in the rose hip.

In three to four months, the seeds had ripened. Robbie removed the seeds and planted them in trays in a half-and-half mix of peat moss and Perlite; he marked them with the names of the roses he had crossed. After refrigerating the trays at 36° to 38°F for four to six weeks to simulate winter, Robbie put them into his garage for a month or so of 50° to 70°F temperatures.

When the seeds germinated, he replanted each one into a three-inch pot. "You reach into the dirt and pull the little seedlings out," he says. "It's a tender moment. I can remember breaking a taproot and feeling so awful, thinking I might just have killed the 'Daddy Frank' rose." But 28 seedlings survived his first trials, and Robbie took those inside. He had talked his wife, Marsha, into letting him use the closet in the guest bedroom as a makeshift greenhouse. He'd lined the walls and floor with plastic sheets and hung fluorescent "grow" lights from the ceiling.

We should mention here that the odds of Robbie's dream coming true—of one of those first 28 seedlings becoming a nationally marketable rose—were long at best. "When you cross two roses," American Rose Society (ARS) vice president Thomas Cairns says, "maybe one seed in 100,000 may have some perfect qualities about it. Part of successful rose breeding is having the intuitive eye and sense of seeing that first bloom and knowing it's something great."

When Robbie saw his first blooms open, they all looked great. "There is nothing more pleasing than to be in the greenhouse, or the closet, or wherever your seeds are germinating," says Robbie, "and watch a rose bloom for the first time. Every seed is genetically different, even if it came out of the same hip, so not one other person in the world is experiencing what you're experiencing at that moment. Most of the new roses aren't going to be marketable, it's true, but I haven't found one yet that wasn't pretty in its own way."

Among Robbie's first blooms, there were five seedlings that he had some hope for. He planted them all in his garden that spring, then watched and waited. After the first year, he thought he might have something: a beautiful red miniature with a deep-pink reverse like none on the market. He took it to the Tenarky District Show in Memphis that fall of 1995. Out of more than 100 seedlings, his won. The next year, it took two more

There is nothing more pleasing than to be in the greenhouse, or the closet, or wherever your seeds are germinating, and watch a rose bloom for the first time.

Essentials FOR Growing THE Best Roses

1. *Water your roses a couple of times a week in the morning or evening hours, giving them the minimum they need of two inches of rain per week.*

2. *Spray your roses once a week in the morning or evening with a strong jet of water, a mite blaster, or a miticide to eliminate spider mites. Another way to slow mites from climbing up your healthy plants is to remove the bottom six to eight inches of leaves. Also rotate in alternate sprays for black spot and other diseases.*

3. *Feed your roses once or twice a month with fertilizer containing nitrogen, phosphorus, and potassium for beautiful foliage, long stems, and big blooms.*

4. *To encourage new growth, deadhead spent blooms, and prune in the spring.*

5. *Talk to rosarians in your area for more localized advice.*

top prizes. Robbie showed his new red miniature to Dennis and Suzy Bridges of Bridges Roses in North Carolina. They took one look, were won over by the little red rose, and agreed to market it.

Because the rose wasn't what he'd had in mind for Daddy Frank, Robbie decided to name his creation 'Miss Flippins'—his father's nickname for Robbie's own 13-year-old daughter, a dancer. In the spring of 1997, Robbie exhibited 'Miss Flippins' in the national rose competition in Minneapolis. It won National Mini Queen. Says Robbie, "I bawled my eyes out."

Robbie had also entered a large white miniature rose for the first time. It took Best Seedling. He registered it as 'Cachet' and took it to the national rose show in Shreveport, Louisiana, that fall. There it also won National Mini Queen. Robbie was on a roll. He expanded his makeshift closet greenhouse to the attic and continued to hybridize. There he came up with a medium-yellow rose that he named for his father. After a two-year trial period, 'Little Tommy Tucker' was chosen for the ARS's highest honor for miniatures: the Award of Excellence.

Robbie waited until Christmas to share the good news with his father. His family gathered to watch Tommy unwrap his package. As the family's practical joker, Tommy was expecting the package to hold a good laugh. What he found instead was a good cry. Inside was the most moving of gifts, an award-winning rose with this dedication:

"A product of the Depression, Tommy Tucker grew up in the small farming community of Clyde, Texas. Due to his father's illness and subsequent death, he became the family's principal breadwinner at the age of 13. Accepting this heavy burden meant giving up much of his own education, but it didn't prevent him from applying his work ethic to ensure that his own children would have the opportunity denied him. . . . In his youth, Dad was often teased about being the 'Little Tommy

Macular Degeneration

The VideoEye® power magnification system combines simplicity and versatility to help people with low vision continue reading and doing everyday tasks.

A self-focusing viewing head on a precision arm moves over anything you want to see. Crisp images are displayed in full color on a high-resolution monitor magnified up to 25 times larger.

Prescription bottles   **Writing checks**

Self care   **Reading**

Knitting, handwork   **Mirror**

FREE information and video!

or George Bush, are
hakes for any othe
— something to be
generously and with a
sonal touch, however fl
The former president
s been a man of le

30 day money-back guarantee
For information or to order call
1-800-416-0758
www.videoeyecorp.com

VideoEye Corporation, Dept. TF 10211 West Emerald • Boise, ID 83704

ph (208) 323-9577 fax (208) 377-1528 ® VideoEye is a registered trademark of VideoEye Corporation Patents pending

Tucker' in the nursery rhyme. We, his children, can affirm that the real Tommy Tucker is a very big man indeed."

*T*he satisfaction of such an achievement spurred Robbie to continue creating. Next came a red-and-white hybrid tea named 'Standing Ovation' (available from Edmunds' Roses) and then a light-pink miniature named 'Amy Grant' for his daughter's hero, the gospel and pop singer (available from Nor' East Miniature Roses).

Robbie grows about 400 roses in his garden now and hybridizes about 5,000 seeds each year. He is still in search of the perfect red rose for his grandfather. His newest rose is a petite red-and-white with medium-green foliage. Robbie named it for Amy Grant's grandmother, Zell, who was a wonderful gardener. Nor' East Miniature Roses will introduce 'Zell' in the spring of 2001. And though it's not the rose Robbie had in mind for his own Daddy Frank, it's the next

best thing: a rose to honor all grandparents throughout the world.

Robbie Tucker Rose Sources

BRIDGES ROSES
734 Toney Rd.
Lawndale, NC 28090
704-538-9412; fax 704-538-1521
www.shelby.net/briroses

EDMUNDS' ROSES
6235 Southwest Kahle Rd.
Wilsonville, OR 97979
888-481-7673 or 503-682-1476;
fax 503-682-1275
www.edmundsroses.com

NOR' EAST MINIATURE ROSES
P.O. Box 307
Rowley, MA 01969
800-426-6485 or 978-948-7964;
fax 978-948-5487
www.noreast-miniroses.com

➡ **Spinning the Web: Go to www.almanac.com and click on Article Links 2001 for Web sites related to this article. *–The Editors*** □ □

Full-Moon Names

■ Historically, the Indians of what are now the northern and eastern United States kept track of the seasons by giving a distinctive name to each recurring full Moon, this name being applied to the entire month in which it occurred. With some variations, the same Moon names were used throughout the Algonquin tribes from New England to Lake Superior.

NAME	MONTH	OTHER NAMES USED
Full Wolf Moon	January	Full Old Moon
Full Snow Moon	February	Full Hunger Moon
Full Worm Moon	March	Full Crow Moon, Full Crust Moon, Full Sugar Moon, Full Sap Moon
Full Pink Moon	April	Full Sprouting Grass Moon, Full Egg Moon, Full Fish Moon
Full Flower Moon	May	Full Corn Planting Moon, Full Milk Moon
Full Strawberry Moon	June	Full Rose Moon, Full Hot Moon
Full Buck Moon	July	Full Thunder Moon, Full Hay Moon
Full Sturgeon Moon	August	Full Red Moon, Full Green Corn Moon
Full Harvest Moon*	September	Full Corn Moon, Full Barley Moon
Full Hunter's Moon	October	Full Travel Moon, Full Dying Grass Moon
Full Beaver Moon	November	Full Frost Moon
Full Cold Moon	December	Full Long Nights Moon

* The Harvest Moon is always the full Moon closest to the autumnal equinox. If the Harvest Moon occurs in October, the September full Moon is usually called the Corn Moon.

Outdoor Planting Table

2 0 0 1

■ The best time to plant flowers and vegetables that bear crops above ground is during the *light* of the Moon; that is, from the day the Moon is new to the day it is full. Flowering bulbs and vegetables that bear crops below ground should be planted during the *dark* of the Moon; that is, from the day after it is full to the day before it is new again. The Moon Favorable columns at right give these Moon days, which are based on the Moon's phases for 2001 and the safe periods for planting in areas that receive frost. Consult **page 178** for dates of frosts and lengths of growing seasons. See the **Left-Hand Calendar Pages 58-84** for the exact days of the new and full Moons.

Aboveground Crops Marked (*)

(E) means Early   (L) means Late

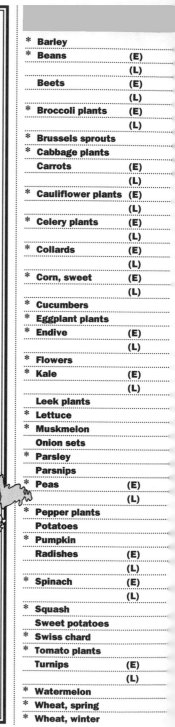

* Barley	
* Beans	(E)
	(L)
Beets	(E)
	(L)
* Broccoli plants	(E)
	(L)
* Brussels sprouts	
* Cabbage plants	
Carrots	(E)
	(L)
* Cauliflower plants	(E)
	(L)
* Celery plants	(E)
	(L)
* Collards	(E)
	(L)
* Corn, sweet	(E)
	(L)
* Cucumbers	
* Eggplant plants	
* Endive	(E)
	(L)
* Flowers	
* Kale	(E)
	(L)
Leek plants	
* Lettuce	
* Muskmelon	
Onion sets	
* Parsley	
Parsnips	
* Peas	(E)
	(L)
* Pepper plants	
Potatoes	
* Pumpkin	
Radishes	(E)
	(L)
* Spinach	(E)
	(L)
* Squash	
Sweet potatoes	
* Swiss chard	
* Tomato plants	
Turnips	(E)
	(L)
* Watermelon	
* Wheat, spring	
* Wheat, winter	

Planting Dates	Moon Favorable	Planting Dates	Moon Favorable	Planting Dates	Moon Favorable	Planting Dates	Moon Favorable
2/15-3/7	2/23-3/7	3/15-4/7	3/24-4/7	5/15-6/21	5/22-6/5, 6/21	6/1-30	6/1-5, 6/21-30
3/15-4/7	3/24-4/7	4/15-30	4/23-30	5/7-6/21	5/7, 5/22-6/5, 6/21	5/30-6/15	5/30-6/5
8/7-31	8/18-31	7/1-21	7/1-5, 7/20-21	6/15-7/15	6/21-7/5	—	—
2/7-28	2/9-22	3/15-4/3	3/15-23	5/1-15	5/8-15	5/25-6/10	6/6-10
9/1-30	9/3-16	8/15-31	8/15-17	7/15-8/15	7/15-19, 8/5-15	6/15-7/8	6/15-20, 7/6-8
2/15-3/15	2/23-3/9	3/7-31	3/7-9, 3/24-31	5/15-31	5/22-31	6/1-25	6/1-5, 6/21-25
9/7-30	9/17-30	8/1-20	8/1-4, 8/18-20	6/15-7/7	6/21-7/5	—	
2/11-3/20	2/23-3/9	3/7-4/15	3/7-9, 3/24-4/7	5/15-31	5/22-31	6/1-25	6/1-5, 6/21-25
2/11-3/20	2/23-3/9	3/7-4/15	3/7-9, 3/24-4/7	5/15-31	5/22-31	6/1-25	6/1-5, 6/21-25
2/15-3/7	2/15-22	3/7-31	3/10-23	5/15-31	5/15-21	5/25-6/10	6/6-10
8/1-9/7	8/5-17, 9/3-7	7/7-31	7/7-19	6/15-7/21	6/15-20, 7/6-19	6/15-7/8	6/15-20, 7/6-8
2/15-3/7	2/23-3/7	3/15-4/7	3/24-4/7	5/15-31	5/22-31	6/1-25	6/1-5, 6/21-25
8/7-31	8/18-31	7/1-8/7	7/1-5, 7/20-8/4	6/15-7/21	6/21-7/5, 7/20-21	—	
2/15-28	2/23-28	3/7-31	3/7-9, 3/24-31	5/15-6/30	5/22-6/5, 6/21-30	6/1-30	6/1-5, 6/21-30
9/15-30	9/17-30	8/15-9/7	8/18-9/2	7/15-8/15	7/20-8/4		
2/11-3/20	2/23-3/9	3/7-4/7	3/7-9, 3/24-4/7	5/15-31	5/22-31	6/1-25	6/1-5, 6/21-25
9/7-30	9/17-30	8/15-31	8/18-31	7/1-8/7	7/1-5, 7/20-8/4	—	
3/15-31	3/24-31	4/1-17	4/1-7	5/10-6/15	5/22-6/5	5/30-6/20	5/30-6/5
8/7-31	8/18-31	7/7-21	7/20-21	6/15-30	6/21-30	—	—
3/7-4/15	3/7-9, 3/24-4/7	4/7-5/15	4/7, 4/23-5/7	5/7-6/20	5/7, 5/22-6/5	5/30-6/15	5/30-6/5
3/7-4/15	3/7-9, 3/24-4/7	4/7-5/15	4/7, 4/23-5/7	6/1-30	6/1-5, 6/21-30	6/15-30	6/21-30
2/15-3/20	2/23-3/9	4/7-5/15	4/7, 4/23-5/7	5/15-31	5/22-31	6/1-25	6/1-5, 6/21-25
8/15-9/7	8/18-9/2	7/15-8/15	7/20-8/4	6/7-30	6/21-30	—	
3/15-4/7	3/24-4/7	4/15-30	4/23-30	5/7-6/21	5/7, 5/22-6/5, 6/21	6/1-30	6/1-5, 6/21-30
2/11-3/20	2/23-3/9	3/7-4/7	3/7-9, 3/24-4/7	5/15-31	5/22-31	6/1-15	6/1-5
9/7-30	9/17-30	8/15-31	8/18-31	7/1-8/7	7/1-5, 7/20-8/4	6/25-7/15	6/25-7/5
2/15-4/15	2/15-22, 3/10-23, 4/8-15	3/7-4/7	3/10-23	5/15-31	5/15-21	6/1-25	6/6-20
2/15-3/7	2/23-3/7	3/1-31	3/1-9, 3/24-31	5/15-6/30	5/22-6/5, 6/21-30	6/1-30	6/1-5, 6/21-30
3/15-4/7	3/24-4/7	4/15-5/7	4/23-5/7	5/15-6/30	5/22-6/5, 6/21-30	6/1-30	6/1-5, 6/21-30
2/1-28	2/9-22	3/1-31	3/10-23	5/15-6/7	5/15-21, 6/6-7	6/1-25	6/6-20
2/20-3/15	2/23-3/9	3/1-31	3/1-9, 3/24-31	5/15-31	5/22-31	6/1-15	6/1-5
1/15-2/4	1/15-23	3/7-31	3/10-23	4/1-30	4/8-22	5/10-31	5/10-21
1/15-2/7	1/24-2/7	3/7-31	3/7-9, 3/24-31	4/15-5/7	4/23-5/7	5/15-31	5/22-31
9/15-30	9/17-30	8/7-31	8/18-31	7/15-31	7/20-31	7/10-25	7/20-25
3/1-20	3/1-9	4/1-30	4/1-7, 4/23-30	5/15-6/30	5/22-6/5, 6/21-30	6/1-30	6/1-5, 6/21-30
2/10-28	2/10-22	4/1-30	4/8-22	5/1-31	5/8-21	6/1-25	6/6-20
3/7-20	3/7-9	4/23-5/15	4/23-5/7	5/15-31	5/22-31	6/1-30	6/1-5, 6/21-30
1/21-3/1	1/21-23, 2/9-22	3/7-31	3/10-23	4/15-30	4/15-22	5/15-6/5	5/15-21
10/1-21	10/3-15	9/7-30	9/7-16	8/15-31	8/15-17	7/10-31	7/10-19
2/7-3/15	2/7-8, 2/23-3/9	3/15-4/20	3/24-4/7	5/15-31	5/22-31	6/1-25	6/1-5, 6/21-25
10/1-21	10/1-2, 10/16-21	8/1-9/15	8/1-4, 8/18-9/2	7/17-9/7	7/20-8/4, 8/18-9/2	7/20-8/5	7/20-8/4
3/15-4/15	3/24-4/7	4/15-30	4/23-30	5/15-6/15	5/22-6/5	6/1-30	6/1-5, 6/21-30
3/23-4/6	3/23	4/21-5/2	4/21-22	5/15-6/15	5/15-21, 6/6-15	6/1-30	6/6-20
2/7-3/15	2/7-8, 2/23-3/9	3/15-4/15	3/24-4/7	5/1-31	5/1-7, 5/22-31	5/15-31	5/22-31
3/7-20	3/7-9	4/7-30	4/7, 4/23-30	5/15-31	5/22-31	6/1-15	6/1-5
1/20-2/15	1/20-23, 2/9-15	3/15-31	3/15-23	4/7-30	4/8-22	5/10-31	5/10-21
9/1-10/15	9/3-16, 10/3-15	8/1-20	8/5-17	7/1-8/15	7/6-19, 8/5-15	—	
3/15-4/7	3/24-4/7	4/15-5/7	4/23-5/7	5/15-6/30	5/22-6/5, 6/21-30	6/1-30	6/1-5, 6/21-30
2/15-28	2/23-28	3/1-20	3/1-9	4/7-30	4/7, 4/23-30	5/15-6/10	5/22-6/5
10/15-12/7	10/16-11/1, 11/15-30	9/15-10/20	9/17-10/2, 10/16-20	8/11-9/15	8/18-9/2	8/5-30	8/18-30

Frosts and Growing Seasons

Courtesy of National Climatic Center

■ Dates given are normal averages for a light freeze (32°F); local weather and topography may cause considerable variations. The possibility of frost occurring after the spring dates and before the fall dates is 50 percent. The classification of freeze temperatures is usually based on their effect on plants, with the following commonly accepted categories: **Light freeze:** 29° to 32°F—tender plants killed; little destructive effect on other vegetation. **Moderate freeze:** 25° to 28°F—widely destructive effect on most vegetation; heavy damage to fruit blossoms and tender and semihardy plants. **Severe freeze:** 24°F and colder—heavy damage to most plants.

CITY	Growing Season (days)	Last Frost Spring	First Frost Fall	CITY	Growing Season (days)	Last Frost Spring	First Frost Fall
Mobile, AL	272	Feb. 27	Nov. 26	North Platte, NE	136	May 11	Sept. 24
Juneau, AK	133	May 16	Sept. 26	Las Vegas, NV	259	Mar. 7	Nov. 21
Phoenix, AZ	308	Feb. 5	Dec. 15	Concord, NH	121	May 23	Sept. 22
Tucson, AZ	273	Feb. 28	Nov. 29	Newark, NJ	219	Apr. 4	Nov. 10
Pine Bluff, AR	234	Mar. 19	Nov. 8	Carlsbad, NM	223	Mar. 29	Nov. 7
Eureka, CA	324	Jan. 30	Dec. 15	Los Alamos, NM	157	May 8	Oct. 13
Sacramento, CA	289	Feb. 14	Dec. 1	Albany, NY	144	May 7	Sept. 29
San Francisco, CA	*	*	*	Syracuse, NY	170	Apr. 28	Oct. 16
Denver, CO	157	May 3	Oct. 8	Fayetteville, NC	212	Apr. 2	Oct. 31
Hartford, CT	167	Apr. 25	Oct. 10	Bismarck, ND	129	May 14	Sept. 20
Wilmington, DE	198	Apr. 13	Oct. 29	Akron, OH	168	May 3	Oct. 18
Miami, FL	*	*	*	Cincinnati, OH	195	Apr. 14	Oct. 27
Tampa, FL	338	Jan. 28	Jan. 3	Lawton, OK	217	Apr. 1	Nov. 5
Athens, GA	224	Mar. 28	Nov. 8	Tulsa, OK	218	Mar. 30	Nov. 4
Savannah, GA	250	Mar. 10	Nov. 15	Pendleton, OR	188	Apr. 15	Oct. 21
Boise, ID	153	May 8	Oct. 9	Portland, OR	217	Apr. 3	Nov. 7
Chicago, IL	187	Apr. 22	Oct. 26	Carlisle, PA	182	Apr. 20	Oct. 20
Springfield, IL	185	Apr. 17	Oct. 19	Williamsport, PA	168	Apr. 29	Oct. 15
Indianapolis, IN	180	Apr. 22	Oct. 20	Kingston, RI	144	May 8	Sept. 30
South Bend, IN	169	May 1	Oct. 18	Charleston, SC	253	Mar. 11	Nov. 20
Atlantic, IA	141	May 9	Sept. 28	Columbia, SC	211	Apr. 4	Nov. 2
Cedar Rapids, IA	161	Apr. 29	Oct. 7	Rapid City, SD	145	May 7	Sept. 29
Topeka, KS	175	Apr. 21	Oct. 14	Memphis, TN	228	Mar. 23	Nov. 7
Lexington, KY	190	Apr. 17	Oct. 25	Nashville, TN	207	Apr. 5	Oct. 29
Monroe, LA	242	Mar. 9	Nov. 7	Amarillo, TX	197	Apr. 14	Oct. 29
New Orleans, LA	288	Feb. 20	Dec. 5	Denton, TX	231	Mar. 25	Nov. 12
Portland, ME	143	May 10	Sept. 30	San Antonio, TX	265	Mar. 3	Nov. 24
Baltimore, MD	231	Mar. 26	Nov. 13	Cedar City, UT	134	May 20	Oct. 2
Worcester, MA	172	Apr. 27	Oct. 17	Spanish Fork, UT	156	May 8	Oct. 12
Lansing, MI	140	May 13	Sept. 30	Burlington, VT	142	May 11	Oct. 1
Marquette, MI	159	May 12	Oct. 19	Norfolk, VA	239	Mar. 23	Nov. 17
Duluth, MN	122	May 21	Sept. 21	Richmond, VA	198	Apr. 10	Oct. 26
Willmar, MN	152	May 4	Oct. 4	Seattle, WA	232	Mar. 24	Nov. 11
Columbus, MS	215	Mar. 27	Oct. 29	Spokane, WA	153	May 4	Oct. 5
Vicksburg, MS	250	Mar. 13	Nov. 18	Parkersburg, WV	175	Apr. 25	Oct. 18
Jefferson City, MO	173	Apr. 26	Oct. 16	Green Bay, WI	143	May 12	Oct. 2
Fort Peck, MT	146	May 5	Sept. 28	Janesville, WI	164	Apr. 28	Oct. 10
Helena, MT	122	May 18	Sept. 18	Casper, WY	123	May 22	Sept. 22
Blair, NE	165	Apr. 27	Oct. 10	*Frosts do not occur every year.			

Septic Helper 2000

If you're a homeowner, you've probably got plenty of headaches already. The last thing you need is trouble from your septic system. That's why we're proud to bring you **SEPTIC HELPER 2000**, the bacteria and enzyme additive that can help you save countless dollars and reduce your worries.

THOUSANDS OF SATISFIED CUSTOMERS HAVE PRAISED SEPTIC HELPER 2000

SEPTIC MAINTENANCE MADE EASY!

Septic Tanks/Cesspools can eventually clog up, back up and become malodorous. Slow drainage sets in and becomes a constant problem. Now there is a product available that can help maintain your system and also help it reach maximum efficiency.

"Can Help to Reduce Pump Outs"

SEPTIC HELPER 2000 can save you money by reducing the frequency of septic tank pumpouts. A small amount of SEPTIC HELPER 2000 used monthly as preventative maintenance can help to liquify your tank by digesting the organic solids. It can help clean the lines leading to and from the septic tank.

100% Money Back Guarantee

The Natural Solution - SEPTIC HELPER 2000 is a natural blend of scientifically enhanced enzyme producing bacteria that act as a catalyst and help speed up the degradation rate of organic waste.The method is natural digestion of natural food by living Friendly Bacteria. Their food is organic waste matter. They recycle wastes back to the simple basic parts of soil, air and water from which they were formed.

FREE 30 DAY TRIAL

You can find more information on our website at: www.kraneproducts.com

For more information, fill out the coupon below, or call toll free: **1-800-614-0066**

SEPTIC HELPER 2000 is packaged in plastic bags, each weighing five ounces. Just follow the easy instructions, pour monthly down the commode and let our product go to work for you.

www.kraneproducts.com

NOT AVAILABLE TO VERMONT RESIDENTS

☐ Yes, I would like more information about **Septic Helper 2000.**

Name _____

Phone (_____)_____

Address _____

_____

City _____ State_____

Zip _____ How many tanks/cesspools _____

MAIL TO: KRANE PRODUCTS, INC.
P.O.BOX 310721 * BOCA RATON, FL * 33431-9916
NOT AVAILABLE TO VERMONT RESIDENTS   OFA

Gardening by the Moon's Sign

■ It is important to note that *the placement of the planets through the signs of the zodiac is not the same in astronomy and astrology.* The *astrological* placement of the Moon, by sign, is given in the table below. (The *astronomical,* or actual, placement is given in the **Left-Hand Calendar Pages 58-84.**)

For planting, the most fertile signs are the three water signs: Cancer, Scorpio, and Pisces. Good second choices are Taurus, Virgo, and Capricorn.

Weeding and plowing are best done when the Moon occupies the sign of Aries, Gemini, Leo, Sagittarius, or Aquarius. Insect pests can also be handled at these times. Transplanting and grafting are best done under a Cancer, Scorpio, or Pisces Moon. Pruning is best done under an Aries, Leo, or Sagittarius Moon, with growth encouraged during waxing (from the day of new to the day of full Moon) and discouraged during waning (from the day after full to the day before new Moon). (The dates of the Moon's phases can be found **on pages 58-84.**) Clean out the garden shed when the Moon occupies Virgo so that the work will flow smoothly. Fences and permanent beds can be built or mended when Capricorn predominates. Avoid indecision when under the Libra Moon.

Moon's Place in the Astrological Zodiac

	NOV. 2000	DEC. 2000	JAN. 2001	FEB. 2001	MAR. 2001	APR. 2001	MAY 2001	JUNE 2001	JULY 2001	AUG. 2001	SEPT. 2001	OCT. 2001	NOV. 2001	DEC. 2001
1	CAP	AQU	PSC	TAU	TAU	CAN	LEO	LIB	SCO	CAP	AQU	PSC	TAU	GEM
2	CAP	AQU	ARI	TAU	GEM	CAN	VIR	SCO	SAG	CAP	PSC	ARI	TAU	CAN
3	AQU	PSC	ARI	GEM	GEM	LEO	VIR	SCO	SAG	AQU	PSC	ARI	GEM	CAN
4	AQU	PSC	TAU	GEM	CAN	LEO	LIB	SCO	CAP	AQU	ARI	TAU	GEM	LEO
5	AQU	ARI	TAU	CAN	CAN	VIR	LIB	SAG	CAP	AQU	ARI	TAU	CAN	LEO
6	PSC	ARI	GEM	CAN	LEO	VIR	SCO	SAG	CAP	PSC	ARI	GEM	CAN	LEO
7	PSC	ARI	GEM	LEO	LEO	LIB	SCO	CAP	AQU	PSC	TAU	GEM	LEO	VIR
8	ARI	TAU	CAN	LEO	VIR	LIB	SAG	CAP	AQU	ARI	TAU	GEM	LEO	VIR
9	ARI	TAU	CAN	VIR	VIR	SCO	SAG	AQU	PSC	ARI	GEM	CAN	VIR	LIB
10	TAU	GEM	LEO	VIR	LIB	SCO	SAG	AQU	PSC	ARI	GEM	CAN	VIR	LIB
11	TAU	GEM	LEO	LIB	LIB	SAG	CAP	AQU	PSC	TAU	CAN	LEO	LIB	SCO
12	GEM	CAN	VIR	LIB	SCO	SAG	CAP	PSC	ARI	TAU	CAN	LEO	LIB	SCO
13	GEM	CAN	VIR	SCO	SCO	CAP	AQU	PSC	ARI	GEM	CAN	VIR	SCO	SAG
14	GEM	LEO	LIB	SCO	SCO	CAP	AQU	ARI	TAU	GEM	LEO	VIR	SCO	SAG
15	CAN	LEO	LIB	SAG	SAG	CAP	AQU	ARI	TAU	CAN	LEO	LIB	SCO	CAP
16	CAN	VIR	LIB	SAG	SAG	AQU	PSC	ARI	TAU	CAN	VIR	LIB	SAG	CAP
17	LEO	VIR	SCO	SAG	CAP	AQU	PSC	TAU	GEM	LEO	VIR	SCO	SAG	CAP
18	LEO	LIB	SCO	CAP	CAP	PSC	ARI	TAU	GEM	LEO	LIB	SCO	CAP	AQU
19	VIR	LIB	SAG	CAP	AQU	PSC	ARI	GEM	CAN	VIR	LIB	SAG	CAP	AQU
20	VIR	SCO	SAG	AQU	AQU	PSC	TAU	GEM	CAN	VIR	SCO	SAG	AQU	PSC
21	LIB	SCO	CAP	AQU	AQU	ARI	TAU	CAN	LEO	LIB	SCO	CAP	AQU	PSC
22	LIB	SCO	CAP	AQU	PSC	ARI	TAU	CAN	LEO	LIB	SAG	CAP	AQU	PSC
23	SCO	SAG	CAP	PSC	PSC	TAU	GEM	LEO	VIR	SCO	SAG	CAP	PSC	ARI
24	SCO	SAG	AQU	PSC	ARI	TAU	GEM	LEO	VIR	SCO	CAP	AQU	PSC	ARI
25	SAG	CAP	AQU	ARI	ARI	GEM	CAN	VIR	LIB	SAG	CAP	AQU	ARI	TAU
26	SAG	CAP	PSC	ARI	ARI	GEM	CAN	VIR	LIB	SAG	CAP	PSC	ARI	TAU
27	SAG	CAP	PSC	ARI	TAU	GEM	LEO	LIB	SCO	SAG	AQU	PSC	ARI	GEM
28	CAP	AQU	PSC	TAU	TAU	CAN	LEO	LIB	SCO	CAP	AQU	PSC	TAU	GEM
29	CAP	AQU	ARI	—	GEM	CAN	VIR	LIB	SAG	CAP	PSC	ARI	TAU	GEM
30	AQU	PSC	ARI	—	GEM	LEO	VIR	SCO	SAG	AQU	PSC	ARI	GEM	CAN
31	—	PSC	TAU	—	CAN	—	LIB	—	SAG	AQU	—	TAU	—	CAN

Especially for Our Gardening Friends...

If you're reading *The Old Farmer's Almanac,* chances are you're either a gardener or you know someone who is. These gardening products from the editors of *The Old Farmer's Almanac* are full
of invaluable advice for everyone from the novice to the expert gardener.

Keep a Beautiful Record of Your Garden!

Our *All-Season Garden Journal* is . . .

- Filled with great gardening ideas, tips, planting schedules, and
  helpful advice for flowers, lawns, and vegetables.

- Undated and arranged by season, with lots of room to keep track
  of gardening successes and "lessons," sources for seeds, and other
  personal garden notes. **Only $12.95***

*Order one
or order many.
Shipping and
handling for each
order is only
$3.95.

Item: OFNDGDN Key: NDJOFAB

Practical, Useful, Time-Tested Gardening Information . . .

2001 Gardening Calendar

Our best-selling calendar includes an outdoor planting
chart, monthly gardening tips, essays, and a large
calendar grid with lots of writing space. **Only $6.99***

Item: OF01CGC Key: NDJOFAB

Gardening Hints and Tips You Can Really Use . . .

Reference Charts for Gardening

Old Farmer's Almanac guides to ... Heirloom Vegetables ... Besting Bugs and Combating Critters in Your
Garden ... Combating Pesky Garden Weeds ... Herb
Companions in the Garden ... Time-Honored Vegetable Gardening Hints. **Get all 5 charts for only $10.00***

Item: OFCPGAR Key: NDJOFAB

BEST BUY **Save 15% when you buy all three items!**
(Journal, Calendar, and 5 Charts). **Only $25*** Item: OFNDGPS Key: NDJOFAB

TERMS:
Payment, including $3.95 shipping and
handling, must be received with your order.
We accept Visa, MasterCard, AmericanEx-
press, and Discover cards. Personal check or
money order also accepted in U.S. funds
drawn on a U.S. bank.

3 WAYS TO ORDER:
1) On-line: www.almanac.com/garden
2) Toll-free: 800-223-3166
3) Mail: The Old Farmer's Almanac
     P.O. Box 37370
     Boone, IA 50037-0370

Home Remedies for Plants,

by Doc and Katy Abraham

Doc and Katy have been writing their syndicated gardening column, "The Green Thumb," since the end of World War II. They garden, landscape, and write from their home in upstate New York. If it lives in a garden, they know about it. Here is some of their best advice.

Doc and Katy Abraham

Look around your kitchen. You have vinegar, baking soda, garlic, and many other products—even a can or two of fruit cocktail—that can help keep house and garden plants healthy. The following remedies for plant problems are safe, inexpensive, and reliable.

ALCOHOL

Alcohol kills **mealybugs, scales, aphids, spider mites, whiteflies, slugs, and earwigs** by acting as a surfactant, or wetting agent, that can penetrate an insect's waxy coat of armor and kill on

Aphids

contact with the body. Methanol (wood alcohol) evaporates a bit too fast. Isopropanol (rubbing alcohol) works fine and is easy to find, but be sure it doesn't have additives. Ethanol (grain alcohol)

Earwigs

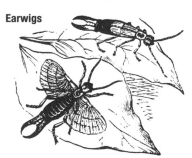

the Old-Fashioned Way

seems to work best. Alcohol usually comes in 70 percent strength in stores (or 95 percent strength purchased commercially). To make an insecticidal spray, mix equal parts 70 percent alcohol and water (or if using 95 percent alcohol, mix 1 part alcohol to 1½ parts water). To kill mealybugs, dip a cotton swab or cotton ball into alcohol and wipe off the infestation.

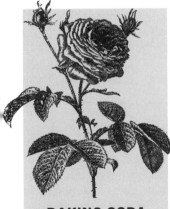

BAKING SODA

Black spot disease causes the leaves of roses to wilt, turn yellow, and drop off. To combat this, mix 3 tablespoons of baking soda into 1 gallon of water and spray the roses. Pick up any fallen rose leaves and burn them or take them to the dump.

BEER

Placed in shallow pans with the top edges flush with the ground, beer is a safe, inexpensive killer of **snails and slugs**. The pests crawl into the pans and drown. In a report to the Entomological Society of America a few years ago, Floyd F. Smith of the U.S. Department of Agriculture said that in a series of four-day greenhouse tests, beer attracted more than 300 slugs, and metaldehyde, a standard bait, attracted only 28.

BORAX

Blisters on geranium leaves, a condition called **edema,** may be caused by a boron deficiency. If the blisters do not clear up as spring advances, mix ⅛ teaspoon of borax into 1 gallon of water and use it to  water the plants two or three times. (For another use of borax, see Epsom Salts.)

BUTTERMILK

Mites are the scourge of many outdoor ornamental plants, as well as some indoor plants. So tiny that it takes 50 of them to cover the head of a pin, mites cause yellowed and stippled foliage and twisted leaf tips. For a simple home cure that works on ornamental plants and fruit trees, mix ½ cup of buttermilk, 4 cups of wheat flour, and 5 gallons of water, and strain the mixture through cheesecloth. Spray it onto affected plants to kill the mites and their eggs.

CANNED FRUIT

You can buy **Japanese beetle** traps of all sorts, but most are no more effective than a can of fruit cocktail. Open the can and let it sit in the sun for a week to ferment. Then place it on top of bricks or wood blocks in a light-colored pail, and fill the pail with water to just below the top of the can. Place the pail about 25 feet from the plants you want to protect. The beetles will head for the

sweet bait, fall into the water, and drown. If rain dilutes the bait, start over.

DISINFECTANT CLEANER

A tiny pest called **thrips** causes gladiolus flowers to turn brown and shrivel up.

Prevent this by soaking corms in a solution of 1 tablespoon of Lysol and 1 gallon of water. Plant corms while still wet.

EPSOM SALTS

If your muskmelons taste flat, the trouble could be a **lack of magnesium** in sandy soil. Sweeten the fruit by spraying the vines with this solution: Dissolve 6½ tablespoons of Epsom salts and 3⅓ tablespoons of borax in 5 gallons of water. Spray the foliage when the vines begin to "run" and again when the fruit is about two inches in diameter.

GARLIC

To keep **dogs and cats** out of the garden, steep 1 chopped garlic bulb and 1 tablespoon of cayenne pepper in 1 quart of water for 1 hour. Add 1 teaspoon of liquid dishwashing soap to help the mixture stick to the plants. Strain the portion you need into a watering can and sprinkle it onto

DETERGENTS AND SOAPS

Here is the best control for **Japanese beetles:** Put 1 tablespoon of liquid dishwashing detergent into a wide-mouthed jar. Add 2 inches of water. Pick or knock the beetles into the jar and they will die in minutes. Many people use Safer's Insecticidal Soap (as directed) or Murphy's Oil Soap (diluted at a rate of ¼ cup of soap to 1 gallon of warm water) as all-purpose bug sprays for indoors and out. Here's another safe bug killer: Mix 1 teaspoon of liquid dishwashing detergent with 1 cup of vegetable oil and shake well; then add it to 1 quart of water. Add 1 cup of rubbing alcohol and shake vigorously to emulsify. Pour this mixture into a spray bottle and use it at ten-day intervals on pests.

Women Are Breaking Down My Door To Get My Wrinkle Creme!

I've just never seen anything like it!

One woman tells another and she tells someone else -- a friend, relative or neighbor. And they all really must be raving about the results they get with my Michelle's Mink Essential Creme. I can't think of any other explanation for the crowds at my door and the stacks of mail orders from all over the country.

It's certainly not because of advertising. You probably haven't seen any of our ads in magazines or newspapers in the last five years.

So many women have been urging me to tell the world about the fantastic difference Michelle's Mink Essential Creme makes I've decided I really should share the good news.

Of course we know that this creme is entirely different. It contains no dangerous hormones, estrogens or steroids -- only fine natural oil and balm. And research scientists say that mink emollients "come closer to the oils of the human skin than any other ingredient."

But the women who use our creme are more interested in results than scientific research. They tell me they actually see exciting changes in their own mirrors.

They are thrilled with how dry, dull skin seems to bloom with a glowing, dewy freshness -- how harsh, aging lines seem to vanish.

A typical letter comes from L. B. of Florida, who's amazed to see how quickly Michelle's Mink Essential Creme works its wonders. "My sister in Missouri gave me a bottle of moisture cream and in three days you could see a vast difference. I thank you."

And from L. H. in Georgia, comes this marvelous endorsement: "I am sure I must be one of your oldest customers. I have been using your cream for many years. I am 78 years old and still haven't any wrinkles. I am sure your cream has played an important part in my good complexion."

Changes in climate, air pollutants, soaps, detergents -- they all contribute to dryness that makes you look so much older.

Michelle's Mink Essential Creme works its miracles by penetrating below the surface of your skin to replace essential oil and restore moisture balance. Your face -- even your throat -- look and feel younger, firmer, more attractive.

Truly, seeing is believing. I am so sure you will be thrilled with Michelle's Mink Essential Creme I make you an unconditional promise.

Try my unique creme. Simply smooth it on your skin at night and let it do its work while you sleep. If, after using it, you are not delighted with the changes in your complexion, just let me know. I'll send you a full refund, no questions asked.

Join the thousands of women who have discovered the secret of smooth, lovely skin. Send for your trial supply of my exclusive complexion beauty aid today. 100% money back guarantee.

Mink oil formula products are considered by research scientists "to come closer to the oils of the human skin than any other ingredient."

MINK ESSENTIAL CREME
Formula No. M-1

1 Jar (4 oz.) $14.95
2 Jars (4 oz. *Save $4*) $25.90
5 Jars (4 oz. *Save $22*). $52.75
Prices include Shipping and Handling

Send check or money order to:

CONTINENTAL QUEST
RESEARCH CORP.
220 W. Carmel Drive
Dept. OFB-01
Carmel, IN 46032

plant leaves. The rest will remain potent for several weeks if kept refrigerated in a covered jar.

MOUTHWASH

An agriculture professor in Texas recommends adding about 2 ounces of Listerine to 1 gallon of water to **extend the life of cut flowers,** including roses. Lister-

ine contains, among other things, sucrose (food for flowers) and a bactericide, and its acidity promotes quicker uptake of water by the stems.

OLIVE OIL

Prevent **mosquitoes** from breeding in rain barrels by floating 1 tablespoon of olive oil on the water's surface.

PETROLEUM JELLY

Whiteflies ("flying dandruff") can be the most difficult plant pest, indoors or out. Trap them with yellow index cards coated with petroleum jelly. To whiteflies (also aphids, scale, and some other insects), the color yellow looks like a mass of new foliage. The bugs are attracted to the cards, get stuck in the jelly, and die.

TALCUM POWDER

To discourage **pesky rabbits,** try dusting your plants with plain talcum powder. It also repels flea beetles on tomatoes, potatoes, peppers, and other plants.

VINEGAR

To keep **insects** away from apple trees, make a solution of 1 cup of vinegar, 1 cup of sugar, and 1 quart of water.

Pour this mixture into a widemouthed plastic jug. Hang the jug, uncovered, in your apple tree. This really works on our 'Northern Spy'.

WOOD ASHES

Slugs and snails hate wood ashes. Sprinkle ashes around flower and vegetable plants. The ashes are a good source of potassium, unlocking nutrients so that plants can take them up. Ashes also check radish maggots: Sprinkle ashes over seeds before covering with soil. ☐☐

Great Gardening Advice All Year Long!

An all-new subscription offer from the editors of *The Old Farmer's Almanac*

Now a quarterly, *The Old Farmer's Almanac Gardener's Companion* is full of practical information for the novice and accomplished gardener alike. Whether you grow annual or perennial flowers or herbs, vegetables, fruit trees, berry bushes, shrubs, a lawn, or houseplants; whether you garden in the North or the South, the East or the West, or anywhere in between; there's information you can use. You will find feature stories relevant to the season, plus plans and projects to take you through the gardening "off-season" (if there *is* such a thing!).

In every issue: Ask the Old Farmer ✦ Growing Tastes and Trends ✦ In the Vegetable Garden ✦ Toward a Better Garden ✦ By Design ✦ Perennial Pleasures ✦ The Natural Observer ✦ Make It Yourself ✦ Report from Canada ✦ Down-to-Earth Advice

Four issues per year/PREMIER ISSUE: Fall 2000
Fall (October) • Early Spring (January) • Spring (April) • Summer (June)

Those FAMOUS Grainger County TOMA

The rocky hills of northeastern Tennessee produce some of the tastiest tomatoes to be found anywhere. Here's how they do it.

In mountainous Grainger County, northeast of Knoxville, Tennessee, a serpentine two-lane blacktop winds along the shore of Cherokee Lake. In late summer, it's lined with hand-lettered signs: TOMATOES. One of my favorite places to buy the county's famous green-shouldered beauties is a little white house where the owner leaves bushel baskets of tomatoes from his field on the porch, along with the price per pound, a scale, and a paper bag where you drop your money. There always seems to be a litter of kittens tumbling around the yard.

Few other foodstuffs—perhaps wine, truffles, and goat cheese—inspire such hot debates over care, cultivation, and taste as do homegrown tomatoes. Somehow, this rural county has become renowned throughout the American heartland for the robust, unique flavor of its tomatoes. So luscious that their interior will ripen to a dark red tinged with purple, Grainger County tomatoes are often rumored to be "the next Vidalia onion." (When cheaper, mass-produced tomatoes from Florida, Georgia, and Arkansas were fraudulently sold as Graingers, the *Knoxville News-Sentinel* covered the story on its front page.)

Grainger County tomato farmers like Steve Longmire and Donnie Morgan say that their profession is both a science and an art. They use the latest agricultural techniques and greenhouses to

Old wives' tales have often maintained that the roughest soil produces the sweetest tomatoes.

TOES

produce near year-round crops of Grainger 'Celebrities' and 'Empires'. "Believe it or not," says Longmire of his hydroponic (indoor) yield, "it's a really good tomato." But no one disputes that the best are the field tomatoes, which go into the ground as early as April and ripen in June.

Longmire estimates that the demand for Grainger tomatoes has more than doubled in the last five years, and local farmers are working hard to meet it. However, Grainger County extension leader Charlie Cavin notes that even the largest Grainger farms still use no automation in packing crops. "That's very unusual," he says. "Most larger producers do. But hand-packing cuts down on bruises. We're more interested in quality than quantity."

The shipping area is also limited by how far these delicate ruby fruits can travel. West Coast destinations are out of the question, which is not true for the mass-produced, pink Styrofoam tomatoes that ship long distances as easily as Ping-Pong balls—and taste about as good.

Ground zero for "Tomato Country," as local vanity plates proudly display, is a five-mile radius around tiny Rutledge, Tennessee. The annual Tomato Festival in July draws

by Krista Reese

–illustrated by
Sara Mintz Zwicker

Don't put

young plants

into the

ground

until

daytime

temperatures

reach

around

60°F.

roughly 15,000 people—an astonishing feat when you consider that there are only 17,400 inhabitants in the entire county. The beauty pageant is now called the Miss Grainger County contest. "We tried Miss Tomato, but it didn't go over too well with the teenagers," says one festival official.

Determining exactly what makes the Grainger tomato so good is an elusive proposition. Dr. Carl Sams, professor of plant and soil science at the University of Tennessee in Knoxville, has been working with the Grainger farmers for years. "There are no easy answers," he says, noting that Grainger County's soil is "well-balanced," with low acidity, not too much nitrogen, and not too much potassium. He believes it could be duplicated.

Perhaps one factor in the tastiness of the Grainger County tomato is its mountainous country and culture. Old wives' tales have often maintained that the roughest soil produces the sweetest tomatoes. You'll certainly find plenty of shale and stone in this area, known as Rocky Top. The rugged foothills may or may not be responsible for the tomatoes' taste, but they certainly account for the fierce independence of the area's farmers. Long isolated in tiny pockets, farmers competed for the best tomatoes and experimented with their own methods.

That's also one reason for a clear consensus on another question: Will the Grainger farmers ever band together to market their product, as the Vidalia onion farmers have? "Well," sighs Cavin, "I wish we could be a little more organized. But I don't think so. They're just . . . competitive."

One local observer put it more succinctly: "It would be easier," she says, "to herd cats."

HOW TO GROW YOUR OWN TOMATO

Tips from the Grainger farmers.

What to Plant

■ The Grainger farmers have many differences, but on tomato variety, they agree almost unanimously. 'Celebrity' and 'Empire' are the best for taste and yield, and 'Mountain Gold' is a good-tasting yellow variety. Choose plants in larger containers rather than egg carton–size seedlings. Regional research has shown that transplants from larger containers (three to four inches) produce a larger root system, bloom earlier, and have a higher yield than those from smaller containers.

(continued)

When to Plant

■ Don't put young plants into the ground until daytime temperatures reach around 60°F. (In Tennessee, that's usually around April 15 to 20.) Some Grainger farmers also watch the signs in *The Old Farmer's Almanac*. Donnie Morgan tries to plant "by the breast or the legs," meaning that he will plant under the astrological signs governing those parts of the body: Cancer for the breast and Aquarius for the legs (see "Gardening by the Moon's Sign," page 180). He warns that under the sign of the heart (Leo), "If you break the root when you're setting the plant, you're done for." He also believes that plants that go into the ground "in the light of the Moon" (during the time of the month when it's waxing) grow taller than those planted "in the dark of the Moon." (See "Outdoor Planting Table," page 176.)

How to Plant

■ Young plants will need to be tied to stakes, so set the stakes at the same time you put in the tomatoes to avoid breaking roots later. Any kind of stake will do, but most of the Grainger farmers use a system that reduces tying. Place square wooden stakes five feet apart, and tie binder twine around the stakes, about ten inches from the ground, so there's a line on both sides of the stake, running parallel. Tie another double line about eight inches above that, and repeat as the plants grow. Plant three tomato plants between every two stakes, and wind them gently through the twine for support as they grow.

How to Water

■ Consistent watering is important. Too little water and good tomatoes won't develop; too much and they'll split. Watering during the heat of the day, especially during a hot spell, can "scald" (crack) them. Most farmers use an irrigation system. If you don't have one, use a drip line or soaker hose, or water from above only in the morning. Moisture on tomato leaves can foster disease. "You need about 1-1/4 inches of rain a week," says farmer Hubert Williams.

How to Mulch

■ Some farmers use black plastic to warm the ground and retard weed growth. But some also note that mud will splash back up onto tomatoes from plastic, so they choose wheat straw instead, which keeps the plant "prettier" and absorbs water.

How to Feed

■ Most Grainger farmers use standard commercial fertilizers like Old Joe or Peters, most opting for 10-10-10 or 20-10-20 in their drip lines. Follow package directions. "Don't put all your fertilizer on at once," says Morgan. "You'll burn up the plants."

Suckering Those Suckers

■ Tomato plants grow new branches in their "joints," which eventually overwhelm the limb beneath it. Some gardeners religiously remove these new branches, called suckers, because they believe they take energy away from producing

tomatoes. Most Grainger farmers "leave two prongs, and that's it," says Williams.

When to Pick

■ Let your homegrowns remain on the vine until they're very red for the best flavor. However, if you need to pick them earlier, be sure they're at least a little pink, and put them into a sunny place until they're ready to eat. Grainger farmers, who must pick early to get their fruit to market, look for the green tomatoes with white stars on the bottom as an indicator that they're ready to ripen in a windowsill at home. And do not ever, ever put your delicious homegrown tomatoes into the refrigerator!

(From Donnie Morgan, Hubert Williams, and Commercial Tomato Production, *published by the University of Tennessee/Agricultural Extension Service.)* □ □

Manure Guide

Type of Manure	Water Content	Primary Nutrients (pounds per ton)		
		Nitrogen	Phosphate	Potash
Cow, horse	60%-80%	12-14	5-9	9-12
Sheep, pig, goat	65%-75%	10-21	7	13-19
Chicken: Wet, sticky, and caked	75%	30	20	10
Moist, crumbly to sticky	50%	40	40	20
Crumbly	30%	60	55	30
Dry	15%	90	70	40
Ashed	None	None	135	100

Type of Garden	Best Type of Manure	Best Time to Apply
Flower	Cow, horse	Early spring
Vegetable	Chicken, cow, horse	Fall, spring
Potato or root crop	Cow, horse	Fall
Acid-loving plants (blueberries, azaleas, mountain laurels, rhododendrons)	Cow, horse	Early fall or not at all

Mr. Smith's MADDENING Mind-Manglers

Test your math and logic skills with these puzzles, compiled for *The Old Farmer's Almanac* by RAYNOR R. SMITH SR., mathematics teacher at Keene Middle School, Keene, New Hampshire.

Answers appear on page 222.

1. Brooke's and Brittany's salaries are in a ratio of 3 to 5, respectively. Brittany's salary is $4,000 per month. By how much money must Brooke's salary increase so that their salaries are in a ratio of 7 to 8?

2. If you roll a die three times, what is the probability that the three rolls will not all show the same number?

3. Jessie took a job washing windows at the Umpire State Building. On the first day, she washed 5 windows; on the second day, 11; on the third day, 17; and on the fourth day, 23. How many windows did she wash on the 75th day?

4. Jordan has 100 yards of fencing for his dog's run. How should he set up the fencing to get the most space for his dog to play in?

5. Math 172A and Math 172B took the same test. The average score of the 20 students in Math 172A was 90 percent, and the average score of the students in Math 172B was 75 percent. If the average score for the combined classes was 81 percent, how many students are in Math 172B?

6. Cassidy invited 17 guests to her party. She assigned each guest a number from 2 to 18, keeping the number 1 for herself. When everyone was dancing, Cassidy noticed that the sum of each couple's numbers was a perfect square. What is the number of Cassidy's partner, and what numbers did the other couples have?

7. Michael, Jordan, Tim, and Duncan are roommates. Michael hates to cook but loves to eat. Jordan doesn't like the beach. Tim often comes home with grease on his clothes. Duncan often shares his work with Michael. One is a lifeguard, one a mechanic, one a chef, and one a teacher. Who has which job?

8. Find two different ways to change the following three toothpicks into the number 10 by adding one additional toothpick.

| | |

9. A videotape can record 2 hours on Short Play, 4 hours on Long Play, or 6 hours on Extra Long Play. If Emily records 30 minutes on SP and 100 minutes on LP, how much recording time is left on ELP?

10. There is three errors in this sentence. What are they?

□ □

Recipes

in the 2000 Recipe Contest

Save the Layer Cake!

Thank you to all the Old Farmer's Almanac *readers who sent in treasured
recipes for old-fashioned layer cakes.
Despite rumors of its demise, the classic layer cake is alive and well. For
more outstanding layer-cake recipes,
go to* **www.almanac.com.**

FIRST PRIZE

Old-Fashioned Buttermilk Wedding Cake

1 cup (2 sticks) butter or margarine, softened
3 cups sugar
4 cups cake flour
1 teaspoon baking soda
2 teaspoons baking powder
1/4 teaspoon salt
2 cups buttermilk
1 teaspoon vanilla extract
1/2 teaspoon butter flavoring
1/2 teaspoon almond extract
6 egg whites

Cream Cheese Frosting:

8 ounces cream cheese, softened
3 cups confectioners' sugar
2 teaspoons vanilla extract

For cake: Preheat oven to 350°F. Grease
and flour three 9-inch round cake pans.
In a large mixing bowl, cream the butter and
sugar until fluffy. Add flour, baking soda,
baking powder, and salt. Pour in buttermilk
and begin mixing slowly. Continue to mix
until well blended. Add flavorings and stir.
In another bowl, beat egg whites until stiff.

Fold the egg whites into the cake batter. Divide the batter evenly among the prepared
pans. Bake for 20 minutes at 350°F, then
lower heat to 300°F and bake for about 25
minutes longer, until a toothpick inserted
near the center comes out clean. Remove
cakes from oven and cool on racks. After 10
minutes, remove from pans and continue
cooling on racks.

For frosting: Combine ingredients in a
mixing bowl and beat until smooth. Spread
frosting between cooled layers and on top
and sides of cake. You don't need a wedding
to enjoy this cake! **Makes 12 to 16 servings.**

Diane Niebling, Overland Park, Kansas

SECOND PRIZE

Peachy Almond Cake

1 cup (2 sticks) butter, softened
2 cups sugar
4 eggs
3 cups flour
3-1/2 teaspoons baking powder
1/2 teaspoon salt
1-1/4 cups milk
1 teaspoon vanilla extract
1 teaspoon almond extract

Filling:

1 cup almond paste (7-ounce package)
2 ripe peaches, pared, pitted, and sliced
**1 cup peach preserves, softened in
microwave oven or stirred**

Frosting:

2 cups heavy cream
1/2 cup confectioners' sugar, or to taste
1/2 teaspoon almond extract, or to taste
1 teaspoon vanilla extract, or to taste

For cake: Preheat oven to 350°F. Grease
and flour two 9-inch round cake pans.
Cream the butter and sugar until fluffy. Beat
in eggs, one at a time, beating until mixture
is as light as whipped cream. Sift together the
flour, baking powder, and salt, and set aside.
Blend the milk and extracts. Alternately add

the dry ingredients and the milk to the butter mixture. Spread the batter in the prepared pans and bake for 30 to 40 minutes, until a toothpick inserted near the center comes out clean. Cool layers on wire racks.

For filling: Place one cake layer onto a serving plate. Divide the almond paste in half, and roll each portion to a 9-inch round (roll paste between two layers of waxed paper or plastic wrap). Place one sheet of almond paste over the first cake layer. Mix the peach slices with ¾ cup of the peach preserves and spread over the almond paste. Add the second cake layer and brush with remaining ¼ cup peach preserves. Top with second round of almond paste.

For frosting: Whip the cream until stiff, then add sugar and extracts to taste. Frost the cake with the whipped cream, and refrigerate until serving time. If desired, drizzle dessert plates with a little caramel sauce, and garnish with a few peach slices and a sprig of fresh mint. **Makes 8 to 10 servings.**

TerryAnn Moore, Oaklyn, New Jersey

THIRD PRIZE

Millennium Chocolate Cake with Mocha Frosting

2/3 cup butter, softened
1-3/4 cups sugar
2 eggs
1 teaspoon vanilla extract
2-1/2 ounces unsweetened baking chocolate, melted and cooled
2-1/2 cups sifted cake flour
1-1/4 teaspoons baking soda
1/2 teaspoon salt
1-1/4 cups sour milk or buttermilk

Mocha Frosting:

6 cups confectioners' sugar
1 cup (2 sticks) unsalted butter, softened
1/2 cup unsweetened cocoa powder
2/3 cup strong brewed coffee (use part coffee-flavored liqueur, if desired)
1 tablespoon vanilla extract

For cake: Preheat oven to 350°F. Line just the bottoms of two 9-inch round cake pans with waxed or parchment paper, and grease the pans and paper well. Dust with flour, and shake out the excess.

In a large bowl, cream the butter and sugar with an electric mixer until fluffy. Add eggs and vanilla, and beat on high speed for 5 minutes, scraping the bowl occasionally. Blend in chocolate. In a separate bowl, whisk flour with baking soda and salt; add alternately to cake batter with sour milk or buttermilk, mixing well after each addition.

Divide the batter between the two prepared pans and bake for 30 to 35 minutes, until a toothpick inserted into the center comes out clean. Let cakes cool in pans on wire racks for 10 minutes, then invert from pans to cool completely on the racks. Carefully peel off the waxed paper.

For frosting: Beat confectioners' sugar with butter; add cocoa, coffee (and coffee liqueur, if using), and vanilla, and beat on low speed until smooth; beat for 1 minute longer at medium speed. Chill for 20 to 30 minutes, until mixture reaches spreading consistency. Use as filling between the layers and to frost top and sides of cake. **Makes about 12 servings.**

Josephine D. Piro, Easton, Pennsylvania

HONORABLE MENTION

Oatmeal Date Cake with Cinnamon Cream-Cheese Frosting

1-1/2 cups boiling water
1 cup rolled oats (uncooked)
1-1/2 cups flour
1 teaspoon baking soda
1 teaspoon cinnamon
1/2 teaspoon grated nutmeg
1/2 cup (1 stick) butter or margarine, softened
1 cup granulated sugar
1 cup brown sugar
2 eggs
1 teaspoon vanilla extract
1/3 cup chopped dates *(continued)*

Cinnamon Cream-Cheese Frosting:

8 ounces cream cheese, softened
1/2 cup (1 stick) butter, softened
4 cups confectioners' sugar, sifted
2 teaspoons vanilla extract
2 teaspoons cinnamon

For cake: Pour boiling water over rolled oats, stir, and let stand for about 40 minutes. Whisk together flour, baking soda, cinnamon, and nutmeg and set aside. In a large bowl with mixer on medium speed, beat butter. Add sugars and beat until fluffy. Beat in eggs one at a time, then add vanilla. Add cooled oat mixture and blend well. On low speed, beat in flour mixture a little at a time. Stir in dates and beat until well blended. Pour batter into two greased and floured 8-inch round cake pans and bake at 350°F until a toothpick inserted into the center comes out clean, about 40 minutes. Cool on racks in pans for 10 minutes, then remove from pans and continue cooling.

For frosting: Whip cream cheese and butter together until fluffy. Add sugar, vanilla, and cinnamon. Mix until smooth. Spread between the layers and on top and sides of cake. **Makes 10 to 12 servings.**

Jennifer Walsh, Creston, Iowa

Special thanks to recipe judge Sylvia Wright.

ANNOUNCING THE 2001
RECIPE CONTEST

Soups and Chowders

■ **What better way to warm the body and soul than with a bowl of hot, homemade soup or chowder? Cash prizes (first prize, $100; second prize, $75; third prize, $50) will be awarded for the best original recipes for soups and chowders. All entries become the property of Yankee Publishing Inc., which reserves all rights to the material. Winners will be announced in the 2002 edition of The** *Old Farmer's Almanac* **and posted on our Web site at www.almanac.com. Deadline is February 1, 2001. Please type all recipes. Address: Recipe Contest, The Old Farmer's Almanac, P.O. Box 520, Dublin, NH 03444. E-mail (subject: Recipe Contest) to almanac@yankeepub.com.**

in the 2000 Essay Contest

What This Country Needs Is...

FIRST PRIZE

What this country needs is a healthy respect for the value of time. Originally, I thought one answer to solving society's ills was to simply show respect to one another. But the problem really comes down to not using time in constructive ways. We know how to be kind and courteous. How often do we take the time to demonstrate these qualities to others? We rush through our days displaying negative behavior to other people. What a waste of a precious gift to use it in such an unkind way. A nasty word spoken aloud may well be the last thing we say on Earth. Let's teach our children how fragile time is: It can't be bought; it can't be given back; it never stands still; and it will run out for each of us. So, America, what I would like to give us is all the time we need to do and say all that we've always wanted to do and say— if only we had enough time.

Marguerite T. Jung, Montville, New Jersey

What this country needs is less iceberg lettuce. I know that in a time of technological bewilderment, crazy cancers, and an overpopulated global village, this might seem to be a trifling matter, but it is not. Iceberg lettuce has become a symbol for the essence of who we have become and what we will offer to the future. It is watery and flavorless. It requires a heaping portion of artificially flavored dressing to hide its blandness and lack of substance. It gives so little nourishment. It is symbolic of how we have lost that wild essence that once coursed through our veins. Real greens, such as spinach, arugula, endive, and dandelion offer us the chance to savor unique and individual flavors. Next spring, plant a garden and grow something you have never tasted. Marvel at what a seed can create, harvest it onto a plate, and share it with a friend.

Daniel Marcou, La Crosse, Wisconsin

THIRD PRIZE

What this country needs is a renewed connection to the rhythms and cycles of Mother Nature. Renewing our bonds to nature through bird-watching, nature walks, star-gazing, and especially gardening teaches many of life's most important values. To grow a plant from seed and observe the newly formed life unfold sparks a reverence for life and an appreciation of its fragility. Taking care of the plants teaches responsibility and the need for constant observation. Nurturing and hard work are learned as the plants mature and the gardener meets their needs. A sense of achievement and improved self-esteem result from the wonderful rewards of flowers, fruits, or vegetables. And the garden as a whole provides a feeling of harmony. Perhaps, just perhaps, the gardener and the coun-

try are better off drawing closer to our Maker by drawing closer to nature.

Michael Walls, Sacramento, California

HONORABLE MENTION

(essays from children)

If someone that works has a family, they need to be with them more. We need more trees to plant. We need to get rid of cigarettes. We need to stop pollution. We need homes that are cheaper for the poor. We need to care for others more. We need to get rid of bad drugs. We need families to stay together so kids can be happy, not sad. People need to remember the Pledge of Allegiance. We need honest people.

We need to turn old buildings into new ones. We need to make things that last longer.

Elizabeth Ann Campbell
Fourth-Grader, St. Frances Cabrini School
Alexandria, Louisiana

ANNOUNCING THE 2001 ESSAY CONTEST

My Most Memorable Family Car Trip

■ **We all have memories—fond and not so fond—of family car trips. Please describe your favorite in 200 words or less. Cash prizes (first prize, $100; second prize, $75; third prize, $50) will be awarded for the best original essay on the subject. All entries become the property of Yankee Publishing Inc., which reserves all rights to the material. Winners will be announced in the 2002 edition of *The Old Farmer's Almanac* and posted on our Web site at www.almanac.com. Deadline is February 1, 2001. Please type all essays. Address: Essay Contest, The Old Farmer's Almanac, P.O. Box 520, Dublin, NH 03444. E-mail (subject: Essay Contest) to almanac@yankeepub.com.**

□□

The *The* PIE LADIES  OF PLAIN CITY, OHIO

Between them, Lena Beachy and Louella Mast have more than 110 years of piemaking experience. The two women mastermind the making of pies at Der Dutchman, a restaurant in the heart of central Ohio's Mennonite country that serves traditional country fare of homemade mashed potatoes and noodles, hearty country soups, fried chicken, and steak. And pie. Last year, Der Dutchman sold more than 53,000 pies—4,200 in the two days before Thanksgiving alone.

The Mennonite restaurant offers 26 varieties of pie, from black

–Leah Feltz

Heartland piemakers Louella Mast *(left)* and Lena Beachy share their expertise— and their recipes.

raspberry and Dutch apple to German chocolate and fresh glazed strawberry. Cream pies are made by prebaking a piecrust, then adding a filling of chocolate cream, chocolate and peanut butter, lemon meringue, coconut cream, banana cream, or butterscotch cream. Fruit, mincemeat, and raisin pies are all made with a top crust. Dutch apple and crumb pies are made with a crumb topping.

Sometimes there are round-the-clock piemakers, crews specially trained to make the homemade crusts, add the homemade fillings, and bake the pies carefully before serving them in the restaurant or selling them through the gift shop next door.

Der Dutchman attracts diners from as far away as Columbus

by Cheryl Heckler-Feltz

*The fruit, cream, and custard pies at Der Dutchman Restaurant
are legendary, thanks to a small handful of Mennonite
women headstrong for perfection in the gentle art of piemaking.*

and Dayton, but it serves primarily a rural, tri-county region known
for prime farmland and Mennonite values. The back roads are dotted with modest farmhouses and nationally ranked dairy herds.
Marked by their prayer caps and understated A-line dresses, women
in this region know how to sew, how to quilt, and how to cook.

LENA AND LOUELLA'S SECRETS FOR PERFECT PIE
*Here are some pearls of wisdom for cooks who want to
improve their pies:*

■ Keep in mind that fruit pies are the easiest to make. Custard and butterscotch pies are the hardest because the ingredients must be cooked to a certain consistency, then cooled quickly. This takes practice.

■ Serve a cream pie as fresh as possible, adding the filling just before serving. This keeps your crust from getting soggy.

■ Use only fresh or frozen fruit. No self-respecting piemaker would consider using canned fruit filling. Even if you try it for fun, remember that a fruit pie made with canned filling should *never* be served to anyone with a discerning taste in pies.

■ Add 1/2 teaspoon of lemon juice to your fruit filling to bring out the taste of the fruit and help the fruit keep its color.

■ Substitute Crisco for lard when making piecrust to reduce cholesterol without forfeiting taste. You can also use up to 1/2 cup of butter-flavored Crisco in the piecrust recipe on the next page.

■ Make the top piecrust slightly thinner than the bottom crust to help maintain the structure of the pie.

■ Make vent holes, which a pie needs in the top crust while it bakes, with artistic markings for certain pies. Carve a couple of small leaves for an apple pie or a heart for a cherry pie.

(c o n t i n u e d)

PIECRUST

FAVORITE

- Bake a pie only in the middle (on the center rack) of the oven—never, under any circumstance, anywhere else in the oven.

- Put canned whipped topping into a bowl first, pour in a small amount of heavy cream and maybe even sugar, and whip it with a whisk to give it a smoother texture and creamier taste for use on a cream pie. Don't simply spray it onto the pie.

- Pay attention to the pie while it's baking. Efficiency in the kitchen is great. However, try not to do too many things at once when you are making pies.

3 cups pastry flour
1 cup shortening
pinch of salt
1/2 cup ice water

Mix flour, shortening, and salt, cutting in shortening until mixture is in crumbs. Toss with water. Do not overmix. Makes enough for two single-crust pies or one double-crust pie.

LOUELLA'S CUSTARD PIE

Louella fills the pie shell only about half full, then moves the pie to the oven rack and adds the rest of the filling using a cup. She prefers Pyrex pie pans to metal.

4 eggs
1 cup sugar
1/2 teaspoon salt
1 teaspoon flour
1 teaspoon vanilla extract
3 cups milk, scalded
1 unbaked 9-inch pie shell
cinnamon, for sprinkling

Separate one of the eggs, whip the white until stiff, and set aside. Beat the yolk and the remaining three eggs; add sugar, salt, flour, and vanilla, and stir well. Add the scalded milk. Stir in the beaten egg white. Pour into pie shell. Sprinkle with cinnamon. Bake at 425°F for 10 minutes, then at 350°F for about 20 minutes, or until set.

LOUELLA'S STRAWBERRY GLAZE PIE

1 box (3 ounces) strawberry gelatin
1/4 teaspoon salt
2 heaping teaspoons cornstarch
1 cup sugar
2 cups cold water
1/2 teaspoon lemon juice
red food coloring, to desired color
1 quart fresh strawberries
1 fully baked 9-inch pie shell
whipped cream or whipped topping

Combine gelatin, salt, cornstarch, and sugar. Slowly add water, stirring well. Cook over medium heat, bringing to a boil, until thick (about 10 minutes); then cool for 1 minute. Add lemon juice and food coloring. Pour into bowl. Put plastic wrap directly onto surface of warm glaze and seal it up against the side of the bowl. Refrigerate until set. When cold, fold in 3 cups halved fresh strawberries. Pour into pie shell. Top with whipped cream or whipped topping. Garnish with fresh strawberries, if desired. Happy eating!

LENA'S PUMPKIN PIE

1/2 cup brown sugar
1/2 cup granulated sugar
2 tablespoons flour
1/2 teaspoon salt
2 teaspoons pumpkin pie spice
1 teaspoon vanilla extract
3/4 cup pumpkin puree
2 eggs, separated
3/4 cup milk
3/4 cup light cream or evaporated milk
1 unbaked 9-inch pie shell

Stir sugars, flour, salt, and spice together. Add vanilla, pumpkin, and egg yolks, and stir until smooth. Heat the milk and cream (or evaporated milk) until hot, and stir into pumpkin mixture. Beat egg whites until stiff, and fold them into the mixture. Pour into pie shell. Bake at 350°F for 15 minutes. Then turn oven to 325°F and bake for 15 minutes longer.

Kitchen Controversies

Mother was right. Too many cooks can indeed spoil the broth—or at least argue about the best way to make it. Often it seems that the simpler the task, the greater the debate it can generate. Take your blood pressure after reading each of the following recommendations from food editor and author **GEORGIA ORCUTT.**

Butter makes the best piecrust.

Countless cookbooks and pie recipes extol the virtues of vegetable shortening for making piecrust. But shortening is made from hydrogenated oils, which worries health watchers. For the best taste, use butter—preferably unsalted. (If you use lard for your piecrusts, keep that secret to yourself.)

Don't bother with tricky weights to keep a pie shell from buckling.

Should you line an empty pie shell with finicky weights, or waxed paper held down by dry beans? Here's the best trick of all for prebaking a pie-crust. Simply place a straight-sided cake pan, just a bit smaller than your pie dish, right down on top of the crust and keep it there as the shell bakes. If you have a 9-inch pie pan, use an 8-inch cake pan; for a 10-inch pie pan, use a 9-inch cake pan. Bake for about 10 minutes, and remove the cake pan. Use a fork to prick any places that still puff up, and bake for 5 minutes longer, or until the crust is a light golden color.

Let asparagus lie down to cook.

Forget about that fancy pot for keeping asparagus upright in bunches. It's a ruse that you have to boil the butt ends while you steam the tips for even cooking. For the best flavor, arrange trimmed asparagus in a big skillet with all the tips going in the same direction. Cover with cold salted water, bring the water to a boil, and cook for

–illustrated by Margo Letourneau

5 to 10 minutes, depending on the thickness of the spears. Taste for doneness. The spears should bend slightly but still be crunchy.

4 Never bake potatoes wrapped in aluminum foil.

When they hit the oven in their tight aluminum coverings, potatoes steam rather than bake, resulting in over-cooked mush. For that nice mealy texture that baked potatoes ought to have, bake them uncovered in a hot oven (400° to 450°F) for about 40 minutes, or until easily pierced with a sharp knife. If you rub the skins first with butter or oil, they will be less crisp than those left plain.

5 Leave out the cream of tartar.

Have you ever started to follow a recipe and suddenly realized that it calls for cream of tartar and you don't have any on hand? Don't rush out to the store; just keep going. If you're beating egg whites, the cream of tartar can prevent them from breaking down when overbeaten. (So don't overdo the beating.) If the cream of tartar is included as a leavening agent (often to ac-company baking soda), just add a bit of baking powder instead, and every-thing should be fine.

6 Get rid of your flour sifter.

Our flour is cleaner these days than it used to be, and we really don't need to screen out lumps, small stones, or in-sects. For most baking that requires

mixing dry ingredients, a whisk will do even better at combining them. Push baking soda through a small sieve if it's lumpy.

7 Never rinse pasta.

Some cookbooks tell readers to rinse cooked pasta under cold running water to stop the cooking process. Ig-nore this. The rinsing only takes away flavor. If you want to keep pasta from getting overcooked, simply drain it before it turns mushy.

8 Bake popovers in a hot oven.

Although the venerable *Joy of Cook-ing* dictates that you must always start popovers in a cold oven, they do fine in a preheated oven if you let all the ingredients come to room tempera-ture before mixing them.

9 It's OK to leave some white on your citrus peels.

Recipes calling for or-ange zest as a flavoring always warn against including any of the peel's bitter white mem-brane. Don't worry about it. If someone can taste the telltale white in your cake or frosting, send them out to the woods to sniff for truffles.

(continued)

Who gave us the idea that salad would be appealing served in a wooden bowl, perhaps one that had first been rubbed with a raw clove of garlic? **IT'S AN APPALLING IDEA.**

10 Buy cheap vanilla.

We'd better qualify this. If you're baking cakes or cookies, use the cheapest vanilla extract you can find. Tests prove that no one can tell the difference between imitation vanilla and the finest pure vanilla in baked goods. But if you're making custard, a fancy icing, or a drink with vanilla flavor, go for the good stuff. There you will taste the difference.

11 Never, ever refrigerate tomatoes.

They hate the cold and give up any ghost of texture and taste if they are sentenced to the refrigerator. Keep juicy fresh tomatoes out on the kitchen counter and eat them up before they go bad.

12 Don't use a wooden salad bowl.

Who gave us the idea that salad would be appealing served in a wooden bowl, perhaps one that had first been rubbed with a raw clove of garlic? It's an appalling idea. Just scrape your fingernail over the bottom of a well-used wooden salad bowl and try to guess the vintage of that gunk. Go for glass or pottery instead.

13 Don't salt meat before you cook it.

Take a tip from the pros. For a juicier steak, salt it on the cooked side after you turn it, and again on the second side before serving. For a roast, use a spice rub that contains salt to create a tasty outer crust.

14 Don't use boiling water to make coffee.

Once you hear the kettle come to a boil, take it off the heat and wait just a bit for the water to back off from a full boil before pouring it over filtered coffee. Water at a rolling boil brings out bitterness in the coffee. (Use boiling water to make tea; to prevent a bitter taste, remove the tea bag or tea leaves from the pot as soon as the tea has steeped.)

–Jill Shaffer

15 Never use butter to cook pancakes.

Even if you apply it to the frying pan with a light hand, butter will make pancakes burn. Use a light vegetable oil or a vegetable oil spray.

16 Buy tuna packed in oil.

Although many of us automatically reach for water-packed tuna, recent studies show that it may contain more fat than the oil-packed variety. The fish itself makes the difference. Fish running in deep, cold water need more fat than those in warmer water; the fat content listed on the can is only an average. Tuna packed in oil tastes like tuna. Take heart in the fact that you'll need relatively little mayonnaise.

17 Don't soak dry beans overnight.

Even though that's how Grandma always did it, beans don't need more than 4 hours of soaking before you cook them. If you need to use them sooner, cover them with water in a large pot, bring to a boil, simmer for 2 minutes, remove from the heat, cover, and let them sit for 1 hour. And don't add baking soda or salt to the soaking or cooking water: Soda depletes their nutritional value and, except for soybeans and lima beans, salt slows down the cooking time.

18 Don't boil "hard-boiled" eggs.

To do it right, put the eggs into a large saucepan, and cover them with one inch of tepid water. Bring just to a boil. Remove from the heat, cover, and let stand 11 minutes for a just-set but tender yolk and 15 minutes for a firm yolk or an extra-large egg.

19 Don't store bread in the refrigerator.

Keep leftover bread in the bread box or on your kitchen counter, tightly sealed in a plastic bag. Experiments show that bread stored at 46°F, the average temperature of a refrigerator, becomes as stale in one day as bread stored at 86°F does in six days.

20 Don't drink water when your mouth is on fire.

If you tangle with a hot pepper that's too spicy for words, reach for some chocolate, or drink milk or beer instead of water to put out the fire. Capsaicin, the alkaloid that is responsible for the heat, is insoluble in water.

21 Don't wait for leftovers to cool before refrigerating them.

The world won't come to an end if you put a warm dish into the refrigerator, nor will your electric or gas bill go up drastically. The notion of waiting for food to cool off before refrigerating it may go back to the days of the real icebox, when something warm would make the ice melt faster.

☐☐

CRAZY FOR CRACKERS

Two hundred years ago, a Boston baker burned a batch of biscuits and called the crisp results crackers. Here's how to make your own, from savory cheddar to comforting graham crackers.

Crackers, as one might imagine, evolved from their more voluminous cousin, bread. Actually, the first recognizable crackers, made by John Pearson of Newburyport, Massachusetts, in 1792 (the year Robert B. Thomas founded our Almanac), were not called crackers at all but pilot bread. Made from two simple ingredients—flour and water—pilot bread stacked easily in barrels aboard sailing ships and boasted a long shelf life. Pearson's pilot bread, which quickly became a staple of nautical life, was also called hardtack, or sea biscuit.

In 1801, another Massachusetts baker, the entrepreneurial Josiah Bent, overcooked a batch of dinner biscuits in his brick oven in Milton, near Boston. Surveying the damage, Bent heard a distinct crackling sound emanating from his wares. Christening the overdone wafers "crackers," he set off to convince the rest of the world of their crunchy charms.

By 1810, naval provisioners stocked barrels of crackers, and Josiah Bent's business was booming. Rival John Pearson's factory made pilot bread until 1898, when his business became the National Biscuit Company. In later years, Josiah Bent's enterprise also was sold to that company, known today as Nabisco.

Several of the old cracker varieties remain favorites. Water crackers, similar to Pearson's pilot bread, still feature only two ingredients, flour and water, although they are more likely to be found at a posh cocktail party than on a clipper ship. Another old variety, called common crackers, is a top-seller at G. H. Bent Company (started by a grandson of old Josiah). One hundred years ago, pillowy common crackers were the main ingredient in the much-loved Common Cracker Pudding.

Another traditional variety is the soda cracker. Similar to common crackers in taste, soda crackers are thinner and crisper and are known to modern snackers as saltines.

One of the best-loved buttery crackers is the famous Ritz, created during the Great Depression by the National Biscuit Company. The cracker was introduced in November of 1934 and was an instant success. Today, Nabisco makes a whopping 16 billion Ritz crackers every year.

A cracker delivery wagon leaving the G. H. Bent factory in Milton, Mass., in 1893. The factory, built only two years earlier, specialized in cold-water "common" crackers.

BY

VICTORIA

DOUDERA

(c o n t i n u e d)

Cracker-Making SECRETS

Cracker maker Joan Harlow of New Hampshire.

–Doug Mindell

With so many crackers available in grocery stores today, it might seem surprising that some folks would even contemplate making them at home. But Joan Harlow, author of *The Harlow's Bread & Cracker Cookbook,* says that making crackers is a rewarding and fun experience.

"Crackers are a wonderful project for cooks who like a challenge and for folks who like to know exactly what's in their snack foods," she says. She owns Harlow's Bread & Cracker Company, an Epping, New Hampshire, business that makes more than a dozen varieties of crackers and many kinds of bread. When asked whether she has ever heard that mysterious crackling sound that inspired Josiah Bent 200 years ago, Harlow laughs. "I hear a wonderful crackling sound all the time," she confesses. "It happens every time my crackers are eaten."

To make up a batch or two of crackers at home, heed these tips from cracker chef Joan Harlow:

- Crackers made with bread flour and yeast will generally roll out the thinnest but may need to be pricked before baking to prevent "pillowing."

- Crackers made with shortening and egg will be "shorter"—that is, not as crisp. Their shelf life is shorter as well.

- For maximum flavor, crush or toast any seeds before adding to cracker dough.

- For truly crispy results, roll the dough as thin as you can, or use a pasta machine. The thinner the cracker, the better the taste and texture.

- If the dough is too sticky or wet, chill it in the refrigerator. Don't work the dough too much: You'll overdevelop the gluten and make a tough cracker.

- If your dough crumbles or tears, it may be too cold. Let it come to room temperature before trying again.

- Line cookie sheets with parchment paper rather than greasing them.

- Bake crackers until you see a blush of tan. Don't undercook.

- Cool crackers on the cookie sheet set onto a cooling rack. The crackers will continue to crispen as they cool.

- Store crackers in an airtight container away from sunlight or heat.

Cream Crackers

A wonderful cracker for a delicate cheese, from The Harlow's Bread & Cracker Cookbook.

1-1/2 cups pastry flour

1 teaspoon salt

1/4 cup sour cream

1/4 cup cold water, more or less

Mix the dry ingredients, then add the sour cream and work in the water a little at a time. Mix until the dough balls up, then divide in half. The dough can be wrapped in plastic and chilled, or rolled immediately.

Preheat oven to 350°F. On parchment paper, roll out the dough into two thin rectangles. For each rectangle, fold the edges in toward the center in overlapping thirds as you would in making a layered pastry. Give the dough a quarter turn and roll it out again. Fold it in thirds, turn and roll once more. Place the paper with the piece of dough onto a cookie sheet, cut into cracker-size portions with a pizza cutter or sharp knife, and bake for about 10 minutes. The crackers will turn a soft biscuity color and be fairly crisp when done. They will finish crisping as they cool on the cookie sheet. **Makes 50 to 60 crackers.**

Spicy Cheddar Crackers

One of Joan Harlow's favorites.

4 cups bread flour

1 pound good Cheddar cheese, grated

1 package dry yeast (1 scant tablespoon)

1 teaspoon dry mustard

1/2 teaspoon cayenne pepper

1 teaspoon salt

1/2 cup vegetable oil

1 container (12 ounces) beer (cheap is OK)

Place all ingredients into the bowl of a mixer. Use the beater attachment and mix on low speed until ingredients are evenly distributed and form a ball. Chill for at least 1 hour.

Preheat oven to 400°F. Line two cookie sheets with parchment paper. Dust your working surface with flour. Divide the dough in half and flatten each half into a disk. Roll it out as you would a piecrust, working from the center to the outside edge until the dough is as thin as you can get it. Place dough onto the lined cookie sheets. Prick dough with a fork. Using a pizza cutter, cut the dough into individual crackers.

Bake one cookie sheet at a time for 12 to 15 minutes, or until golden, turning the sheet halfway through if your oven has hot spots. Dump the crackers onto a wire rack and let them cool completely before storing them in an airtight container. **Makes about 80 crackers.**

(c o n t i n u e d)

Graham Crackers

An eccentric American clergyman named Sylvester Graham invented this classic snack in 1829. An advocate of temperance, vegetarianism, and unsifted, coarsely ground wheat flour, Graham created his cracker using winter wheat berries, ground with just the right combination of fine, medium, and coarse granules. His crackers were an immediate sensation with people of all ages, so popular that the crackers and the coarse flour were both named for their inventor.

1 cup white flour
1-1/4 cups whole wheat flour
5 tablespoons sugar
1/2 teaspoon salt
1/2 teaspoon baking soda
1 teaspoon baking powder
1/4 teaspoon ground cinnamon
3 tablespoons cold butter, cut into small pieces
1/4 cup solid vegetable shortening
2 tablespoons honey
1 tablespoon molasses
1/4 cup water, more or less
1 teaspoon vanilla extract

Combine flours, sugar, salt, baking soda, baking powder, and cinnamon in a large bowl. Work in the butter and shortening with your fingers until the mixture has the consistency of coarse crumbs.

In a separate bowl, mix the honey, molasses, water, and vanilla. Sprinkle this mixture over the dry ingredients, and toss with a fork until well blended. Form the dough into a ball. (If dough is too dry, sprinkle on more water until you can form it into a ball.) Cover and chill for several hours.

Cut the dough in half and let it sit for 15 minutes at room temperature. Sprinkle a piece of parchment paper with whole wheat flour. Roll out one of the dough pieces on the paper to about 7x15 inches. If the dough cracks or breaks, just pinch the edges back together.

Poke a fork into the dough at ½- to 1-inch intervals. Then cut dough into 2½-inch squares. Use a spatula to move the squares to a large ungreased baking sheet. You can place them close together. Repeat with the other half of the dough. Bake in the center of the oven for 15 minutes at 350°F, or until lightly browned on the edges. Remove crackers from sheet before they are completely cool. Store in an airtight container at room temperature for up to a month.

For a sweeter treat: Sprinkle a mixture of sugar and cinnamon over the top of the crackers before baking.

Makes about 36 crackers.

Ugly Crackers

Don't let the name fool you—Joan Harlow claims that these best-selling crackers have a lovely taste!

6 cups all-purpose flour
1 cup sesame seeds, crushed or toasted
1 tablespoon salt
1 tablespoon baking powder
3/4 cup crumbled blue cheese
2 cups milk

Mix flour, sesame seeds, salt, and baking powder together. Cut in blue cheese until it is well distributed. Stir in milk and form dough into a ball. Wrap the dough in plastic and chill for at least 1 hour.

Preheat oven to 350°F. Roll out the dough as thin as you can get it. Place large sheets of dough onto parchment-lined cookie sheets and cut across and down into squares.

Bake for 8 to 10 minutes. These crackers will turn golden around the edges of the pan, or anywhere that you have a significantly thinner place in the dough. **Makes about 120 crackers.**

For even more cracker recipes (and recipes for bagels, scones, tea breads, and other treats), order a copy of *The Harlow's Bread & Cracker Cookbook* by sending $12.95 to Harlow's Bread & Cracker Company, Rte. 27, Epping, NH 03042. (Your payment includes postage.)

Great Recipes from
The Old Farmer's Almanac!

More than 50 mouthwatering cookie recipes!

NEW! This new cookbook has our favorite cookie recipes plus some great tips to make even the best cookie baker better. We've included kitchen-tested, easy-to-follow recipes for bar cookies, dropped cookies, hand-shaped, and cutout cookies from noted bakers Flo Braker, Ken Haedrich, and Susan Peery, plus award-winning recipes from Almanac cooking contests. There's even room for you to add your favorite cookie recipes to make this the only cookie book for your kitchen.

The Old Farmer's Almanac Favorite Cookies
Spiral binding, durable cover, colorfully illustrated.
Item: OFNDCCK Key: NDCOFAB

Only $12.95 (+ shipping and handling*)

Also included . . .
- 10 things every cookie baker needs to know
- Ingredient substitution list
- Measurement conversions
- Oodles of useful tips for baking, packaging, shipping, and more . . .

Buy Both and Save 15%!

Only $22.00 (+shipping and handling*)
Item: OFNDCKS Key: NDCOFAB
*One small charge of $3.95 for shipping and handling per order!

Seasonal cooking at its best!

We've collected more than 100 of our seasonal favorites and added many useful tips for planning and preparation. Whether sweet or savory, these kitchen-tested recipes are easy to follow, and the tasty results will certainly bring compliments to the cook!

The Old Farmer's Almanac Kitchen-Tested
Recipes for Every Season
Spiral binding, durable cover, colorfully illustrated.
Item: OFNDREC Key: NDCOFAB

Only $12.95
(+ shipping and handling*)

Handy tips and reference charts include . . .
- The party planner
- Substitutions for common and uncommon ingredients
- Rainy-day grilling conversions
- Slow-cooker tips, and more . . .

Best Fishing Days, 2001

(and other fishing lore from the files of *The Old Farmer's Almanac*)

Probably the best fishing times are when the ocean tides are restless before their turn and in the first hour of ebbing. All fish in all waters —salt and fresh—feed most heavily at those times.

The best temperatures for fish species vary widely, of course, and are chiefly important if you are going to have your own fishpond. The best temperatures for brook trout are 45° to 65°F. Brown trout and rainbow trout are more tolerant of higher temperatures. Smallmouth black bass do best in cool water. Horned pout take what they find.

Most of us go fishing when we can get time off, not because it is the best time. But there *are* best times:

■ One hour before and one hour after high tides, and one hour before and one hour after low tides. (The times of high tides for Boston are given on pages 58-84 and corrected for your locality on pages 232-233. Inland, the times for high tides correspond with the times the Moon is due south. Low tides are halfway between high tides.)

■ During "the morning rise" (after sunup for a spell) and "the evening rise" (just before sundown and the hour or so after).

■ When the barometer is steady or on the rise. (But, of course, even in a three-day driving northeaster, the fish aren't going to give up feeding. Their hunger clock keeps right on working, and the smart fisherman will find just the right bait.)

■ When there is a hatch of flies—caddis flies or mayflies, commonly. (The fisherman will have to match the hatching flies with *his* fly or go fishless.)

■ When the breeze is from a westerly quarter rather than from the north or east.

■ When the water is still or rippled, rather than during a wind.

■ Starting on the day the Moon is new and continuing through the day it is full.

Moon Between New & Full, 2001

- January 1-9
- January 24-February 8
- February 23-March 9
- March 24-April 7
- April 23-May 7
- May 22-June 5
- June 21-July 5
- July 20-August 4
- August 18-September 2
- September 17-October 2
- October 16-November 1
- November 15-30
- December 14-30

What People Fish for Most (freshwater)	
Bass	35%
Trout	18%
Catfish	11%
All species	9%
Bream	6%
Crappie	6%
Carp/muskie/panfish/ pike/shad/steelhead/ striper	5%
Walleye	5%
Perch	3%
Salmon	2%

–courtesy American Sportfishing Association

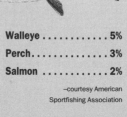

New lure out-fishes live bait 3 to 1; could be banned from tournaments.

Automatically simulates movement of a live worm

by Charlie Allen

VERO BEACH, FL — In a recent bass competition near this Florida coast town, a champion fisherman used an imitation lure not yet on the market and humbled another champion who was using live bait. Both were in the same boat under the supervision of official observers. The new lure caught three times more bass than the live bait.

The size of the lure's win is great news for anyone who loves fresh-water fishing, but because bass tournaments are getting richer and richer, a new issue arises. Should such a lure be allowed in competition where prizes have reached the $1,000,000 level? Most tournaments already prohibit live bait, and this new lure out-fished live bait three to one.

I asked one of the sponsors of the Vero Beach contest why the lure was so effective, and about its future in tournaments."The Walking Worm™ (the lure's name) works because fish love worms more than any other food. Worms are scale-less and easier to digest than other live bait. To a fish they're a treat. But they must be alive, and that means movement. If a worm or any other prey stops moving for a moment, as regular plastic worms do, fish smell a rat. They know it's a fake. Even if the prey resumes moving, say, when a fisherman reels in a regular plastic worm, it's too late. Their mind's made up.

"Ichthyologists—a fancy word for a fish professor—say that constant movement excites a predatory response in a fish. They strike because they're programmed that way. Constant movement presents a temptation so overwhelming it triggers larger, less aggressive fish to strike, even fish that have just fed.

"The Walking Worm's genius is a multi-flex construction that traps air between tail segments. This causes the worm's tail to constantly curl, as if it were strolling across the bottom or through middle or top water. To a bass or other predatory fish, this constant curling is ice cream. They go berserk.

"I was recently down in Alabama where I saw three imitation lures – crank bait, a plastic worm and the Walking Worm – dropped in a huge fish tank with bass in it. They swam right by the other two then darted for the Walking Worm. Why? Well, the crank bait was moving, but it wasn't a worm. The regular plastic worm looked tasty, but it stopped moving for awhile when it hit the bottom and that convinced the fish it was dead. To the bass, the Walking Worm was a juicy live worm, and they went for it hook, line and sinker, literally.

"Yes, I suppose the Walking Worm could cause some regulation. The money is so big now fisherman will look for any advantage. The Walking Worm caught more bass today in an hour than the winner of a $600,000 prize caught over in Cypress Gardens. Now there's a $1,000,000 prize coming up. If I were eligible for that tournament, I know what I would use."

To order a box of 30 worms (one color per box, e.g. June Bug) call **1-800-873-4415** anytime or day, or mail your name, address and check or money order (or cc number and exp. date) to NGC Sports **(Dept. W-56)**, 60 Church St., Yalesville, CT 06492. One color costs $19.95, two or more are $18.00 each, all six colors are only $89.00 (add $5.00 s/h). The Walking Worm can be Texas and Carolina rigged. There's a 30-day money-back guarantee, if you return them.

WW-3   © Bost Enterprises, Inc. 2000 **Dept. W-56**

One hundred years ago, on a cold

Queen of

The Mist

"I Felt As Though All Nature Were Being Annihilated"

October afternoon, Annie Edson Taylor conquered Niagara Falls.

"reat Heaven, what a fall of bright-green water!" wrote Charles Dickens in 1843, upon stepping to the brink of Niagara Falls. Niagara's terrible beauty has challenged the pens of countless writers, but for some visitors, the cataract represents the ultimate challenge—risking all to conquer nature. Throughout the 1800s, daring souls took on the Niagara River's gaping gorge and raging rapids, upping the ante with each feat until only one breathtaking stunt remained: riding the river over the falls itself.

In 1829, Sam Patch, the Yankee Leaper, jumped from a platform erected between Niagara's American and Horseshoe Falls. His successful 130-foot plunge thrilled thousands of onlookers. In the summer of 1859, a Frenchman who called himself "The Great Blondin" crossed the gorge 21 times on a rope, the first of several Niagara tightrope walkers. By the 1880s, daredevils were literally barreling their way down the dangerous Whirlpool Rapids below the falls or swimming across the treacherous river. Whirlpool-riding culminated in 1901 when two women took turns making the trip on consecutive days using the same barrel. After Martha Wagenfuhrer's ride on September 6, Maud Willard set out the next day accompanied by her fox terrier. When the barrel in which the two were riding became stuck in the whirlpool and drifted for hours, Maud Willard suffocated, but her pet managed to survive by sticking its nose into the barrel's single airhole.

The time was ripe for challenging the falls itself, and Annie Edson Taylor, a teacher from Bay City, Michigan, determined to be the first. She chose to make the trip on her birthday, October 24, 1901. *(continued)*

Annie Taylor pets a furry friend perched atop a replica of her oak barrel. Annie hoped to cash in on her daring exploit.

by Randy Miller

photos: Niagara Falls Public Library, Local History Department

Horseshoe Falls (above) c. 1901; Annie (left), bruised and dazed, makes her way to shore just moments after emerging from the barrel.

Many of the details of Annie's early life are unknown. She was elusive about her background or gave conflicting information. She said she was 43 years old in 1901, but genealogical records later revealed she was born in 1838, making her 63 years old at the time of her exploit. Orphaned by age 14, Annie claimed to have been trained to teach piano, dancing, and "physical culture." She said she was married at 18, bore a child who lived only a few days, and became a widow at 21 (although no written records of these events have been found). What is known for sure is that she was an unmarried woman, childless, well educated, independent, and poor.

And one thing more: Annie had a full deck of courage. In short, she possessed all the characteristics that made her a suspect woman of her day, a

A s I reached the brink, the barrel did what I predicted it would do, paused for a moment and then made the awful plunge of 158 feet to the boiling cauldron below."

What Is the Risk?

Besides wooden, metal, and plastic barrels, people have used rubber devices, a kayak, and a jet ski to go over Niagara Falls. (Today, local laws forbid all such attempts.) Including Annie Taylor's historic first trip in 1901, there have been 17 instances in which people have risked their lives going over the falls, involving 2 women and 13 men (two of the men made two attempts each). Five people lost their lives, which means that there is about a 70 percent chance of surviving a plunge over Niagara Falls.

maverick, a female to fear or even to ridicule. Thomas Carlyle summed up one of the anxieties of the age: that the spread of democracy would unleash the debasing force of individualism. He concluded that full political rights (for men *and* women) would bring only "unspeakable Chaos."

Annie Taylor, growing up in nearby Auburn, New York, would have known of the well-publicized catastrophes associated with Niagara Falls. Newspaper reports of severed limbs and headless torsos being found in the gorge—the effects of tangling with the raging Niagara River—were not uncommon. Annie made careful preparations, planning her ride "on scientific principles." She drew a barrel pattern, cut it out of paper, and sewed it together with twine. This she took to a cooper, who fashioned the 4½-foot barrel out of "white Kentucky oak, with ten hoops," Annie recalled in her 1902 booklet. She inspected each stave and insisted on the finest craftsmanship, knowing the shock her barrel would be subjected to. She had cloth straps installed inside the barrel and packed several pil-

Norman Candler (left), designer of "The Thing," and Red Hill Jr. pose for this 1951 photo, a day before Hill lost his life going over the falls.

lows for cushioning. A heavy anvil was bolted to the outside bottom of the barrel to keep it upright as much as possible.

On the chosen day, Annie had rivermen row her and her barrel from the American side above the falls to an island near the shore. Here the cask was placed into the water. "I took off my hat, street skirt, and coat, and entered the barrel," she wrote. The lid was screwed down tight, and a bicycle pump was used to fill the barrel with fresh air. The men towed the barrel across the river to the current that would bring her over the Canadian Horseshoe Falls. Cut loose at 4:05 P.M., Annie vividly recalled what happened next:

"I was started on a trip no traveler had ever taken, my heart swelled, and for some moments, I felt as though I were being suffocated, but I determined to be brave. By a supreme effort of will, I calmed myself at once and began earnestly to pray. . . . The trip through the Rapids was nothing but a pleasant sensation. . . . As I reached the brink, the barrel did what I predicted it would do, paused for a moment and then made the awful plunge of 158 feet to the boiling cauldron below. I thought for a moment my senses were lost. The feeling was one of absolute horror, but still I knew when I struck the water of the lower river. . . . I went down, down. . . . Below the surface, *all was still*. . . . On coming to the surface, the barrel was carried into a cave back of the falls, whirled like a dasher in a churn, dropped among the rocks, and turned with the velocity of a top until the anvil ground with such force

Annie, who felt defrauded by her managers, survived by selling mementos herself.

as to generate electricity, which penetrated and illumined the barrel. . . . I felt as though all nature were being annihilated."

Several thousand people had watched Annie's barrel shoot over the waterfall, and soon it bobbed close to shore, where it was brought up onto a rock. Exactly 50 minutes after the cover was secured, it was frantically removed. "My God, she's alive!" a man shouted, as later reported in the *Niagara Falls Gazette*. "The word soon reached the top of the gorge. A tremendous roar went up from the crowd and was heard on the American side of the river. They gave an answering cheer and both boats of the Maid of the Mist Company blew their whistles in salute to the brave woman, who was soon dubbed Queen of the Mist."

Annie Taylor emerged from the barrel dazed, bruised, and frigid from the cold water that had managed to leak into the barrel. She had no broken bones but complained of a pain between her shoulders. She needed several days to recuperate. While she was on the mend, her manager failed to protect the historic barrel, and souvenir hunters trashed it. He apparently found other uses for the money collected for Annie along the banks of the river.

Annie had hoped to capitalize on her ride by attracting people who were attending the great Pan American Exposition being held in Buffalo. She appeared at the fair, greeted an endless line of people for a day, and later went on the lecture tour with her refurbished barrel.

But something wasn't working. People found her uninspiring as a speaker and wished she looked somehow younger and more fragile. Her manager booked her in out-of-the-way places and used the income to pay off expenses that always seemed to match the profits. Eventually, he stole the barrel and then substituted a young woman, a fake, for Annie.

How Much Water Goes Over Niagara Falls?

The volume of water 100 years ago, when Annie Taylor surveyed the raging torrent, was immense, even though a small portion of the river above the falls began to be diverted to generate electricity in 1895. The average flow at the head of the Niagara River for the month of October 1901 was 1.4 million gallons of water per second, according to data compiled by the Great Lakes Environmental Research Laboratory. Because an estimated 80 to 90 percent of the river flows over the larger of Niagara's two cascades, the Horseshoe Falls, Annie's barrel was catapulted and pummeled by some 1.2 million gallons of water, or about 5,000 tons, per second.

If we changed that green water into a river of green peas, for example, enough peas would fall in one second to serve 50 million people. Or put peas onto a railroad train perched all along the 2,200-foot curved brink of Horseshoe Falls, and it would take 45 fully loaded boxcars tumbling over the edge each second to equal the force Annie faced.

Today, because anywhere from about 50 to 75 percent of the Niagara River can be diverted for hydroelectric power (depending on regulations established by a 1950 American/Canadian treaty that protects the scenic value of the falls), Niagara Falls is a greatly diminished cataract compared with the natural wonder challenged by Annie Taylor.

Annie recovered the barrel in Chicago and hired another manager, but it ended the same way. He deserted her and took the barrel. It all might have worked out better if she had gotten her first choice for a manager. "Annie wanted her nephew, Charles Edson, who was my father, to manage her exploit," recalls 92-year-old Willard Edson of Toledo, Ohio. "But he didn't like the idea of her going over the falls, so he said no."

In the following years, Annie Taylor descended deeper into poverty, never realizing her dream of wealth. In the summer tourist season, she set up a booth on a sidewalk in Niagara Falls and sold postcards and her ten-cent booklet, sitting next to a replica of her barrel. In the dead of winter, she trudged along the snowy streets offering her wares to well-dressed pedestrians.

By the spring of 1921, the Queen of the Mist was unable to care for herself. She was taken to a charitable institution in Lockport, New York, where she lived the remaining weeks of her life. Annie Edson Taylor died on April 30 at the age of 82, penniless, blind, and broken in health. Shortly before her death, she expressed the belief that her strength had never fully returned in the 20 years since the horrific ordeal of riding over the falls.

America loves its mythical figures, the likes of Paul Bunyan, John Henry, and Pecos Bill. These larger-than-life heroes all tackled the terrible forces of nature with superhuman strength and will. But there is one figure yet to be fully celebrated, who took on the mighty force of Niagara Falls with mythical courage. Though her feat seems larger than life, Annie Taylor is no myth—she was a real woman. □ □

➤ Spinning the Web: Go to www.almanac.com and click on Article Links 2001 for Web sites related to this article. *–The Editors*

ANSWERS TO Mr. Smith's MADDENING Mind-Manglers

From page 194.

1. It must increase by $1,100.

Brooke's $\frac{3}{5} = \frac{x}{4,000}$ $\frac{7}{8} = \frac{x}{4,000}$
Brittany's

$$5x = 12,000 \qquad 8x = 28,000$$

$$\frac{5x}{5} = \frac{12,000}{5} \qquad \frac{8x}{8} = \frac{28,000}{8}$$

$$x = 2,400 \qquad x = 3,500$$

$$\$3,500 - \$2,400 = \$1,100$$

2. The probability is 35 out of 36. You must first find the possibility of all three rolls being the same number. You have no idea what the first number rolled will be, but you have a 6 out of 6 chance of getting a number. You will then have a 1 out of 6 chance of getting the same number on your second roll, and a 1 out of 6 chance of getting the same number on your third roll. Thus you have a 1 out of 36 chance of getting the same number three times in a row. Therefore, you have a 35 out of 36 chance of their all not being the same!

$$\frac{6}{6} \times \frac{1}{6} \times \frac{1}{6} = \frac{6}{216} = \frac{1}{36}$$

3. 449 windows. Each day the number of windows increased by 6, so you can work out the pattern. But to save time, find an algebraic rule that works:

$5 + 6(n - 1)$ [That is, 5 (the constant number of windows Jessie washed every day) plus 6 (the number of windows increased every day, beginning on the second day) times the result of n (the day number) minus 1.]

Day 1 = 5 + 6(1 − 1) = 5 + 0 = 5
Day 2 = 5 + 6(2 − 1) = 5 + 6 = 11
Day 75 = 5 + 6(75 − 1) = 5 + 444
           = 449

4. He should set up the fence as a circle to get the maximum space. Any other shape—square, rectangle, etc.—will not provide as much space as the circle, or 796.1 square yards. (Area of a circle = πr^2.)

5. 30 students.

$$81 = \frac{90(20) + 75(n)}{n + 20}$$

$$81(n + 20) = \frac{1{,}800 + 75n}{n + 20} \times (n + 20)$$

$$81n + 1{,}620 = 1{,}800 + 75n$$
$$6n = 180$$
$$n = 30$$

6. Cassidy's partner is number 15. The pairs are:

1 + 15 = 16	6 + 10 = 16
2 + 14 = 16	7 + 18 = 25
3 + 13 = 16	8 + 17 = 25
4 + 12 = 16	9 + 16 = 25
5 + 11 = 16	

7.

	Lfgrd	Cook	Mech	Teach
Michael	Yes	X	X	X
Jordan	X	X	X	Yes
Tim	X	X	Yes	X
Duncan	X	Yes	X	X

8.

X̲   II − I

9. 120 minutes. Method: 30 minutes SP = 90 minutes ELP, because ELP is 3 times SP. 100 minutes LP = 150 minutes ELP, because ELP is 1.5 times LP. Thus 240 of the 360 minutes of ELP has been used, leaving 120 minutes.

10. (1) There "are" . . .
(2) errors
(3) There are only two errors!

☐ ☐

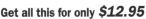

Secrets of the Zodiac

Ancient astrologers associated each of the signs with a part of the body over which they felt the sign held some influence. The first sign of the zodiac—Aries—was attributed to the head, with the rest of the signs moving down the body, ending with Pisces at the feet.

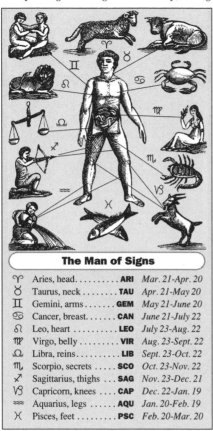

The Man of Signs

♈	Aries, head.........	**ARI**	*Mar. 21-Apr. 20*
♉	Taurus, neck.......	**TAU**	*Apr. 21-May 20*
♊	Gemini, arms......	**GEM**	*May 21-June 20*
♋	Cancer, breast......	**CAN**	*June 21-July 22*
♌	Leo, heart.........	**LEO**	*July 23-Aug. 22*
♍	Virgo, belly........	**VIR**	*Aug. 23-Sept. 22*
♎	Libra, reins.........	**LIB**	*Sept. 23-Oct. 22*
♏	Scorpio, secrets.....	**SCO**	*Oct. 23-Nov. 22*
♐	Sagittarius, thighs ...	**SAG**	*Nov. 23-Dec. 21*
♑	Capricorn, knees	**CAP**	*Dec. 22-Jan. 19*
♒	Aquarius, legs	**AQU**	*Jan. 20-Feb. 19*
♓	Pisces, feet.........	**PSC**	*Feb. 20-Mar. 20*

Astrology and Astronomy

■ Astrology is a tool we use to time events according to the *astrological* placement of the two luminaries (the Sun and the Moon) and eight planets in the 12 signs of the zodiac. Astronomy, on the other hand, is the charting of the *actual* placement of the known planets and constellations, taking into account precession of the equinoxes. As a result, *the placement of the planets in the signs of the zodiac are not the same astrologically and astronomically.* (The Moon's astronomical place is given in the **Left-Hand Calendar Pages 58-84,** and its astrological place is given in **Gardening by the Moon's Sign, page 180.**)

Modern astrology is a study of synchronicities. The planetary movements do not cause events. Rather, they explain the "flow," or trajectory, that events tend to follow. Because of free will, you can choose to plan a schedule in harmony with the flow, or you can choose to swim against the current.

The dates given in the **Astrological Timetable (page 225)** have been chosen with particular care to the astrological passage of the Moon. However, because other planets also influence us, it's best to take a look at all indicators before seeking advice on major life decisions. A qualified astrologer can study the current relationship of the planets and your own personal birth chart to assist you in the best possible timing for carrying out your plans.

When Mercury Is Retrograde

■ Sometimes when we look out from our perspective here on Earth, the other planets appear to be traveling backward through the zodiac. (They're not actually moving backward; it just looks that way to us.) We call this *retrograde motion.*

Mercury's retrograde periods, which occur three or four times a year, can cause travel delays and misconstrued communications. Plans have a way of unraveling, too. However, this is an excellent time to research or look into the past. Intuition is high during these periods, and coincidences can be extraordinary.

When Mercury is retrograde, astrologers advise us to keep plans flexible, allow extra time for travel, and avoid signing contracts. It's OK and even useful to look over projects and plans, because we may see them with different eyes at these times. However, our normal system of checks and balances might not be active, so it's best to wait until Mercury is direct again to make any final decisions. In 2001, Mercury will be retrograde from February 4 to 25, June 4 to 28, and October 1 to 23.

–Celeste Longacre

Astrological Timetable, 2001

■ The following month-by-month chart is based on the Moon's sign and shows the most favorable times each month for certain activities. *by Celeste Longacre*

	JAN.	FEB.	MAR.	APR.	MAY	JUNE	JULY	AUG.	SEPT.	OCT.	NOV.	DEC.
Give up smoking	11, 15	11, 12, 20, 21	11, 12, 20, 21	16, 17, 21, 22	14, 15, 19, 20	10, 11, 15, 16	7, 8, 12, 13	8, 9, 17, 18	5, 6, 14, 15	3, 11, 12, 15, 16	7, 8, 12, 13	5, 6, 9, 10
Begin diet to lose weight	11, 15	11, 20, 21	11, 12, 20, 21	16, 17, 21, 22	14, 15, 19, 20	10, 11, 15, 16	7, 8, 12, 13	8, 9, 17, 18	5, 6, 14, 15	3, 11, 12, 15, 16	7, 8, 12, 13	5, 6, 9, 10
Begin diet to gain weight	2, 3, 29, 30	7, 25, 26	6, 7, 25, 26	3, 4, 30	1, 4, 5, 27, 28	1, 24, 28, 29	21, 22, 25, 26	21, 22, 31	27, 28	24, 25, 29, 30	20, 21, 25, 26	18, 19, 23, 24
Cut hair to encourage growth	4, 5, 28	1, 2, 28	1, 27, 28	7, 24	4, 28	1, 2, 28, 29	21, 25, 26	21, 22	18, 19, 30	1, 27, 28	23, 24, 28, 29	20, 21, 25, 26
Cut hair to discourage growth	11, 12, 15, 16	11, 12, 23	10, 11, 22, 23	18, 20	16, 17, 21	12, 13, 17, 18	10, 11, 14, 15	6, 7, 11, 12, 18	7, 8, 14, 15	4, 5, 15	2, 7, 8, 12, 13	5, 6, 9, 10
Have dental care	12, 13	9, 10	8, 9	5, 6	2, 3, 29, 30	26, 27	23, 24	19, 20	16, 17	13, 14	9, 10, 11	7, 8
End old projects	22, 23	21, 22	23, 24	21, 22	21, 22	19, 20	18, 19	17, 18	15, 16	14, 15	13, 14	12, 13
Start new projects	25, 26	24, 25	26, 27	24, 25	24, 25	22, 23	21, 22	20, 21	18, 19	17, 18	16, 17	15, 16
Entertain	10, 11	7, 8	6, 7	3, 4, 31	1, 27, 28	23, 24	21, 22	17, 18	14, 15	11, 12	7, 8	4, 5, 6
Go camping	19, 20	15, 16, 17	15, 16	11, 12	8, 9, 10	5, 6	2, 3, 29, 30	26, 27	22, 23	19, 20	16, 17	13, 14
Plant above-ground crops	1, 4, 5, 27, 28	5, 6, 24, 28	1, 4, 5, 27, 28	1, 2, 5, 28, 29	2, 3, 25, 26, 30	3, 4, 21, 22, 30	1, 24, 27, 28	23, 24, 28, 29	20, 21, 26, 30	1, 17, 18, 27, 28	23, 24, 28, 29	20, 21, 25, 26
Plant below-ground crops	12, 13, 17, 18	9, 10, 13, 14	13, 14, 22	9, 10, 19, 20	11, 12, 16, 17, 21	12, 13, 17, 18	10, 11, 14, 15, 19	6, 7, 11, 12, 15, 16	3, 7, 8, 12, 13	4, 5, 9, 10	2, 5, 6, 10	2, 3, 7, 8, 11, 12
Destroy pests and weeds	2, 3, 29, 30	26, 27	25, 26	21, 22	18, 19	15, 16	12, 13	8, 9	5, 6	2, 3, 29, 30	25, 26, 27	23, 24
Graft or pollinate	8, 9	5, 6	4, 5, 31	1, 2, 28, 29	25, 26	21, 22	19, 20	15, 16	12, 13	9, 10	5, 6	2, 3, 30, 31
Prune to encourage growth	2, 3, 29, 30	7, 25, 26, 27	6, 7, 26	3, 4, 30	1, 27, 28	5, 23, 24	2, 3, 29, 30	26, 27	22, 23	19, 20, 29, 30	16, 17, 25, 26, 27	14, 23, 24
Prune to discourage growth	10, 11, 20	15, 16	15, 16	11, 12, 21, 22	9, 10, 18, 19	15, 16	12, 13	8, 9, 10, 17	5, 6, 14, 15	11, 12	7, 8	5, 6, 13
Harvest above-ground crops	4, 5, 27, 28	1, 2, 28	1, 8, 27, 28	5, 6, 24	2, 3, 29, 30	25, 26	23, 24	28, 29	24, 25	22, 23, 31	18, 19, 28, 29	15, 16, 25, 26
Harvest below-ground crops	12, 13, 22, 23	9, 10, 18, 19	17, 18	14, 15	11, 12, 21, 22	7, 8, 17, 18	6, 14, 15	11, 12	7, 8, 16	4, 5, 13, 14	2, 9, 10	7, 8
Cut hay	2, 3, 29, 30	26, 27	25, 26	21, 22	18, 19	15, 16	12, 13	8, 9	5, 6	2, 3, 29, 30	25, 26, 27	23, 24
Begin logging	22, 23	18, 19	17, 18	14, 15	11, 12	7, 8	5, 6	1, 2, 28, 29	24, 25	22, 23	18, 19	15, 16
Set posts or pour concrete	22, 23	18, 19	17, 18	14, 15	11, 12	7, 8	5, 6	1, 2, 28, 29	24, 25	22, 23	18, 19	15, 16
Breed	17, 18	13, 14	12, 13, 14	9, 10	6, 7	3, 4	1, 27, 28	23, 24	20, 21	17, 18	14, 15	11, 12
Wean	11, 15	11, 12, 20, 21	11, 12, 20, 21	16, 17, 21, 22	14, 15, 19, 20	10, 11, 15, 16	7, 8, 12, 13	8, 9, 17, 18	5, 6, 14, 15	3, 11, 12, 15, 16	7, 8, 12, 13	5, 6, 9, 10
Castrate animals	24, 25	21, 22	20, 21	16, 17	13, 14, 15	10, 11	7, 8	3, 4, 30, 31	1, 27, 28	24, 25	20, 21, 22	18, 19
Slaughter	17, 18	13, 14	12, 13, 14	9, 10	6, 7	3, 4	1, 27, 28	23, 24	20, 21	17, 18	14, 15	11, 12

Time Corrections

■ Times of sunrise/sunset and moonrise/moonset, selected times for observing the visible planets, and transit times of the bright stars are given for Boston **on pages 58-84, 50-51, and 54.** Use the Key Letter shown to the right of each time on those pages with this table to find the number of minutes, already adjusted for different time zones, that you must add to or subtract from Boston time to get the correct time for your city. (Because of complex calculations for different locales, times may not be precise to the minute.) If your city is not listed, find the city closest to you in latitude and longitude and use those figures. Boston's latitude is 42° 22' and its longitude is 71° 03'. Canadian cities appear at the end of the table. For further information on the use of Key Letters and this table, see **How to Use This Almanac, page 40.**

Time Zone Code: Codes represent *standard time.* Atlantic is –1, Eastern is 0, Central is 1, Mountain is 2, Pacific is 3, Alaska is 4, and Hawaii-Aleutian is 5.

City	North Latitude ° '		West Longitude ° '		Time Zone Code	Key Letters				
						A (min.)	B (min.)	C (min.)	D (min.)	E (min.)
Aberdeen, SD	45	28	98	29	1	+37	+44	+49	+54	+59
Akron, OH	41	5	81	31	0	+46	+43	+41	+39	+37
Albany, NY	42	39	73	45	0	+ 9	+10	+10	+11	+11
Albert Lea, MN	43	39	93	22	1	+24	+26	+28	+31	+33
Albuquerque, NM	35	5	106	39	2	+45	+32	+22	+11	+ 2
Alexandria, LA	31	18	92	27	1	+58	+40	+26	+ 9	– 3
Allentown–Bethlehem, PA	40	36	75	28	0	+23	+20	+17	+14	+12
Amarillo, TX	35	12	101	50	1	+85	+73	+63	+52	+43
Anchorage, AK	61	10	149	59	4	–46	+27	+71	+122	+171
Asheville, NC	35	36	82	33	0	+67	+55	+46	+35	+27
Atlanta, GA	33	45	84	24	0	+79	+65	+53	+40	+30
Atlantic City, NJ	39	22	74	26	0	+23	+17	+13	+ 8	+ 4
Augusta, GA	33	28	81	58	0	+70	+55	+44	+30	+19
Augusta, ME	44	19	69	46	0	–12	– 8	– 5	– 1	0
Austin, TX	30	16	97	45	1	+82	+62	+47	+29	+15
Bakersfield, CA	35	23	119	1	3	+33	+21	+12	+ 1	– 7
Baltimore, MD	39	17	76	37	0	+32	+26	+22	+17	+13
Bangor, ME	44	48	68	46	0	–18	–13	– 9	– 5	– 1
Barstow, CA	34	54	117	1	3	+27	+14	+ 4	– 7	–16
Baton Rouge, LA	30	27	91	11	1	+55	+36	+21	+ 3	–10
Beaumont, TX	30	5	94	6	1	+67	+48	+32	+14	0
Bellingham, WA	48	45	122	29	3	0	+13	+24	+37	+47
Bemidji, MN	47	28	94	53	1	+14	+26	+34	+44	+52
Berlin, NH	44	28	71	11	0	– 7	– 3	0	+ 3	+ 7
Billings, MT	45	47	108	30	2	+16	+23	+29	+35	+40
Biloxi, MS	30	24	88	53	1	+46	+27	+11	– 5	–19
Binghamton, NY	42	6	75	55	0	+20	+19	+19	+18	+18
Birmingham, AL	33	31	86	49	1	+30	+15	+ 3	–10	–20
Bismarck, ND	46	48	100	47	1	+41	+50	+58	+66	+73
Boise, ID	43	37	116	12	2	+55	+58	+60	+62	+64
Brattleboro, VT	42	51	72	34	0	+ 4	+ 5	+ 5	+ 6	+ 7
Bridgeport, CT	41	11	73	11	0	+12	+10	+ 8	+ 6	+ 4
Brockton, MA	42	5	71	1	0	0	0	0	0	– 1
Brownsville, TX	25	54	97	30	1	+91	+66	+46	+23	+ 5
Buffalo, NY	42	53	78	52	0	+29	+30	+30	+31	+32
Burlington, VT	44	29	73	13	0	0	+ 4	+ 8	+12	+15
Butte, MT	46	1	112	32	2	+31	+39	+45	+52	+57
Cairo, IL	37	0	89	11	1	+29	+20	+12	+ 4	– 2
Camden, NJ	39	57	75	7	0	+24	+19	+16	+12	+ 9
Canton, OH	40	48	81	23	0	+46	+43	+41	+38	+36
Cape May, NJ	38	56	74	56	0	+26	+20	+15	+ 9	+ 5
Carson City–Reno, NV	39	10	119	46	3	+25	+19	+14	+ 9	+ 5

City	North Latitude °	'	West Longitude °	'	Time Zone Code	A (min.)	B (min.)	C (min.)	D (min.)	E (min.)
Casper, WY	42	51	106	19	2	+19	+19	+20	+21	+22
Charleston, SC	32	47	79	56	0	+64	+48	+36	+21	+10
Charleston, WV	38	21	81	38	0	+55	+48	+42	+35	+30
Charlotte, NC	35	14	80	51	0	+61	+49	+39	+28	+19
Charlottesville, VA	38	2	78	30	0	+43	+35	+29	+22	+17
Chattanooga, TN	35	3	85	19	0	+79	+67	+57	+45	+36
Cheboygan, MI	45	39	84	29	0	+40	+47	+53	+59	+64
Cheyenne, WY	41	8	104	49	2	+19	+16	+14	+12	+11
Chicago–Oak Park, IL	41	52	87	38	1	+ 7	+ 6	+ 6	+ 5	+ 4
Cincinnati–Hamilton, OH	39	6	84	31	0	+64	+58	+53	+48	+44
Cleveland–Lakewood, OH	41	30	81	42	0	+45	+43	+42	+40	+39
Columbia, SC	34	0	81	2	0	+65	+51	+40	+27	+17
Columbus, OH	39	57	83	1	0	+55	+51	+47	+43	+40
Cordova, AK	60	33	145	45	4	−55	+13	+55	+103	+149
Corpus Christi, TX	27	48	97	24	1	+86	+64	+46	+25	+ 9
Craig, CO	40	31	107	33	2	+32	+28	+25	+22	+20
Dallas–Fort Worth, TX	32	47	96	48	1	+71	+55	+43	+28	+17
Danville, IL	40	8	87	37	1	+13	+ 9	+ 6	+ 2	0
Danville, VA	36	36	79	23	0	+51	+41	+33	+24	+17
Davenport, IA	41	32	90	35	1	+20	+19	+17	+16	+15
Dayton, OH	39	45	84	10	0	+61	+56	+52	+48	+44
Decatur, AL	34	36	86	59	1	+27	+14	+ 4	− 7	−17
Decatur, IL	39	51	88	57	1	+19	+15	+11	+ 7	+ 4
Denver–Boulder, CO	39	44	104	59	2	+24	+19	+15	+11	+ 7
Des Moines, IA	41	35	93	37	1	+32	+31	+30	+28	+27
Detroit–Dearborn, MI	42	20	83	3	0	+47	+47	+47	+47	+47
Dubuque, IA	42	30	90	41	1	+17	+18	+18	+18	+18
Duluth, MN	46	47	92	6	1	+ 6	+16	+23	+31	+38
Durham, NC	36	0	78	55	0	+51	+40	+31	+21	+13
Eastport, ME	44	54	67	0	0	−26	−20	−16	−11	− 8
Eau Claire, WI	44	49	91	30	1	+12	+17	+21	+25	+29
Elko, NV	40	50	115	46	3	+ 3	0	− 1	− 3	− 5
Ellsworth, ME	44	33	68	25	0	−18	−14	−10	− 6	− 3
El Paso, TX	31	45	106	29	2	+53	+35	+22	+ 6	− 6
Erie, PA	42	7	80	5	0	+36	+36	+35	+35	+35
Eugene, OR	44	3	123	6	3	+21	+24	+27	+30	+33
Fairbanks, AK	64	48	147	51	4	−127	+ 2	+61	+131	+205
Fall River– New Bedford, MA	41	42	71	9	0	+ 2	+ 1	0	0	− 1
Fargo, ND	46	53	96	47	1	+24	+34	+42	+50	+57
Flagstaff, AZ	35	12	111	39	2	+64	+52	+42	+31	+22
Flint, MI	43	1	83	41	0	+47	+49	+50	+51	+52
Fort Myers, FL	26	38	81	52	0	+87	+63	+44	+21	+ 4
Fort Scott, KS	37	50	94	42	1	+49	+41	+34	+27	+21
Fort Smith, AR	35	23	94	25	1	+55	+43	+33	+22	+14
Fort Wayne, IN	41	4	85	9	0	+60	+58	+56	+54	+52
Fresno, CA	36	44	119	47	3	+32	+22	+15	+ 6	0
Gallup, NM	35	32	108	45	2	+52	+40	+31	+20	+11
Galveston, TX	29	18	94	48	1	+72	+52	+35	+16	+ 1
Gary, IN	41	36	87	20	1	+ 7	+ 6	+ 4	+ 3	+ 2
Glasgow, MT	48	12	106	38	2	− 1	+11	+21	+32	+42
Grand Forks, ND	47	55	97	3	1	+21	+33	+43	+53	+62
Grand Island, NE	40	55	98	21	1	+53	+51	+49	+46	+44
Grand Junction, CO	39	4	108	33	2	+40	+34	+29	+24	+20
Great Falls, MT	47	30	111	17	2	+20	+31	+39	+49	+58
Green Bay, WI	44	31	88	0	1	0	+ 3	+ 7	+11	+14
Greensboro, NC	36	4	79	47	0	+54	+43	+35	+25	+17

City	North Latitude ° '		West Longitude ° '		Time Zone Code	Key Letters				
						A (min.)	B (min.)	C (min.)	D (min.)	E (min.)
Hagerstown, MD..........	39	39	77	43	0	+35	+30	+26	+22	+18
Harrisburg, PA	40	16	76	53	0	+30	+26	+23	+19	+16
Hartford–New Britain, CT..	41	46	72	41	0	+ 8	+ 7	+ 6	+ 5	+ 4
Helena, MT..............	46	36	112	2	2	+27	+36	+43	+51	+57
Hilo, HI	19	44	155	5	5	+94	+62	+37	+ 7	−15
Honolulu, HI	21	18	157	52	5	+102	+72	+48	+19	− 1
Houston, TX	29	45	95	22	1	+73	+53	+37	+19	+ 5
Indianapolis, IN...........	39	46	86	10	0	+69	+64	+60	+56	+52
Ironwood, MI	46	27	90	9	1	0	+ 9	+15	+23	+29
Jackson, MI..............	42	15	84	24	0	+53	+53	+53	+52	+52
Jackson, MS	32	18	90	11	1	+46	+30	+17	+ 1	−10
Jacksonville, FL	30	20	81	40	0	+77	+58	+43	+25	+11
Jefferson City, MO	38	34	92	10	1	+36	+29	+24	+18	+13
Joplin, MO...............	37	6	94	30	1	+50	+41	+33	+25	+18
Juneau, AK	58	18	134	25	4	−76	−23	+10	+49	+86
Kalamazoo, MI	42	17	85	35	0	+58	+57	+57	+57	+57
Kanab, UT...............	37	3	112	32	2	+62	+53	+46	+37	+30
Kansas City, MO..........	39	1	94	20	1	+44	+37	+33	+27	+23
Keene, NH...............	42	56	72	17	0	+ 2	+ 3	+ 4	+ 5	+ 6
Ketchikan, AK............	55	21	131	39	4	−62	−25	0	+29	+56
Knoxville, TN	35	58	83	55	0	+71	+60	+51	+41	+33
Kodiak, AK	57	47	152	24	4	0	+49	+82	+120	+154
LaCrosse, WI.............	43	48	91	15	1	+15	+18	+20	+22	+25
Lake Charles, LA	30	14	93	13	1	+64	+44	+29	+11	− 2
Lanai City, HI	20	50	156	55	5	+99	+69	+44	+15	− 6
Lancaster, PA	40	2	76	18	0	+28	+24	+20	+17	+13
Lansing, MI..............	42	44	84	33	0	+52	+53	+53	+54	+54
Las Cruces, NM	32	19	106	47	2	+53	+36	+23	+ 8	− 3
Las Vegas, NV	36	10	115	9	3	+16	+ 4	− 3	−13	−20
Lawrence–Lowell, MA.....	42	42	71	10	0	0	0	0	0	+ 1
Lewiston, ID	46	25	117	1	3	−12	− 3	+ 2	+10	+17
Lexington–Frankfort, KY...	38	3	84	30	0	+67	+59	+53	+46	+41
Liberal, KS	37	3	100	55	1	+76	+66	+59	+51	+44
Lihue, HI	21	59	159	23	5	+107	+77	+54	+26	+ 5
Lincoln, NE..............	40	49	96	41	1	+47	+44	+42	+39	+37
Little Rock, AR...........	34	45	92	17	1	+48	+35	+25	+13	+ 4
Los Angeles–Pasadena– Santa Monica, CA	34	3	118	14	3	+34	+20	+ 9	− 3	−13
Louisville, KY............	38	15	85	46	0	+72	+64	+58	+52	+46
Macon, GA	32	50	83	38	0	+79	+63	+50	+36	+24
Madison, WI	43	4	89	23	1	+10	+11	+12	+14	+15
Manchester–Concord, NH..	42	59	71	28	0	0	0	+ 1	+ 2	+ 3
McAllen, TX..............	26	12	98	14	1	+93	+69	+49	+26	+ 9
Memphis, TN	35	9	90	3	1	+38	+26	+16	+ 5	− 3
Meridian, MS	32	22	88	42	1	+40	+24	+11	− 4	−15
Miami, FL	25	47	80	12	0	+88	+57	+37	+14	− 3
Miles City, MT	46	25	105	51	2	+ 3	+11	+18	+26	+32
Milwaukee, WI	43	2	87	54	1	+ 4	+ 6	+ 7	+ 8	+ 9
Minneapolis–St. Paul, MN..	44	59	93	16	1	+18	+24	+28	+33	+37
Minot, ND	48	14	101	18	1	+36	+50	+59	+71	+81
Moab, UT................	38	35	109	33	2	+46	+39	+33	+27	+22
Mobile, AL	30	42	88	3	1	+42	+23	+ 8	− 8	−22
Monroe, LA..............	32	30	92	7	1	+53	+37	+24	+ 9	− 1
Montgomery, AL	32	23	86	19	1	+31	+14	+ 1	−13	−25
Muncie, IN...............	40	12	85	23	0	+64	+60	+57	+53	+50
Nashville, TN	36	10	86	47	1	+22	+11	+ 3	− 6	−14
Newark–East Orange, NJ...	40	44	74	10	0	+17	+14	+12	+ 9	+ 7

City	North Latitude °	North Latitude '	West Longitude °	West Longitude '	Time Zone Code	A (min.)	B (min.)	C (min.)	D (min.)	E (min.)
New Haven, CT	41	18	72	56	0	+11	+ 8	+ 7	+ 5	+ 4
New London, CT	41	22	72	6	0	+ 7	+ 5	+ 4	+ 2	+ 1
New Orleans, LA	29	57	90	4	1	+52	+32	+16	− 1	−15
New York, NY	40	45	74	0	0	+17	+14	+11	+ 9	+ 6
Norfolk, VA	36	51	76	17	0	+38	+28	+21	+12	+ 5
North Platte, NE	41	8	100	46	1	+62	+60	+58	+56	+54
Norwalk–Stamford, CT	41	7	73	22	0	+13	+10	+ 9	+ 7	+ 5
Oakley, KS	39	8	100	51	1	+69	+63	+59	+53	+49
Ogden, UT	41	13	111	58	2	+47	+45	+43	+41	+40
Ogdensburg, NY	44	42	75	30	0	+ 8	+13	+17	+21	+25
Oklahoma City, OK	35	28	97	31	1	+67	+55	+46	+35	+26
Omaha, NE	41	16	95	56	1	+43	+40	+39	+37	+36
Orlando, FL	28	32	81	22	0	+80	+59	+42	+22	+ 6
Ortonville, MN	45	19	96	27	1	+30	+36	+40	+46	+51
Oshkosh, WI	44	1	88	33	1	+ 3	+ 6	+ 9	+12	+15
Palm Springs, CA	33	49	116	32	3	+28	+13	+ 1	−12	−22
Parkersburg, WV	39	16	81	34	0	+52	+46	+42	+36	+32
Paterson, NJ	40	55	74	10	0	+17	+14	+12	+ 9	+ 7
Pendleton, OR	45	40	118	47	3	− 1	+ 4	+10	+16	+21
Pensacola, FL	30	25	87	13	1	+39	+20	+ 5	−12	−26
Peoria, IL	40	42	89	36	1	+19	+16	+14	+11	+ 9
Philadelphia–Chester, PA	39	57	75	9	0	+24	+19	+16	+12	+ 9
Phoenix, AZ	33	27	112	4	2	+71	+56	+44	+30	+20
Pierre, SD	44	22	100	21	1	+49	+53	+56	+60	+63
Pittsburgh–McKeesport, PA	40	26	80	0	0	+42	+38	+35	+32	+29
Pittsfield, MA	42	27	73	15	0	+ 8	+ 8	+ 8	+ 8	+ 8
Pocatello, ID	42	52	112	27	2	+43	+44	+45	+46	+46
Poplar Bluff, MO	36	46	90	24	1	+35	+25	+17	+ 8	+ 1
Portland, ME	43	40	70	15	0	− 8	− 5	− 3	− 1	0
Portland, OR	45	31	122	41	3	+14	+20	+25	+31	+36
Portsmouth, NH	43	5	70	45	0	− 4	− 2	− 1	0	0
Presque Isle, ME	46	41	68	1	0	−29	−19	−12	− 4	+ 2
Providence, RI	41	50	71	25	0	+ 3	+ 2	+ 1	0	0
Pueblo, CO	38	16	104	37	2	+27	+20	+14	+ 7	+ 2
Raleigh, NC	35	47	78	38	0	+51	+39	+30	+20	+12
Rapid City, SD	44	5	103	14	2	+ 2	+ 5	+ 8	+11	+13
Reading, PA	40	20	75	56	0	+26	+22	+19	+16	+13
Redding, CA	40	35	122	24	3	+31	+27	+25	+22	+19
Richmond, VA	37	32	77	26	0	+41	+32	+25	+17	+11
Roanoke, VA	37	16	79	57	0	+51	+42	+35	+27	+21
Roswell, NM	33	24	104	32	2	+41	+26	+14	0	−10
Rutland, VT	43	37	72	58	0	+ 2	+ 5	+ 7	+ 9	+11
Sacramento, CA	38	35	121	30	3	+34	+27	+21	+15	+10
St. Johnsbury, VT	44	25	72	1	0	− 4	0	+ 3	+ 7	+10
St. Joseph, MI	42	5	86	26	0	+61	+61	+60	+60	+59
St. Joseph, MO	39	46	94	50	1	+43	+38	+35	+30	+27
St. Louis, MO	38	37	90	12	1	+28	+21	+16	+10	+ 5
St. Petersburg, FL	27	46	82	39	0	+87	+65	+47	+26	+10
Salem, OR	44	57	123	1	3	+17	+23	+27	+31	+35
Salina, KS	38	50	97	37	1	+57	+51	+46	+40	+35
Salisbury, MD	38	22	75	36	0	+31	+23	+18	+11	+ 6
Salt Lake City, UT	40	45	111	53	2	+48	+45	+43	+40	+38
San Antonio, TX	29	25	98	30	1	+87	+66	+50	+31	+16
San Diego, CA	32	43	117	9	3	+33	+17	+ 4	− 9	−21
San Francisco–Oakland– San Jose, CA	37	47	122	25	3	+40	+31	+25	+18	+12
Santa Fe, NM	35	41	105	56	2	+40	+28	+19	+ 9	0

City	North Latitude ° '		West Longitude ° '		Time Zone Code	Key Letters A (min.)	B (min.)	C (min.)	D (min.)	E (min.)
Savannah, GA 32	5	81	6	0	+70	+54	+40	+25	+13
Scranton–Wilkes-Barre, PA 41	25	75	40	0	+21	+19	+18	+16	+15
Seattle–Tacoma–									
Olympia, WA 47	37	122	20	3	+ 3	+15	+24	+34	+42
Sheridan, WY 44	48	106	58	2	+14	+19	+23	+27	+31
Shreveport, LA 32	31	93	45	1	+60	+44	+31	+16	+ 4
Sioux Falls, SD 43	33	96	44	1	+38	+40	+42	+44	+46
South Bend, IN 41	41	86	15	0	+62	+61	+60	+59	+58
Spartanburg, SC 34	56	81	57	0	+66	+53	+43	+32	+23
Spokane, WA 47	40	117	24	3	−16	− 4	+ 4	+14	+23
Springfield, IL. 39	48	89	39	1	+22	+18	+14	+10	+ 6
Springfield–Holyoke, MA . . 42	6	72	36	0	+ 6	+ 6	+ 6	+ 5	+ 5
Springfield, MO 37	13	93	18	1	+45	+36	+29	+20	+14
Syracuse, NY. 43	3	76	9	0	+17	+19	+20	+21	+22
Tallahassee, FL 30	27	84	17	0	+87	+68	+53	+35	+22
Tampa, FL. 27	57	82	27	0	+86	+64	+46	+25	+ 9
Terre Haute, IN 39	28	87	24	0	+74	+69	+65	+60	+56
Texarkana, AR 33	26	94	3	1	+59	+44	+32	+18	+ 8
Toledo, OH 41	39	83	33	0	+52	+50	+49	+48	+47
Topeka, KS 39	3	95	40	1	+49	+43	+38	+32	+28
Traverse City, MI 44	46	85	38	0	+49	+54	+57	+62	+65
Trenton, NJ 40	13	74	46	0	+21	+17	+14	+11	+ 8
Trinidad, CO 37	10	104	31	2	+30	+21	+13	+ 5	0
Tucson, AZ 32	13	110	58	2	+70	+53	+40	+24	+12
Tulsa, OK 36	9	95	60	1	+59	+48	+40	+30	+22
Tupelo, MS 34	16	88	34	1	+35	+21	+10	− 2	−11
Vernal, UT. 40	27	109	32	2	+40	+36	+33	+30	+28
Walla Walla, WA 46	4	118	20	3	− 5	+ 2	+ 8	+15	+21
Washington, DC 38	54	77	1	0	+35	+28	+23	+18	+13
Waterbury–Meriden, CT . . . 41	33	73	3	0	+10	+ 9	+ 7	+ 6	+ 5
Waterloo, IA 42	30	92	20	1	+24	+24	+24	+25	+25
Wausau, WI. 44	58	89	38	1	+ 4	+ 9	+13	+18	+22
West Palm Beach, FL 26	43	80	3	0	+79	+55	+36	+14	− 2
Wichita, KS 37	42	97	20	1	+60	+51	+45	+37	+31
Williston, ND 48	9	103	37	1	+46	+59	+69	+80	+90
Wilmington, DE 39	45	75	33	0	+26	+21	+18	+13	+10
Wilmington, NC 34	14	77	55	0	+52	+38	+27	+15	+ 5
Winchester, VA. 39	11	78	10	0	+38	+33	+28	+23	+19
Worcester, MA 42	16	71	48	0	+ 3	+ 2	+ 2	+ 2	+ 2
York, PA 39	58	76	43	0	+30	+26	+22	+18	+15
Youngstown, OH 41	6	80	39	0	+42	40	+38	+36	+34
Yuma, AZ 32	43	114	37	2	+83	+67	+54	+40	+28
CANADA									
Calgary, AB. 51	5	114	5	2	+13	+35	+50	+68	+84
Edmonton, AB 53	34	113	25	2	− 3	+26	+47	+72	+93
Halifax, NS 44	38	63	35	−1	+21	+26	+29	+33	+37
Montreal, QC. 45	28	73	39	0	− 1	+ 4	+ 9	+15	+20
Ottawa, ON 45	25	75	43	0	+ 6	+13	+18	+23	+28
Peterborough, ON 44	18	78	19	0	+21	+25	+28	+32	+35
Saint John, NB 45	16	66	3	−1	+28	+34	+39	+44	+49
Saskatoon, SK 52	10	106	40	1	+37	+63	+80	+101	+119
Sydney, NS 46	10	60	10	−1	+ 1	+ 9	+15	+23	+28
Thunder Bay, ON 48	27	89	12	0	+47	+61	+71	+83	+93
Toronto, ON 43	39	79	23	0	+28	+30	+32	+35	+37
Vancouver, BC 49	13	123	6	3	0	+15	+26	+40	+52
Winnipeg, MB. 49	53	97	10	1	+12	+30	+43	+58	+71

The Old Farmer's Almanac

2001 Engagement Calendar

New Expanded Page Format

FREE GIFT—A softcover edition of *The 2001 Old Farmer's Almanac* is our gift to you with each Engagement Calendar ordered†.

❖ Beautifully designed to use as a date book, daily journal, or planner for a wedding or other special event.

❖ New format with two pages per week provides even more space to keep track of appointments or make daily journal entries. We've added room for reminders, too!

❖ Weekly doses of pithy advice and folklore, along with holiday, seasonal, and astronomical information, plus two pages each month that are full of useful and amusing Almanac wit and wisdom.

❖ Hardcover with concealed wire binding lies flat on your desk and withstands the wear and tear of carrying the calendar from place to place or keeping it from year to year.

Only $12.95 * *includes FREE Almanac*

*(+ $3.95 s&h) Order Item: OF01CEGC/Key: EGBOFAB

3 ways to order:

1) On-line **www.almanac.com/engagement**

2) Phone toll-free **800-223-3166**

3) Mail order with payment to The Old Farmer's Almanac, P.O. Box 37370, Boone, IA 50037-0370

---

†Your order qualifies you for enrollment in our Engagement Calendar Continuity Program. You will automatically receive the next year's calendar plus a FREE copy of *The Old Farmer's Almanac* for a preview. We'll send you a notice before we are ready to mail it to remind you and give you the opportunity to tell us if you'd like to change your program. If you're not completely satisfied, just return the calendar and keep the Almanac as our gift. **You may cancel this program at any time.**

Tide Corrections

■ Many factors affect the times and heights of the tides: the coastal configuration, the time of the Moon's southing (crossing the meridian), and the Moon's phase. The High Tide column on the **Left-Hand Calendar Pages 58-84** lists the times of high tide at Commonwealth Pier in Boston Harbor. The heights of some of these tides, reckoned from Mean Lower Low Water, are given on the **Right-Hand Calendar Pages 59-85**. Use this table to calculate the approximate times and heights of high water at the places shown. Apply the time difference to the times of high tide at Boston **(pages 58-84)** and the height difference to the heights at Boston **(pages 59-85)**.

Estimations derived from this table are not meant to be used for navigation. The Old Farmer's Almanac accepts no responsibility for errors or any consequences ensuing from the use of this table.

Tide predictions for North America's East and West Coasts and the Caribbean region are printed by Thomas Reed Publications, Inc., 800-995-4995. Predictions for many other stations can be found at the National Ocean Service Web site, http://co-ops.nos.noaa.gov, and at Canada's Department of Fisheries and Oceans Web site, www.chshq.dfo.ca/chs_hq/nautpubl/PRED.html.

Coastal Site	Difference: Time (h. m.)	Height (ft.)
Canada		
Alberton, PE	−5 45**	−7.5
Charlottetown, PE	−0 45**	−3.5
Halifax, NS	−3 23	−4.5
North Sydney, NS	−3 15	−6.5
Saint John, NB	+0 30	+15.0
St. John's, NF	−4 00	−6.5
Yarmouth, NS	−0 40	+3.0
Maine		
Bar Harbor	−0 34	+0.9
Belfast	−0 20	+0.4
Boothbay Harbor	−0 18	−0.8
Chebeague Island	−0 16	−0.6
Eastport	−0 28	+8.4
Kennebunkport	+0 04	−1.0
Machias	−0 28	+2.8
Monhegan Island	−0 25	−0.8
Old Orchard	0 00	−0.8
Portland	−0 12	−0.6

Coastal Site	Difference: Time (h. m.)	Height (ft.)
Rockland	−0 28	+0.1
Stonington	−0 30	+0.1
York	−0 09	−1.0
New Hampshire		
Hampton	+0 02	−1.3
Portsmouth	+0 11	−1.5
Rye Beach	−0 09	−0.9
Massachusetts		
Annisquam	−0 02	−1.1
Beverly Farms	0 00	−0.5
Boston	0 00	0.0
Cape Cod Canal		
East Entrance	−0 01	−0.8
West Entrance	−2 16	−5.9
Chatham Outer Coast	+0 30	−2.8
Inside	+1 54	*0.4
Cohasset	+0 02	−0.07
Cotuit Highlands	+1 15	*0.3
Dennis Port	+1 01	*0.4
Duxbury–Gurnet Point	+0 02	−0.3
Fall River	−3 03	−5.0
Gloucester	−0 03	−0.8
Hingham	+0 07	0.0
Hull	+0 03	−0.2
Hyannis Port	+1 01	*0.3
Magnolia–Manchester	−0 02	−0.7
Marblehead	−0 02	−0.4
Marion	−3 22	−5.4
Monument Beach	−3 08	−5.4
Nahant	−0 01	−0.5
Nantasket	+0 04	−0.1
Nantucket	+0 56	*0.3
Nauset Beach	+0 30	*0.6
New Bedford	−3 24	−5.7
Newburyport	+0 19	−1.8
Oak Bluffs	+0 30	*0.2
Onset–R.R. Bridge	−2 16	−5.9
Plymouth	+0 05	0.0
Provincetown	+0 14	−0.4
Revere Beach	−0 01	−0.3
Rockport	−0 08	−1.0
Salem	0 00	−0.5
Scituate	−0 05	−0.7
Wareham	−3 09	−5.3
Wellfleet	+0 12	+0.5
West Falmouth	−3 10	−5.4
Westport Harbor	−3 22	−6.4
Woods Hole		
Little Harbor	−2 50	*0.2
Oceanographic Inst.	−3 07	*0.2
Rhode Island		
Bristol	−3 24	−5.3
Narragansett Pier	−3 42	−6.2

Coastal Site	Difference: Time (h. m.)	Height (ft.)	Coastal Site	Difference: Time (h. m.)	Height (ft.)
Newport	−3 34	−5.9	Norfolk	−2 06	−6.6
Point Judith	−3 41	−6.3	Virginia Beach	−4 00	−6.0
Providence	−3 20	−4.8	Yorktown	−2 13	−7.0
Sakonnet	−3 44	−5.6	**North Carolina**		
Watch Hill	−2 50	−6.8	Cape Fear	−3 55	−5.0
Connecticut			Cape Lookout	−4 28	−5.7
Bridgeport	+0 01	−2.6	Currituck	−4 10	−5.8
Madison	−0 22	−2.3	Hatteras		
New Haven	−0 11	−3.2	Inlet	−4 03	−7.4
New London	−1 54	−6.7	Kitty Hawk	−4 14	−6.2
Norwalk	+0 01	−2.2	Ocean	−4 26	−6.0
Old Lyme			**South Carolina**		
Highway Bridge	−0 30	−6.2	Charleston	−3 22	−4.3
Stamford	+0 01	−2.2	Georgetown	−1 48	*0.36
Stonington	−2 27	−6.6	Hilton Head	−3 22	−2.9
New York			Myrtle Beach	−3 49	−4.4
Coney Island	−3 33	−4.9	St. Helena		
Fire Island Light	−2 43	*0.1	Harbor Entrance	−3 15	−3.4
Long Beach	−3 11	−5.7	**Georgia**		
Montauk Harbor	−2 19	−7.4	Jekyll Island	−3 46	−2.9
New York City–Battery	−2 43	−5.0	St. Simon's Island	−2 50	−2.9
Oyster Bay	+0 04	−1.8	Savannah Beach		
Port Chester	−0 09	−2.2	River Entrance	−3 14	−5.5
Port Washington	−0 01	−2.1	Tybee Light	−3 22	−2.7
Sag Harbor	−0 55	−6.8	**Florida**		
Southampton			Cape Canaveral	−3 59	−6.0
Shinnecock Inlet	−4 20	*0.2	Daytona Beach	−3 28	−5.3
Willets Point	0 00	−2.3	Fort Lauderdale	−2 50	−7.2
New Jersey			Fort Pierce Inlet	−3 32	−6.9
Asbury Park	−4 04	−5.3	Jacksonville		
Atlantic City	−3 56	−5.5	Railroad Bridge	−6 55	*0.1
Bay Head–Sea Girt	−4 04	−5.3	Miami Harbor Entrance	−3 18	−7.0
Beach Haven	−1 43	*0.24	St. Augustine	−2 55	−4.9
Cape May	−3 28	−5.3			
Ocean City	−3 06	−5.9			
Sandy Hook	−3 30	−5.0			
Seaside Park	−4 03	−5.4			
Pennsylvania					
Philadelphia	+2 40	−3.5			
Delaware					
Cape Henlopen	−2 48	−5.3			
Rehoboth Beach	−3 37	−5.7			
Wilmington	+1 56	−3.8			
Maryland					
Annapolis	+6 23	−8.5			
Baltimore	+7 59	−8.3			
Cambridge	+5 05	−7.8			
Havre de Grace	+11 21	−7.7			
Point No Point	+2 28	−8.1			
Prince Frederick					
Plum Point	+4 25	−8.5			
Virginia					
Cape Charles	−2 20	−7.0			
Hampton Roads	−2 02	−6.9			

* Where the difference in the Height column is so marked, height at Boston should be multiplied by this ratio.

** Varies widely; accurate only within 1½ hours. Consult local tide tables for precise times and heights.

Example: The conversion of the times and heights of the tides at Boston to those of Cape Fear, North Carolina, is given below:

Sample tide calculation July 1, 2001:

High tide Boston (p. 74)	8:45 A.M.	EDT
Correction for Cape Fear	−3:55 hrs.	
High tide Cape Fear	4:50 A.M.	EDT
Tide height Boston (p. 75)	9.4 ft.	
Correction for Cape Fear	−5.0 ft.	
Tide height Cape Fear	4.4 ft.	

The Twilight Zone

How to determine the length of twilight and the times of dawn and dark.

■ Twilight is the period of time between dawn and sunrise, and again between sunset and dark. Both dawn and dark are defined as moments when the Sun is 18 degrees below the horizon. The latitude of a place and the time of year determine the length of twilight. To find the latitude of your city or the city nearest you, consult the **Time Corrections table, page 226.** Use that figure in the chart below with the appropriate date, and you will have the length of twilight in your area.

Latitude	Length of Twilight (hours and minutes)								
	Jan. 1 to Apr. 10	Apr. 11 to May 2	May 3 to May 14	May 15 to May 25	May 26 to July 22	July 23 to Aug. 3	Aug. 4 to Aug. 14	Aug. 15 to Sept. 5	Sept. 6 to Dec. 31
25° N to 30° N	1 20	1 23	1 26	1 29	1 32	1 29	1 26	1 23	1 20
31° N to 36° N	1 26	1 28	1 34	1 38	1 43	1 38	1 34	1 28	1 26
37° N to 42° N	1 33	1 39	1 47	1 52	1 59	1 52	1 47	1 39	1 33
43° N to 47° N	1 42	1 51	2 02	2 13	2 27	2 13	2 02	1 51	1 42
48° N to 49° N	1 50	2 04	2 22	2 42	—	2 42	2 22	2 04	1 50

■ To determine when dawn will break and when dark will descend, apply the length of twilight to the times of sunrise and sunset. Follow the instructions given in **How to Use This Almanac, page 40,** to determine sunrise/sunset times for your locality. Subtract the length of twilight from the time of sunrise for dawn. Add the length of twilight to the time of sunset for dark. (See examples at right.)

	Boston, Mass. (latitude 42° 22')	Oshkosh, Wis. (latitude 44° 1')
Sunrise, August 1	5:37 A.M.	5:40 A.M.
Length of twilight	−1:52	−2:13
Dawn breaks	3:45 A.M. EDT	3:27 A.M. CDT
Sunset, August 1	8:04 P.M.	8:16 P.M.
Length of twilight	+1:52	+2:13
Dark descends	9:56 P.M. EDT	10:29 P.M. CDT

Tidal Glossary

Apogean Tide: A monthly tide of decreased range that occurs when the Moon is at apogee (farthest from Earth).

Diurnal Tide: A tide with one high water and one low water in a tidal day of approximately 24 hours.

Mean Lower Low Water: The arithmetic mean of the lesser of a daily pair of low waters, observed over a specific 19-year cycle called the National Tidal Datum Epoch.

Neap Tide: A tide of decreased range that occurs twice a month, when the Moon is in quadrature (during its first and last quarter, when the Sun and the Moon are at right angles to each other relative to Earth).

Perigean Tide: A monthly tide of increased range that occurs when the Moon is at perigee (closest to Earth).

Semidiurnal Tide: A tide with one high water and one low water every half day. East

Coast tides, for example, are semidiurnal, with two highs and two lows during a tidal day of approximately 24 hours.

Spring Tide: A tide of increased range that occurs at times of syzygy each month. Named not for the season of spring but from the German *springen* ("to leap up"), a spring tide also brings a lower low water.

Syzygy: The nearly straight-line configuration that occurs twice a month, when the Sun and the Moon are in conjunction (on the same side of Earth at the new Moon) and when they are in opposition (on opposite sides of Earth at the full Moon). In both cases, the gravitational effects of the Sun and the Moon reinforce each other, and tidal range is increased.

Vanishing Tide: A mixed tide of considerable inequality in the two highs and two lows, so that the lower high (or higher low) may become indistinct or appear to vanish.

The Old Farmer's
General Store

The Old Farmer's
General Store

For information about advertising in *The Old Farmer's Almanac,* call Donna Stone at 800-729-9265, ext. 214.

Classified Advertising

ALTERNATIVE ENERGY

YOUR OWN ELECTRIC COMPANY. 60% less than grid power. Use anywhere. Diesel generators, trace inverters. Alternative power generation since 1985. Brochures. Imperial-A, 8569 Ward North Rd., Kinsman OH 44428-9536. 800-830-0498.

BUILD SUN-, WIND-, WATER- powered appliances. 30 plans. Details $3. MCOD, 3203 Bordero, Thousand Oaks CA 91362.

ALTERNATIVE TRANSPORTATION

BICYCLE ENGINES, MOPEDS, MOTORIZED TRIKES! Catalog $2. Motorbikes, 7621 Pineforest, Pensacola FL 32526-8768. 850-941-2080. www.fiveflagsmotorbikes.com.

ANTIQUES

ANTIQUE LIQUIDATORS, VISIT OUR ON-LINE WEB STORE at www.antiqueliquidators.com. Mention *The Old Farmer's Almanac* for 20% discount.

ASTROLOGY/OCCULT

BIORHYTHMS. Your physical, emotional, intellectual cycles charted in color. Interpretation guide. Six months ($14). Twelve months ($20). Send name, birth date. CYCLES, Dept. FAB, 2251 Berkely Ave., Schenectady NY 12309.

PSYCHIC SPIRITUAL ADVISOR helps restore broken love, health, happiness. Telephone readings help even miles away. Remarkable results. $3/reading. 707-579-5123.

FREE OCCULT CATALOG! Books, jewelry, bumper stickers, ritual items, incense. Azure-Green, PO Box 48-OFA, Middlefield MA 01243. 413-623-2155. www.azuregreen.com.

WITCH WORKS™. Empowered moon-cultivated herbal potions, essences. Box 1839A, Royal Oak MI 48068-1839. 248-542-3113. www.witchworks.com.

MISS LISA, astrology reader and advisor. Extraordinary powers. 3810 Memorial Dr., Waycross GA 31501. 912-283-3206.

FREE! ONE BLACK OR WHITE MAGIC SPELL! Tell me what you need! EKSES, PO Box 9315(B), San Bernardino CA 92427-9315.

FREE MINI READINGS. Psychic Diana has the ability to solve all problems. Removes spells and reunites loved ones. Toronto, Ontario; 416-226-5418.

ASTROLOGY. Personalized, comprehensive natal chart ($14). Progressed chart for current year ($14). Both ($20). Send name, birth date, birth time, birthplace. CYCLES, Dept. FAA, 2251 Berkely Ave., Schenectady NY 12309.

MRS. KING, spiritual reader and advisor, will help in all matters of life, where all others have failed. Call 912-283-0635.

ASTROLOGY—FREE CATALOG: books, tapes, tarot, spirituality. 800-500-0453 or 714-255-9218. Church of Light at www.light.org.

WICCA/MAGIC—Seminary of Wicca offers home-study course and degree programs. PO Box 1366, Nashua NH 03061.

ASTROLOGY—Natal ($15). Moving? Relocation chart for potential of location ($15). Need questions answered? Horary ($25). Compatibility ($15). Biorhythm ($10). Numerology ($15). Transits ($35). Send name, birth date/time/place, and city/state/ country for relocation; written question for horary to: Star-Trak, 20-A Woburn St., Reading MA 01867. Web site: www.s-trak.com.

"DISPENSATIONAL TRUTH" BY CLARENCE LARKIN! Available through amazon.com or Sunbooks, Box 5588(OFA), Santa Fe NM 87502-5588.

FREE LUCKY NUMBERS. Send birth date, self-addressed stamped envelope. Mystic, Box 2009-R, Jamestown NC 27282.

THE MOST COMPLETE metaphysical, magical, psychic-power correspondence course ever. Become a recognized professional. Earn unlimited income with our university doctoral degree program. Reasonable rates. University of Metaphysical Arts & Sciences, 2110 Artesia Blvd., Admissions #B-264, Redonda Beach CA 90278-3014. 310-398-1638. E-mail: mysticadamad@mediaone.net.

POWERFUL SPELLS performed by Gabrielle. Specializing in reuniting lovers. Guaranteed in two hours. 504-471-2693.

OCCULT POWER CATALOG: Large selection herbs, oils, incense, books, etc. $3. Power Products, Box 442, Mars Hill NC 28754.

FREE METAPHYSICAL CATALOG. Feng shui, incense, oils, tarot, and candles. Moonrise Magic. 505-332-2665. Web site: www.moonrisebooks.com.

INCREDIBLY ACCURATE telephone readings by Stephen & Tasha Halpert. Clairvoyance, tarot, astrology. Visa/MC. 508-839-0111. www.peacenow4u.com.

SECRET MAYA INDIAN MAGIC discovered in Chichen Itza. Assure happiness and love. Enhance health and beauty. Obtain wealth. $3. EC Schneider, 154A W. Foothill 240, Upland CA 91786. www.SecretMayanMagic.com.

AUTOMOTIVE

AUTOMOBILE/TRUCK/MOTORCYCLE literature wanted: 1900-1975. I buy sales brochures, manuals, toys, racing memorabilia, etc. Walter Miller, 6710 Brooklawn, Syracuse NY 13211. 315-432-8282. Fax 315-432-8256. E-mail: info@autolit.com.

BIRDHOUSES

PURPLE MARTIN BIRDHOUSES only $29.95. Free catalog. 800-764-8688. www.purplemartin.net

BEER & WINE MAKING

WINEMAKERS-BEERMAKERS. Free illustrated catalog. Fast service. Since 1967. Kraus, Box 7850-YB, Independence MO 64054. 800-841-7404.

BOOKS/MAGAZINES/CATALOGS

HAWAIIAN LUAU of taste treats. Original Macadamia Nut Korn Krunch, 100% Kona Coffee, scrumptious chocolates, Hawaiian macadamias; factory-direct prices. Free catalog 800-437-7477. Kona Confections, 74-5467 Kaiwi St., Kailua-Kona HI 96745. Check out our Web site www.konaconfections.com.

BECOME A PUBLISHED AUTHOR. Publisher with 80-year tradition. Author's Guide to Subsidy Publishing 800-695-9599.

FAMILY FUN. 100-year-old book of children's manners, *Goops and How to Be Them*. www.TheGoops.com.

GRACE LIVINGSTON HILL BOOK COLLECTORS! We stock them all! Phone 800-854-8571 for free lists.

TORNADO SHELTER. Build your own. Multiple designs. (Book and free plans.) $19.95 plus $2 s/h. Tornado Shelter, PO Box 36, Strafford MO 65757.

FREE BOOKLETS: Life, death, soul, resurrection, pollution crisis, hell, Judgment Day, restitution. BIBLE STANDARD(OF), PO Box 67, Chester Springs PA 19425-0067.

GIANT PUMPKINS. Grow your biggest ever with help from books and competition-strain seeds. For information, write to: Giant Pumpkins, Box 247-OFA, Norton MA 02766, or call 800-985-7878. Web site: www.giantpumpkin.com.

WHOLESOME FAMILY FUN! Inspirational stories, cookbook reviews, recipes, contests, home business opportunities, more. Sample $2. 12-issue subscription, $20. SHOESTRING MAGAZINE, PO Box FA-609, Kechi KS 67067.

BOSTON

BOSTON TROLLEYS AND TRAINS—books and videos. Catalog and membership information from Boston Street Railway Association, PO Box 102, Cambridge MA 02238.

BUSINESS OPPORTUNITIES

LET THE GOVERNMENT FINANCE your small business. Grants/loans to $800,000. Free recorded message: 707-448-0270 (KE1). Web site: www.usgovernmentinformation.com.

FREE INTERNET ACCESS! www.businessline.net—Pin #72102. Moneymaking CDs! www.ordercom.com/T15/2243 .htm. Fax-on-demand number 281-398-5611, #487.

$400 WEEKLY ASSEMBLING PRODUCTS from home. For free information, send SASE to Home Assembly-FA, PO Box 216, New Britain CT 06050-0216.

PIANO TUNING PAYS: Learn at home. American School correspondence course. 800-497-9793. www.piano-tuning.com.

LET THE GOVERNMENT START YOUR BUSINESS. Grants, loans; HUD Tracer, $800/week; free incorporation; free merchant account for accepting credit cards. 800-306-0873. www.capitalpublications.com.

EARN SUBSTANTIAL INCOME LOCATING DISTRESSED PROPERTY. Use our money. No financial risk to you. Split big profits. No experience needed. Complete training provided. Unlimited earnings potential. Call for free information package. 800-331-4555 ext. 7830.

MAKE $575 WEEKLY! Guaranteed. Mail list advertisements from home! Free supplies. Send stamped envelope: Superior (#FA-21), Box 7, Bedford Park IL 60499.

GET PAID $268.20/roll taking easy snapshots at home! Photowealth, Box 3706-FO, Idyllwild CA 92549. 909-659-9757. Web site: www.photowealth.com.

RECORD VIDEOTAPES AT HOME! Easy $1,800 weekly income! Free start-up information kit! CMSVIDEO, Dept. 174, 210 Lorna Square, Birmingham AL 35216-5439. 205-663-9888.

$80,000 FROM ONE ACRE! Grow ginseng and goldenseal. Information. Long SASE. Herbs, 5712-FA Cooper Rd., Indianapolis IN 46228.

PROFIT FROM ON-LINE shopping and commission. www.Quixtar.com. IBO#00001466093. Shelton, 4447 Penrose, Saint Louis MO 63115. E-mail: Diane17177@msn.com.

NATIONAL DIRECTORY: Home workers wanted by over 100 companies. Good pay. Free newsletter. Gulf Books, 23110 SR-54, Lutz FL 33549-6933. Web site: www.gulfbooks.com.

BUY IT WHOLESALE

49,457 PRODUCTS, FACTORY DIRECT. Taiwan, Hong Kong, Mexico! Save 500%-900%. Echomark, Box 739-FA0, Shalimar FL 32579-0739.

CARNIVOROUS PLANTS

CARNIVOROUS (insect-eating) plants, seeds, supplies, and books. Peter Paul's Nurseries, Canandaigua NY 14424-8713. www.peterpauls.com.

COLLECTIBLES/NOSTALGIA

NORMAN ROCKWELL prints, posters. Catalog $4. Refundable. Rockwell Gallery Collection, Box 126OF, Huntingdon Valley PA 19006. 215-969-5619. www.rockwellsite.com.

COLLECTIBLE BIRDHOUSES. 40 differenet styles. 912-982-4868. www.giftsandblrdhouses.com.

CRAFTS

REPLITIQUES produces handmade wood reproductions of colonial kitchen and household items, including clocks and cabinets. Brochure available $3. 120 Orchard Ave., York Haven PA 17370. Web site: www.replitiques.com.

DEER CONTROL

DEER PROBLEMS? We can help! Free catalog. Call Deerbusters, 888-422-3337. Web site: www.deerbusters.com.

EDUCATION/INSTRUCTION

COMPLETE HIGH SCHOOL AT HOME. Diploma awarded. Low tuition. Est. 1897—accredited. Telephone 800-531-9268 for free information, or write to AMERICAN SCHOOL, Dept. #348, 220 E. 170th St., Lansing IL 60438.

BECOME A PRIVATE INVESTIGATOR. Approved home study. Free literature. P.C.D.I., Atlanta, Georgia. 800-362-7070, Dept. JRK554.

BECOME A HOME INSPECTOR. Approved home study. Free literature. P.C.D.I., Atlanta, Georgia. 800-362-7070, Dept. PPK554.

LEARN TO RESOLVE YOUR IRS problems (liens, garnishments, returns). SASE. Preferred $ervices, 203 Argonne B209, Long Beach CA 90803. www.preferredservices.org.

BECOME A MEDICAL TRANSCRIPTIONIST. Home study. Free career literature. P.C.D.I., Atlanta, Georgia. 800-362-7070, Dept. YYK554.

BECOME A VETERINARY ASSISTANT/animal care specialist. Home study. Exciting careers for animal lovers. Free literature package. 800-362-7070, Dept. CCK554.

BECOME A BRIDAL CONSULTANT. Home study. Free career literature. P.C.D.I., Atlanta, Georgia. Call today at 800-362-7070, Dept. MRK554.

LEARN LANDSCAPING AT HOME. Free brochure. Call 800-326-9221 or write Lifetime Career Schools, Dept. OB0190, 101 Harrison St., Archbald PA 18403. www.lifetime-career.com.

COMPUTER CAREERS are among the highest paying! Train at home in just a few months! Call 800-326-9221 or write Lifetime Career Schools, Dept. OB1190, 101 Harrison St., Archbald PA 18403.

FARM & GARDEN

CANNING SUPPLIES. Extensive selection. Canners, dryers, jars, ingredients, tools, books. Free catalog. 800-776-0575. www.kitchenkrafts.com.

TROY-BILT® OWNERS. Discount parts catalog, send stamp. Replacement tines $64. Kelley's, Manilla IN 46150. 317-398-9042. Web site: www.svs.net/kelley/index.htm.

FERTILIZER

NEPTUNE'S HARVEST ORGANIC FERTILIZERS: Extremely effective. Commercially proven. Outperforms chemicals. Wholesale/retail/farm. Catalog. 800-259-4769. www.neptunesharvest.com.

FINANCIAL/LOANS BY MAIL

FREE CASH! Wealthy families unloading millions to help minimize their taxes. Fortune, PM B 249F, 1626 North Wilcox Ave., Hollywood CA 90028.

FOOD & RECIPES

TOTALLY NUTS brand peanuts, cashews, and other assorted nuts. Call us at 888-489-6887 or E-mail totalynutzz@aol.com.

YUMMY CHOCOLATE TREATS. Heavenly recipes. $3. PO Box 28621, 4050 Hastings St., Burnaby BC V5C 6J4 Canada.

EXOTIC JERKY, gourmet quality. Alligator, ostrich, venison, buffalo, etc. Free list. Samples available. C.S.W., PO Box 104F, Collins NY 14034.

HIGH HIMALAYAN GOAT-MILK CAKE, a Tibetan keepsake. Recipe intriguingly delicious, yet a profound mystical experience added to your meal. $5/US, $8/ Canadian. Dennis Montgomery, 2948 Lake Angelus Rd., Waterford MI 48329.

GRATED SWEET-POTATO PUDDING. Genuine old south flavor. $2 to Wolf Den Books, PMB 221, 5783 S.W. 40th St., Miami FL 33155.

FUND-RAISING

MAKE GOOD MONEY for your school, group, or organization selling The Old Farmer's Almanac publications and calendars to friends and neighbors. Great products sell themselves! Great prices! Great opportunity! Call today 800-424-6906. The Old Farmer's Almanac Fund-Raising, 220 South St., Bernardston MA 01337. www.gbimarketing.com.

GIFTS

ODD AND UNUSUAL GIFTS. Some one-of-a-kind handmade. Some country. All enchanting. www.rooki.com.

BE LUCKY, BE HAPPY AT theluckshop.com. Curios, treasures for your joy, comfort, and fun.

PERSONALIZED CANDY BARS and children's books for all occasions. Call for free color catalogs 888-869-7116, or visit www.readingforkids.com.

MAINE LOBSTERS. Buy direct off the dock in Maine; unique gifts. www.MaineLobsterDirect.com or call us at 800-556-2783.

A PERFECT GIFT for him or her. Easy listening by pianist Vincent. Order CD or cassette. 609-490-0004.

AMAZING GIFTS: Christmas, mothers, birthdays, animals. Buy three, get a fourth item free! 410-661-6260. www.armugifts.com.

GINSENG

GINSENG. First-year roots. $20/100. Seed $12/oz. Information $1. Ginseng, OFAG, Flag Pond TN 37657.

HEALTH CARE

LOSE WEIGHT! Feel full with all-natural, vegetable-based, easy-to-make slimming soup recipe. Contains no calories! Send $3: JS, PO Box 218, Clifton CO 81520.

MICROHYDRIN! A powerful all-natural antioxidant dietary supplement, of negative hydrogen ions, gives you antiaging benefits and more. Call now 877-539-5450 (toll-free).

FREE MEDITERRANEAN HERBS. Ultimate health, youth, sexual rejuvenation, natural disease termination. Register today; call 631-595-1553.

HERBAL EYE PILLOWS really do work! Brochure $1. SASE to Real Dreams, PO Box 299, Fairfield CA 94533.

DENTURES: "Everything You Want To Know About Getting, Wearing & Living Comfortably With Dentures." $14 (p/h included) money order to SASUWEH PUBLICATIONS, PO Box 9156, Midland TX 79708-9156. Web site: www.hometown.aol.com/sayersrmt/myhomepage/business.html.

MAGNETIC PRODUCTS. Free reports and catalog. American Health Service Magnetics. 800-635-7070.

DIABETICS WHO TEST BLOOD GLUCOSE. Home delivery of your testing supplies. We bill Medicare/private insurance directly at no cost to you. Toll-free 877-430-8094.

HELP WANTED

EASY WORK! EXCELLENT PAY! Assemble products at home. Call toll-free 800-467-5566 ext. 12627.

WARNING! Don't fall for home working scams. Free consumer newsletter helps you find legitimate home employment. Toll-free 888-800-6732 (document 501).

INVENTIONS/PATENTS

INVENTIONS, IDEAS, NEW PRODUCTS! Presentation to industry/exhibition at national innovation exposition. Patent services. 888-439-IDEA (4332).

LAMPS

ALADDIN KEROSENE MANTLE LAMPS. Smokeless, odorless, and bright! Color catalog $2. Jack's Country Store, Box 710, Ocean Park WA 98640. www.jackscountrystore.com.

REPLACEMENT GLASS LAMP SHADES, including chimneys, student shades, and hurricanes. Send $1 for catalog. Lamp Glass, PO Box 400791, Cambridge MA 02140. www.lampglass.nu.

MUSIC/RECORDS/TAPES

ACCORDIONS, CONCERTINAS, button boxes. New, used, buy, sell, trade, repair. Hohners, Martin guitars. Catalog $5. Castiglione, Box 40-A, Warren MI 48090. 810-755-6050.

NURSERY STOCK

EVERGREEN TREE SEEDLINGS direct from grower. Free catalog. Carino Nurseries, Box 538, Dept. AL, Indiana PA 15701. Web site: www.carinonurseries.com.

OF INTEREST TO ALL

TWELVE-MONTH BIORHYTHM CHARTS. $8. Send birth date and year. John Morgan, 1208 Harris, Bartlesville OK 74006.

UNMARRIED CATHOLICS. Nationwide club. Huge membership. Newsletter. Free information. Sparks, Box 872-FA, Troy NY 12181.

OUTDOOR SPORTS/ACTIVITIES

BAIT SECRETS for freshwater and saltwater fishing detailed in eight pocket booklets. Gulf Books, 23110 SR-54 #323, Lutz FL 33549-6933. www.gulfbooks.com.

PERSONALS

MEET WOMEN WORLDWIDE FOR LOVE AND MARRIAGE. World's #1 personal ad service since 1974! Free 32-page photomagazine. Cherry Blossoms, PO Box 190FA, Kapaau HI 96755. 800-322-3267 ext. 71. E-mail: cherry@blossoms.com. Web site: www.cherryblossoms.com/?adid=07.

SINGLE NONSMOKERS make a date to find a health-minded mate. 603-256-8686. sniusa@together.net.

SISTER RUBY helps in all problems. One free reading by phone. Removes bad luck. 912-776-3069.

REVEREND DEWBERRY, spiritualist healer, helps in all problems. Brings back lovers; financial blessings; removes unnatural sickness, nature, hair loss; guarantees help 24 hours. 800-989-1059 or 912-264-3259. 4488 New Jesup Hwy., Brunswick GA 31520.

MOTHER DORA can influence others. Bring luck. Help with all problems. Correct wrongs. Results! 912-888-5999.

SISTER ROGERS, psychic reader and advisor. Can help you with problems, love, business, marriage, and health. 903-454-4406.

RUSSIAN LADIES, truly beautiful, educated, seek relationships. 8,000 selected from 120,000 plus ladies. Exciting tours, videos. Free color catalog—500 photos! Euro182; PO Box 888851, Atlanta GA 30356. 770-458-0909. Web site: www.euroladies.com.

BEAUTIFUL ASIAN LADIES overseas seek love, marriage. Lowest rates! Free brochure: PR, Box 1245FA, Benicia CA 94510. 707-747-6906.

MRS. NANCY, INDIAN HEALER. Are you facing difficult problems? Are you sick, suffering, in pain and misery? Has your loved one left you? Are you unhappy? Mrs. Nancy reunites lovers fast. Will give you options you never considered. Call now at 803-981-7679 for total answers. 2146 Celanese Rd., Rock Hill SC 29732.

SISTER JOSIE can solve all problems in life such as love, business, health, marriage, financial. 706-548-8598.

NICE SINGLES with Christian values. Free magazine. Singles-OFA, Allardt TN 38504-0310. Web site: www.nicesingles.com.

LONELY? UNLUCKY? UNHAPPY? Lost nature? Lost love? Linda solves all problems quickly. Free readings. 912-995-3611.

MEET LATIN WOMEN! Seeking men of all ages. Mexican–South American introductions. Magazines, videos, single vacations. Free brochures! TLC, Box 924994-AM, Houston TX 77292-4994. 713-896-9224. www.tlcworldwide.com.

ATTENTION: SISTER LIGHT, Spartanburg, South Carolina. One free reading when you call. I will help in all problems. 864-576-9397 or 864-978-6767.

REVEREND PASTOR LEWIS, reader and advisor, can solve all problems in life such as love, business, health, marriage, financials. 404-755-1301; 970-266-0499.

ASIAN DREAM GIRLS abroad desire love, marriage. Lowest price! Tours! Free brochure. ADG, Box 4821FA, Sanford FL 32772. 407-321-8558.

DOMINIQUE REVEALS FUTURE, love, finances; helps all problems. Reunites lovers immediately. One free reading. 423-472-3035.

FREE MONEY RELEASED! Wealthy families and foundations unloading billions! Blessing, Box 47, Springfield MO 65801.

MRS. RUTH, southern-born spiritualist, removes evil, bad luck. Helps in all problems. Free sample reading. 334-616-6363.

MOTHER DOROTHY KAY, reader and advisor. Advice on all problems—love, marriage, health, business, and nature. Gifted healer, she will remove your sickness, sorrow, pain, bad luck. ESP. Results in three days. Write or call about your problems. 1214 Gordon St., Atlanta GA 30310. 404-755-1301; 970-266-0499.

POULTRY

GOSLINGS, DUCKLINGS, CHICKS, turkeys, guineas, books. Picture catalog $1, deductible. Pilgrim Goose Hatchery, OF-21, Williamsfield OH 44093.

REAL ESTATE

ARKANSAS LAND. Free lists! Recreational, investment, retirement homes, acreages. Gatlin Farm Agency, Box 790, Waldron AR 72958. Toll-free 800-562-9078 ext. OFA. E-mail: gfahaleb@ipa.net.

GOVERNMENT LAND NOW AVAILABLE for claim. 160 acres/person. Free recorded message: 707-448-1887 (4KE1). www.usgovernmentinformation.com.

ESCAPE TO THE HILLS OF SOUTH-CENTRAL KENTUCKY. Secluded country properties. Inexpensive homes. Call Century 21, Vibbert Realty, 800-267-2600 for free brochure.

LET THE GOVERNMENT PAY for your new or existing home. Hundreds of programs. Free recorded message: 707-448-3210 (8KE1). www.usgovernmentinformation.com.

RELIGION

ROSICRUCIANS: a mystical tradition/home study available. PO Box 4764, Dallas TX 75208. www.arcgl.org.

REVELATION: HOW TO STUDY IT and have it make sense. Keys to unlocking its symbols. Clearwater Bible Students, PO Box 8216, Clearwater FL 33758.

SATELLITE TV

FREE 18" SATELLITE TV SYSTEM. Echostar model 3720 (regularly $199). Free installation. Call 626-568-0903 for details. Mention serial No. S-1707491. Expires December 31, 2000.

SEEDS

TOBACCO SEEDS AND SUPPLIES. Grow tobacco anywhere in the USA for cigarettes, cigars, and chew! Kits, rolling machines, and more. Free catalog. 800-793-8186. www.tobaccosupply.com.

HEIRLOOM VEGETABLE, HERB, and flower seeds. Eternal Seeds, 1301 Stn. B., Ottawa ON K1P 5R4 Canada. 819-827-2795. E-mail: edecas@travel-net.com.

DRY GOURDS AND SEEDS! 20 varieties of gourds plus many other unique garden items from seed. For complete listing: Gourdgeous Farm, LLC., 1470 12th St. E, Palmetto FL 34221, or visit our Web site www.gourdgeousfarm.com.

THE ORIGINAL "GROW YOUR OWN" seed company. Tobacco, medicinal plants, houseplants, and more. Free catalog. EONS, Dept. FA, PO Box 4604, Hallandale FL 33008. 954-455-0229. www.eonseed.com.

HEIRLOOM TOMATO SEEDS, 400 varieties! Catalog $1. Pomodori Di Marianna, 1955 CCC Rd., Dickson TN 37055.

Index to Advertisers

Cursive!
FOILED AGAIN

Isn't it time to get a handle on our handwriting? You can type your grocery list on a Palm Pilot, but what about a love letter, or a sympathy note? Handwriting—perhaps our messiest invention—still matters, and there's hope for us all.

BY BARBARA GETTY AND ART MAIER

"A true source of human happiness lies in taking a genuine interest in all the details of daily life and elevating them by art."

—William Morris (1834-1896)

Top: Austin Norman Palmer. **Above:** Platt Rogers Spencer. **Below (both pages):** Getty/Dubay style of basic and cursive italic.

Aa Bb Cc Dd Ee Ff Gg Hh Ii Jj Kk Ll Mm Nn Oo F

ll letters written in one stroke unless otherwise indicated.

Aa Bb Cc Dd Ee Ff Gg Hh Ii Jj Kk Ll M

ana bnb cnc dnd ene fnf gng hnh ini jnj knk lnl mr

How We Got to Where We Are

Do the names Platt Rogers Spencer, Charles Paxton Zaner, E. W. Bloser, or Austin Norman Palmer mean anything to you? All are "penmasters" who developed methods of teaching handwriting during the past 200 years. Theirs are the classic American hands, with varying degrees of loops and swirls and flourishes, that have tortured generations of schoolchildren.

In the late 19th century, penmanship had the status of today's computer studies—it was taught to everyone as a basic skill. Beautiful, uniform handwriting was essential in business and a mark of fine upbringing. The main style of penmanship taught throughout the 19th century was a descendant of British script called the round hand. Platt Rogers Spencer (1800-1864), an influential teacher, gave the British round hand a slant and simplified the letters somewhat, but Spencerian writing was still fairly ornate, a close relative of the elaborate fantasies used by copperplate engravers.

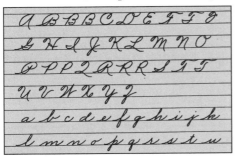

A fine example of Spencerian flourishes, from an 1860s autograph book.

Then along came Austin Norman Palmer, who, along with other writing "reformers" of his day (including Zaner, Bloser, and others), streamlined the Spencerian system for practical business use and for teaching children. After the Roman Catholic teaching order and the New York City school system adopted his method around the turn of the 20th century, Palmer's career took off. By 1920, the majority of public and parochial schools in the United States used Palmer materials. He not only sold penmanship magazines and school lesson books, but also pens, paper, and even ink powder that dissolved in tap water.

Look familiar? It's classic Palmer style, loops and all.

If you went to elementary school anytime from the 1920s through the 1950s, chances are you learned the Palmer method of handwriting, a muscular, whole-arm experience involving endless drills at the blackboard and on paper—long lines of identical loops and ovals, vigorous push-pulls at the

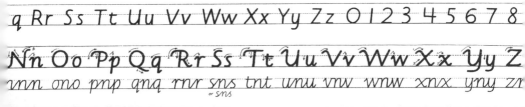

chalkboard, hours of perfecting capital *Q*'s (like big, blowsy *2*'s) and lower-case *z*'s (not to be confused with *g*'s). If you were left-handed, you probably were corrected and coerced into using your right hand instead. As late as 1940, left-handed children were classified as "special needs" in some schools and were taught to slant their paper and letters as if they were right-handed.

Very few schoolchildren could do those infamous loops and coils to Palmer's standards. But for those who could, and who submitted writing samples to his magazine, *The Western Penman,* Palmer awarded beautifully engraved certificates of recognition. Exceptional talent won a prized Palmer medal.

Getty/Dubay cursive simply links the basic italic forms with short lines.

Complicating the handwriting scene in the era between the World Wars was the new insistence among many educators that students learn to print before they learn cursive. Marjorie Wise began teaching the ball and stick, or manuscript, method of writing for beginners in 1922. Before this, all children had to learn cursive from the start.

Manuscript, based on the skeletal geometric forms of 15th-century hand lettering, called Bookhand, was seen as a major breakthrough. However, most children (except those in progressive schools, mostly private ones) still had to switch to cursive in third grade, abandoning their new skills and learning 52 new, complicated letters! As one handwriting historian noted, "Teaching ball and stick printing and then switching to cursive is like teaching math entirely in Roman numerals up into third grade, then turning to Arabic numerals."

As educational practices and pressures changed in the last decades of the 20th century, penmanship classes slid far down the pecking order. Palmer fell out of favor; lefties were allowed to do their own thing; and no one style prevailed. Colleges dropped penmanship courses from their teacher-training requirements. In the 1960s, the plump, slanted forms of the D'Nealian system were adopted in many schools, but this simplified form of cursive still required the third-grade switch.

The first real innovation in handwriting since 1922 came in 1974, when Charles Lehman's

POOR HANDWRITING CAN BE HAZARDOUS TO YOUR HEALTH!

■ **If it's your doctor's handwriting that's unreadable, watch out. According to Kate Gladstone, who runs a handwriting-repair business in Albany, New York, 93 percent of prescriptions can be read only with difficulty by pharmacists, and 20 percent cannot be deciphered at all.**

Family Pharmacist **magazine features a monthly "puzzle" column consisting of the most strikingly illegible "mystery Rx's" sent in by readers.**

Simple Italic Handwriting, a teacher's guide, was chosen as one of the official public-school texts in Oregon. Lehman's system used the same letters for both printing and cursive, simply joining the printing with short lines. Finally, cursive was ready to reinvent itself.

CURSIVE MAKES A COMEBACK

hat's old is always new, and this computer age is seeing a growing interest in beautiful and legible handwriting. Now colleges are offering penmanship courses again, sales of stationery and fancy pens are on the upswing, and handwritten business letters have a new cachet. If the loops and dips of the Palmer method drove you to distraction, there's hope in new styles for new times.

Following Charles Lehman's lead, and yet reaching back 500 years to the Vatican scribes who developed the "Italique" style, a simple variation of italic handwriting is growing in popularity. Two of its leading proponents—and teachers—are Barbara Getty and Inga Dubay of Portland, Oregon. They have developed a simple system for teaching rapid, legible handwriting to children and adults, with special legibility workshops for doctors. (They also offer a free course on National Handwriting Day, which falls on the Saturday in January closest to January 23, John Hancock's birthday.)

Getty and Dubay teach a basic italic style in which most letters (21 out of 26) can be written with one continuous stroke; for cursive, the letters are joined in the simplest and most direct way. There are no extra loops on ascenders and descenders, no backtracking to cross the *t*, and no extreme slant. It's efficient, it's legible, and for people who use Getty and Dubay's self-teaching manual, *Write Now* (Continuing Education Press, Portland State University, Portland, OR), or attend one of their classes, it's transforming. People have even been known to practice their penmanship.

SEVEN WAYS TO SIMPLIFY YOUR CURSIVE

■ Cross lowercase *t*'s as you write them. Don't wait to go back after the entire word is written.

■ Emphasize the downstrokes of letters and use only about a 5 to 15 degree slant to the right (too much slant causes poor legibility).

■ Eliminate loops wherever possible. Simply retrace your initial stroke on ascenders, or lift the pen without looping on descenders. (Most adults who write fast but legibly normally eliminate some or many loops and joiners in their handwriting.)

■ Join letters with straight lines, not curves. For examply, join *o* to *n* with a straight, short horizontal line.

■ Use "print" forms of capitals in cursive writing, with the same slant as the cursive, especially for twisty letters like *S*, *G*, *J*, and others. Remember, capitals form only 2 percent of ordinary prose text.

■ Strongly consider print-like forms for the lowercase letters *b*, *f*, *r*, *s*, and *z*.

■ Position the paper in front of the writing-arm's shoulder.

Barbara Getty is a calligrapher and handwriting instructor; Art Maier is an expert on the Palmer method. ☐☐

Anecdotes AND Pleasantries

A sampling from the hundreds of letters, clippings, and e-mails sent to us by Almanac readers from all over the United States and Canada during the past year.

The 12 Steps to Giving Your Cat a Pill

The following (slightly abridged from the original version) was sent to us by C.R.S. of Sacramento, California. It was written by Bob Story for a California newspaper.

1 Pick up cat and cradle it in the crook of your left arm as though holding a baby. Position right forefinger and thumb on both sides of cat's mouth and gently apply pressure to its cheeks. When cat opens up, pop pill into mouth. Cat will then close mouth and swallow.

2 Retrieve pill from floor and cat from behind sofa. Repeat the process.

3 Retrieve cat from bedroom, and throw soggy pill away.

4 Remove second pill from foil wrap, cradle cat in left arm, holding rear paws tightly with left hand. Force jaws open, and push pill to back of throat with forefinger. Hold mouth shut for a count of 10, if you are able. Hold cat's mouth closed as well.

5 Retrieve pill from goldfish bowl and cat from top of wardrobe.

6 Kneel on floor with cat wedged firmly between knees, immobilizing front and rear paws. Ask assistant to hold cat's head firmly with one hand while forcing wooden ruler into cat's throat. Flick pill down ruler with forefinger, and rub cat's throat vigorously.

7 Retrieve cat from living-room curtain valance.

8 Carefully sweep shattered figurines from hearth and set them aside for later gluing. Remove third pill from foil wrap.

9 Wrap cat in beach towel and ask assistant to lie prone on cat with cat's head visible under assistant's armpit. Put pill in end of paper tube you've made for this purpose. Then force cat's mouth open with pencil, and blow.

10 Check label to make sure pill is not lethal to humans. Sip water to take taste away. Apply bandage to assistant's forearm, and remove blood from carpet with soap and cold water.

11 Retrieve cat from neighbor's roof.

12 Telephone your veterinarian. Or, better still, drop your cat, along with a generous donation, at an animal shelter and buy yourself a couple of goldfish.

How to Change Your Pants in the Woods

Courtesy of Jon Vara of Marshfield, Vermont.

There are any number of respectable reasons for needing to change your pants outdoors. Maybe the weather has turned too cold for shorts. Maybe you accidentally sat in a puddle. Whatever the cause, though, there's a right way and a wrong way.

First, the wrong way: Take off your shoes and remove your pants. (For the sake of clarity, we'll refer to this pair of pants as Pants A and the second pair as Pants B.) Throw Pants A to one side and put on Pants B one leg at a time, while attempting to keep your socks dry by hopping rapidly up and down on whichever foot is in contact with the damp ground. When Pants B are up around your waist, continue to hop in place while jamming a foot into one shoe. Step down on the newly shod foot, and brush the leaves, grass, pebbles, and other debris from the sock on the unshod foot. Put on that shoe,

Fooling Around with WORDS

The first six facts are courtesy of A.J. of Lexington, Kentucky. The spelling list is courtesy of M.J. of Fargo, North Dakota.

- The longest word you can spell without repeating a letter: **uncopyrightable**

- The longest word with just one vowel: **strengths**

- The only English word with a triple letter: **goddessship**

- The word with the longest definition in most dictionaries: **set**

- The shortest "ology" (study of) word: **oology** (the study of birds' eggs)

- The only word in which an "f" is pronounced like a "v": **of**

Ten of the most commonly misspelled words in America:

1. accommodate
2. committee
3. definitely
4. embarrass
5. harass
6. millennium
7. misspell
8. noticeable
9. receive
10. separate

remove the first, and shake out the debris. Put the first back on, tie both shoes, fasten your belt, and look up with a confident expression, as if unaware that those around you have been fighting back laughter throughout the whole performance.

Here's the right way: Take off one shoe, then—while standing on the other, still-shod foot—withdraw that leg from the leg of Pants A. Insert it into the corresponding leg of Pants B, put your shoe back on, and calmly tie it. You are now wearing both shoes and have one leg in each of two different pairs of pants. This is a good time to pause for a moment, glance up at any onlookers, and savor the puzzled expressions on their faces.

Their puzzlement will turn to open admiration as you finish the sequence. Untie and remove your other shoe (that is, the shoe on the foot of the leg that's still within the leg of Pants A), slip out of the second half of Pants A, and step into the other half of Pants B. Pull Pants B up to your waist. If you've followed the procedure correctly, you'll now be standing on one shod foot with both legs fully enclosed in Pants B, having arrived at that point without ever setting a sock onto the ground. Put on your second shoe, tie it, stand up, and take a bow.

As We Begin the 21st Century...
Let's Remember "Amazing Grace," the Mother of All Computers (1906-1992)

The following three readers, who enjoy the Almanac Web site (www.almanac.com), e-mailed information to us about the late Grace Hopper, born 95 years ago: M.J. of Munsonville, New Hampshire; R.D.H. of Tucson, Arizona; and F.J.H. of Newton, Massachusetts.

Known to everyone as "Amazing Grace," Navy Rear Admiral Grace Hopper, born in 1906 in New York City, was a programmer on the first large-scale digital computer in the United States, the Mark I. "It was 51 feet long, 8 feet high, and 8 feet deep," she recalled years later. "And it had 72 words of storage and could perform three additions a second."

Among Admiral Hopper's other accomplishments:

She coined the term "computer bug" in 1951, when an actual bug—a moth—shorted out two tubes in an experimental computer she was working on. (She taped the two-inch moth into the UNIVAC I logbook; you can see it at http://ei.cs.vt.edu/~history/Bug.GIF.)

She built the first A-0 compiler, which went live on November 4, 1952, on the UNIVAC I to predict the Eisenhower win after only 7 percent of the votes were in.

At her retirement from the Navy in 1986, she was the oldest officer on active duty.

Quote: "It's easier to ask forgiveness than to get permission." *–Grace Hopper*

The Day John Kennedy Announced He Was a Jelly-Filled Pastry

And Other Historic Misstatements

Courtesy of G.E.O of Cambridge, Massachusetts.

When President John F. Kennedy declared "Ich bin ein Berliner" at the climax of his famous speech in Berlin in 1963, he was literally saying, "I am a jelly-filled pastry." (He should have said "Ich bin Berliner.")

Others in the odd remark hall of fame:

"If Lincoln were alive today, he'd roll over in his grave." *–President Gerald Ford*

"A zebra does not change its spots." *–Vice President Al Gore*

"If we don't succeed, we run the risk of failure." *–Vice President Dan Quayle*

"Outside of the killings, we have one of the lowest crime rates in the nation." *–Marion Barry, mayor of Washington, D.C.*

"Baseball is 90 percent mental; the other half is physical." *–Yogi Berra*

"Anybody who goes to a psychiatrist ought to have his head examined." *–Samuel Goldwyn, Hollywood producer*

"This is the worst disaster to hit California since I was elected." *–Governor Pat Brown, referring to flooding*

"I'm the football coach around here and don't you remember it." *–Bill Peterson, Florida State University football coach*

"I have nothing to say and I'm going to say it just once." *–Frank Smith, Toronto Maple Leafs coach*

Does This Old 19th-Century Poem Ring True Today?

(You decide!)

Courtesy of H.T.S. of Moosup, Connecticut.

When Pa Is Sick

When Pa is sick,
he's scared to death,
An' Ma an' us just holds our breath.
He crawls in bed an' puffs and grunts,
An' does all kind of crazy stunts.
He wants Doc Brown, an' "mighty quick,"
For when Pa's ill, he's awful sick.
He gasps an' groans, an' sort of sighs;
He talks so queer, and rolls his eyes.
Ma jumps an' runs, an' all of us,
An' peace an' joy is mighty skeerce—
When Pa is sick, it's somthin' fierce!

When Ma Is Sick

When Ma is sick,
she pegs away;
She's quiet,
though, not much to say.
She goes right on a-doin' things,
An' sometimes laughs and even sings.
She says she don't feel extra well;
But then, it's just a kinda spell.
She'll be all right tomorrow, sure.
A good old sleep will be the cure.
An' Pa, he sniffs and makes no kick,
"For women-folks is 'always sick!'"
An' Ma, she smiles, lets on she's glad;
When Ma is sick, it ain't so bad!

(continued)

For Those Partial to Pirate Jokes

Courtesy of B.R.H., Bangor, Maine.

A sailor meets a pirate in a bar. The pirate has a peg leg, a hook, and an eye patch. "How'd you end up with a peg leg?" asks the sailor. "I was swept overboard in a storm," says the pirate. "A shark bit off me whole leg."

"Wow!" said the sailor. "What about the hook?"

"We were boarding an enemy ship, battling the other seamen with swords. One of them cut me hand clean off."

"Incredible!" remarked the sailor. "And the eye patch?"

"A seagull dropping fell in me eye," replied the pirate.

"You lost your eye to a seagull dropping?" the sailor asked incredulously.

Said the pirate, "It was me first day with the hook."

The Five Best "Bests" of the Year

1 The best color to wear while deer hunting?

ANSWER: No, not red—nor orange. Although they're both safe colors, deer can see them like a neon sign. Deer cannot see battleship gray, but on the other hand, neither can other hunters, so it's not safe. Therefore, the best color to wear while deer hunting is—are you ready for this?—shocking pink! Deer can barely see it at all (because it is a blend from opposite ends of the rainbow and is not found in nature), but other hunters can spot you for what you are in less time than it takes to say hi. So it's very safe.

Courtesy of S.T.M. of Denver, Colorado, who gleaned the information from an article written by George Reiger in Field & Stream.

2 The best way to blow a really huge bubble with your bubble gum?

ANSWER: Chew at least five pieces mixed with a teaspoon of peanut butter.

Courtesy of Adult Peanut Butter Lovers' Fan Club of Tifton, Georgia.

3 The best way to know you're getting along in age?

ANSWER: When you realize you don't really care where your spouse goes on any given day just as long as you don't have to go, too.

4 The best (or, perhaps, near-best) riddle?

ANSWER: Name the creature we eat before it's born and after it's dead. (Hint: Although no one knows why, it often crosses the road.)

Courtesy of R. J. of Dublin, New Hampshire.

5 The best type of lawn to put in?

ANSWER: A lawn that grows to a certain height and no higher and therefore never needs mowing. No, it's not on the market as yet—but it may well be in a few years. Recently, scientists have discovered a gene known as BAS-1 that appears to control the production of an important growth hormone in the plant thale cress *(Arabidopsis).*

Courtesy of R. G. of Tulsa, Oklahoma, who credits Henry Fountain of The New York Times.

.00000000
000000000
000000000
000000001

The Smallest Anything Can Possibly Be

Courtesy of C.R.G. of Rochester, New York, who sent us the following excerpt from an article written by George Johnson in The New York Times "Science Times."

Slightly smaller than what Americans quaintly insist on calling half an inch, a centimeter (one hundredth of a meter) is easy enough to see. Divide this small length into ten equal slices and you are looking, or probably squinting, at a millimeter (one thousandth, or 10 to the minus 3 meters). By the time you divide one of these tiny units into a thousand minuscule micrometers, you have far exceeded the limits of the finest bifocals.

But in the mind's eye, let the cutting continue, chopping the micrometer into a thousand nanometers and the nanometers into a thousand picometers, and those in steps of a thousandfold into femtometers, attometers, zeptometers, and yoctometers. At this point, 10 to the minus 24 meters, about one billionth the radius of a proton, the roster of convenient Greek names runs out. But go ahead and keep dividing, again and again, until you reach a length only a hundred billionth as large as that tiny amount: 10 to the minus 35 meters, or a decimal point followed by 34 zeroes and then a 1.

You have finally hit rock bottom: a span called the Planck length, the shortest anything can get.

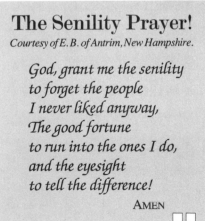

The Senility Prayer!
Courtesy of E. B. of Antrim, New Hampshire.

God, grant me the senility
to forget the people
I never liked anyway,
The good fortune
to run into the ones I do,
and the eyesight
to tell the difference!

AMEN

2000

January
S	M	T	W	T	F	S
						1
2	3	4	5	6	7	8
9	10	11	12	13	14	15
16	17	18	19	20	21	22
23	24	25	26	27	28	29
30	31					

February
S	M	T	W	T	F	S
		1	2	3	4	5
6	7	8	9	10	11	12
13	14	15	16	17	18	19
20	21	22	23	24	25	26
27	28	29				

March
S	M	T	W	T	F	S
			1	2	3	4
5	6	7	8	9	10	11
12	13	14	15	16	17	18
19	20	21	22	23	24	25
26	27	28	29	30	31	

April
S	M	T	W	T	F	S
						1
2	3	4	5	6	7	8
9	10	11	12	13	14	15
16	17	18	19	20	21	22
23	24	25	26	27	28	29
30						

May
S	M	T	W	T	F	S
	1	2	3	4	5	6
7	8	9	10	11	12	13
14	15	16	17	18	19	20
21	22	23	24	25	26	27
28	29	30	31			

June
S	M	T	W	T	F	S
				1	2	3
4	5	6	7	8	9	10
11	12	13	14	15	16	17
18	19	20	21	22	23	24
25	26	27	28	29	30	

July
S	M	T	W	T	F	S
						1
2	3	4	5	6	7	8
9	10	11	12	13	14	15
16	17	18	19	20	21	22
23	24	25	26	27	28	29
30	31					

August
S	M	T	W	T	F	S
		1	2	3	4	5
6	7	8	9	10	11	12
13	14	15	16	17	18	19
20	21	22	23	24	25	26
27	28	29	30	31		

September
S	M	T	W	T	F	S
					1	2
3	4	5	6	7	8	9
10	11	12	13	14	15	16
17	18	19	20	21	22	23
24	25	26	27	28	29	30

October
S	M	T	W	T	F	S
1	2	3	4	5	6	7
8	9	10	11	12	13	14
15	16	17	18	19	20	21
22	23	24	25	26	27	28
29	30	31				

November
S	M	T	W	T	F	S
			1	2	3	4
5	6	7	8	9	10	11
12	13	14	15	16	17	18
19	20	21	22	23	24	25
26	27	28	29	30		

December
S	M	T	W	T	F	S
					1	2
3	4	5	6	7	8	9
10	11	12	13	14	15	16
17	18	19	20	21	22	23
24	25	26	27	28	29	30
31						

2001

January
S	M	T	W	T	F	S
	1	2	3	4	5	6
7	8	9	10	11	12	13
14	15	16	17	18	19	20
21	22	23	24	25	26	27
28	29	30	31			

February
S	M	T	W	T	F	S
				1	2	3
4	5	6	7	8	9	10
11	12	13	14	15	16	17
18	19	20	21	22	23	24
25	26	27	28			

March
S	M	T	W	T	F	S
				1	2	3
4	5	6	7	8	9	10
11	12	13	14	15	16	17
18	19	20	21	22	23	24
25	26	27	28	29	30	31

April
S	M	T	W	T	F	S
1	2	3	4	5	6	7
8	9	10	11	12	13	14
15	16	17	18	19	20	21
22	23	24	25	26	27	28
29	30					

May
S	M	T	W	T	F	S
		1	2	3	4	5
6	7	8	9	10	11	12
13	14	15	16	17	18	19
20	21	22	23	24	25	26
27	28	29	30	31		

June
S	M	T	W	T	F	S
					1	2
3	4	5	6	7	8	9
10	11	12	13	14	15	16
17	18	19	20	21	22	23
24	25	26	27	28	29	30

July
S	M	T	W	T	F	S
1	2	3	4	5	6	7
8	9	10	11	12	13	14
15	16	17	18	19	20	21
22	23	24	25	26	27	28
29	30	31				

August
S	M	T	W	T	F	S
			1	2	3	4
5	6	7	8	9	10	11
12	13	14	15	16	17	18
19	20	21	22	23	24	25
26	27	28	29	30	31	

September
S	M	T	W	T	F	S
						1
2	3	4	5	6	7	8
9	10	11	12	13	14	15
16	17	18	19	20	21	22
23	24	25	26	27	28	29
30						

October
S	M	T	W	T	F	S
	1	2	3	4	5	6
7	8	9	10	11	12	13
14	15	16	17	18	19	20
21	22	23	24	25	26	27
28	29	30	31			

November
S	M	T	W	T	F	S
				1	2	3
4	5	6	7	8	9	10
11	12	13	14	15	16	17
18	19	20	21	22	23	24
25	26	27	28	29	30	

December
S	M	T	W	T	F	S
						1
2	3	4	5	6	7	8
9	10	11	12	13	14	15
16	17	18	19	20	21	22
23	24	25	26	27	28	29
30	31					

2002

January
S	M	T	W	T	F	S
		1	2	3	4	5
6	7	8	9	10	11	12
13	14	15	16	17	18	19
20	21	22	23	24	25	26
27	28	29	30	31		

February
S	M	T	W	T	F	S
					1	2
3	4	5	6	7	8	9
10	11	12	13	14	15	16
17	18	19	20	21	22	23
24	25	26	27	28		

March
S	M	T	W	T	F	S
					1	2
3	4	5	6	7	8	9
10	11	12	13	14	15	16
17	18	19	20	21	22	23
24	25	26	27	28	29	30
31						

April
S	M	T	W	T	F	S
	1	2	3	4	5	6
7	8	9	10	11	12	13
14	15	16	17	18	19	20
21	22	23	24	25	26	27
28	29	30				

May
S	M	T	W	T	F	S
			1	2	3	4
5	6	7	8	9	10	11
12	13	14	15	16	17	18
19	20	21	22	23	24	25
26	27	28	29	30	31	

June
S	M	T	W	T	F	S
						1
2	3	4	5	6	7	8
9	10	11	12	13	14	15
16	17	18	19	20	21	22
23	24	25	26	27	28	29
30						

July
S	M	T	W	T	F	S
	1	2	3	4	5	6
7	8	9	10	11	12	13
14	15	16	17	18	19	20
21	22	23	24	25	26	27
28	29	30	31			

August
S	M	T	W	T	F	S
				1	2	3
4	5	6	7	8	9	10
11	12	13	14	15	16	17
18	19	20	21	22	23	24
25	26	27	28	29	30	31

September
S	M	T	W	T	F	S
1	2	3	4	5	6	7
8	9	10	11	12	13	14
15	16	17	18	19	20	21
22	23	24	25	26	27	28
29	30					

October
S	M	T	W	T	F	S
		1	2	3	4	5
6	7	8	9	10	11	12
13	14	15	16	17	18	19
20	21	22	23	24	25	26
27	28	29	30	31		

November
S	M	T	W	T	F	S
					1	2
3	4	5	6	7	8	9
10	11	12	13	14	15	16
17	18	19	20	21	22	23
24	25	26	27	28	29	30

December
S	M	T	W	T	F	S
1	2	3	4	5	6	7
8	9	10	11	12	13	14
15	16	17	18	19	20	21
22	23	24	25	26	27	28
29	30	31				

A Reference Compendium

compiled by Mare-Anne Jarvela

Total Solar Eclipses (2001-2024)

Date		Regions with Visible Totality
2001	June 21	Atlantic Ocean, southern Africa
2002	Dec. 4	southern Africa, Indian Ocean, Australia
2003	Nov. 23	Antarctica
2005	Apr. 8	S. Pacific Ocean
2006	Mar. 29	Africa, Turkey, Russia
2008	Aug. 1	Greenland, Siberia, China
2009	July 22	India, China, S. Pacific Ocean
2010	July 11	S. Pacific Ocean, southern South America
2012	Nov. 13	Australia, S. Pacific Ocean
2013	Nov. 3	Atlantic Ocean, Central Africa
2015	Mar. 20	N. Atlantic Ocean, Arctic
2016	Mar. 9	Southeast Asia, N. Pacific Ocean
2017	Aug. 17	United States
2019	July 2	S. Pacific Ocean, South America
2020	Dec. 14	S. Pacific Ocean, South America
2021	Dec. 4	Antarctica
2023	Apr. 20	Indonesia
2024	Apr. 8	Mexico, United States, Canada

Easter Sunday (2001-2005)

■ Christian churches that follow the Gregorian calendar (Eastern Orthodox churches follow the Julian calendar) celebrate Easter on the first Sunday after the full Moon that occurs on or just after the vernal equinox.

In	Easter will fall on
2001	April 15
2002	March 31
2003	April 20
2004	April 11
2005	March 27

When Will the Moon Rise Today?

■ A lunar puzzle involves the timing of moonrise. Folks who enjoy the out-of-doors and the wonders of nature may wish to commit to memory the following gem:

**The new Moon always rises at sunrise
And the first quarter at noon.
The full Moon always rises at sunset
And the last quarter at midnight.**

Moonrise occurs about 50 minutes later each day than the day before. The new Moon is invisible because its illuminated side faces away from Earth, which occurs when the Moon lines up between Earth and the Sun. One or two days after the date of the new Moon, you can see it in the western sky as a thin crescent setting just after sunset. (See pages 58-84 for exact moonrise times.)

Triskaidekaphobia

Here are a few conclusions on Friday the 13th:

Of the 14 possible configurations for the annual calendar (see any perpetual calendar), the occurrence of Friday the 13th is this:

■ 6 of 14 years have one Friday the 13th.
 6 of 14 years have two Friday the 13th.
 2 of 14 years have three Friday the 13th.

There is no year without one Friday the 13th, and no year with more than three.

■ There are two Fridays the 13th in 2001. The next year to have three Fridays the 13th is 2009.

■ The reason we say "Fridays the 13th" is that no one can pronounce "Friday the 13ths."

Glossary of Almanac Oddities

■ Many readers have expressed puzzlement over the rather obscure notations that appear on our Right-Hand Calendar Pages (pages 59-85). These "oddities" have long been fixtures in the Almanac, and we are pleased to provide some definitions. (Once explained, it may seem that they are not so odd after all!)

■ Ember Days (Movable)

The Almanac traditionally marks the four periods formerly observed by the Roman Catholic and Anglican churches for prayer, fasting, and the ordination of clergy. These Ember Days are the Wednesdays, Fridays, and Saturdays that follow in succession after 1) the First Sunday in Lent; 2) Pentecost (Whitsunday); 3) the Feast of the Holy Cross (September 14); and 4) the Feast of St. Lucy (December 13). The word *ember* is perhaps a corruption of the Latin *quatuor tempora,* "four times."

Folklore has it that the weather on each of the three days foretells the weather for three successive months—that is, for September's Ember Days, Wednesday forecasts weather for October, Friday for November, and Saturday for December.

■ Plough Monday (January)

The first Monday after the Epiphany; so called because it was the end of the Christmas holidays, when men returned to their plough—or daily work. It was customary for farm laborers to draw a plough through the village, soliciting money for a "plough-light," which was kept burning in the parish church all year. In some areas, the custom of blessing the plough is maintained.

■ Three Chilly Saints (May)

Mammertius, Pancratius, and Gervatius, three early Christian saints, whose feast days occur on May 11, 12, and 13, respectively. Because these days are traditionally cold (an old French saying goes: "St. Mammertius, St. Pancras, and St. Gervais do not pass without a frost"), they have come to be known as the Three Chilly Saints.

■ Midsummer Day (June 24)

Although it occurs near the summer solstice, to the farmer it is the midpoint of the growing season, halfway between planting and harvest and an occasion for festivity. The English church considered it a "Quarter Day," one of the four major divisions of the liturgical year. It also marks the feast day of St. John the Baptist.

■ Cornscateous Air (July)

A term first used by the old almanac makers to signify warm, damp air. Though it signals ideal climatic conditions for growing corn, it also poses a danger to those affected by asthma, pneumonia, and other respiratory problems.

■ Dog Days (July-August)

The hottest and most unhealthy days of the year. Also known as "Canicular Days," the name derives from the Dog Star, Sirius. The Almanac lists the traditional timing of Dog Days: The 40 days beginning July 3 and ending August 11, coinciding with the heliacal (at sunrise) rising of Sirius.

■ Cat Nights Begin (August)

The term harks back to the days when people believed in witches. An old Irish legend has it that a witch could turn herself into a cat eight times and then regain herself, but on the ninth time—August 17—she couldn't change back. Hence the saying, "A cat has nine lives." Since August is a "yowly" time for cats, this may have prompted the speculation about witches on the prowl in the first place.

■ Harvest Home (September)

In both Europe and Britain, the conclusion of the harvest each autumn was once marked by great festivals of fun, feasting, and thanksgiving known as "Harvest Home." It was also a time to hold elections, pay workers, and collect rents. These festivals usually took place around the time of the autumnal equinox. Certain ethnic groups in this country, particularly the Pennsylvania Dutch, have kept the tradition alive.

■ St. Luke's Little Summer (October)

A spell of warm weather occurring about the time of the saint's feast day, October 18. This period is sometimes referred to as "Indian summer."

■ Indian Summer (November)

A period of warm weather following a cold spell or a hard frost. Though there are differing dates for the time of occurrence, for more than 200 years the Almanac has adhered to the saying, "If

All Saints brings out winter, St. Martin's brings out Indian summer." Accordingly, Indian summer can occur between St. Martin's Day (November 11) and November 20. As for the origin of the term, some say it comes from the early Indians, who believed the condition was caused by a warm wind sent from the court of their southwestern God, Cautantowwit.

■ Halcyon Days (December)

A period (about 14 days) of calm weather, following the blustery winds of autumn's end. The ancient Greeks and Romans believed them to occur around the time of the winter solstice when the halcyon, or kingfisher, was brooding. In a nest floating on the sea, the bird was said to have charmed the wind and waves so the waters were especially calm during this period.

■ Beware the Pogonip (December)

The word *pogonip* is a meteorological term used to describe an uncommon occurrence—frozen fog. The word was coined by American Indians to describe the frozen fogs of fine ice needles that occur in the mountain valleys of the western United States. According to Indian tradition, breathing the fog is injurious to the lungs.

Phases of the Moon

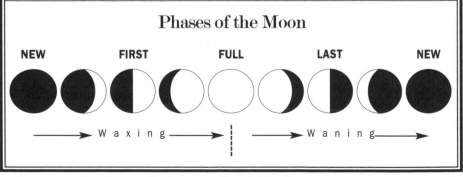

NEW   FIRST   FULL   LAST   NEW

Waxing →   ┊   → Waning →

Month Names

January	Named for the Roman god Janus, protector of gates and doorways. Janus is depicted with two faces, one looking into the past, the other into the future.
February	From the Latin word *februa*, "to cleanse." The Roman Februalia was a month of purification and atonement.
March	Named for the Roman god of war, Mars. This was the time of year to resume military campaigns that had been interrupted by winter.
April	From the Latin word *aperio*, "to open (bud)," because plants begin to grow in this month.
May	Named for the Roman goddess Maia, who oversaw the growth of plants. Also from the Latin word *maiores*, meaning "elders," who were celebrated during this month.
June	Named for the Roman goddess Juno, patroness of marriage and the well-being of women. Also from the Latin word *juvenis*, "young people."
July	Named to honor Roman dictator Julius Caesar (100 B.C.- 44 B.C.). In 46 B.C., Julius Caesar made one of his greatest contributions to history: With the help of Sosigenes, he developed the Julian calendar, the precursor to the Gregorian calendar we use today.
August	Named to honor the first Roman emperor (and grandnephew of Julius Caesar), Augustus Caesar (63 B.C.-A.D. 14).
September	From the Latin word *septem*, "seven," because this had been the seventh month of the early Roman calendar.
October	From the Latin word *octo*, "eight," because this had been the eighth month of the early Roman calendar.
November	From the Latin word *novem*, "nine," because this had been the ninth month of the early Roman calendar.
December	From the Latin word *decem*, "ten," because this had been the tenth month of the early Roman calendar.

Dining by the Calendar
Traditional foods for feasts and fasts.

■ **January**

Feast of the Circumcision: Black-eyed peas and pork (United States); oat-husk gruel or oatmeal porridge (Scotland).

Epiphany: Cake with a lucky bean baked in it; the one who finds the bean is the king or queen of the feast, in memory of the three Wise Men (France).

Robert Burns Day: Haggis—sheep's stomach stuffed with suet, chopped organ meat (heart, lungs, liver), onions, oatmeal, and seasonings (Scotland). Haggis is a traditional Scottish delicacy served on all holidays of national importance.

(continued)

■ February

Candlemas Day: Pancakes eaten today will prevent hemorrhoids for a full year (French American).

St. Agatha: Round loaves of bread blessed by a priest (southern Europe).

Shrove Tuesday: Pancakes (England); oatcakes (Scotland); rabbit (Ireland). Rich foods are eaten to usher in the Lenten fast; pancakes use up the last of the eggs and butter.

Lent: Simnel, a large fruitcake baked so hard it has sometimes been mistaken by recipients for a hassock or footstool (Great Britain).

■ March

St. David: Leeks, to be worn (Wales) or eaten raw (England). Recalls a Welsh victory over the Saxons in A.D. 640; the Welsh wore leeks in their hats to distinguish them from the enemy.

St. Benedict: Nettle soup (ancient monastic practice). Picking nettles, which irritate the skin, was a penance in keeping with the spirit of the monastic rule of St. Benedict.

Purim: Strong drink and three-cornered cookies flavored with poppy seeds (Jewish). These cookies, called hamantaschen, are said to represent the three-cornered hat of Haman, the enemy of the Jewish people, whose downfall is celebrated on this holiday.

Maundy Thursday: Green foods or foods colored green (southern Europe). The medieval liturgical observance called for green vestments; in some parts of Europe, it is still called Green Thursday.

Good Friday: Hot cross buns. If made properly on this day, they will never get moldy (England).

■ April

Easter: Lamb as symbol of sacrifice; also ham.

Beltane, May Day Eve: Strong ale (England); oatcakes with nine knobs to be broken off one by one and offered to each of nine supernatural protectors of domestic animals (Scotland).

■ May

Ascension Day: Fowl, or pastries molded into the shape of birds, to commemorate the taking of Jesus into the skies (medieval Europe).

Whitsunday (Pentecost): Dove or pigeon in honor of the Holy Spirit (southern Europe); strong ale (England).

St. Dunstan: Beer. Cider pressed today will go bad (England).

Corpus Christi: Orange peel dipped in chocolate, chicken stuffed with sauerkraut (Basque Provinces).

■ June

St. Anthony of Padua: Liver, possibly based on the pre-Christian custom of eating liver on the summer solstice.

Feast of St. John the Baptist: First fruits of spring harvest.

■ July

St. Swithin: Eggs, because the saint miraculously restored intact a basket of eggs that had been broken by a poor woman taking them to market; he also looks after apples (medieval England).

St. James: Oysters, because James was a fisherman (England).

■ August

Lammas Day: Oatcakes (Scotland); loaves made from new grain of the season (England); toffee; seaweed pudding. Blueberries in baskets as an offering to a sweetheart are the last vestige of this holiday as a pagan fertility festival (Ireland).

St. Lawrence of Rome: Because the saint was roasted to death on a gridiron, it is courteous to serve only cold meat today (southern Europe).

Feast of the Assumption: Onions, possibly because they have always been considered wholesome and potent against evil (Polish American).

■ September

St. Giles: Tea loaf with raisins (Scotland).

Nativity of Mary: Blackberries, possibly because the color is reminiscent of the depiction of the Virgin's blue cloak (Brittany).

Michaelmas Day: New wine (Europe); goose, originally a sacrifice to the saint (Great Britain); cake of oats, barley, and rye (Scotland); carrots (Ireland).

■ October

Rosh Hashanah: Sweet foods; honey; foods colored orange or yellow to represent a bright, joyous, and sweet new year (Jewish).

Yom Kippur: Fast day; the day before, eat kreplach (filled noodles), considered by generations of mothers to be good and filling (Jewish).

St. Luke: Oatcakes flavored with anise and cinnamon (Scotland).

Sts. Simon and Jude: Dirge cakes, simple fried buns made for distribution to the poor. Also apples or potatoes, for divination (Scotland and England). Divination with apples is accomplished by peeling the fruit in one long strip and tossing the peel over one's shoulder. The letter formed by the peel is then interpreted.

All Hallows Eve: Apples and nuts for divination (England); buttered oat-husk gruel (Scotland); bosty, a mixture of potatoes, cabbage, and onions (Ireland).

■ November

All Saints Day: Chestnuts (Italy); gingerbread and oatcakes (Scotland); milk (central Europe); doughnuts, whose round shape indicates eternity (Tyrol).

All Souls Day: Skull-shaped candy (Mexico); beans, peas, and lentils, considered food of the poor, as penance for souls in purgatory (southern Europe).

St. Martin: Last religious feast day before the beginning of the Advent fast. Goose, last of fresh-killed meat before winter; blood pudding (Great Britain).

St. Andrew: Haggis—stuffed sheep's stomach (Scotland).

■ December

St. Nicholas: Fruit, nuts, candy for children (Germany). Commemorates, in part, the miracle by which the saint restored to life three young boys who had been murdered by a greedy innkeeper.

St. Lucy: Headcheese; cakes flavored with saffron or cardamom, raisins, and almonds (Sweden). The saffron imparts a yellow color to the cakes, representing sunlight, whose return is celebrated at the solstice.

Christmas: Boar's head or goose, plum pudding, nuts, oranges (England); turkey (United States); spiced beef (Ireland).

St. John the Evangelist: Small loaves of bread made with blessed wine (medieval Europe). This is a feast on which wine is ritually blessed in memory of the saint, who drank poisoned wine and miraculously survived.

Chanukah: Latkes—potato pancakes (Jewish).

Holy Innocents Day: Baby food, pablum, farina, in honor of the children killed by King Herod of Judea (monastic observance).

St. Sylvester: Strong drink (United States); haggis, oatcakes and cheese, oat-husk gruel or porridge (Scotland).

–E. Brady

How to Find the Day of the Week for Any Given Date

To compute the day of the week for any given date as far back as the mid-18th century, proceed as follows:

■ Add the last two digits of the year to one-quarter of the last two digits (discard any remainder if it doesn't come out even), the given date, and the month key from the key box below. Divide the sum by 7; the number left over is the day of the week (1 is Sunday, 2 is Monday, and so on). If it comes out even, the day is Saturday. If you go back before 1900, add 2 to the sum before dividing; before 1800, add 4. Don't go back before 1753. From 2000 to 2099, subtract 1 from the sum before dividing.

Example: **The Dayton Flood was on Tuesday, March 25, 1913.**

Last two digits of year:	13
One-quarter of these two digits:	3
Given day of month:	25
Key number for March:	4
Sum:	45

45 ÷ 7 = 6, with a remainder of 3. The flood took place on Tuesday, the third day of the week.

KEY	
January	1
leap year	0
February...........	4
leap year	3
March	4
April...............	0
May	2
June	5
July	0
August.............	3
September	6
October	1
November...........	4
December	6

Day Names

■ The Romans named the days of the week after the Sun, the Moon, and the five known planets. These names have survived in European languages, but English names also reflect an Anglo-Saxon influence.

LATIN	FRENCH	ITALIAN	SPANISH	SAXON	ENGLISH
Solis (Sun)	dimanche	domenica	domingo	Sun	Sunday
Lunae (Moon)	lundi	lunedì	lunes	Moon	Monday
Martis (Mars)	mardi	martedì	martes	Tiw (the Anglo-Saxon god of war, the equivalent of the Norse Tyr or the Roman Mars)	Tuesday
Mercurii (Mercury)	mercredi	mercoledì	miércoles	Woden (the Anglo-Saxon equivalent of the Norse Odin or the Roman Mercury)	Wednesday
Jovis (Jupiter)	jeudi	giovedì	jueves	Thor (the Norse god of thunder, the equivalent of the Roman Jupiter)	Thursday
Veneris (Venus)	vendredi	venerdì	viernes	Frigg (the Norse god of love and fertility, the equivalent of the Roman Venus)	Friday
Saturni (Saturn)	samedi	sabato	sábado	Saterne (Saturn, the Roman god of agriculture)	Saturday

Chinese Zodiac

■ The animal designations of the Chinese zodiac follow a 12-year cycle and are always used in the same sequence. The Chinese year of 354 days begins three to seven weeks into the western 365-day year, so the animal designation changes at that time, rather than on January 1.

Rat

Ambitious and sincere, you can be generous with your financial resources. Compatible with the dragon and the monkey. Your opposite is the horse.

1900	1960
1912	1972
1924	1984
1936	1996
1948	2008

Rabbit (Hare)

Talented and affectionate, you are a seeker of tranquility. Compatible with the sheep and the pig. Your opposite is the rooster.

1903	1963
1915	1975
1927	1987
1939	1999
1951	2011

Horse

Physically attractive and popular, you like the company of others. Compatible with the tiger and the dog. Your opposite is the rat.

1906	1966
1918	1978
1930	1990
1942	2002
1954	2014

Rooster (Cock)

Seeking wisdom and truth, you have a pioneering spirit. Compatible with the snake and the ox. Your opposite is the rabbit.

1909	1969
1921	1981
1933	1993
1945	2005
1957	2017

Ox (Buffalo)

A leader, you are bright and cheerful. Compatible with the snake and the rooster. Your opposite is the sheep.

1901	1961
1913	1973
1925	1985
1937	1997
1949	2009

Dragon

Robust and passionate, your life is filled with complexity. Compatible with the monkey and the rat. Your opposite is the dog.

1904	1964
1916	1976
1928	1988
1940	2000
1952	2012

Sheep (Goat)

Aesthetic and stylish, you enjoy being a private person. Compatible with the pig and the rabbit. Your opposite is the ox.

1907	1967
1919	1979
1931	1991
1943	2003
1955	2015

Dog

Generous and loyal, you have the ability to work well with others. Compatible with the horse and the tiger. Your opposite is the dragon.

1910	1970
1922	1982
1934	1994
1946	2006
1958	2018

Tiger

Forthright and sensitive, you possess great courage. Compatible with the horse and the dog. Your opposite is the monkey.

1902	1962
1914	1974
1926	1986
1938	1998
1950	2010

Snake

Strong-willed and intense, you display great wisdom. Compatible with the rooster and the ox. Your opposite is the pig.

1905	1965
1917	1977
1929	1989
1941	2001
1953	2013

Monkey

Persuasive and intelligent, you strive to excel. Compatible with the dragon and the rat. Your opposite is the tiger.

1908	1968
1920	1980
1932	1992
1944	2004
1956	2016

Pig (Boar)

Gallant and noble, your friends will remain at your side. Compatible with the rabbit and the sheep. Your opposite is the snake.

1911	1971
1923	1983
1935	1995
1947	2007
1959	2019

Clouds

1. High clouds (bases starting at an average of 20,000 feet)

Cirrus: thin feather-like crystal clouds.

Cirrostratus: thin white clouds that resemble veils.

Cirrocumulus: thin clouds that appear as small "cotton patches."

2. Middle clouds (bases starting at about 10,000 feet)

Altostratus: grayish or bluish layer of clouds that can obscure the Sun.

Altocumulus: gray or white layer or patches of solid clouds with rounded shapes.

3. Low clouds (bases starting near Earth's surface to 6,500 feet)

Stratus: thin, gray sheet-like clouds with low base; may bring drizzle and snow.

Stratocumulus: rounded cloud masses that form on top of a layer.

Nimbostratus: dark, gray shapeless cloud layers containing rain, snow, and ice pellets.

4. Clouds with vertical development (high clouds that form at almost any altitude and that reach up to 14,000 feet)

Cumulus: fair-weather clouds with flat bases and domeshaped tops.

Cumulonimbus: large, dark, vertical clouds with bulging tops that bring showers, thunder, and lightning.

Snowflakes

■ Snowflakes are made up of six-sided crystals. If you look carefully at the snowflakes during the next snowstorm, you might be able to find some of the crystal types below. The temperature at which a crystal forms mainly determines the basic shape. Sometimes a snowflake is a combination of more than one type of crystal.

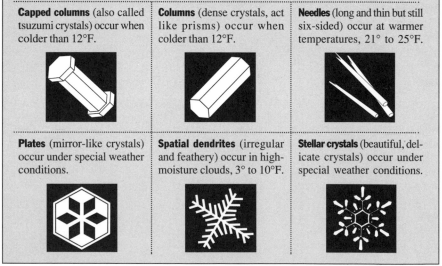

Capped columns (also called tsuzumi crystals) occur when colder than 12°F.	**Columns** (dense crystals, act like prisms) occur when colder than 12°F.	**Needles** (long and thin but still six-sided) occur at warmer temperatures, 21° to 25°F.
Plates (mirror-like crystals) occur under special weather conditions.	**Spatial dendrites** (irregular and feathery) occur in high-moisture clouds, 3° to 10°F.	**Stellar crystals** (beautiful, delicate crystals) occur under special weather conditions.

Windchill Table

■ As wind speed increases, the air temperature against your body falls. The combination of cold temperature and high wind creates a cooling effect so severe that exposed flesh can freeze. (Inanimate objects, such as cars, do not experience windchill.)

To gauge wind speed: At 10 miles per hour, you can feel wind on your face; at 20, small branches move and dust or snow is raised; at 30, large branches move and wires whistle; at 40, whole trees bend. –courtesy Mount Washington Observatory

Wind Velocity (mph)	Temperature (°F)											
	50	41	32	23	14	5	–4	–13	–22	–31	–40	–49	–58
	Equivalent Temperature (°F) (Equivalent in cooling power on exposed flesh under calm conditions)											
5	48	39	28	19	10	1	–9	–18	–27	–36	–51	–56	–65
10	41	30	18	7	–4	–15	–26	–36	–49	–60	–71	–81	–92
20	32	19	7	–6	–18	–31	–44	–58	–71	–83	–96	–108	–121
30	28	14	1	–13	–27	–40	–54	–69	–81	–96	–108	–123	–137
40	27	12	–2	–17	–31	–45	–60	–74	–89	–103	–116	–130	–144
50	25	10	–4	–18	–33	–47	–62	–76	–90	–105	–119	–134	–148
	Little Danger			Increasing Danger			Great Danger					
	Danger from freezing of exposed flesh (for properly clothed person)											

Heat Index

■ As humidity increases, the air temperature feels hotter to your skin. The combination of hot temperature and high humidity reduces your body's ability to cool itself. For example, the heat you feel when the actual temperature is 90°F with a relative humidity of 70 percent is 106°.

Humidity (%)	Temperature (°F)										
	70	75	80	85	90	95	100	105	110	115	120
	Equivalent Temperature (°F)										
0	64	69	73	78	83	87	91	95	99	103	107
10	65	70	75	80	85	90	95	100	105	111	116
20	66	72	77	82	87	93	99	105	112	120	130
30	67	73	78	84	90	96	104	113	123	135	148
40	68	74	79	86	93	101	110	123	137	152	
50	69	75	81	88	96	107	120	135	150		
60	70	76	82	90	100	114	132	149			
70	70	77	85	93	106	124	144				
80	71	78	86	97	113	136					
90	71	79	88	102	122						
100	72	80	91	108							

Is It Raining, Drizzling, or Misting?

	Drops (per sq. ft. per sec.)	Diameter of Drops (mm)	Intensity (in. per hr.)
Cloudburst	113	2.85	4.00
Excessive rain	76	2.40	1.60
Heavy rain	46	2.05	.60
Moderate rain	46	1.60	.15
Light rain	26	1.24	.04
Drizzle	14	.96	.01
Mist	2,510	.10	.002
Fog	6,264,000	.01	.005

A Table Foretelling the Weather Through All the Lunations of Each Year (Forever)

■ This table is the result of many years of actual observation and shows what sort of weather will probably follow the Moon's entrance into any of its quarters. For example, the table shows that the week following February 9, 2001, will have hard frost, unless wind is south or west, because the Moon becomes full that day at 12:24 A.M. EST. (See Left-Hand Calendar Pages 58-84 for 2001 Moon phases.)

Editor's note: Although the data in this table is taken into consideration in the yearlong process of compiling the annual long-range weather forecasts for The Old Farmer's Almanac, we rely far more on our projections of solar activity.

Time of Change	Summer	Winter
Midnight to 2 A.M.	Fair	Hard frost, unless wind is south or west
2 A.M. to 4 A.M.	Cold, with frequent showers	Snow and stormy
4 A.M. to 6 A.M.	Rain	Rain
6 A.M. to 8 A.M.	Wind and rain	Stormy
8 A.M. to 10 A.M.	Changeable	Cold rain if wind is west; snow if east
10 A.M. to noon	Frequent showers	Cold with high winds
Noon to 2 P.M.	Very rainy	Snow or rain
2 P.M. to 4 P.M.	Changeable	Fair and mild
4 P.M. to 6 P.M.	Fair	Fair
6 P.M. to 10 P.M.	Fair if wind is northwest; rain if wind is south or southwest	Fair and frosty if wind is north or northeast; rain or snow if wind is south or southwest
10 P.M. to midnight	Fair	Fair and frosty

This table was created more than 160 years ago by Dr. Herschell for the Boston Courier; *it first appeared in* The Old Farmer's Almanac *in 1834.*

Beaufort Wind Force Scale

"Used Mostly at Sea but of Help to All Who Are Interested in the Weather"

■ A scale of wind velocity was devised by Admiral Sir Francis Beaufort of the British Navy in 1805. The numbers 0 to 12 were arranged by Beaufort to indicate the strength of the wind from a calm, force 0, to a hurricane, force 12. Here's a scale adapted to land.

Beaufort Force	Description	When You See This	mph	km/h
0	Calm	Smoke goes straight up. No wind.	less than 1	less than 2
1	Light air	Direction of wind is shown by smoke drift but not by wind vane.	1-3	2-5
2	Light breeze	Wind felt on face. Leaves rustle. Wind vane moves.	4-7	6-11
3	Gentle breeze	Leaves and small twigs move steadily. Wind extends small flag straight out.	8-12	12-19
4	Moderate breeze	Wind raises dust and loose paper. Small branches move.	13-18	20-29
5	Fresh breeze	Small trees sway. Waves form on lakes.	19-24	30-39
6	Strong breeze	Large branches move. Wires whistle. Umbrellas are hard to use.	25-31	40-50
7	Moderate gale	Whole trees are in motion. Hard to walk against the wind.	32-38	51-61
8	Fresh gale	Twigs break from trees. Very hard to walk against wind.	39-46	62-74
9	Strong gale	Small damage to buildings. Roof shingles are removed.	47-54	75-87
10	Whole gale	Trees are uprooted.	55-63	88-101
11	Violent storm	Widespread damage from wind.	64-72	102-116
12	Hurricane	Widespread destruction from wind.	73+	117+

Atlantic Hurricane Names for 2001

Allison	Erin	Jerry	Noel	Tanya
Barry	Felix	Karen	Olga	Van
Chantal	Gabrielle	Lorenzo	Pablo	Wendy
Dean	Humberto	Michelle	Rebekah	
	Iris		Sebastien	

East-Pacific Hurricane Names for 2001

Adolph	Flossie	Kiko	Priscilla	Wallis
Barbara	Gil	Lorena	Raymond	Xina
Cosme	Henriette	Manuel	Sonia	York
Dalilia	Israel	Narda	Tico	Zelda
Erick	Juliette	Octave	Velma	

Retired Atlantic Hurricane Names

■ These are some of the most destructive and costly storms whose names have been retired from the six-year rotating hurricane list.

Year Retired	Name	Year Retired	Name	Year Retired	Name	Year Retired	Name
1970	Celia	1979	David	1985	Gloria	1990	Klaus
1972	Agnes	1979	Frederic	1988	Gilbert	1991	Bob
1974	Carmen	1980	Allen	1988	Joan	1992	Andrew
1975	Eloise	1983	Alicia	1989	Hugo	1995	Opal
1977	Anita	1985	Elena	1990	Diana	1995	Roxanne

Fujita Scale (or F Scale) for Tornadoes

■ This is a system developed by Dr. Theodore Fujita to classify tornadoes based on wind damage. All tornadoes, and most other severe local windstorms, are assigned a single number from this scale according to the most intense damage caused by the storm.

F0 (weak) . . . . . . 40-72 mph, light damage
F1 (weak). . 73-112 mph, moderate damage
F2 (strong) . . . . 113-157 mph, considerable damage
F3 (strong) . . 158-206 mph, severe damage
F4 (violent). . . . . 207-260 mph, devastating damage
F5 (violent) . . . . 261-318 mph (rare), incredible damage

Richter Scale for Measuring Earthquakes

Magnitude	Possible Effects
1	Detectable only by instruments
2	Barely detectable, even near the epicenter
3	Felt indoors
4	Felt by most people; slight damage
5	Felt by all; damage minor to moderate
6	Moderately destructive
7	Major damage
8	Total and major damage

Devised by American geologist Charles W. Richter in 1935 to measure the magnitude of an earthquake.

Winter Weather Terms

Winter Storm Watch
■ Possibility of a winter storm. Be alert to changing weather conditions. Avoid unnecessary travel.

Winter Storm Warning
■ A severe winter storm has started or is about to begin in the forecast area. You should stay indoors during the storm. If you must go outdoors, wear several layers of lightweight clothing, which will keep you warmer than a single heavy coat. In addition, wear gloves or mittens and a hat to prevent loss of body heat. Cover your mouth to protect your lungs.

Heavy Snow Warning
■ Snow accumulations are expected to approach or exceed six inches in 12 hours but will not be accompanied by significant wind. This warning could also be issued if eight inches or more of snow accumulation is expected in a 24-hour period. During a heavy snow warning, freezing rain and sleet are not expected.

Blizzard Warning
■ Sustained winds or frequent gusts of 35 miles per hour or greater will occur in combination with considerable falling and/or blowing snow for a period of at least three hours. Visibility will often be reduced to less than ¼ mile in a blizzard.

Ice Storm Warning
■ A significant coating of ice, ½ inch thick or more, is expected.

Windchill Warning
■ Windchills reach life-threatening levels of -50°F or lower.

Windchill Advisory
■ Windchill factors fall between -35° and -50°F.

Sleet
■ Frozen or partially frozen rain in the form of ice pellets hit the ground so fast they bounce off with a sharp click.

Freezing Rain
■ Rain falls as a liquid but turns to ice on contact with a frozen surface to form a smooth ice coating called glaze.

Safe Ice Thickness*

Ice Thickness	Permissible Load
2 inches	One person on foot
3 inches	Group in single file
7-1/2 inches	Passenger car (2-ton gross)
8 inches	Light truck (2-1/2-ton gross)
10 inches	Medium truck (3-1/2-ton gross)
12 inches	Heavy truck (8-ton gross)
15 inches	10 tons
20 inches	25 tons
30 inches	70 tons
36 inches	110 tons

*Solid clear blue/black pond and lake ice

■ Slush ice has only half the strength of blue ice.

■ Strength value of river ice is 15 percent less.

Source: American Pulpwood Association

A Beginner Garden

■ A good size for a beginner vegetable garden is 10x16 feet and features crops that are easy to grow. A plot this size, planted as suggested below, can feed a family of four for one summer, with a little extra for canning and freezing (or giving away).

Make your garden 11 rows of ten feet each of the following:

ROW	
1	Zucchini (4 plants)
2	Tomatoes (5 plants, staked)
3	Peppers (6 plants)
4	Cabbage
5	Bush beans
6	Lettuce
7	Beets
8	Carrots
9	Chard
10	Radishes
11	Marigolds (to discourage rabbits!)

Ideally the rows should run north and south to take full advantage of the Sun.

Plants with Interesting Foliage

■ **Airy/fine foliage**
Barrenwort, *Epimedium* spp.
Maidenhair fern, *Adiantum pedatum*
Meadow rue, *Thalictrum* spp.
Silver mound, *Artemisia schmidtiana*

■ **Linear foliage**
Blazing star, *Liatris* spp.
Daylily, *Hemerocallis* spp.
Iris, *Iris* spp.
Yucca, *Yucca* spp.

■ **Textured foliage**
Lamb's-ear, *Stachys byzantina*
Sea holly, *Eryngium* spp.
Silver sage, *Salvia argentea*
Woolly thyme, *Thymus pseudolanuginosus*

■ **Foliage with attractive shapes**
Cranesbill, *Geranium* spp.
Foamflower, *Tiarella cordifolia*
Hybrid lupine, *Lupinus* x *rus selianus*
Lady's-mantle, *Alchemilla vulgaris*

Perennials for Cutting Gardens

Aster *(Aster)*

Baby's-breath *(Gypsophila)*

Bellflower *(Campanula)*

Black-eyed Susan
  (Rudbeckia)

Blanket flower *(Gaillardia)*

Chrysanthemum
  (Chrysanthemum)

Delphinium *(Delphinium)*

False sunflower *(Heliopsis)*

Flowering onion *(Allium)*

Foxglove *(Digitalis)*

Gay-feather *(Liatris)*

Globe thistle *(Echinops)*

Goldenrod *(Solidago)*

Iris *(Iris)*

Lavender *(Lavandula)*

Meadow rue *(Thalictrum)*

Peony *(Paeonia)*

Phlox *(Phlox)*

Purple coneflower
  (Echinacea)

Sea holly *(Eryngium)*

Speedwell *(Veronica)*

Tickseed *(Coreopsis)*

Yarrow *(Achillea)*

Herb Gardening

Name	Height (inches)	Part Used	Name	Height (inches)	Part Used
Anise	18	Seeds	Hyssop	14	Leaves
Basil	20	Leaves	Lemon balm	20	Leaves
Borage	18	Leaves, flowers	Marjoram	18	Leaves
Caraway	18	Seeds	Mint	24	Leaves
Catnip	24	Leaves	Rosemary	18	Leaves
Chamomile	10	Flowers	Sage	16	Leaves
Chevril	15	Leaves	Savory	16	Leaves
Chive	12	Leaves	Tarragon	20	Leaves
Coriander	20	Leaves, seeds	Thyme	7	Leaves
Dill	36	Leaves, seeds			

Herbs to Plant in Lawns

■ Choose plants that suit your soil and your climate. All these can withstand mowing and considerable foot traffic.

- ❀ Ajuga or bugleweed *(Ajuga reptans)*
- ❀ Corsican mint *(Mentha requienii)*
- ❀ Dwarf cinquefoil *(Potentilla tabernaemontani)*
- ❀ English pennyroyal *(Mentha pulegium)*
- ❀ Green Irish moss *(Sagiona subulata)*
- ❀ Pearly everlasting *(Anaphalis margaritacea)*
- ❀ Roman chamomile *(Chamaemelum nobile)*
- ❀ Rupturewort *(Herniaria glabra)*
- ❀ Speedwell *(Veronica officinalis)*
- ❀ Stonecrop *(Sedum ternatum)*
- ❀ Sweet violets *(Viola odorata* or *tricolor)*
- ❀ Thyme *(Thymus serpyllum)*
- ❀ White clover *(Trifolium repens)*
- ❀ Wild strawberries *(Fragaria virginiana)*
- ❀ Wintergreen or partridgeberry *(Mitchella repens)*

Herbs That Attract Butterflies

Catmint	*Nepeta*
Creeping thyme	*Thymus serpyllum*
Dill	*Anethum graveolens*
Mealy-cup sage	*Salvia farinacea*
Mint	*Mentha*
Oregano	*Origanum vulgare*
Parsley	*Petroselinum crispum*
Sweet marjoram	*Origanum majorana*

Heat-Loving Wildflowers

Bee balm *(Monarda)*

Black-eyed Susan *(Rudbeckia)*

Blazing star *(Liatris)*

Butterfly weed *(Asclepias tuberosa)*

Four-o'clock *(Mirabilis)*

Prairie coneflower *(Ratibida pinnata)*

Purple coneflower *(Echinacea purpurea)*

Wild indigo *(Baptisia)*

Flowers That Attract Butterflies

Allium . . . . *Allium*	Helen's flower . . *Helenium*	Purple coneflower
Aster . . . . *Aster*	Hollyhock . . . . *Alcea*	. . . . *Echinacea purpurea*
Bee balm . . . . . . *Monarda*	Honeysuckle . . . . *Lonicera*	Purple loosestrife . . *Lythrum*
Butterfly bush . . . *Buddleia*	Lavender . . . . . *Lavendula*	Rock cress . . . . *Arabis*
Clove pink . . . . . *Dianthus*	Lilac . . . . *Syringa*	Sea holly . . . . *Eryngium*
Cornflower . . . . *Centaurea*	Lupine . . . . *Lupinus*	Shasta daisy *Chrysanthemum*
Daylily . . . . *Hemerocallis*	Lychnis . . . . *Lychnis*	Snapdragon . . *Antirrhinum*
False indigo . . . . . *Baptisia*	Mallow . . . . *Malva*	Stonecrop . . . . *Sedum*
Fleabane . . . . *Erigeron*	Milkweed . . . . . *Asclepias*	Sweet alyssum . . *Lobularia*
Floss flower . . . *Ageratum*	Pansy . . . . *Viola*	Sweet rocket . . . . . *Hesperis*
Globe thistle . . . . *Echinops*	Phlox . . . . *Phlox*	Tickseed . . . . *Coreopsis*
Goldenrod . . . . . . *Solidago*	Privet . . . . *Ligustrum*	Zinnia . . . . *Zinnia*

Flowers That Attract Hummingbirds

Beard tongue . . . . *Penstemon*	Lily . . . . *Lilium*
Bee balm . . . . *Monarda*	Lupine . . . . *Lupinus*
Butterfly bush . . . . *Buddleia*	Petunia . . . . *Petunia*
Catmint . . . . *Nepeta*	Pincushion flower . . . . *Scabiosa*
Clove pink . . . . *Dianthus*	Red-hot poker . . . . *Kniphofia*
Columbine . . . . *Aquilegia*	Scarlet sage . . . . *Salvia splendens*
Coral bells . . . . *Heuchera*	Soapwort . . . . *Saponaria*
Daylily . . . . *Hemerocallis*	Summer phlox . . . . *Phlox paniculata*
Desert candle . . . . *Yucca*	Trumpet honeysuckle . . . . *Lonicera*
Flag . . . . *Iris*	*sempervirens*
Flowering tobacco . . . . . . *Nicotiana alata*	Verbena . . . . *Verbena*
Foxglove . . . . *Digitalis*	Weigela . . . . *Weigela*
Larkspur . . . . *Delphinium*	**Note: Choose varieties in red and orange shades.**

Forcing Blooms Indoors

■ Here is a list of some shrubs and trees that can be forced to flower indoors. (The trees tend to be stubborn and their blossoms may not be as rewarding as those of the shrubs.) The numbers indicate the approximate number of weeks they will take to flower.

Buckeye 5	Flowering quince 4	Red maple 2
Cherry 4	Forsythia 1	Redbud 2
Cornelian dogwood 2	Honeysuckle 3	Red-twig dogwood 5
Crab apple 4	Horse chestnut 5	Spicebush 2
Deutzia 3	Lilac 4	Spirea 4
Flowering almond 3	Magnolia 3	Wisteria 3
Flowering dogwood 5	Pussy willow 2	Source: Purdue University Cooperative Extension Service

Fall-Planted Bulbs

	Planting Depth (inches)	Spacing (inches)	Flower Height (inches)
Early-Spring Blooms			
Crocus	3	2-3	4-6
Glory-of-the-snow	3	2-3	6-10
Grape hyacinth	3-4	3	8-10
Snowdrop	4	2-3	6
Mid-Spring Blooms			
Daffodil	7	3-4	6-18
Squill	2	4-6	8
Tulip	8	3-6	6-28
Windflower	2	3-4	3-18
Late-Spring Blooms			
Dutch iris	4	3-6	15-24
Hyacinth	6	6-8	4-12
Ornamental onion	6	4-6	6-24
Spanish bluebell	3	3-6	15-20

Spring-Planted Bulbs

	Planting Depth (inches)	Spacing (inches)	Flower Height (inches)
Summer Blooms			
Begonia	2	12	8-18
Blazing star	3-4	6	18
Caladium	2	8-12	12-24
Canna lily	5	16	18-72
Dahlia	4-6	16	12-60
Freesia	2	2-4	12-24
Gladiolus	5	4	24-34
Gloxinia	4	15	12-24
Lily	6-8	12	24-72

Forcing Bulbs Indoors

■ The technique is simple. Plant bulbs in pots of rich soil so tips are just even with pot rims. Store in a cold frame, cellar, or refrigerator at a cold temperature for two to several months. Water bulbs just enough to keep them from drying out. When roots can be seen poking out through bottoms of pots, bring them into a lighted room to flower.

The table below shows estimated times for rooting and ideal temperatures for flowering for some of the most common spring bulbs.

Name of Bulb	Time for Rooting	Temperature for Flowering
Crocus *(Crocus)*	8-12 weeks	55-60°F
Daffodil *(Narcissus)*	10-12 weeks	50-60°F
Freesia *(Freesia)*	8-12 weeks	50-55°F
Glory-of-the-snow *(Chionodoxa)*	10-14 weeks	55-60°F
Grape hyacinth *(Muscari)*	10-12 weeks	55-60°F
Hyacinth *(Hyacinthus)*	8-10 weeks	55-60°F
Lily-of-the-valley *(Convallaria)*	10-12 weeks	60-65°F
Netted iris *(Iris reticulata)*	10-14 weeks	55-60°F
Snowdrop *(Galanthus)*	9-12 weeks	55-60°F
Squill *(Scilla)*	12-16 weeks	55-60°F
Striped squill *(Puschkinia)*	8-12 weeks	50-55°F
Tulip *(Tulipa)*	12-16 weeks	55-60°F

Planning Your Garden

Sow or plant in cool weather	Beets/chard, broccoli, Brussels sprouts, cabbage, lettuce, onions, parsley, peas, radishes, spinach, turnips
Sow or plant in warm weather	Beans, carrots, corn, cucumbers, eggplant, melons, okra, peppers, squash, tomatoes
One crop per season	Corn, eggplant, leeks, melons, peppers, potatoes, spinach (New Zealand), squash, tomatoes
Resow for additional crops	Beans, beets, cabbage family, carrots, kohlrabi, lettuce, radishes, rutabagas, spinach, turnips

Vegetable Seeds Best Sown in the Ground

Beans, bush and pole
Beets
Carrots
Collards
Corn
Cucumbers
Endive
Kale
Kohlrabi
Mustard greens
Parsnips
Peas
Potatoes
Radishes
Spinach
Squash, summer and
    winter
Swiss chard
Turnips

Vegetables and Herbs Best Started Indoors

Seeds	Weeks Before Last Frost in Spring
Basil	6
Broccoli	6-8
Brussels sprouts	4-8
Cabbage	6-8
Cauliflower	6-8
Celeriac	6-8
Celery	6-8
Chives	8-12
Eggplant	8-10
Leeks	8-12
Lettuce	4-6
Onions	10-12
Parsley	8
Peppers	8-10
Sweet marjoram	8
Tomatoes	6-8

Minimum Soil Temperature for Seeds to Germinate

Vegetable	Minimum Soil Temperature (°F)
Beans	48-50
Beets	39-41
Cabbage	38-40
Carrots	39-41
Corn	46-50
Melons	55-60
Onions	34-36
Peas	34-36
Radishes	39-41
Squash	55-60
Tomatoes	50-55

The Healthiest Vegetables

■ These results come from adding up the percent of the USRDA for six nutrients (vitamin A, vitamin C, folate, iron, copper, calcium) plus fiber for each vegetable.

1	Sweet potatoes	6	Kale
2	Carrots	7	Dandelion greens
3	Spinach	8	Broccoli
4	Collard greens	9	Brussels sprouts
5	Red peppers	10	Potatoes

Critical Low Temperatures for Frost Damage to Vegetables

Vegetable	Temperature (°F)
Artichokes	31-32
Asparagus	30-31
Beans	31-32
Beets (roots)	29-30
Beets (tops)	31-32
Broccoli	29-30
Cabbage	26-28
Carrots	28-30
Cauliflower	27-29
Celery	31-32
Cucumbers	30-32
Kale	27-29
Muskmelon	33-34
Okra	29-30
Peas	28-30
Potato tubers	28-30
Pumpkins	31-32
Radishes	30-32
Spinach	30-32
Squash (summer)	31-33
Squash (winter)	30-32
Sweet corn	32-33
Sweet potatoes	32-33
Tomatoes	32-34
Watermelon	32-33

When Is a Good Time to Fertilize Your Vegetables?

Crop	Time of Application
Asparagus	Before growth starts in spring.
Beans	After heavy blossom and set of pods.
Broccoli	Three weeks after transplanting.
Cabbage	Three weeks after transplanting.
Cauliflower	Three weeks after transplanting.
Corn	When eight to ten inches tall and again when silk first appears.
Cucumbers	One week after blossoming and again three weeks later.
Eggplant	After first fruit-set.
Kale	When plants are one-third grown.
Lettuce, head	Two to three weeks after transplanting.
Muskmelon	One week after blossoming and again three weeks later.
Onions	When bulbs begin to swell and again when plants are one foot tall.
Peas	After heavy bloom and set of pods.
Peppers	After first fruit-set.
Potatoes	At blossom time or time of second hilling.
Spinach	When plants are one-third grown.
Squash	Just before vines start to run, when plants are about one foot tall.
Tomatoes	One to two weeks before first picking and again two weeks after first picking.
Watermelon	Just before vines start to run, when plants are about one foot tall.

Fertilizer Formulas

■ Fertilizers are labeled to show the percentages by weight of nitrogen (N), phosphorus (P), and potassium (K). Nitrogen is needed for leaf growth. Phosphorus is associated with root growth and fruit production. Potassium helps the plant fight off diseases. A 100-pound bag of 10-5-10 contains 10 pounds of nitrogen, 5 pounds of phosphorus, and 10 pounds of potassium. The rest is filler.

Lawn Fertilizing Tips

■ Test your soil: The pH balance should be 7.0 or more—6.2 to 6.7 puts your lawn at risk for fungal diseases. If the pH is too low, correct it with liming, best done in the fall.

■ Control weeds by promoting healthy lawn growth with natural fertilizers in spring and early fall.

■ If you put lime and fertilizer on your lawn, spread half of it as you walk north to south, the other half as you walk east to west to cut down on missed areas.

General Rules for Pruning

What	When	How
Apple	Early spring	Prune moderately. Keep tree open with main branches well spaced. Avoid sharp V-shaped crotches.
Cherry	Early spring	Prune the most vigorous shoots moderately.
Clematis	Spring	Cut weak growth. Save as much old wood as possible.
Flowering dogwood	After flowering	Remove dead wood only.
Forsythia	After flowering	Remove old branches at ground. Trim new growth.
Lilac	After flowering	Remove diseased, scaly growth, flower heads, and suckers.
Peach	Early spring	Remove half of last year's growth. Keep tree headed low.
Plum	Early spring	Cut dead, diseased branches; trim rank growth moderately.
Rhododendron	After flowering	Prune judiciously. Snip branches from weak, leggy plants to induce growth from roots.
Rose (except climbers)	Spring, after frosts	Cut dead and weak growth; cut branches or canes to four or five eyes.
Rose (climbers)	After flowering	Cut half of old growth; retain new shoots for next year.
Rose of Sharon	When buds begin	Cut all winter-killed wood to swell growth back to live wood.
Trumpet vine	Early spring	Prune side branches severely to main stem.
Virginia creeper	Spring	Clip young plants freely. Thin old plants and remove dead growth.
Wisteria	Spring, summer	Cut new growth to spurs at axils of leaves.

Soil Fixes

■ **CLAY SOIL:** Add coarse sand (not beach sand) and compost.

■ **SILT SOIL:** Add coarse sand (not beach sand) or gravel and compost, or well-rotted horse manure mixed with fresh straw.

■ **SANDY SOIL:** Add humus or aged manure, or sawdust with some extra nitrogen. Heavy, clay-rich soil can also be added to improve the soil.

Soil Amendments

■ **Bark, ground:** Made from various tree barks. Improves soil structure.

■ **Compost:** Excellent conditioner.

■ **Leaf mold:** Decomposed leaves that add nutrients and structure to soil.

■ **Lime:** Raises the pH of acid soil and helps loosen clay soil.

■ **Manure:** Best if composted. Good conditioner.

■ **Sand:** Improves drainage in clay soil.

■ **Topsoil:** Usually used with another amendment. Replaces existing soil.

Lawn Tips

■ Moss and sorrel in lawns usually means poor soil, poor aeration or drainage, or excessive acidity.

■ During a drought, let the grass grow longer between mowings, and reduce fertilizer.

■ Raise the level of your lawn-mower blades during the hot summer days. Taller grass better resists drought.

■ Water your lawn early in the morning or in the evening.

■ The best time to apply fertilizer is just before it rains.

■ You can reduce mowing time by redesigning your lawn, reducing sharp corners and adding sweeping curves.

■ Any feeding of lawns in the fall should be done with a low-nitrogen, slow-acting fertilizer.

■ In areas of your lawn where tree roots compete with the grass, apply some extra fertilizer to benefit both.

Vegetable Gardening in Containers

■ Lack of yard space is no excuse for not gardening, because many vegetables can be readily grown in containers. In addition to providing five hours or more of full sun, attention must be given to choosing the proper container, using a good soil mix, planting and spacing requirements, fertilizing, watering, and variety selection.

Vegetable	Type of Container	Recommended Varieties
Beans, snap	5-gallon window box	Bush 'Romano', Bush 'Blue Lake', 'Tender Crop'
Broccoli	1 plant/5-gallon pot; 3 plants/15-gallon tub	'Green Comet', 'DeCicco'
Carrots	5-gallon window box at least 12 inches deep	'Short 'n Sweet', 'Danvers Half Long', 'Tiny Sweet'
Cucumbers	1 plant/1-gallon pot	'Patio Pik', 'Spacemaster', 'Pot Luck'
Eggplant	5-gallon pot	'Slim Jim', 'Ichiban', 'Black Beauty'
Lettuce	5-gallon window box	'Salad Bowl', 'Ruby'
Onions	5-gallon window box	'White Sweet Spanish', 'Yellow Sweet Spanish'
Peppers	1 plant/2-gallon pot; 5 plants/15-gallon tub	'Sweet Banana', 'Yolo', 'Wonder', 'Long Red', 'Cayenne'
Radishes	5-gallon window box	'Cherry Belle', 'Icicle'
Tomatoes	Bushel basket	'Tiny Tim', 'Small Fry', 'Early Girl', 'Sweet 100', 'Patio'

–courtesy North Carolina Cooperative Extension Service

Fall Palette

TREE	COLOR
Sugar maple and sumac	Flame red and orange
Red maple, dogwood, sassafras, and scarlet oak	Dark red
Poplar, birch, tulip tree, willow	Yellow
Ash	Plum purple
Oak, beech, larch, elm, hickory, and sycamore	Tan or brown
Locust	Stays green (until leaves drop)
Black walnut and butternut	Drops leaves before turning color

Weed Combat

USE MULCH. Reduce weed growth in your garden by covering the soil between plants and along rows with mulch, a covering that blocks daylight and inhibits growth under it.

SAVE THOSE YOUNG PLANTS. It's critical to keep weeds away from newly emerging seedlings. Keep your crops weed-free for the first four weeks of their life.

CLOSE RANKS. If your soil is rich and well tilled, plant your crops closer together than is commonly recommended to further cut down on weed growth.

CUT THEM OFF AT THE PASS. Another method is to encourage weeds to grow—and remove them from the soil before you plant your garden.

OFF WITH THEIR HEADS! Use a grass whip or string trimmer and cut off their heads before they flower.

TRIM THE EDGES. Keep the edges of your property mowed to cut down on invasions of weeds into your fertile garden soil.

Buckhorn plantain
Stem length: 4 to 12 inches. Treatment: Hand-weed and destroy.

Pepperweed
Stem length: 6 to 8 inches. Treatment: Pull out before it seeds.

Bull thistle
Stem length: 2 to 5 feet. Treatment: Pull or cultivate out before it seeds.

Purslane
Stem length: 2 to 12 inches. Treatment: Pull out and destroy.

Common burdock
Stem length: 2 to 6 feet. Treatment: Pull out before it seeds.

Quackgrass
Stem length: 1 to 3 feet. Treatment: Dig out.

Field bindweed, or wild morning glory
Stem length: 1 to 4 feet. Treatment: Dig out before it flowers.

Redroot pigweed
Stem length: 1 to 6 feet. Treatment: Pull out before it flowers.

Lamb's-quarter
Stem length: 1 to 6 feet. Treatment: Cultivate out.

Stinging nettle
Stem length: 3 to 6 feet. Treatment: Pull out with gloved hands.

Large crabgrass
Stem length: 8 inches to 3 feet. Treatment: Pull or cultivate out before it seeds.

How Much Water Is Enough?

■ When confronted with a dry garden and the end of a hose, many gardeners admit to a certain insecurity about just how much water those plants really need. Here's a guide to help you estimate when and how much to water, assuming rich, well-balanced soil. Increase frequency during hot, dry periods.

Vegetable	Critical time(s) to water for a 5-foot row
● **Beans**	When flowers form and during pod-forming and picking.
■ **Beets**	Before soil gets bone-dry.
■ **Broccoli**	Don't let soil dry out for 4 weeks after transplanting.
■ **Brussels sprouts**	Don't let soil dry out for 4 weeks after transplanting.
▲ **Cabbage**	Water frequently in dry weather for best crop.
■ **Carrots**	Before soil gets bone-dry.
▲ **Cauliflower**	Water frequently for best crop.
▲ **Celery**	Water frequently for best crop.
● **Corn**	When tassels form and when cobs swell.
▲ **Cucumbers**	Water frequently for best crop.
▲ **Lettuce/ Spinach**	Water frequently for best crop.
■ **Onions**	In dry weather, water in early stage to get plants going.
■ **Parsnips**	Before soil gets bone-dry.
● **Peas**	When flowers form and during pod-forming and picking.
● **Potatoes**	When the size of marbles.
▲ **Squash (all types)**	Water frequently for best crop.
● **Tomatoes**	For 3 to 4 weeks after transplanting and when flowers and fruit form.

▲ Needs a lot of water during dry spells. ● Needs water at critical stages of development.

Number of gallons of water needed	Comments
2 per week depending on rainfall	Dry soil when pods are forming will adversely affect quantity and quality.
1 at early stage; 2 every 2 weeks	Water sparingly during early stages to prevent foliage from becoming too lush at the expense of the roots; increase water when round roots form.
1 to 1-1/2 per week	Best crop will result with no water shortage.
1 to 1-1/2 per week	Plants can endure dry conditions once they are established. Give 2 gallons the last 2 weeks before harvest for most succulent crop.
2 per week	If crop suffers some dry weather, focus efforts on providing 2 gallons 2 weeks before harvest. (Too much water will cause heads to crack.)
1 at early stage; 2 every 2 weeks as roots mature	Roots may split if crop is watered after soil has become too dry.
2 per week	Give 2 gallons before harvest for best crop.
2 per week	If conditions are very dry, water daily.
2 at important stages (left)	Cob size will be smaller if plants do not receive water when ears are forming.
1 per week	Water diligently when fruits form and throughout growth; give highest watering priority.
2 per week	Best crop will result with no water shortage.
1/2 to 1 per week if soil is very dry	Withhold water from bulb onions at later growth stages to improve storage qualities; water salad onions anytime soil is very dry.
1 per week in early stages	Water when dry to keep plants growing steadily. Too much water will encourage lush foliage and small roots.
2 per week	To reduce excess foliage and stem growth, do not water young seedlings unless wilting.
2 per week	In dry weather, give 2 gallons throughout the growing season every 10 days. Swings from very dry to very wet produce oddly shaped and cracked tubers.
1 per week	Water diligently when fruits form and throughout their growth; give highest watering priority.
1 twice a week or more	Frequent watering may increase yield but adversely affect flavor.

■ Does not need frequent watering.

References and Resources

Bulbs

American Daffodil Society
4126 Winfield Rd.
Columbus, OH 43220-4606
www.mc.edu/~adswww

Netherlands Flower Bulb
Information Center
30 Midwood St.
Brooklyn, NY 11225
718-693-5400
www.bulb.com

Ferns

American Fern Society
326 West St. NW
Vienna, VA 22180-4151
www.visuallink.net/fern/
index.html

The Hardy Fern Foundation
P.O. Box 166
Medina, WA 98036-0166
http://darkwing.uoregon.edu/
~sueman

Flowers

Hardy Plant Society
Mid-Atlantic Group
801 Concord Rd.
Glen Mills, PA 19342

National Wildflower Research
Center
4801 La Crosse Ave.
Austin, TX 78739
512-292-4200
www.wildflower.org

Perennial Plant Association
3383 Schirtzinger Rd.
Hilliard, OH 43026
614-771-8431

Fruits

California Rare Fruit Growers
The Fullerton Arboretum-CSUF
P.O. Box 6850
Fullerton, CA 92834-6850
www.crfg.org

Home Orchard Society
P.O. Box 230192
Tigard, OR 97281-0192

North American Fruit Explorers
1716 Apples Rd.
Chapin, IL 62628
www.nafex.org

Herbs

American Herb Association
Kathi Keville, Editor
P.O. Box 1673
Nevada City, CA 95959-1673
530-265-9552; fax 530-274-3140

The Flower and Herb Exchange
3076 North Winn Rd.
Decorah, IA 52101
319-382-5990

Herb Research Foundation
1007 Pearl St., Ste. 200
Boulder, CO 80302
303-449-2265; 800-748-2617
www.herbs.org

Herb Society of America
9019 Kirtland Chardon Rd.
Kirtland, OH 44094
440-256-0514
www.herbsociety.org

Vegetables

The Cook's Garden
P.O. Box 535
Londonderry, VT 05148
802-824-3027; 800-457-9703
www.cooksgarden.com

National Hot Pepper Association
Betty Payton
400 Northwest 20th St.
Ft. Lauderdale, FL 33311-3818
954-565-4972
http://inter-linked.com/org/nhpa

Seeds of Change
P.O. Box 15700
Santa Fe, NM 87506-5700
888-762-7333
www.seedsofchange.com

Shepherd's Garden Seeds
30 Irene St.
Torrington, CT 06790-6658
860-482-3638
www.shepherdseeds.com

Tomato Growers Supply
Company
P.O. Box 2237
Fort Myers, FL 33902
888-478-7333
www.tomatogrowers.com

Miscellaneous

Biological Urban Gardening
Services (BUGS)
Steven Zien, Executive Director
P.O. Box 76
Citrus Heights, CA 95611-0076
916-726-5377
Organization devoted to reducing
the use of pesticides, particu-
larly in urban landscape
environments.

Internet Gardening Links:
http://learning.lib.vt.edu/
garden.html

The Lawn Institute:
www.lawninstitute.com

Lists of Gardening Catalogs:
http://pbmfaq.dvol.com/list
www.cog.brown.edu/gardening

The Official Seedstarting Home
Page:
www.chestnutsw.com/seedhp.htm

The U.S. National Arboretum
"Web Version" of the USDA
Plant Hardiness Zone Map:
www.ars-grin.gov/ars/Beltsville/
na/hardzone/ushzmap.html?

Water-Wise Gardening:
www.ebmud.com/watercon/
garden.htm

Cooperative Extension Services

Alabama
www.acenet.auburn.edu

Alaska
http://zorba.uafadm.alaska
.edu/coop-ext/index.html

Arizona
http://ag.arizona.edu/
extension

Arkansas
www.uaex.edu

California
www.ucce-north.ucdavis.edu
www.uckac.edu/danrscr

Colorado
www.arapcsuext.org/horti/
indxhort.html

Connecticut
www.lib.uconn.edu/canr/ces/
index.html

Delaware
http://bluehen.ags.udel.edu/
deces

Florida
www.ifas.ufl.edu/www/
agator/htm/ces.htm

Georgia
www.ces.uga.edu

Hawaii
www.ctahr.hawaii.edu

Idaho
www.uidaho.edu/ag/
extension

Illinois
www.ag.uiuc.edu/~robsond/
solutions/hort.html

Indiana
http://info.aes.purdue.edu/
agresearch/agreswww.html

Iowa
www.exnet.iastate.edu

Kansas
www.oznet.ksu.edu

Kentucky
www.ca.uky.edu

Louisiana
www.agctr.lsu.edu/wwwac/
lces.html

Maine
www.umext.maine.edu

Maryland
www.agnr.umd.edu/ces

Massachusetts
www.umass.edu/umext

Michigan
www.msue.msu.edu/msue

Minnesota
www.mes.umn.edu

Mississippi
http://ext.msstate.edu

Missouri
http://extension.missouri.edu

Montana
http://extn.msu.montana.edu

Nebraska
www.ianr.unl.edu/ianr/
coopext/coopext.htm

Nevada
www.nce.unr.edu/nce/
extnhome.htm

New Hampshire
http://ceinfo.unh.edu

New Jersey
www.rce.rutgers.edu

New Mexico
www.cahe.nmsu.edu/ces

New York
www.cce.cornell.edu

North Carolina
www.ces.ncsu.edu

North Dakota
www.ext.nodak.edu

Ohio
www.ag.ohio-state.edu

Oklahoma
www.okstate.edu/OSU_Ag/
oces

Oregon
http://wwwagcomm.ads.orst
.edu/AgComWebFile/
extser/index.html

Pennsylvania
www.cas.psu.edu/docs/coext/
coopext.html

Rhode Island
www.edc.uri.edu

South Carolina
http://virtual.clemson.edu/
groups/extension

South Dakota
www.abs.sdstate.edu/ces

Tennessee
www.utextension.utk.edu

Texas
http://agextension.tamu.edu

Utah
http://ext.usu.edu

Vermont
http://ctr.uvm.edu/ext

Virginia
www.ext.vt.edu

Washington
http://gardening.wsu.edu
http://gardening.wsu.edu/
eastside

West Virginia
www.wvu.edu/~exten

Wisconsin
www.uwex.edu/ces

Wyoming
www.uwyo.edu/ag/ces/
ceshome.htm

Table of Measures

Apothecaries'

1 scruple = 20 grains
1 dram = 3 scruples
1 ounce = 8 drams
1 pound = 12 ounces

Avoirdupois

1 ounce = 16 drams
1 pound = 16 ounces
1 hundredweight = 100
    pounds
1 ton = 2,000 pounds
1 long ton = 2,240 pounds

Cubic Measure

1 cubic foot = 1,728 cubic
    inches
1 cubic yard = 27 cubic feet
1 cord = 128 cubic feet
1 U.S. liquid gallon = 4
    quarts = 231 cubic inches
1 Imperial gallon = 1.20 U.S.
    gallons = 0.16 cubic feet
1 board foot = 144 cubic
    inches

Dry Measure

2 pints = 1 quart
4 quarts = 1 gallon
2 gallons = 1 peck
4 pecks = 1 bushel

Liquid Measure

4 gills = 1 pint
2 pints = 1 quart
4 quarts = 1 gallon
63 gallons = 1 hogshead
2 hogsheads = 1 pipe or butt
2 pipes = 1 tun

Linear Measure

1 foot = 12 inches
1 yard = 3 feet
1 rod = 5½ yards
1 mile = 320 rods = 1,760
    yards = 5,280 feet
1 Int. nautical mile =
    6,076.1155 feet
1 knot = 1 nautical mile
    per hour

1 furlong = ⅛ mile = 660 feet
    = 220 yards
1 league = 3 miles = 24
    furlongs
1 fathom = 2 yards = 6 feet
1 chain = 100 links = 22 yards
1 link = 7.92 inches
1 hand = 4 inches
1 span = 9 inches

Square Measure

1 square foot = 144 square
    inches
1 square yard = 9 square feet
1 square rod = 30¼ square
    yards = 272¼ square feet
1 acre = 160 square rods =
    43,560 square feet
1 square mile = 640 acres
    = 102,400 square rods
1 square rod = 625 square
    links
1 square chain = 16 square
    rods
1 acre = 10 square chains

Household Measures

120 drops of water = 1
    teaspoon
60 drops thick fluid = 1
    teaspoon
2 teaspoons = 1 dessertspoon
3 teaspoons = 1 tablespoon
16 tablespoons = 1 cup
1 cup = 8 ounces
2 cups = 1 pint
2 pints = 1 quart
4 quarts = 1 gallon
3 tablespoons flour = 1 ounce
2 tablespoons butter = 1 ounce
2 cups granulated sugar =
    1 pound

3¾ cups confectioners' sugar
    = 1 pound
3½ cups wheat flour = 1
    pound
5⅓ cups dry coffee = 1 pound
6½ cups dry tea = 1 pound
2 cups shortening = 1 pound
1 stick butter = ½ cup
2 cups cornmeal = 1 pound
2¾ cups brown sugar = 1
    pound
2⅜ cups raisins = 1 pound
9 eggs = 1 pound
1 ounce yeast = 1 scant
    tablespoon

Metric

1 inch = 2.54 centimeters
1 centimeter = 0.39 inch
1 meter = 39.37 inches
1 yard = 0.914 meters
1 mile = 1,609.344 meters
    = 1.61 kilometers
1 kilometer = .62 mile
1 square inch = 6.45 square
    centimeters
1 square yard = 0.84 square
    meter
1 square mile = 2.59 square
    kilometers
1 square kilometer = 0.386
    square mile
1 acre = 0.40 hectare
1 hectare = 2.47 acres
1 cubic yard = 0.76 cubic
    meter
1 cubic meter = 1.31 cubic
    yards
1 liter = 1.057 U.S. liquid
    quarts
1 U.S. liquid quart = 0.946
    liter
1 U.S. liquid gallon = 3.78
    liters
1 gram = 0.035 ounce
1 ounce = 28.349 grams
1 kilogram = 2.2 pounds
1 pound avoirdupois = 0.45
    kilogram

Proper Canning Practices

- Carefully select and wash fresh food.
- Peel some fresh foods.
- Hot-pack many foods.
- Add acids (lemon juice or vinegar) to some foods.

- Use acceptable jars and self-sealing lids.
- Process jars in a boiling-water or pressure canner for the correct amount of time.

Quantities Needed per Quart Canned

	Quantity per Quart Canned (pounds)
Fruits	
Apples	2½ to 3
Blackberries	1½ to 3½
Blueberries	1½ to 3
Cherries	2 to 2½
Grapes	4
Peaches	2 to 3

	Quantity per Quart Canned (pounds)
Pears	2 to 3
Raspberries	1½ to 3
Strawberries	1½ to 3
Vegetables	
Asparagus	2½ to 4½
Beans	1½ to 2½
Beets	2 to 3½

	Quantity per Quart Canned (pounds)
Cauliflower	3
Corn	3 to 6
Peas	3 to 6
Peppers	3
Spinach	2 to 3
Tomatoes	2½ to 3½

How to Order Two Bun Halves Filled with Cheese, Meat, Onions, Peppers, and Other Stuff

Place	Name	Place	Name
Norfolk, VA	Submarine	Norristown, PA	Zeppelin
Akron, OH	"	Mobile, AL	Poor boy
Jacksonville, FL	"	Sacramento, CA	"
Los Angeles, CA	"	Houston, TX	"
Philadelphia, PA	Hoagie	Montgomery, AL	"
Ann Arbor, MI	"	New Orleans, LA	Poor boy or musalatta
Knoxville, TN	"	Gary, IN	Submarine or torpedo
Newark, NJ	"	Allentown, PA	Hoagie or Italian sandwich
Providence, RI	"	Cheyenne, WY	Hoagie, submarine, or rocket
Des Moines, IA	Grinder	Cincinnati, OH	Hoagie, submarine, or rocket
Hartford, CT	"	Buffalo, NY	Hoagie, submarine, or bomber
Chester, PA	"	Dublin, NH	Two bun halves filled with cheese, meat, onions, peppers, and other stuff
Cleveland, OH	"		
Madison, WI	Garibaldi		

Pan Sizes and Equivalents

■ In the midst of cooking but without the right pan? You can substitute one size for another, keeping in mind that when you change the pan size, you must sometimes change the cooking time. For example, if a recipe calls for using an 8-inch round cake pan and baking for 25 minutes, and you substitute a 9-inch pan, the cake may bake in only 20 minutes, because the batter forms a thinner layer in the larger pan. (Use a toothpick inserted into the center of the cake to test for doneness. If it comes out clean, the cake has finished baking.) Also, specialty pans such as tube and Bundt pans distribute heat differently; you may not get the same results if you substitute a regular cake pan for a specialty one, even if the volume is the same.

Pan Size	Volume	Substitute
9-inch pie pan	4 cups	■ 8-inch round cake pan
8x4x2-1/2-inch loaf pan	6 cups	■ Three 5x2-inch loaf pans ■ Two 3x1-1/4-inch muffin tins ■ 12x8x2-inch cake pan
9x5x3-inch loaf pan	8 cups	■ 8x8-inch cake pan ■ 9-inch round cake pan
15x10x1-inch jelly roll pan	10 cups	■ 9x9-inch cake pan ■ Two 8-inch round cake pans ■ 8x3-inch springform pan
10x3-inch Bundt pan	12 cups	■ Two 8x4x2-1/2-inch loaf pans ■ 9x3-inch angel food cake pan ■ 9x3-inch springform pan
13x9x2-inch cake pan	14-15 cups	■ Two 9-inch round cake pans ■ Two 8x8-inch cake pans

■ If you are cooking a casserole and don't have the correct size dish, here are some baking-pan substitutions. Again, think about the depth of the ingredients in the dish and lengthen or shorten the baking time accordingly.

CASSEROLE SIZE	BAKING-PAN SUBSTITUTE
1-1/2 quarts	9x5x3-inch loaf pan
2 quarts	8x8-inch cake pan
2-1/2 quarts	9x9-inch cake pan
3 quarts	13x9x2-inch cake pan
4 quarts	14x10x2-inch cake pan

Food for Thought

Food	Calories
Piece of pecan pie	580
Grilled cheese sandwich	440
Chocolate shake	364
Bagel with cream cheese	361
20 potato chips	228
10 french fries	214
Half a cantaloupe	94
Corn on the cob (no butter)	70
Carrot	30

Don't Freeze These

Bananas
Canned hams
Cooked eggs
Cooked potatoes
Cream fillings and puddings
Custards
Fried foods
Gelatin dishes
Mayonnaise
Raw vegetables, such as cabbage, celery, green onions, radishes, and salad greens
Soft cheeses, cottage cheese
Sour cream
Yogurt

Appetizing Amounts

Occasion	Number of Bites per Person
Hors d'oeuvres (with meal following)	4
Cocktail party	10
Grand affair, no dinner following (e.g., wedding reception)	10-15

The Party Planner

How much do you need when you're cooking for a crowd?

■ If you're planning a big meal, these estimates can help you determine how much food you should buy. They're based on "average" servings; adjust quantities upward for extra-big eaters and downward if children are included.

Food	To Serve 25	To Serve 50	To Serve 100
MEATS			
Chicken or turkey breast	12-1/2 pounds	25 pounds	50 pounds
Fish (fillets or steaks)	7-1/2 pounds	15 pounds	30 pounds
Hamburgers	8 to 9 pounds	15 to 18 pounds	30 to 36 pounds
Ham or roast beef	10 pounds	20 pounds	40 pounds
Hot dogs	6 pounds	12-1/2 pounds	25 pounds
Meat loaf	6 pounds	12 pounds	24 pounds
Oysters	1 gallon	2 gallons	4 gallons
Pork	10 pounds	20 pounds	40 pounds
MISCELLANEOUS			
Bread (loaves)	3	5	10
Butter	3/4 pound	1-1/2 pounds	3 pounds
Cheese	3/4 pound	1-1/2 pounds	3 pounds
Coffee	3/4 pound	1-1/2 pounds	3 pounds
Milk	1-1/2 gallons	3 gallons	6 gallons
Nuts	3/4 pound	1-1/2 pounds	3 pounds
Olives	1/2 pound	1 pound	2 pounds
Pickles	1/2 quart	1 quart	2 quarts
Rolls	50	100	200
Soup	5 quarts	2-1/2 gallons	5 gallons
SIDE DISHES			
Baked beans	5 quarts	2-1/2 gallons	5 gallons
Beets	7-1/2 pounds	15 pounds	30 pounds
Cabbage for cole slaw	5 pounds	10 pounds	20 pounds
Carrots	7-1/2 pounds	15 pounds	30 pounds
Lettuce for salad (heads)	5	10	20
Peas (fresh)	12 pounds	25 pounds	50 pounds
Potatoes	9 pounds	18 pounds	36 pounds
Potato salad	3 quarts	1-1/2 gallons	3 gallons
Salad dressing	3 cups	1-1/2 quarts	3 quarts
DESSERTS			
Cakes	2	4	8
Ice cream	1 gallon	2 gallons	4 gallons
Pies	4	9	18
Whipping cream	1 pint	2 pints	4 pints

Substitutions for Common Ingredients

ITEM	QUANTITY	SUBSTITUTION
Allspice	1 teaspoon	½ teaspoon cinnamon plus ⅛ teaspoon ground cloves
Arrowroot, as thickener	1½ teaspoons	1 tablespoon flour
Baking powder	1 teaspoon	¼ teaspoon baking soda plus ⅝ teaspoon cream of tartar
Bread crumbs, dry	¼ cup	1 slice bread
Bread crumbs, soft	½ cup	1 slice bread
Buttermilk	1 cup	1 cup plain yogurt
Chocolate, unsweetened	1 ounce	3 tablespoons cocoa plus 1 tablespoon butter or fat
Cracker crumbs	¾ cup	1 cup dry bread crumbs
Cream, heavy	1 cup	¾ cup milk plus ⅓ cup melted butter (this will not whip)
Cream, light	1 cup	⅞ cup milk plus 3 tablespoons melted butter
Cream, sour	1 cup	⅞ cup buttermilk or plain yogurt plus 3 tablespoons melted butter
Cream, whipping	1 cup	⅔ cup well-chilled evaporated milk, whipped; **or** 1 cup nonfat dry milk powder whipped with 1 cup ice water
Egg	1 whole	2 yolks
Flour, all-purpose	1 cup	1⅛ cups cake flour; **or** ⅝ cup potato flour; **or** 1¼ cups rye or coarsely ground whole grain flour; **or** 1 cup cornmeal
Flour, cake	1 cup	1 cup minus 2 tablespoons sifted all-purpose flour
Flour, self-rising	1 cup	1 cup all-purpose flour plus 1¼ teaspoons baking powder plus ¼ teaspoon salt
Garlic	1 small clove	⅛ teaspoon garlic powder; **or** ½ teaspoon instant minced garlic
Herbs, dried	½ to 1 teaspoon	1 tablespoon fresh, minced and packed
Honey	1 cup	1¼ cups sugar plus ½ cup liquid

Measuring Vegetables

Asparagus: 1 pound = 3 cups chopped

Beans (string): 1 pound = 4 cups chopped

Beets: 1 pound (5 medium) = 2-1/2 cups chopped

Broccoli: 1/2 pound = 6 cups chopped

Cabbage: 1 pound = 4-1/2 cups shredded

Carrots: 1 pound = 3-1/2 cups sliced or grated

Celery: 1 pound = 4 cups chopped

Cucumbers: 1 pound (2 medium) = 4 cups sliced

Eggplant: 1 pound = 4 cups chopped (6 cups raw, cubed = 3 cups cooked)

Garlic: 1 clove = 1 teaspoon chopped

Leeks: 1 pound = 4 cups chopped (2 cups cooked)

Mushrooms: 1 pound = 5 to 6 cups sliced = 2 cups cooked

Onions: 1 pound = 4 cups sliced = 2 cups cooked

Parsnips: 1 pound unpeeled = 1-1/2 cups cooked, pureed

Peas: 1 pound whole = 1 to 1-1/2 cups shelled

Potatoes: 1 pound (3 medium) sliced = 2 cups mashed

Pumpkin: 1 pound = 4 cups chopped = 2 cups cooked and drained

Spinach: 1 pound = 3/4 to 1 cup cooked

ITEM	QUANTITY	SUBSTITUTION
Lemon	1	1 to 3 tablespoons juice, 1 to 1½ teaspoons grated rind
Lemon juice	1 teaspoon	½ teaspoon vinegar
Lemon rind, grated	1 teaspoon	½ teaspoon lemon extract
Milk, skim	1 cup	⅓ cup instant nonfat dry milk plus about ¾ cup water
Milk, to sour	1 cup	Add 1 tablespoon vinegar or lemon juice to 1 cup milk minus 1 tablespoon. Stir and let stand 5 minutes.
Milk, whole	1 cup	½ cup evaporated milk plus ½ cup water; **or** 1 cup skim milk plus 2 teaspoons melted butter
Molasses	1 cup	1 cup honey
Mustard, prepared	1 tablespoon	1 teaspoon dry or powdered mustard
Onion, chopped	1 small	1 tablespoon instant minced onion; **or** 1 teaspoon onion powder; **or** ¼ cup frozen chopped onion
Sugar, granulated	1 cup	1 cup firmly packed brown sugar; **or** 1¾ cups confectioners' sugar (do not substitute in baking); **or** 2 cups corn syrup; **or** 1 cup superfine sugar
Tomatoes, canned	1 cup	½ cup tomato sauce plus ½ cup water; **or** 1⅓ cups chopped fresh tomatoes, simmered
Tomato juice	1 cup	½ cup tomato sauce plus ½ cup water plus dash each salt and sugar; **or** ¼ cup tomato paste plus ¾ cup water plus salt and sugar
Tomato ketchup	½ cup	½ cup tomato sauce plus 2 tablespoons sugar, 1 tablespoon vinegar, and ⅛ teaspoon ground cloves
Tomato puree	1 cup	½ cup tomato paste plus ½ cup water
Tomato soup	1 can (10¾ oz.)	1 cup tomato sauce plus ¼ cup water
Vanilla	1-inch bean	1 teaspoon vanilla extract
Yeast	1 cake (⅗ oz.)	1 package active dried yeast (1 scant tablespoon)
Yogurt, plain	1 cup	1 cup buttermilk

Squash (summer): 1 pound = 4 cups grated = 2 cups salted and drained

Squash (winter): 2 pounds = 2-1/2 cups cooked, pureed

Sweet potatoes: 1 pound = 4 cups grated = 1 cup cooked, pureed

Swiss chard: 1 pound = 5 to 6 cups packed leaves = 1 to 1-1/2 cups cooked

Tomatoes: 1 pound (3 or 4 medium) = 1-1/2 cups seeded pulp

Turnips: 1 pound = 4 cups chopped = 2 cups cooked, mashed

Measuring Fruits

Apples: 1 pound (3 or 4 medium) = 3 cups sliced
Bananas: 1 pound (3 or 4 medium) = 1-3/4 cups mashed
Berries: 1 quart = 3-1/2 cups
Dates: 1 pound = 2-1/2 cups pitted
Lemon: 1 whole = 1 to 3 tablespoons juice; 1 to 1-1/2 teaspoons grated rind
Lime: 1 whole = 1-1/2 to 2 tablespoons juice
Orange: 1 medium = 6 to 8 tablespoons juice; 2 to 3 tablespoons grated rind
Peaches: 1 pound (4 medium) = 3 cups sliced
Pears: 1 pound (4 medium) = 2 cups sliced
Rhubarb: 1 pound = 2 cups cooked
Strawberries: 1 quart = 3 cups sliced

Substitutions for Uncommon Ingredients

*Cooking an ethnic dish but can't find a special ingredient?
Here are a few ideas for alternatives.*

ITEM	SUBSTITUTION
Balsamic vinegar, 1 tablespoon	1 tablespoon red wine vinegar plus ½ teaspoon sugar
Bamboo shoots	Asparagus (in fried dishes)
Bergamot	Mint
Chayotes	Yellow summer squash **or** zucchini
Cilantro	Parsley (for color only; flavor cannot be duplicated)
Coconut milk	2½ cups water plus 2 cups shredded, unsweetened coconut. Combine and bring to a boil. Remove from heat; cool. Mix in a blender for 2 minutes; strain. Makes about 2 cups.
Delicata squash	Butternut squash **or** sweet potato
Green mangoes	Sour, green cooking apples
Habanero peppers	5 jalapeño peppers **or** serrano peppers
Italian seasoning	Equal parts basil, marjoram, oregano, rosemary, sage, and thyme
Lemon grass	Lemon zest (zest from 1 lemon equals 2 stalks lemon grass)
Limes or lime juice	Lemons or lemon juice
Lo Mein noodles	Egg noodles
Mascarpone, 1 cup	3 tablespoons heavy cream plus ¾ cup cream cheese plus 4 tablespoons butter
Neufchâtel	Cream cheese **or** Boursin
Palm sugar	Light brown sugar
Rice wine	Pale, dry sherry **or** white vermouth
Red peppers	Equal amount pimientos
Romano cheese	Parmesan cheese
Saffron	Turmeric (for color; flavor is different)
Shallots	Red onions **or** Spanish onions
Shrimp paste	Anchovy paste
Tamarind juice	5 parts ketchup to 1 part vinegar

Knots

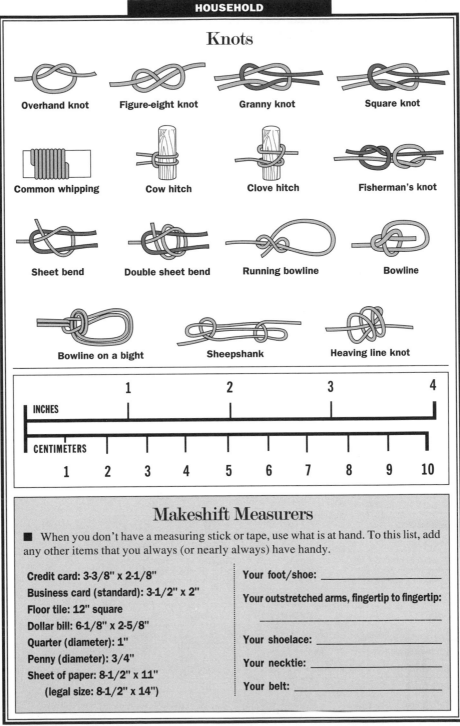

Overhand knot   **Figure-eight knot**   **Granny knot**   **Square knot**

Common whipping   **Cow hitch**   **Clove hitch**   **Fisherman's knot**

Sheet bend   **Double sheet bend**   **Running bowline**   **Bowline**

Bowline on a bight   **Sheepshank**   **Heaving line knot**

INCHES   1   2   3   4

CENTIMETERS   1   2   3   4   5   6   7   8   9   10

Makeshift Measurers

■ When you don't have a measuring stick or tape, use what is at hand. To this list, add any other items that you always (or nearly always) have handy.

Credit card: 3-3/8" x 2-1/8"
Business card (standard): 3-1/2" x 2"
Floor tile: 12" square
Dollar bill: 6-1/8" x 2-5/8"
Quarter (diameter): 1"
Penny (diameter): 3/4"
Sheet of paper: 8-1/2" x 11"
   (legal size: 8-1/2" x 14")

Your foot/shoe: _____

Your outstretched arms, fingertip to fingertip:

_____

Your shoelace: _____

Your necktie: _____

Your belt: _____

Hand Thermometer for Outdoor Cooking

■ Hold your palm close to where the food will be cooking: over the coals or in front of a reflector oven. Count "one-and-one, two-and-two," and so on, for as many seconds as you can hold your hand still.

Seconds Counted	Heat	Temperature
6-8	Slow	250°-350°F
4-5	Moderate	350°-400°F
2-3	Hot	400°-450°F
1 or less	Very hot	450°-500°F

Life Expectancy by Current Age

If your age now is . . . **You can expect to live to age . . .**

If your age now is . . .	Men	Women
0	72	79
20	74	80
25	74	80
30	75	80
35	75	81
40	76	81
45	76	81
50	77	82
55	78	82
60	79	83
65	80	84
70	82	86
75	85	87
80	87	89
85	90	92

Source: U.S. Department of Health and Human Services, 1995

Is It a Cold or the Flu?

Symptoms	Flu	Cold	Allergy	Sinusitis
Headache	Always	Occasionally	Occasionally	Always
Muscle aches	Always	Usually	Rarely	Rarely
Fatigue, weakness	Always	Usually	Rarely	Rarely
Fever	Always	Occasionally	Never	Occasionally
Cough	Usually	Occasionally	Occasionally	Usually
Runny, stuffy nose	Occasionally	Usually	Usually	Always
Nasal discharge	Occasionally	Usually	Usually	Always
Sneezing	Rarely	Occasionally	Usually	Rarely
Sore throat	Rarely	Usually	Occasionally	Rarely
Itchy eyes, nose, throat	Rarely	Rarely	Usually	Never

Are You Skinny, Just Right, or Overweight?

■ Here's an easy formula to figure your Body Mass Index (BMI), now thought to be a more accurate indicator of relative body size than the old insurance charts. **W** is your weight in pounds and **H** is your height in inches.

$$BMI = \frac{(W \times 705) \div H}{H}$$

■ If the result is 25 or less, you are within a healthy weight range.

■ If it's 19 or below, you are too skinny.

■ Between 25 and 27, you are as much as 8 percent over your healthy weight.

■ Between 27 and 30, you are at increased risk for health problems.

■ Above 30, you are more than 20 percent over your healthy weight. It puts you at a dramatically increased risk for serious health problems.

There are a couple of exceptions to the above. Very muscular people with a high BMI generally have nothing to worry about, and extreme skinniness is generally a symptom of some other health problem, not the cause.

Here's another way to see if you are dangerously overweight. Measure your waistline. A waist measurement of 35 inches or more in women and 41 inches or more in men, regardless of height, suggests a serious risk of weight-related health problems.

Calorie Burning

■ If you hustle through your chores to get to the fitness center, relax. You're getting a great workout already. The left-hand column lists "chore" exercises, the middle column shows number of calories you burn per minute per pound of your body weight, the right-hand column lists comparable "recreational" exercises. For example, a 150-pound person forking straw bales burns 9.45 calories per minute, the same workout he/she would get playing basketball.

Chopping with an ax, fast.	0.135	Skiing, cross country, uphill
Climbing hills, with 44-pound load	0.066	Swimming, crawl, fast
Digging trenches	0.065	Skiing, cross country, steady walk
Forking straw bales	0.063	Basketball
Chopping down trees	0.060	Football
Climbing hills, with 9-pound load	0.058	Swimming, crawl, slow
Sawing by hand	0.055	Skiing, cross country, moderate
Mowing lawns	0.051	Horseback riding, trotting
Scrubbing floors	0.049	Tennis
Shoveling coal	0.049	Aerobic dance, medium
Hoeing	0.041	Weight training, circuit training
Stacking firewood	0.040	Weight lifting, free weights
Shoveling grain	0.038	Golf
Painting houses	0.035	Walking, normal pace, asphalt road
Weeding	0.033	Table tennis
Shopping for food	0.028	Cycling, 5.5 mph
Mopping floors	0.028	Fishing
Washing windows	0.026	Croquet
Raking	0.025	Dancing, ballroom
Driving a tractor	0.016	Drawing, standing position

How Much Paint Will You Need?

■ Estimate your room size and paint needs before you go to the store. Running out of a custom color halfway through the job could mean disaster. For the sake of the following exercise, assume you have a 10x15-foot room with an 8-foot ceiling. The room has two doors and two windows.

For Walls

■ Measure the total distance (perimeter) around the room:
(10 ft. + 15 ft.) x 2 = 50 ft.

■ Multiply the perimeter by the ceiling height to get the total wall area:
50 ft. x 8 ft. = 400 sq. ft.

■ Doors are usually 21 square feet (there are two in this exercise):
21 sq. ft. x 2 = 42 sq. ft.

■ Windows average 15 square feet (there are two in this exercise):
15 sq. ft. x 2 = 30 sq. ft.

■ Take the total wall area and subtract the area for the doors and windows to get the wall surface to be painted:
400 sq. ft. (wall area)
– 42 sq. ft. (doors)
– 30 sq. ft. (windows)
_____
328 sq. ft.

■ As a rule of thumb, one gallon of quality paint will usually cover 400 square feet. One quart will cover 100 square feet. Since you need to cover 328 square feet in this example, one gallon will be adequate to give one coat of paint to the walls. (Coverage will be affected by the porosity and texture of the surface. In addition, bright colors may require a minimum of two coats.)

For Ceilings

■ Using the rule of thumb for coverage above, you can calculate the quantity of paint needed for the ceiling by multiplying the width by the length:
10 ft. x 15 ft. = 150 sq. ft.

This ceiling will require approximately two quarts of paint. (A flat finish is recommended to minimize surface imperfections.)

For Doors, Windows, and Trim

■ The area for the doors and windows has been calculated above. Determine the baseboard trim by taking the perimeter of the room, less 3 feet per door (3 ft. x 2 = 6 ft.), and multiplying this by the average trim width of your baseboard, which in this example is 6 inches (or 0.5 feet).

50 ft. (perimeter) - 6 ft. = 44 ft.
44 ft. x 0.5 ft. = 22 sq. ft.

■ Add the area for doors, windows, and baseboard trim.
42 sq. ft. (doors)
+30 sq. ft. (windows)
+22 sq. ft. (baseboard trim)
_____
94 sq. ft.

One quart will probably be sufficient to cover the doors, windows, and trim in this example.

–courtesy M.A.B. Paints

Exterior Paint

■ Here's how to estimate the number of gallons needed for one-coat coverage of a home that is 20 feet wide by 40 feet long, has walls that rise 16 feet to the eaves on the 40-foot sides, and has full-width gables on the 20-foot sides rising 10 feet to the peaks.

■ First, find the area of the walls. Add the width to the length:

20 ft. + 40 ft. = 60 ft.

Double it for four sides:

60 ft. x 2 = 120 ft.

Multiply that by the height of the walls:

120 ft. x 16 ft. = 1,920 sq. ft.

The area of the walls is 1,920 square feet.

■ Next, find the area of the gables. Take half the width of one gable at its base:

20 ft. ÷ 2 = 10 ft.

Multiply that by the height of the gable:

10 ft. x 10 ft. = 100 sq. ft.

Multiply that by the number of gables:

100 sq. ft. x 2 = 200 sq. ft.

The area of the gables is 200 square feet.

■ Add the two figures together for the total area:

1,920 sq. ft. + 200 sq. ft. = 2,120 sq. ft.

■ Finally, divide the total area by the area covered by a gallon of paint (400 square feet) to find the number of gallons needed:

2,120 sq. ft. ÷ 400 sq. ft./gal. = 5.3 gal.

Buy five gallons of paint to start with. The sixth gallon might not be necessary.

How Much Wallpaper Will You Need?

■ Measure the length of each wall, add these figures together, and multiply by the height of the walls to get the area (square footage) of the room.

■ Calculate the square footage of each door, window, or other opening in the room. Add these figures together and subtract the total from the area of the room.

■ Take that figure and multiply by 1.15, to account for a waste rate of about 15 percent in your wallpaper project.

■ Wallpaper is sold in single, double, and triple rolls. (Average coverage for a double roll, for example, is 56 square feet.) Divide the coverage figure (from the label) into the total square footage of the room you're papering. Round the answer up to the nearest whole number. This is the number of rolls you need to buy.

■ Save leftover wallpaper rolls, carefully wrapped to keep them clean.

Guide to Lumber and Nails

Lumber Width and Thickness in Inches

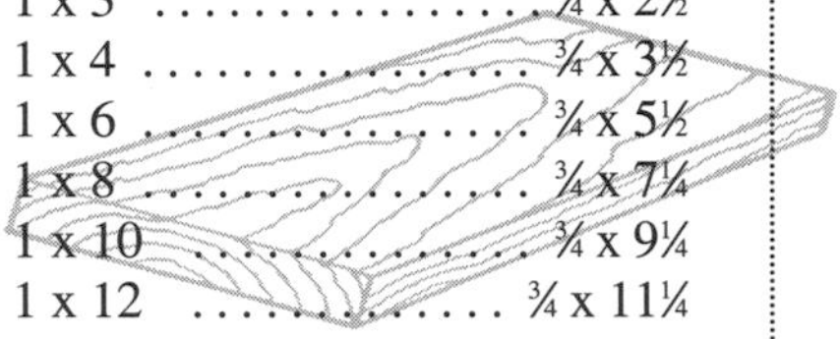

NOMINAL SIZE	ACTUAL SIZE Dry or Seasoned
1 x 3	¾ x 2½
1 x 4	¾ x 3½
1 x 6	¾ x 5½
1 x 8	¾ x 7¼
1 x 10	¾ x 9¼
1 x 12	¾ x 11¼
2 x 3	1½ x 2½
2 x 4	1½ x 3½
2 x 6	1½ x 5½
2 x 8	1½ x 7¼
2 x 10	1½ x 9¼
2 x 12	1½ x 11¼

Nail Sizes

The nail on the left is a 5d (penny) finish nail; on the right, 20d common. The numerals below the nail sizes indicate the approximate number of common nails per pound.

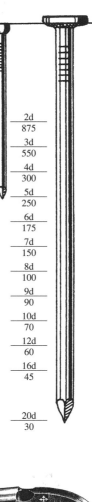

2d	875
3d	550
4d	300
5d	250
6d	175
7d	150
8d	100
9d	90
10d	70
12d	60
16d	45
20d	30

Lumber Measure in Board Feet

Size in Inches	LENGTH 12 ft.	14 ft.	16 ft.	18 ft.	20 ft.
1 x 4	4	4⅔	5⅓	6	6⅔
1 x 6	6	7	8	9	10
1 x 8	8	9⅓	10⅔	12	13⅓
1 x 10	10	11⅔	13⅓	15	16⅔
1 x 12	12	14	16	18	20
2 x 3	6	7	8	9	10
2 x 4	8	9⅓	10⅔	12	13⅓
2 x 6	12	14	16	18	20
2 x 8	16	18⅔	21⅓	24	26⅔
2 x 10	20	23⅓	26⅔	30	33⅓
2 x 12	24	28	32	36	40
4 x 4	16	18⅔	21⅓	24	26⅔
6 x 6	36	42	48	54	60
8 x 8	64	74⅔	85⅓	96	106⅔
10 x 10	100	116⅔	133⅓	150	166⅔
12 x 12	144	168	192	216	240

Firewood Heat Values

High Heat Value

1 CORD = 200-250 GALLONS OF FUEL OIL

American beech
Apple
Ironwood
Red oak
Shagbark hickory
Sugar maple
White ash
White oak
Yellow birch

Medium Heat Value

1 CORD = 150-200 GALLONS OF FUEL OIL

American elm
Black cherry
Douglas fir
Red maple
Silver maple
Tamarack
White birch

Low Heat Value

1 CORD = 100-150 GALLONS OF FUEL OIL

Aspen
Cottonwood
Hemlock
Lodgepole pine
Red alder
Redwood
Sitka spruce
Western red cedar
White pine

How Many Trees in a Cord of Wood?

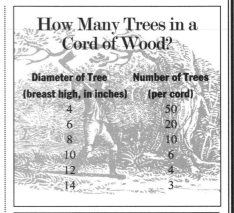

Diameter of Tree (breast high, in inches)	Number of Trees (per cord)
4	50
6	20
8	10
10	6
12	4
14	3

Heat Values of Fuels

(approximate)

Fuel	BTU	Unit of Measure
Oil	141,000	Gallon
Coal	31,000	Pound
Natural gas	1,000	Cubic foot
Steam	1,000	Cubic foot
Electricity	3,413	Kilowatt-hour
Gasoline	124,000	Gallon

How to Find the Number of Bricks in a Wall or Building

(or how to estimate how many nonmodular standard bricks will be needed for a project)

Rule

■ Multiply the length of the wall in feet by its height in feet, and that by its thickness in feet, and then multiply that result by 20. The answer will be the number of bricks in the wall.

Example

■ 30 feet (length) x 20 feet (height) x 1 foot (thickness) = 600 x 20 = 12,000 bricks

Animal Terminology

Animal	Male	Female	Young
Ant	Male ant (reproductive)	Queen (reproductive), worker (nonreproductive)	Antling
Antelope	Ram	Ewe	Calf, fawn, kid, yearling
Ass	Jack, jackass	Jenny	Foal
Bear	Boar, he-bear	Sow, she-bear	Cub
Beaver	Boar	Sow	Kit, kitten
Bee	Drone	Queen or queen bee, worker (nonreproductive)	Larva
Buffalo	Bull	Cow	Calf, yearling, spike-bull
Camel	Bull	Cow	Calf, colt
Caribou	Bull, stag, hart	Cow, doe	Calf, fawn
Cat	Tom, tomcat, gib, gibcat, boarcat, ramcat	Tabby, grimalkin, malkin, pussy, queen	Kitten, kit, kitling, kitty, pussy
Cattle	Bull	Cow	Calf, stot, yearling, bullcalf, heifer
Chicken	Rooster, cock, stag, chanticleer	Hen, partlet, biddy	Chick, chicken, poult, cockerel, pullet
Deer	Buck, stag	Doe	Fawn
Dog	Dog	Bitch	Whelp
Duck	Drake, stag	Duck	Duckling, flapper
Elephant	Bull	Cow	Calf
Fox	Dog	Vixen	Kit, pup, cub
Giraffe	Bull	Cow	Calf
Goat	Buck, billy, billie, billy goat, he-goat	She-goat, nanny, nannie, nanny goat	Kid
Goose	Gander, stag	Goose, dame	Gosling
Horse	Stallion, stag, horse, stud	Mare, dam	Colt, foal, stot, stag, filly, hog-colt, hogget
Kangaroo	Buck	Doe	Joey
Leopard	Leopard	Leopardess	Cub
Lion	Lion, tom	Lioness, she-lion	Shelp, cub, lionet
Moose	Bull	Cow	Calf
Partridge	Cock	Hen	Cheeper
Quail	Cock	Hen	Cheeper, chick, squealer
Reindeer	Buck	Doe	Fawn
Seal	Bull	Cow	Whelp, pup, cub, bachelor
Sheep	Buck, ram, male sheep, mutton	Ewe, dam	Lamb, lambkin, shearling, yearling, cosset, hog
Swan	Cob	Pen	Cygnet
Swine	Boar	Sow	Shoat, trotter, pig, piglet, farrow, suckling
Termite	King	Queen	Nymph
Walrus	Bull	Cow	Cub
Whale	Bull	Cow	Calf
Zebra	Stallion	Mare	Colt, foal

Collective
Colony, nest, army, state, swarm
Herd
Pace, drove, herd
Sleuth, sloth
Family, colony
Swarm, grist, cluster, nest, hive, erst
Troop, herd, gang
Flock, train, caravan
Herd
Clowder, clutter (kindle or kendle of kittens)
Drove, herd
Flock, run, brood, clutch, peep
Herd, leash
Pack (cry or mute of hounds, leash of greyhounds)
Brace, team, paddling, raft, bed, flock, flight
Herd
Leash, skulk, cloud, troop
Herd, corps, troop
Tribe, trip, flock, herd
Flock (on land), gaggle, skein (in flight), gaggle or plump (on water)
Haras, stable, remuda, herd, string, field, set, pair, team
Mob, troop, herd
Leap
Pride, troop, flock, sawt, souse
Herd
Covey
Bevy, covey
Herd
Pod, herd, trip, rookery, harem
Flock, drove, hirsel, trip, pack
Herd, team, bank, wege, bevy
Drift, sounder, herd, trip (litter of pigs)
Colony, nest, swarm, brood
Pod, herd
Gam, pod, school, herd
Herd

More Animal Collectives

army of caterpillars, frogs
bale of turtles
band of gorillas
bed of clams, oysters
brood of jellyfish
business of flies
cartload of monkeys
cast of hawks
cete of badgers
charm of goldfinches
chatter of budgerigars
cloud of gnats, flies, grasshoppers, locusts
colony of penguins
congregation of plovers
convocation of eagles
crash of rhinoceri
descent of woodpeckers
dole of turtles
down of hares
dray of squirrels
dule of turtle doves
exaltation of larks
family of sardines
flight of birds
flock of lice
gang of elks
hatch of flies
horde of gnats
host of sparrows

hover of trout
husk of hares
knab of toads
knot of toads, snakes
murder of crows
murmuration of starlings
mustering of storks
nest of vipers
nest or nide of pheasants
pack of weasels
pladge of wasps
plague of locusts
scattering of herons
sedge or siege of cranes
smuck of jellyfish
span of mules
spring of teals
steam of minnows
tittering of magpies
troop of monkeys
troubling of goldfish
volery of birds
watch of nightingales
wing of plovers
yoke of oxen

Dogs: Gentle, Fierce, Smart, Popular

Gentlest Breeds	Fiercest Breeds	Smartest Breeds	Most Popular Breeds
Golden retriever	Pit bull	Border collie	Labrador retriever
Labrador retriever	German shepherd	Poodle	Rottweiler
Shetland sheepdog	Husky	German shepherd	Cocker spaniel
Old English sheepdog	Malamute	(Alsatian)	German shepherd
Welsh terrier	Doberman pinscher	Golden retriever	Poodle
Yorkshire terrier	Rottweiler	Doberman pinscher	Golden retriever
Beagle	Great Dane	Shetland sheepdog	Beagle
Dalmatian	Saint Bernard	Labrador retriever	Dachshund
Pointer		Papillon	Shetland sheepdog
		Rottweiler	Chow chow
		Australian cattle dog	

Don't Poison Your Pussycat!

■ Certain common houseplants are poisonous to cats. They should not be allowed to eat the following:

- Azalea *(Rhododendron)*
- Common or cherry laurel *(Prunus laurocerasus)*
- Dumb cane *(Dieffenbachia)*
- Elephant's ears *(Caladium)*
- Mistletoe *(Ficus deltoidea)*
- Oleander *(Nerium oleander)*
- Philodendron *(Philodendron)*
- True ivy *(Hedera)*
- Winter or false Jerusalem cherry *(Solanum capiscastrum)*

Ten Most Intelligent Animals

(besides humans)

■ According to Edward O. Wilson, behavioral biologist, professor of zoology, Harvard University, they are:

1. Chimpanzee (two species)
2. Gorilla
3. Orangutan
4. Baboon (seven species, including drill and mandrill)
5. Gibbon (seven species)
6. Monkey (many species, especially the macaques, the patas, and the Celebes black ape)
7. Smaller toothed whale (several species, especially killer whale)
8. Dolphin (many of the approximately 80 species)
9. Elephant (two species)
10. Pig

Nutritional Value of Various Insects per 100 Grams

Insect	Protein (g)	Fat (g)	Carbohydrate (g)	Calcium (mg)	Iron (mg)
Giant water beetle	19.8	8.3	2.1	43.5	13.6
Red ant	13.9	3.5	2.9	47.8	5.7
Silkworm pupa	9.6	5.6	2.3	41.7	1.8
Dung beetle	17.2	4.3	0.2	30.9	7.7
Cricket	12.9	5.5	5.1	75.8	9.5
Small grasshopper	20.6	6.1	3.9	35.2	5.0
Large grasshopper	14.3	3.3	2.2	27.5	3.0
June beetle	13.4	1.4	2.9	22.6	6.0
Termite	14.2	—	—	—	35.5
Weevil	6.7	—	—	—	13.1
Compared with:					
Beef (lean ground)	27.4	—	—	—	3.5
Fish (broiled cod)	28.5	—	—	—	1.0

–courtesy Department of Entomology, Iowa State University

Gestation and Mating Table

	Proper Age for First Mating	Period of Fertility (years)	Number of Females for One Male	Period of Gestation (days) AVERAGE	RANGE
Ewe	90 lb. or 1 yr.	6		147 / 151[8]	142-154
Ram	12-14 mo., well matured	7	50-75[2] / 35-40[3]		
Mare	3 yr.	10-12		336	310-370
Stallion	3 yr.	12-15	40-45[4] / Record 252[5]		
Cow	15-18 mo.[1]	10-14		283	279-290[6] 262-300[7]
Bull	1 yr., well matured	10-12	50[4] / Thousands[5]		
Sow	5-6 mo. or 250 lb.	6		115	110-120
Boar	250-300 lb.	6	50[2] / 35-40[3]		
Doe goat	10 mo. or 85-90 lb.	6		150	145-155
Buck goat	Well matured	5	30		
Bitch	16-18 mo.	8		63	58-67
Male dog	12-16 mo.	8			
She cat	12 mo.	6		63	60-68
Doe rabbit	6 mo.	5-6		31	30-32
Buck rabbit	6 mo.	5-6	30		

[1]Holstein and beef: 750 lb.; Jersey: 500 lb. [2]Hand-mated. [3]Pasture. [4]Natural. [5]Artificial. [6]Beef; 8-10 days shorter for Angus. [7]Dairy. [8]For fine wool breeds.

Maximum Life Spans of Animals in Captivity (years)

Ant (queen)	18+	Chimpanzee	36	Kangaroo	30	Quahog	150
Badger	26	Coyote	21+	Goat (domestic)	20	Lion	29	Rabbit	18+
Beaver	15+	Dog (domestic)	29	Goldfish	41	Monarch butterfly	1+	Squirrel, gray	23
Box turtle (Eastern)	138	Dolphin	25	Goose (domestic)	20	Mouse (house)	6	Tiger	26
Camel	35+	Duck (domestic)	23	Gorilla	50+	Mussel		Toad	40
Cat (domestic)	34	Eagle	55	Horse	62	(freshwater)	70-80	Tortoise(Marion's)	152+
Chicken (domestic)	25	Elephant	75	Housefly	17 days	Octopus	2-3	Turkey (domestic)	16

Incubation Periods of Birds and Poultry (days)

Canary	14-15	Goose	30-34	Pheasant	22-24
Chicken	21	Guinea	26-28	Swan	42
Duck	26-32	Parakeet	18-20	Turkey	28

Gestation Periods of Wild Animals (days)

Black bear	210	Otter	270-300	Squirrel, gray	44
Hippo	225-250	Reindeer	210-240	Whale, sperm.	480
Moose	240-250	Seal	330	Wolf	60-63

	Estral (estrous) Cycle Including Heat Period AVERAGE	RANGE	Length of Heat (estrus) AVERAGE	RANGE	Usual Time of Ovulation	When Cycle Recurs if Not Bred
Mare	21 days	10-37 days	5-6 days	2-11 days	24-48 hours before end of estrus	21 days
Sow	21 days	18-24 days	2-3 days	1-5 days	30-36 hours after start of estrus	21 days
Ewe	16½ days	14-19 days	30 hours	24-32 hours	12-24 hours before end of estrus	16½ days
Goat	21 days	18-24 days	2-3 days	1-4 days	Near end of estrus	21 days
Cow	21 days	18-24 days	18 hours	10-24 hours	10-12 hours after end of estrus	21 days
Bitch	24 days		7 days	5-9 days	1-3 days after first acceptance	Pseudo-pregnancy
Cat		15-21 days	3-4 days, if mated	9-10 days, in absence of male	24-56 hours after coitus	Pseudo-pregnancy

Know Your Angels

I. First Group— nearest to God	Seraphim Cherubim Thrones
II. Second Group— receives the reflection of Divine Presence from the first group	Dominions Virtues Powers
III. Angelic Group— ministers directly to human beings	Principalities Archangels Angels

Famous Last Words of Real People

"My exit is the result of too many entrees."
–Richard Monckton Milnes (Victorian politician)

"I'm dying, as I have lived, beyond my means."
–Oscar Wilde

"I am going to the great perhaps."
–Rabelais (writer, priest, physician)

"Well, if this is dying, there is nothing unpleasant about it."
–Maria Mitchell (professor of astronomy)

"Just pull my legs straight, and place me as a dead man; it will save trouble for you shortly."   –Dr. Fidge

"I am about to—or I am going to—die: either expression is used."
–Dominique Bouhours (philosopher and grammarian)

The Golden Rule
(It's true in all faiths.)

Brahmanism:
This is the sum of duty: Do naught unto others which would cause you pain if done to you.
Mahabharata 5:1517

Buddhism:
Hurt not others in ways that you yourself would find hurtful.
Udana-Varga 5:18

Confucianism:
Surely it is the maxim of loving-kindness: Do not unto others what you would not have them do unto you.   *Analects 15:23*

Taoism:
Regard your neighbor's gain as your own gain and your neighbor's loss as your own loss.
T'ai Shang Kan Ying P'ien

Zoroastrianism:
That nature alone is good which re-frains from doing unto another what-soever is not good for itself.
Dadistan-i-dinik 94:5

Judaism:
What is hateful to you, do not to your fellowman. That is the entire Law; all the rest is commentary.
Talmud, Shabbat 31a

Christianity:
All things whatsoever ye would that men should do to you, do ye even so to them; for this is the law and the prophets.
Matthew 7:12

Islam:
No one of you is a believer until he desires for his brother that which he desires for himself.
Sunnah

–courtesy Elizabeth Pool